THOMAS F. VAN LAAN is a member of the Department of English at Rutgers University.

The idea that the world is a theatre in which each individual human being plays out the part assigned to him by God, who is both the playwright and the producer of the drama of life, was one of the great commonplaces of the Renaissance and one to which Shakespeare alluded frequently.

Shakespeare's plays, however, transformed this familiar notion from a cliché to a fertile source of invention. In the past two decades, and especially since the publication of Anne Righter's *Shakespeare and the Idea of the Play* in 1962, the idea has received considerable critical attention. This new work supplements and extends recent studies by examining in detail the function of the histrionic metaphors, both verbal and other, in Shakespeare's plays.

In *Role-playing in Shakespeare*, Professor Van Laan argues that the theatrical allusions, disguises, impersonations, and conscious or unconscious self-misrepresentations which abound in these plays exemplify a basic concern with role-playing that substantially affects characterization, action, structure, and theme. Surveying the evidence contained in the plays themselves, he defines the term 'role' and proceeds to explore some important general aspects of the topic, including the conception of identity implicit in Shakespearian characterization, the relation of role-playing to dramatic structure, and the recurring theme of the discrepancy between the actor and his part. He then describes the patterns that the role-playing materials assume in the various dramatic genres, comedy, history, and tragedy. The final chapter is a study of one of the primary sources of action in Shakespeare, the internal dramatist.

The wide scope of this enquiry, taking in all of Shakespeare's plays, and the thoroughness with which Van Laan has pursued his argument provide a coherent and illuminating perspective on two of the most intriguing qualities of Shakespeare's work as a whole: the sense of continuity and the sense of an underlying unity within such great variety.

Role-playing in Shakespeare

THOMAS F. VAN LAAN

University of Toronto Press
Toronto Buffalo London

©   University of Toronto Press 1978
Toronto Buffalo London
Printed in Canada

Canadian Cataloguing in Publication Data

Van Laan, Thomas F., 1931–
   Role-playing in Shakespeare

   Bibliography: p.
   Includes index.
   ISBN 0-8020-5356-4

   1. Shakespeare, William, 1564–1616 – Criticism and interpretation.
   2. Role-playing in literature. I. Title

PR 2976.V27   822.3'3   C 77-001422-4

---

for Krista, Thomas, and Marcy

Contents

Preface

Totus mundus agit histrionem

One of the dubious anecdotes that Sir William Oldys, the eighteenth-century antiquarian, recorded about Shakespeare identifies the words quoted above as the motto of the Globe Theatre, and even though this report may not be true, it is nonetheless intriguing. For as several studies of individual plays by Shakespeare, and especially Anne Righter's more comprehensive *Shakespeare and the Idea of the Play*, have begun to demonstrate during the past decade or so, if this *was* the motto of the Globe, it provided not only a clever justification of theatrical endeavours and a reassuring echo of a familiar Renaissance cliché but also an incisive allusion to the content of many of the plays performed there. The *theatrum mundi* concept – the idea that 'the world's a stage' – was one of the many popular tropes bequeathed by the Middle Ages to the Renaissance, whose writers, both dramatic and non-dramatic, made it very much their own through constant repetition. From Aristophanes on, moreover, especially in comedy, dramatists have tended not simply to echo this trope but to dramatize it by having their characters occasionally speak about experience in theatrical terms and sometimes even behave as if the world they inhabited were indeed a stage. In Shakespeare, this occasional tendency becomes standard practice; his plays transform the familiar trope from a cliché to a fertile source of invention.

 The chapters that follow seek to supplement and extend the recent studies alluded to above by examining in detail the function of the histrionic metaphors, both verbal and otherwise, in Shakespeare's plays. My argument, briefly put, is that the theatrical allusions, disguises, impersonations, and conscious or unconscious self-misrepresentations which abound in Shakespeare's plays exemplify a basic concern with role-playing that substantially affects characterization, action, structure, and theme; Shakespearian man, whatever else he may be, is a role-playing animal, and the plays that dramatize his experiences emphasize role-playing as a central focus of considerable significance. Chapter 1, by way of introduction, surveys the evidence from the plays and defines the term 'role.' Drawing mainly on the comedies, chapters 2, 3, and 4 explore some important general aspects of the topic: the place of role-playing in Shakespearian characterization, the contribution of role-playing materials to dramatic structure, and the specific, oft-recurring theme of the discrepancy between the actor and his part. Chapters 5 to 8 describe the patterns that the role-playing materials assume in the various dramatic genres, comedy, history, and tragedy. The final chapter is a study of one of the primary sources of action in Shakespeare, the internal dramatist, and especially of the manifestations of this figure in the last two major plays, *The Winter's Tale* and *The Tempest*.

Shakespeare's plays are cited from the edition of Peter Alexander (London 1951). My understanding of Shakespeare and my readings of individual plays owe a great deal to previous Shakespeare criticism and to my former teachers, my colleagues, and my students, though I have not attempted the impossible task of sorting out and registering specific items of indebtedness. Nor have I attempted to provide a running account, through footnotes, of the relation of my work to that of others who have also studied the histrionic and theatrical metaphors in Shakespeare, to indicate which of my insights have already been recorded by others or exactly how my analysis of the role-playing imagery of a particular play distinguishes itself from the other existing analyses with similar focus. What I have tried to do instead is to provide as complete a bibliography as possible of books and articles substantially concerned not just with the presence of role-playing imagery in the plays but in some important way with its implications.

The section on *King Lear* in chapter 8 has already appeared in much the same form under the title 'Acting as Action in *King Lear*' in *Some Facets of King Lear: Essays in Prismatic Criticism*, ed. Rosalie L. Colie and F.T. Flahiff (University of Toronto Press 1974), and I am indebted to the University of Toronto Press for permission to reprint. I am grateful to the Publications Fund of the University of Toronto Press and the University of Toronto, which helped finance the publication of this book, and to the Research Council of Rutgers University for grants-in-aid which supported my research, gave me the free time to complete it, and helped meet the cost of publication. David J. Kalstone, Bridget Gellert Lyons, and Robert B. Lyons have given me valuable advice, not all of which I have been able to follow but for all of which and for their kind reading of the manuscript I am deeply grateful. I am also grateful to Prudence Tracy, of the University of Toronto Press, for her kindness and helpfulness, to Margaret Parker, my editor, for her meticulous work on the manuscript, and to my typist, Judy von Loewe. Finally, I must acknowledge a special debt of gratitude to my children Thomas and Marcy, who (usually) performed their roles in proof-reading the manuscript with diligence and fidelity.

ROLE-PLAYING IN SHAKESPEARE

1 Introduction

> All the world's a stage,
> And all the men and women merely players;
> They have their exits and their entrances;
> And one man in his time plays many parts,
> His acts being seven ages.
> *(As You Like It*, II.vii.139-43)

Jaques' speech on the seven ages of man has specific functions within its immediate context – as both a revelation of character and one key to the play's design – yet at the same time it is also the most fully formulated example of a verbal motif ubiquitous in Shakespeare: a motif that likens the experience being dramatized on the stage to histrionic activity. Other examples, fully as explicit as this by Jaques, immediately come to mind. Jaques' speech is itself preceded and inspired by Duke Senior's realization that 'we are not alone unhappy':

> This wide and universal theatre
> Presents more woeful pageants than the scene
> Wherein we play in. (II.vii.137-9)

Antonio, in *The Merchant of Venice*, holds 'the world but as the world' –

> A stage, where every man must play a part,
> And mine a sad one. (I.i.77-9)

And Northumberland, deeply moved by the news that his son, Hotspur, has been killed and their rebellion thwarted, eagerly anticipates what would now be called 'the final curtain':

> Let order die!
> And let this world no longer be a stage
> To feed contention in a ling'ring act;

> But let one spirit of the first-born Cain
> Reign in all bosoms, that, each heart being set
> On bloody courses, the rude scene may end
> And darkness be the burier of the dead! (*2 Henry IV*, I.i.154-60)

Primarily, however, this motif is established and sustained not through such speeches as these, which flatly equate the world with the stage or assert that man is an actor playing a part, but through the virtually constant passages that imply the same conceptions. Shakespearian characters seldom *do* something; instead, they 'play' the abstract type normally associated with the kind of action they are performing (e.g., 'play the eaves-dropper,' *Richard III*, V.iii.221; 'play the humble host,' *Macbeth*, III.iv.4). A character's activity or some portion of it is frequently labelled a 'part' (e.g., *Winter's Tale*, I.ii.188). An individual segment of action – occasionally a play's action as a whole – is often defined as a 'scene' (e.g., *Julius Caesar*, III.i.113), an 'act' in the full theatrical sense (e.g., *Richard III*, II.ii.39), a 'play' (e.g., *As You Like It*, III.iv.54), a 'pageant' (e.g., *Midsummer Night's Dream*, III.ii.114), or a 'tragedy' (e.g., *Henry V*, I.ii.106).

Throughout Shakespeare's plays, in other words, one confronts almost constantly a highly interesting implication about the characters and their experience, an implication that can perhaps be spelled out most readily through a brief examination of the verb 'play' (when it carries a histrionic sense), and especially of the formula 'play the – ,' as in 'play the man,' 'play the tyrant,' 'play the porter,' 'play the flouting Jack,' and so forth. I count seventy-four instances of this formula in Shakespeare, an average of two instances per play, with only two plays (*A Midsummer Night's Dream* and *Julius Caesar*) not represented. Only three times does Shakespeare employ the verb 'play' to denote pretence or dissembling: in Hamlet's admission that his outer manifestations of grief 'are actions that a man might play' (*Hamlet*, I.ii.84), in Cleopatra's appeal to Antony to 'play one scene / Of excellent dissembling, and let it look / Like perfect honour' (*Antony and Cleopatra*, I.iii.78-80), and, less explicitly, in Viola's claim, 'I am not that I play' (*Twelfth Night*, I.v.173-4). Against these passages, moreover, can be placed two others that establish a clear distinction between pretence and playing, Richard III's boast about his ability to 'seem a saint when most I play the devil' (*Richard III*, I.iii.338) and Coriolanus' attempt to convince his mother that he should not humble himself before the people: 'Would you have me / False to my nature? Rather say I play / The man I am' (*Coriolanus*, III.ii.14-16). And in no instance of the formula is there the least suggestion that the designated agent does not sincerely strive to become or resemble that which he is said to 'play.' This formula, then, especially as it is reinforced by other uses of the verb 'play' and by the many references to parts, scenes, acts, plays, pageants, and tragedies, helps to establish a world in which *action* equals *acting*, in which to do something is to take on a particular role with fixed attributes.

Or nearly always. For there is an additional formula in Shakespeare – 'play false' (*Tempest*, v.i.172; *Two Gentlemen of Verona*, iv.ii.57; *Comedy of Errors*, ii.ii.141; *Merchant of Venice*, i.ii.39; *King John*, i.i.118; and *Macbeth*, i.v.18) – which adds further implications. This formula would seem to derive from cheating at games, and that is its most obvious signification in the instance from *The Tempest;* but as the instances from *The Comedy of Errors*, *The Merchant of Venice*, *King John*, and especially *The Two Gentlemen of Verona* clearly indicate, the formula also involves strong histrionic connotations. In *The Two Gentlemen of Verona*, for example, when the disguised Julia and the Host are observing Proteus' wooing of Silvia, and the Host asks Julia why she dislikes the song in praise of Silvia, her reply that 'he plays false' only seems to be criticizing the skill of the musician. The 'he' actually refers to Proteus, and Julia's use of the formula is her way of saying that Proteus behaves in a manner inappropriate to his status as her lover. Julia, as she adds a few lines later, 'would always have one play but one thing' (iv.ii.69). These instances of the formula, and perhaps those in *The Tempest* and *Macbeth* as well, imply that some actions are to be conceived of less as assumptions of particular roles than as violations of more fundamental roles that ought to be adhered to. And this implication in turn suggests that the basic structure to which a character adds a temporary role when he plays the murderer or the orator is itself some kind of role.

These implications about character and experience derive even further significance from the fact that the equating of action and histrionic activity in Shakespeare's plays by no means results only from explicit or nearly explicit verbal images. Here, to illustrate what I have in mind, is the beginning of the episode from *Twelfth Night* in which Viola first meets Olivia:

> OLIVIA Give me my veil; come, throw it o'er my face;
> We'll once more hear Orsino's embassy.
> *(Enter Viola.)*
> VIOLA The honourable lady of the house, which is she?
> OLIVIA Speak to me; I shall answer for her. Your will?
> VIOLA Most radiant, exquisite, and unmatchable beauty – I pray you
> tell me if this be the lady of the house, for I never saw her. I would be
> loath to cast away my speech; for, besides that it is excellently well
> penn'd, I have taken great pains to con it. Good beauties, let me sustain
> no scorn; I am very comptible, even to the least sinister usage.
> OLIVIA Whence came you, sir?
> VIOLA I can say little more than I have studied, and that question's out

of my part. Good gentle one, give me modest assurance if you be the lady of the house, that I may proceed in my speech.

OLIVIA Are you a comedian?

VIOLA No, my profound heart; and yet, by the very fangs of malice I swear, I am not that I play. Are you the lady of the house?

OLIVIA If I do not usurp myself, I am.

VIOLA Most certain, if you are she, you do usurp yourself; for what is yours to bestow is not yours to reserve. But this is from my commission. I will on with my speech in your praise, and then show you the heart of my message.

OLIVIA Come to what is important in't. I forgive you the praise.

VIOLA Alas, I took great pains to study it, and 'tis poetical.

OLIVIA It is the more like to be feigned; I pray you keep it in. I hear you were saucy at my gates, and allow'd your approach rather to wonder at you than to hear you. If you be not mad, be gone; if you have reason, be brief; 'tis not that time of moon with me to make one in so skipping a dialogue. (I.v.156-89)

The verbal motif is here much in evidence, of course; Viola's talk of the 'speech' that 'is excellently well penn'd' and that she 'took great pains to study' as well as of her 'part' refers to her current business as Orsino's 'embassy.' So also does Olivia's 'skipping ... dialogue' and – in so far as it takes meaning from its immediate context – Viola's 'I am not that I play,' for to Olivia this line can make sense only in relation to Viola's later protestations that her parentage is 'Above my fortunes, yet my state is well: / I am a gentleman' (262-3) and that 'I am no fee'd post, lady' (268). These terms clearly define Viola's current business as a temporary role that she, though no 'comedian,' is playing. Nor is this the only role explicitly referred to: for the spectators, who possess more information than Olivia, Viola's 'I am not that I play' assigns the same status to the fictitious identity 'Cesario' that Viola is also playing.

No other examples of histrionic activity are explicitly defined, but the interest and excitement of the scene derive from the tensions produced by the interplay of several different kinds of role-playing, and all this talk of conned speeches, of parts, of playing, and of dialogues has the additional function of alerting the spectators to the further roles involved in the interplay. Olivia, as the opening line of the quoted passage indicates, wears a veil throughout most of this scene, thereby upholding the vow reported in I.i by Valentine:

The element itself, till seven years' heat,
Shall not behold her face at ample view;
But like a cloistress she will veiled walk,
And water once a day her chamber round

[handwritten marginalia: Does he connect it with ① theatre ② psych ③ sonal role ?]

> With eye-offending brine; all this to season
> A brother's dead love, which she would keep fresh
> And lasting in her sad remembrance. (I.i.26-32)

Her 'sad remembrance' is also, perhaps, one source of her objection to having to participate 'in so skipping a dialogue,' though of course the sentence as a whole by no means dispenses with the witty tone she maintains throughout. These details – the veil and the speech – remind the spectators that Olivia has her own disguise, corresponding to Viola's impersonation of Cesario; she too is playing a self-conceived role, that of the cloistered mourner.

What primarily defines Olivia's response to her brother's death as a role is the manner in which others regard this response. Before Viola's entrance Feste has called Olivia a fool for mourning her brother's death (I.v.65-7), and Viola, when Olivia finally unveils, also disapproves of her behaviour:

> Lady, you are the cruell'st she alive,
> If you will lead these graces to the grave,
> And leave the world no copy. (225-7)

These objections brand Olivia's behaviour as inappropriate to what she should be doing, and therefore they point to a further role, one that she is violating. Olivia may be the sister of a dead brother, but she is also, and more basically, the beautiful and eligible young woman she reveals herself to be when she unveils. Her way of mourning her brother thus prevents her from fulfilling what is also, in terms of the conventions of comedy as well as those of society, a role with its own specific dictates. Once more, there is a parallel between Olivia and Viola. To the spectators, Viola's 'I am not that I play' points not only to the role-like quality of the projected identity 'Cesario' but also to a discrepancy similar to that in Olivia's behaviour. What Viola actually is, in contrast to what she plays, is the same as that which Olivia basically is, a beautiful and eligible young woman. Viola too possesses a dramatic and social role that she cannot properly fulfil because she has assumed a conflicting role.

This role shared by the two characters is also implied by Olivia's ultimate response to Viola within the scene. As the meeting continues, Olivia begins to feel 'this youth's perfections / With an invisible and subtle stealth / To creep in at mine eyes' (280-2); she begins, in other words, to play her basic role of eligible young woman. The problem is, of course, that since another woman rather than a man inspires her performance, she actually misplays the dictates of her womanhood. And thus she is made to play the scene's final role, a new inappropriate role, one that structurally parallels Viola's 'part' as Orsino's 'embassy.'

This scene from *Twelfth Night* effectively demonstrates that explicit

verbal images constitute but one means, and not necessarily the most important, through which Shakespeare likens the experience being dramatized on
the stage to histrionic activity. The plays also abound in explicit *stage* images
- the cases of actual role-playing in which the characters engage. Viola's assumption of the guise of Cesario is but one example from a vast number of impersonations, which range in degree from full-dress performances like hers –
and Julia's, and Portia's, and Rosalind's, and Kent's, and Edgar's, and so on –
through conscious and deliberate misrepresentations of the self without benefit
of changes in name and costume - like those of Iago, or Richard III, or Petruchio, or Beatrice and Benedick - to the far less conscious adoptions of fictional, and often borrowed, self-misrepresentations - like those of Othello and of
most of the characters in *Twelfth Night*. Constantly, moreover, Shakespeare's
characters delight in producing plays and playlets of their own devising - some
fully rehearsed, as in *Love's Labour's Lost* and *A Midsummer Night's Dream*;
some wholly impromptu, as in *1 Henry IV*; some a curious mixture of both,
as in the opening scene of *King Lear* - and even when they are not so engaged
they are in danger of having their activity given the appearance of being a playlet through the presence of onstage spectators - as frequently in *Much Ado
About Nothing*, or in the first moments of *Antony and Cleopatra*.

Most of the plays contain one or more instances of obvious role-playing;
among the comedies, for example, only *Pericles* and *The Tempest* contain
neither a full-dress impersonation nor a clearly defined, finite internal playlet
of the sort just mentioned. In the typical Shakespeare play, therefore, a concern with role-playing is very much in evidence. The obvious stage images and
the recurring verbal theatrical metaphors are in themselves sufficient to establish role-playing as a significant dramatic theme. At the same time, through
the emphasis they give this theme they produce two further effects that help
to amplify it. They direct the spectators' attention to the less obvious instances
of impersonative role-playing, the unconscious self-misrepresentations that often betray themselves only through the character's manner or through his adoption of familiar vocabularies and rhythms. And they prompt the spectators to
realize and experience the countless examples of an additional kind of role-
playing, to perceive *as role-playing* the characters' fulfilment or violation,
through their behaviour, of the roles they possess by virtue of their social situation or their dramatic function. The consistency with which this pattern recurs in play after play demonstrates Shakespeare's considerable interest in
role-playing, both as a conception of character and as the basis for an action.
It suggests, in fact, that he thought of dramatic man as a role-playing animal.

In the chapters that follow I explore the various definitions of this term
which the plays themselves provide, but, as my analysis of the scene from
Twelfth Night and my subsequent comments have probably indicated, some
preliminary clarification is necessary, specifically an elucidation of the term

'role.' What comes next, therefore, is intended to designate the various types of phenomena my use of the term encompasses, and to suggest why I think Shakespeare and the members of his audience would have felt comfortable in regarding each of these types as a role.

I distinguish four kinds of roles in Shakespeare. Type one is a role in the literal sense, a part in a play, pageant, or other entertainment – for example, the role of Pyramus that Bottom assumes for the performance of 'The Most Lamentable Comedy and Most Cruel Death of Pyramus and Thisby.' Type two, which includes such diverse examples as Viola impersonating Cesario, 'honest' Iago, and the more unconsciously assumed self-misrepresentations of an Olivia or an Othello, is also a nonce-role, a role temporarily assumed, but rather than arising from formal theatrical activity, it constitutes one dimension of its performer's interrelation with the rest of his world. It is an alien identity that he appropriates as a means of controlling, or of trying to cope with, some aspect of his total situation.

With the possible exception of the unconsciously assumed self-misrepresentation, the authenticity of the types I have thus far isolated admits of no argument; in one case (type one) the character literally becomes an actor, in the other (type two) the relation between his primary identity and that which he projects to the world is unquestionably parallel to the relation of an actor to his external, pre-formulated part, and, like an actor, in assuming a nonce-role the character tacitly agrees to accept its dictates, of dress (when this is relevant), of speech, of gesture, and of behaviour, for so long as the performance shall last. In turning to those roles that the character possesses or acquires by virtue of his place in a dramatic design or a mimetic social structure, however, I take up less obvious and therefore more problematic conceptions of role. Nevertheless, the types I now introduce involve the same kind of externally imposed pattern as that inherent in the nonce-role.

The first of these problematic types (type three) is the dramatic role. Viola and Olivia, as I have said, both portray the beautiful and eligible young woman of comedy. Falstaff, among other things, is a *Miles Gloriosus*, a Lord of Misrule, and a morality-play Vice. Hamlet is a dramatic revenger. Richard III determines 'to prove a villain' (i.i.30), and with this speech he foreordains not only his infamous career but also his ignominious end. This type of role is likely to be the most basic and influential type for a particular character because in most cases, of course, he does not realize he is playing it, and he can escape its dictates only rarely and then only with the utmost difficulty. Some characters, it is true, manage to evade these dictates, or some of them, and this evasion constitutes an important element in their definition. But for most characters the dramatic role fixes at least the general limits within which action is possible. It determines the kind of thing that can (and sometimes must) happen to the character, the responses he can appropriately make, and especially

the ultimate fortune he is to suffer or enjoy. Where established dramatic practice, literary convention, or the Renaissance doctrine of decorum have been
particularly influential, the dramatic role will also dictate attributes of a more
specific kind, even to the extent of prescribing costume, language, and gesture.

In one respect my name for type three may be misleading, because drama
is by no means an insulated form; it draws not only upon itself but also upon
the literary tradition as a whole. Type three also includes, therefore, roles
whose specific dictates have been established less by dramatic convention than
by the evolution of general literary stereotype. One of the more familiar examples of this category is the conventional lover, whose various attributes were
thoroughly codified and amply detailed in writing of all kinds. The following
illustration, taken from the 'Characters' affixed to *Sir Thomas Overbury his
Wife* (1614), is more severely satiric than the norm, but otherwise it is wholly
typical:

> He is never without verses and musk confects, and sighs to the hazard of
> his buttons. His eyes are all white, either to wear the livery of his mistress'
> complexion or to keep Cupid from hitting the black. He fights with
> passion, and loseth much of his blood by his weapon; dreams, thence
> his paleness. His arms are carelessly used, as if their best use was nothing
> but embracements. He is untrussed, unbuttoned, and ungartered, not
> out of carelessness, but care; his farthest end being but going to bed ...
> Her favor lifts him up as the sun moisture; when he disfavors, unable to
> hold that happiness, it falls down in tears. His fingers are his orators,
> and he expresseth much of himself upon some instrument. He answers
> not, or not to the purpose, and no marvel, for he is not at home. He
> scotcheth time with dancing with his mistress, taking up of her glove,
> and wearing her feather, he is confined to her color, and dares not pass
> out of the circuit of her memory. His imagination is a fool, and it goeth
> in a pied coat of red and white. Shortly he is translated out of a man
> into folly; his imagination is the glass of lust, and himself the traitor to
> his own discretion. (*A Book of Seventeenth-Century Prose*, ed. Robert
> P. Tristram Coffin and Alexander M. Witherspoon [New York 1929]
> p. 223)

Forgetting to 'say / The perfect ceremony of love's rite,' according to
Sonnet 23, likens the lover to 'an unperfect actor on the stage / Who with his
fear is put besides his part.' This is as much as to say that the lover's behaviour
is a kind of fixed role, and as one listens to descriptions of the lover (or a particular lover) like those by Speed (*The Two Gentlemen of Verona*, II.i.16-23),
Moth (*Love's Labour's Lost*, III.i.10-19), and Benedick (*Much Ado About Nothing*, II.iii.11-19), or as one watches the behaviour of most of the lovers with

whom these speakers associate, it becomes clear that in many of the plays, especially the early comedies, to fall in love is to adopt a 'ceremony' remarkably like that depicted in the Overburyan 'Character.' One important distinction is in order, however. In *The Two Gentlemen of Verona*, Shakespeare accepts the literary stereotype as an adequate representation of the dramatic role of lover: his lovers there may be open to ridicule for their behaviour, but if so the reason is that love tends to make one ridiculous. In *Much Ado About Nothing* or *Twelfth Night*, on the other hand, the literary stereotype calls for ridicule not because love is intrinsically absurd but because the lover who performs this 'ceremony' lacks the imagination to invent a fresh and meaningful expression of the feeling his dramatic role obliges him to demonstrate. In this case the stereotype is actually an example not of a type three role but of the self-misrepresentations that belong to type two.

Playing the lover does not always involve an appropriate response to dramatic role, however, for 'the lover' is also an example of the fourth and most problematic type of role, that which a character possesses by virtue of his position in a mimetic social structure. Since this conception of role is by far the most difficult to acknowledge and may seem to involve a mere play on words, it requires for its validation some proof that the Elizabethans, whose social structure provided the model for the plays to imitate, regarded or at least responded to their social positions as if they were indeed akin to theatrical parts. I turn, then, to a consideration of the highest social role of all, the king, about whom James I writes in the *Basilicon Doron*, 'It is a true olde saying, That a King is as one set on a stage, whose smallest actions and gestures, all the people gazinglie doe beholde' (ed. James Craigie, London 1944, p. 163; cf. p. 12). The two excerpts that follow are designed to expand James's comparison, to provide some sense of just how apt it is.

Paul Hentzner, a German who travelled through England in 1598, has left the following account of his visit to the Royal Palace of Greenwich:

We were admitted by an order, which Mr. Rogers (Daniel Rogerius) had procured from the Lord Chamberlain, into the Presence-Chamber hung with rich tapestry, and the floor, after the English fashion, strewed with hay, through which the Queen commonly passes in her way to chapel. At the door stood a gentleman dressed in velvet, with a gold chain, whose office was to introduce to the Queen any person of distinction that came to wait on her. It was Sunday, when there is usually the greatest attendance of nobility. In the same hall were the Archbishop of Canterbury, the Bishop of London, a great number of Counsellors of State, Officers of the Crown, and Gentlemen, who waited the Queen's coming out, which she did from her own apartment when it was time to go to prayers, attended in the following manner:–

First went Gentlemen, Barons, Earls, Knights of the Garter, all richly dressed and bareheaded; next came the Lord High Chancellor of England, bearing the seals in a red silk purse, between two, one of whom carried the royal sceptre, the other the sword of state in a red scabbard, studded with golden fleur-de-lis, the point upwards; next came the Queen, in the 65th year of her age (as we were told), very majestic; her face oblong, fair but wrinkled; her eyes small, yet black and pleasant; her nose a little hooked, her lips narrow, and her teeth black, (a defect the English seem subject to, from their too great use of sugar); she had in her ears two pearls with very rich drops; her hair was of an auburn colour, but false (*crinem fulvum, sed factitium*); upon her head she had a small crown, reported to be made of some of the gold of the celebrated Luneburg table; her bosom was uncovered, as all the English ladies have it till they marry; and she had on a necklace of exceeding fine jewels; her hands were slender, her fingers rather long, and her stature neither tall nor low; her air was stately, her manner of speaking mild and obliging. That day she was dressed in white silk, bordered with pearls of the size of beans, and over it a mantle of black silk shot with silver threads; her train was very long, the end of it borne by a marchioness; instead of a chain, she had an oblong collar of gold and jewels. As she went along in all this state and magnificence, she spoke very graciously, first to one, then to another (whether foreign ministers, or those who attend for different reasons), in English, French, and Italian; for besides being well skilled in Greek, Latin, and the languages I have mentioned, she is mistress of Spanish, Scotch, and Dutch (*Belgicum*). Whoever speaks to her, it is kneeling; now and then she raises some with her hand. While we were there, William Slawata, a Bohemian Baron, had letters to present to her; and she, after pulling off her glove, gave him her right hand to kiss, sparkling with rings and jewels – a mark of particular favour. Wherever she turned her face as she was going along, everybody fell down on their knees. The ladies of the court followed next to her, very handsome and well-shaped, and for the most part dressed in white. She was guarded on each side by the gentlemen pensioners, fifty in number, with gilt halberds. In the ante-chapel, next the hall where we were, petitions were presented to her, and she received them most graciously, which occasioned the acclamation of *God save the Quene Elizabeth!* She answered it with *I thancke you myn good peupel.* In the chapel was excellent music; as soon as it and the service were over, which scarcely exceeded half-an-hour, the Queen returned in the same state and order, and prepared to go to dinner. But while she was still at prayers, we saw her table set out with the following solemnity:– A gentleman entered the room bearing a rod, and along with him another .

who had a table-cloth, which after they had both knelt three times, with the utmost veneration, he spread upon the table, and after kneeling again, they both retired. Then came two others, one with the rod again, the other with a salt-cellar, a plate and bread; when they had knelt as the others had done, and placed what was brought upon the table, they too retired with the same ceremonies performed by the first. At last came an unmarried lady of extraordinary beauty (we were told that she was a countess) and along with her a married one, bearing a tasting-knife; the former was dressed in white silk, who, when she had prostrated herself three times, in the most graceful manner approached the table and rubbed the plates with bread and salt with as much awe as if the Queen had been present. When they had waited there a little while, the yeomen of the guard entered, bareheaded, clothed in scarlet, with a golden rose upon their backs, bringing in at each turn a course of twenty-four dishes, served in silver most of it gilt; these dishes were received by a gentleman in the same order as they were brought and placed upon the table, while the lady-taster gave to each of the guard a mouthful to eat of the particular dish he had brought, for fear of any poison. During the time that this guard, which consists of the tallest and stoutest men that can be found in all England, 100 in number, being carefully selected for this service, were bringing dinner, twelve trumpets and two kettle-drums made the hall ring for half-an-hour together. At the end of this ceremonial, a number of unmarried ladies appeared, who with particular solemnity lifted the meat off the table, and conveyed it into the Queen's inner and more private chamber, where after she had chosen for herself, the rest goes to the ladies of the Court. (*England as Seen by Foreigners*, ed. William Brenchley Rye, London 1865, pp. 103-7)

Hentzner's glimpse of Elizabeth's court may be profitably supplemented with the following extracts from a contemporary Spanish description of the 'Banquet and Entertainment Given by James I to the Constable of Castile at Whitehall Palace, on Sunday, Aug. 19, 1604':

The dishes were brought in by gentlemen and servants of the King, who were accompanied by the Lord Chamberlain, and before placing them on the table they made four or five obeisances. The Earls of Pembroke (*Panbrue*) and of Southampton officiated as gentlemen-ushers. Their Majesties with the Prince [Henry] entered after the Constable and the others, and placed themselves at their throne, and all stood in a line to hear the grace said; the Constable being at the King's side and the Count de Villamediana on the Queen's. Their Majesties washed their hands in the same basin, the Lord Treasurer handing the towel to the King, and the High Admiral to the Queen. The Prince washed in another basin, in which water was also taken to the Constable, who was waited upon by the same gentlemen. They took their seats in the following manner: their Majesties sat at the head of the table, at a distance from each other, under the canopy of state, the Queen being on the right hand, on chairs of brocade with cushions; and at her side, a little apart, sat the Constable, on a tabouret of brocade with a high cushion of the same, and on the side of the King the Prince was seated in like manner ...

There was plenty of instrumental music, and the banquet was sumptuous and profuse. The first thing the King did was to send the Constable a melon and half a dozen of oranges on a very green branch, telling him that they were the fruit of Spain transplanted into England; to which the latter, kissing his hand, replied that he valued the gift more as coming from his Majesty than as being the fruit of his own country; he then divided the melon with their Majesties, and Don Blasco de Aragon handed the plate to the Queen, who politely and graciously acknowledged the attention. Soon afterwards the King stood up, and with his head uncovered drank to the Constable the health of their Spanish Majesties, and may the peace be happy and perpetual! The Constable pledged him in like manner, and replied that he entertained the same hope and that from the peace the greatest advantages might result to both crowns and to christendom. The toast was then drunk by the Count Villamediana and the others present, to the delight and applause of their Majesties. Immediately afterwards, the Constable, seeing that another opportunity might not be afforded him, rose and drank to the King the health of the Queen from the lid of a cup of agate of extraordinary beauty and richness, set with diamonds and rubies, praying his Majesty would condescend to drink the toast from the cup, which he did accordingly, and ordered it to be passed round to the Prince and the others; and the Constable directed that the cup should remain in his Majesty's buffet. At this period the people shouted out: *Peace, peace, peace! God save the King! God save the King! God save the King!* and a king at arms presented himself before the table, and after the drums, trumpets, and other instruments had sounded, with a loud voice said in English:– 'that the kingdom returned many thanks to his Majesty for having concluded with the King of Spain so advantageous a peace, and he prayed to God that it might endure for many ages, and his subjects hoped that his Majesty would endeavour with all his might to maintain it, so that they might enjoy from it tranquillity and repose, and that security and advantage might result to all his people; and therefore they prayed him to allow the same to be published in the kingdoms and dominions of his Majesty.' The King gave permission accordingly and the peace was forthwith proclaimed in that city, the proclamation being repeated at every fifty paces ... (Rye, pp. 118-21)

I have quoted these accounts at length for two reasons. Both Hentzner and the anonymous Spanish writer lend substance to James I's image of the king 'as one set on a stage' by conveying an unmistakable sense of a staged action going on before an audience (this impression is enhanced in the second account by the presence of 'the people' at the banquet) and of the participants acting out rather than spontaneously executing their various speeches and gestures. Nonetheless, I am more interested in these accounts for their concrete presentation of much of the 'thrice gorgeous ceremony' (*Henry V,* IV.i.262) that appertains to the king: the special treatment he receives from others, the special language and gestures he employs, his being propertied, costumed, and endowed with

> the balm, the sceptre, and the ball,
> The sword, the mace, the crown imperial,
> The intertissued robe of gold and pearl,
> The farced title running fore the king,
> The throne he sits on ... the tide of pomp
> That beats upon the high shore of this world. (256-61)

This ceremony belongs not to the individual king but to the abstract idea of *the King* which exists prior to the accession of the individual king and lives on after his death; the ceremony is an attribute of what James I and the many other Elizabethan writers on kingship call 'the King's office': the whole pattern of representational divinity, glory, rights, responsibilities, and requirements which the individual king must learn and adapt himself to. James wrote the *Basilicon Doron,* for example, to train his son Henry 'in all the pointes of a Kings office' (p.7), and in it he makes clear that the king's own contribution to the royal ceremony has nothing to do with his personal choice. He tells Henry how, what, and how much he must eat and drink, how he must sleep, what 'rayment' he must wear, and what forms his speaking, language, and gesture must take. Here, to illustrate, are excerpts from his instructions on language and on gesture:

> In your language be plaine, honest, naturall, comelie, cleane, short, and sentencious: eschewing both the extremities, aswell in not using any rusticall corrupt leide [manner of speaking], as booke-language, and pen and inke-horne tearmes: and least of all mignarde [dainty] & effœminate tearmes. (p. 179)

Use also the like forme in your gesture; neither looking sillelie, like a stupide pedant; nor unsetledlie, with an uncouth morgue [haughty demeanour], like a new-com-over Cavalier: but let your behavior be naturall, grave, and according to the fashion of the countrie. Be not over sparing in your courtesies; for that will be imputed to in-civility & arrogancie: nor yet over prodigal in jowking or nodding at every step; for that forme of being populare, becommeth better aspiring *Absalons*, then lawfull Kings: framing every your gesture according to your present actions: looking gravelie & with a majestie when ye sit in judgement, or gives audience to Embassadours; homely, when ye are in private with your owne servantes; merelie, when ye are at any pastime or merrie discourse; and let your countenance smell of courage and magnanimitie when ye are at the warres. (p. 181)

But it is not alone through its attendant ceremony that kingship qualifies as a role. The 'pointes of a Kings office' include not only those rules that the king must observe in defining his kingliness ritualistically but also further rules dictating both the functions that go with his office and the strategies through which he must perform them. James is, naturally, less specific in telling Henry how, as he once puts it, to 'play the wise Kings part' (p. 101), but the main requirements are abundantly clear. The 'lawfull good King,' he informs Henry,

thinking his highest honor to consist in the due discharge of his calling, employeth all his studie and paines, to procure and maintaine, by the making and execution of good lawes, the well fare and peace of his people; and as their naturall father & kindly maister, thinketh his greatest contentment standeth in their prosperity, and his greatest suretie in having their harts, subjecting his owne private affections and appetites to the weale and standing of his subjectes, ever thinking the common interesse his cheefest particulare ... (p. 55).

And he goes on to declare how the king should behave when first ascending his throne, how he should treat each of the three estates, how he should conduct himself towards other princes, and when and how he should wage war. 'But it is not ynough to a good King,' James adds, 'by the scepter of good lawes well execute to governe, & by the force of armes to protect his people; if he joyne not therewith his vertuous life in his owne person, and in the person of his Court and companie: by good example alluring his subjectes to the love of vertue, and hatred of vice' (pp. 103, 105). And in this context he instructs Henry on the choosing and wise ruling of courtiers, the selection of a queen, and the virtues that the king must make his own, concluding as follows:

'But above all vertues, study to knowe well your owne craft, which is to rule your people. And when I say this I bid you knowe all craftes. For except ye knowe everie one, howe can ye controlle every one, whiche is your proper office?' (p. 143).

The extensive ceremony appertaining to kingship simplifies a perception of the role-like qualities of the king's office; what is true of the king, however, is also true of the other social positions: each has its 'proper office,' which its occupant must learn and uphold. The accounts by Hentzner and the anonymous Spanish writer also indicate, for example, some of the ceremony defining the office of courtier, and for confirmation that the courtier, like his master, had a fairly fixed role to play, one need only glance at some of the items in the 'brief rehearsal of the chief conditions and qualities in a Courtier' which Sir Thomas Hoby appended to his translation of Castiglione's *Il Cortegiano:*

> To speak and write the language that is most in use among the common people, without inventing new words, inkhorn terms, or strange phrases, and such as be grown out of use by long time ...
>
> To speak always of matters likely, lest he be counted a liar in reporting of wonders and strange miracles ...
>
> To use evermore toward his Prince or Lord the respect that becometh the servant toward his master ...
>
> To be handsome and cleanly in his apparel ...
>
> To make his garments after the fashion of the most, and those to be black, or of some darkish and sad color, not garish ...
>
> The final end of a courtier, whereto all his good conditions and honest qualities tend, is to become an instructor and teacher of his Prince or Lord, inclining him to virtuous practices; and to be frank and free with him, after he is once in favor, in matters touching his honor and estimation, always putting him in mind to follow virtue and to flee vice, opening unto him the commodities of the one and inconveniences of the other; and to shut his ear against flatterers, which are the first beginning of self-seeking and all ignorance. (*Tudor Poetry and Prose*, ed. J. William Hebel et al. [New York 1953] pp. 712, 714-15)

But the ultimate test of my claims about the social role involves, of course, the nature of the less public social positions – those of lover, friend, servant, and the various familial relationships. These also qualify as roles in my sense, for the notion of 'office' pervaded the entire Elizabethan social fabric. To illustrate the role-like qualities of these less public 'offices,' I draw on T.B.'s English translation of *The French Academie* by Pierre de la Primaudaye. This book was written to teach its readers how they ought to govern themselves 'wisely and dutifully in all humane actions and affaires, and in all

charges and places whatsoever, either publike or private whereunto [they] shall
be called' (third edition 1594, Sig B4v.), and, like most other courtesy books
as well as *The Courtier* and the *Basilicon Doron*, rather than merely presuming
to give advice it instead spells out what it assumes to be unequivocal and unal-
terable facts of life. The most illuminating of its many chapters is number 48,
'Of the dutie of a Wife towards hir Husband.' This chapter prescribes the proper costume of a wife:

> A wife ought to be modest in hir garments and ornaments of hir body,
> and not use such sumptuous apparel as the law or custom of the coun-
> trey permitteth; (p. 516)

it prescribes how and what she must speak:

> Moreover a woman must have a speciall care to be silent, and to speake
> as seldome as she may, unlesse it be to hir husband, or at his bidding ...
> Like wise a woman that respecteth hir honour, ought to be ashamed to
> utter any dishonest speeches, floutes & jests, and no lesse ashamed to
> give eare unto them ... She must bestow as much time as she can steale
> from domesticall affaires, in the studie of notable sayings, and of the
> morall sentences of auncient Sages and good men. And it were a seem-
> ely and honorable thing to heare a woman speake to hir husband in this
> sort: Husband, you are my teacher, my governour and master in Philo-
> sophie, and in the knowledge of most excellent and heavenly sciences;
> (pp. 517, 518)

it prescribes her proper response to her husband:

> So is she a bad wife and unreasonable, which frowneth when hir husband
> is desirous to be mery with her, & to take some honest recreation: or
> contrarywise, which laugheth and sporteth hir selfe when she seeth him
> full of busines and greatly troubled ... A wife must have no proper and
> peculiar passion or affection to hir self, but must be partaker of the
> pastimes, affaires, thoughts & laughters of hir husband ... A wife must
> not trust too much either to hir wealth, or to the nobilitie of hir race,
> or to hir beautie, but to that which setteth nearest hir husbands hart,
> that is, to hir behavior, maners and conversation, taking order that these
> things be not hard, troublesom, or irksom to hir husband every day, but
> such as please him and agree with his conditions; (pp. 513-14)

and it gives numerous directions, of which the following are representative, on
how she must conduct herself in her day-to-day affairs:

A wise woman that loveth hir husband as becometh hir, somtime toller-
ateth & dissembleth an evil intreatie, trusting so much to hir constancie
& vertue, that by continuing in hir dutie she is able to bring him back
again to his. She must governe hir selfe so discreetly, that neither hir
neighbours, nor other of hir familiar friends be made acquainted in any
sort with hir complaints & grievances ... (p. 514)

And seeing it is the duty of an honest woman to take upon hir the care
& oversight of household affaires, she must keep at home, and not love
to gad abroad, or be desirous of meetings ... (pp. 515-16)

Wives should avoid plaies, dancing, masking, hunting and discharging
of harquebuzes, with such other dealings very unmeete for their sexe.
(p. 518)

Like the king and the courtier, therefore, the wife had a fixed role from which
she could not justifiably deviate, and for her to have ignored its dictates would
have been 'to play the ill huswife' (p. 515). Once again, moreover, it is not a
question of a single social position, for *The French Academie* has similar chapters on the duties of the husband, the master, the servant, and the child, as
well as sections on how to fulfil – or play – the offices of friend and lover.
    The kind of role I have listed first – the actual theatrical part – requires
no further definition. Types two to four, on the other hand – the nonce-role,
the literary-dramatic role, and the social role – call for at least one additional
comment. In labelling an example of these types a 'role,' I do not have in mind,
of course, the usual theatrical sense of the term, that of a part in a play whose
every word, gesture, and movement have been established or implied by its
creator; nor, on the other hand, do I mean anything so vague and general as
the current rather loose sense of the term, in which everything we do becomes
a role and any theatrical connection is but dimly perceived if it is perceived at
all. An analogy for what I have in mind exists in the sense of 'role' that has
been disseminated by the Commedia dell'arte. A Commedia dell'arte role, such
as Harlequin or 'the lean and slipper'd pantaloon' (*As You Like It*, II.vii.158),
was never fully scripted because the plays including it were merely scenarios.
Full scripting was unnecessary because the role itself was established by tradition and comprised both a complete set of 'gestures' – characteristic costume,
language, and mannerisms – and an equally complete set of 'moves' – appropriate responses, verbal or visual, to whatever situation the scenarist might
concoct. The actor that played Harlequin might modify the role to suit his
own personality, but he could do so only within a fixed range of possibilities.
Once he entered a scene his 'gestures' would have to conform to the familiar
pattern characteristic of Harlequin, and once an action involving him began he

could cope with it only as Harlequin might. For if he adopted other 'gestures' and 'moves' he would project an uncomfortable discrepancy between his own image and the conventions of the part he pretended to play.

To what extent Shakespeare had knowledge of the Commedia dell'arte roles is an unanswerable question, but it is also an irrelevant one. What is relevant is that Shakespeare, as a practising dramatist and a highly mobile member of the social structure of his time, was in a remarkable position not only to experience all the types of roles I have outlined but also to be especially alert to the phenomenon of role-playing and its various ramifications. As a practising dramatist, he knew well, of course, the traditional dramatic roles, and since he wrote for a fairly stable company of players, he also constantly faced the task of fitting the parts he created to given actors – and thus must often have unavoidably realized some of the difficulties involved in the relation between a role and its performer. As a highly mobile member of the social structure of his time, he not only experienced all the social roles at first hand, but with his dramatist's eye he must also have experienced them *as roles*, particularly on those occasions when he attended functions at court and would have had to be especially careful about getting his own part right; nor, surely, was his dramatist's eye blind to the endless playing of nonce-roles that goes on in all societies, though probably never more so than in the extremely histrionic milieu in which he lived. It is no wonder, then, that his plays are so alive to the various issues of roles and role-playing and that these issues are so fundamental to them.

2 Identity and role

Am not I Christopher Sly, old Sly's son of Burton Heath; by birth a pedlar, by education a cardmaker, by transmutation a bearherd, and now by present profession a tinker? Ask Marian Hacket, the fat ale-wife of Wincot, if she know me not.

(The Taming of the Shrew, Ind.ii.16-19)

The Comedy of Errors is in all probability Shakespeare's first comedy, perhaps even his first play, and, not surprisingly, it lacks the explicit emphasis on role-playing that was to become characteristic as early as *Richard III* and *The Taming of the Shrew*. Few clear-cut verbal metaphors of the theatre occur in *The Comedy of Errors*, and although the play contains much impersonation, most of it unwilling, stage images like Julia's disguise in *The Two Gentlemen of Verona* or the Show of the Nine Worthies in *Love's Labour's Lost* are conspicuously lacking; as the play's language tends to suggest, Shakespeare at this point seems far more conscious of social reality than of the reality of his profession. But *The Comedy of Errors* is nonetheless well worth examining here because of what it reveals about Shakespeare's sense of dramatic character and of the relation between a character's identity and role-playing. Identity is of course an important dramatic issue throughout Shakespeare, yet it is nowhere more explicitly so than in this play. Oddly enough, the play offers not one but two definitions of identity, the first perceivable through focusing upon action, the second through focusing on character.

The action of *The Comedy of Errors* derives, of course, from Plautus' *Menaechmi*, but by adding the second pair of twins and by other means Shakespeare has brought into central focus a type of activity that Plautus had shown surprisingly little interest in. The most recurrent as well as the most characteristic action in Shakespeare's play is the attribution of identity to someone who does not correspond to it. Early on the misattributed identity is simply that of a second character with whom the first has been confused, but before long the process grows more complicated, and thus throughout most of the play the falsely attributed identity is a fiction even within the world of the play, a new creation, a bizarre composite of the actual identity of one character, certain statements and actions of another, and the wild imaginings of a third. On three occasions, moreover, a character's claim to a particular identity is rejected, and in the process a third kind of misattributed identity emerges, for the character is implicitly identified as an impostor. Whichever of these three kinds of false identity is involved in any given case, however, the basic pattern remains the same. The spectators are continually presented with a discrepancy between the projected identity and the character to whom it is attributed.

What complicates this basic pattern is that, although the discrepancy is always obvious to the spectators and usually apparent to the mistaken character, it often carries no real weight in the action. Time and time again, it is the attributed rather than the actual identity that determines the experience of the character, whether he notes the discrepancy or not. In II.i, the visiting Antipholus beats the local Dromio because he supposes him to be *his* Dromio and does not care to be flouted by a servant. That he has erred in his rather forceful attribution of identity is true enough, but for all practical purposes this fact is irrelevant as far as poor Dromio is concerned: the beating has been administered; in existence if not in essence, Dromio of Ephesus has become his Syracusan twin. Dromio here has no idea that he is the victim of error, but knowledge of the discrepancy would probably not have saved him, since it seldom does the mistaken character any good. In III.i, the local Antipholus knows full well that he is not the impostor his wife Adriana and the visiting Dromio imply him to be, but he must nevertheless leave without gaining entry to his house. Later he is equally sure he is not the man – he thinks there is no such person – who is guilty of all the charges levelled against him, but he must nevertheless submit to arrest for debt in IV.i and to being subdued as a madman in IV.iv. This complication, in which the mistaken character is made to undergo experiences appropriate to the identity imposed on him, combines well with the fictitiousness of most of the imposed identities. Identity *per se* begins to look like a kind of role that one might play as if one were an actor portraying the part of some fictional character.

Other aspects of the play help to intensify this effect. Shakespeare introduces the whole series of errors by emphasizing through the plight of Aegeon the danger of being a Syracusan in Ephesus, and when the focus shifts to Antipholus of Syracuse in I.ii, the first words of the scene are spoken by an anonymous merchant who advises Antipholus to 'give out' that he is 'of Epidamnum' – in other words, to play a role – 'Lest that your goods too soon be confiscate' (1-2). Antipholus never has an opportunity to attempt this stratagem, and the danger of being a Syracusan is forgotten as the play concerns itself exclusively with the kaleidoscopic sequence of confusions, but in effect he improves on the merchant's advice, however unintentionally, by playing the role not of an Epidamnian but of an Ephesian – the local Antipholus.

The notion of identity as a role becomes fully explicit in II.ii, when Ad-

riana and her sister, Luciana, mistake Antipholus and Dromio of Syracuse for
their Ephesian twins. After reproaching her supposed husband for his infidelity, Adriana orders him home to dinner, where Dromio, according to her command, is to 'keep the gate' and 'let no creature enter' (205, 209). She then repeats this command with 'Dromio, play the porter well' (210), and Dromio's
response – 'Master, shall I be porter at the gate?' (216) – suggests that in this
world there is no real difference between being something and playing something. More important, Adriana's command is interestingly ambiguous. 'Porter' clearly means the office of gatekeeper, which is indeed something that
can be 'played,' since it has a number of traditional functions, including those
that Adriana specifically mentions. At the same time, however, 'the porter' also denotes Dromio of Ephesus, and hence her command has the additional effect of directing Dromio to 'play' a particular identity. The sequel indicates
that both of these meanings are operative. In driving away the two Ephesians
in III.i, Dromio fulfils Adriana's sense of playing the porter, and in the process
he also manages to appropriate the identity of the other Dromio, not only by
obeying Adriana but also, and more persuasively, by falling into the clutches
of Nell the kitchen-wench, his twin's sweetheart. Antipholus, Dromio's master,
responds in a similar fashion. He is bewildered by the presumptuous behaviour
of these strange women and especially by their commands to himself and
Dromio, but he decides to 'say as they say, and persever so' (II.ii.214). He too,
therefore, agrees to play a role, to take direction from others and speak the
lines they expect from him; and, like Dromio, he is successful in playing his
assigned part. He refuses to treat Adriana as a wife, for he instead vigorously
woos Luciana, but this behaviour, rather than exposing the imposture, is inter-
preted by Adriana as merely the latest and the most outrageous example of
her husband's philandering.

Oddly enough, the characters' attitudes towards their own identities further help to establish this notion of identity as role. When Dromio of Syracuse
finds an alien identity imposed on him by Adriana and Luciana, he does not,
even when he gets the chance, insist on the authenticity of his own; instead, he
fears he has been 'transformed' (II.ii.194), and later, after his experience with
Nell, he can no longer regard himself as 'Dromio,' Antipholus' 'man,' or 'myself': 'I am an ass, I am a woman's man, and besides myself' (III.ii.73-7). Antipholus usually tries to explain his peculiar experience by speculating about
the nature of those who mistake him, but, under the compulsion of his feeling
for Luciana, even he entertains the possibility of transformation:

> Against my soul's pure truth why labour you
> To make it wander in an unknown field?
> Are you a god? Would you create me new?
> Transform me, then, and to your pow'r I'll yield.

> But *if that I am I*, then well I know
> Your weeping sister is no wife of mine. (37-42; my italics)

Despite this talk about his 'soul's pure truth,' he acknowledges that he may not be who he thinks he is. Like his servant, he sees his identity, that which should be his most intrinsic possession, as perhaps no more an essential part of himself than a dramatic role is of the actor who performs it.

The definition of identity emerging from a focus on character, which owes even less to Plautus, can most readily be extrapolated from the long speech in II.ii in which Adriana mistakes the visiting Antipholus for her husband and proceeds to upbraid him. Her opening lines succinctly establish the basic issue:

> Ay, ay, Antipholus, look strange and frown.
> Some other mistress hath thy sweet aspects;
> I am not Adriana, nor thy wife. (109-11)

The third line contains more than sarcasm, for Adriana intends a firm cause-and-effect relationship; in her mind she is no longer Adriana because Adriana is the wife of Antipholus and Antipholus no longer behaves like a husband. When she then goes on to argue that, 'being strange' to her, Antipholus is therefore 'estranged' from himself, since she, as his wife, is 'better than thy dear self's better part' (119-22), she indicates that the marriage relationship also helps determine the identity of the husband; but, naturally, she is more interested in her own situation, which she further expounds in the 'drop of water' passage:

> For know, my love, as easy mayst thou fall
> A drop of water in the breaking gulf,
> And take unmingled thence that drop again
> Without addition or diminishing,
> As take from me thyself, and not me too. (124-8)

In fact, she concludes, her identity is so intricately dependent on her link with her husband that his philandering necessarily alters her very nature:

> For if we two be one, and thou play false,
> I do digest the poison of thy flesh,
> Being strumpeted by thy contagion. (141-3)

Adriana is by no means the only one to perceive identity in this way, nor is the marriage tie the only relationship regarded by the characters as a crucial factor in defining their identities. Antipholus of Syracuse extols Luciana as

> mine own self's better part;
> Mine eye's clear eye, my dear heart's dearer heart,
> My food, my fortune, and my sweet hope's aim,
> My sole earth's heaven, and my heaven's claim;

and when Luciana, thinking him to be her sister's husband, objects, 'All this my sister is, or else should be,' he replies, 'Call thyself sister, sweet, for I am thee' (III.ii.61-6). For Dromio of Syracuse, identity depends on his relation to his master: 'Do you know me, sir? Am I Dromio? Am I your man? Am I myself?' (73-4). For Antipholus of Ephesus, apparently, it depends in part on his relation to the community as a whole – at least he refrains from breaking in his own door when Balthazar warns him that 'Herein you war against your reputation' (III.i.86). It is, however, in the final scene of the play that Shakespeare most clearly establishes the overwhelming importance of external relationships in the composition of identity. Here all the characters are properly identified, but only in terms of their links with one another, that is, as husbands, wives, fathers, sons, mothers, masters, servants, and – most important of all – brothers. The celebration called for by Aemilia is properly a nativity feast because the central characters are truly reborn; each of them has gained new relationships and thus in the metaphysics of the play transformed his identity.

A focus on character reveals, therefore, that identity consists of the various functions a character acquires through participating in a number of social relationships. 'Antipholus of Ephesus,' for example, is by the end of the play a label designating the point of intersection where a number of separate identities converge, though not without the possibility of collision. To be Antipholus of Ephesus is to be husband of Adriana, brother-in-law of Luciana, master of Dromio of Ephesus, 'friend' of the Courtesan (this 'identity' will probably dissolve), business acquaintance of Balthazar and Angelo, respected member of Ephesian society, loyal soldier of the Duke, son of Aegeon and Aemilia, and brother of Antipholus of Syracuse. Similar points of intersection, involving similar functions, form the identities of all the other characters in the play.

These functions are, of course, 'roles' in the sense I establish in the introduction, and my term is fully justified by the dialogue of the play, which often speaks of the various functions as if they were dramatic parts dictating definite moves to the characters possessing them. Adriana's charge that her husband strumpets her by playing false establishes this conception quite explicitly. Her phrase 'play false' not only denotes a failure to live up to certain obligations imposed by the state of being a husband; through the histrionic metaphor it also suggests that this failure is analogous to the ineffective performance of a dramatic part, that her husband is a bad actor in more senses than one. The play's word for what I have called a 'function' is the usual Elizabethan term, 'office.' Luciana employs it, for example, in a long speech of advice in which, still mistaking the visiting Antipholus for his Ephesian twin, she reminds him of the 'husband's office' (III.ii.2). This office requires, she asserts, that regardless of the husband's true feeling for his wife, he must still 'use her with ... kindness' (6). He must maintain a specified manner toward her ('Look sweet,' 11; 'Bear a fair presence, though your heart be tainted,' 13; assume 'the carriage of a holy saint,' 14) and address her in a specified way ('Speak fair,' 11; 'Be not thy tongue thy own shame's orator,' 10). Luciana here sounds much like *The French Academie* – or, especially in her conclusion, like a director instructing an actor: 'Then, gentle brother, get you in again; / Comfort my sister, cheer her, call her wife' (25-6).

Other functions are similarly defined. Adriana calls her wifehood an 'office' and specifies some of its attributes (v.i.98-100). Both Antipholus of Syracuse and his Dromio focus on some of the obligations the office of servant imposes (II.ii.32-4, 63-4; IV.i.113-14). The Duke of Ephesus pities Aegeon and would gladly help him, 'were it not against our laws, / Against my crown, my oath, my dignity, / Which princes, would they, may not disannul' (I.i.143-5). And Pinch, according to the local Antipholus, was not merely conjuring in IV.iv; more precisely, he 'took on him as a conjurer' (v.i.242).

For Pinch and the Duke, identity is equivalent to a single role. For most of the others, however, it is a more complicated matter because in each case several roles are involved. Yet not even for these others is identity some kind of unified personality ('character' in the psychological sense) but rather the nexus of the various social roles that they are given to play.

Any attempt to penetrate beneath this nexus in search of the 'essential man' is doomed to failure. Antipholus of Syracuse mentions at one point his 'soul's pure truth' (III.ii.37), but it is an empty, undramatized cliché without any validity. Antipholus has no inner substance; apart from his ability to perform properly whichever of his roles the immediate situation seems to call for, or his capacity to express bewilderment in response to bewildering events, he is devoid of 'personality.' The reason is obvious. Antipholus of Syracuse must lack inner substance because the play requires that he be interchangeable with his Ephesian twin. To the spectator, the only discernible difference between them is that Antipholus of Ephesus is more irascible and Antipholus of Syracuse more likely to feel bafflement than outrage. Partly this difference is a result of their contrasting experiences, but partly, also, it is a dramatic necessity: the irascibility of Antipholus of Ephesus serves him – and Shakespeare – a useful turn by prompting his escape from bondage so that he can seek out the Duke, demand satisfaction, and thus bring about the resolution of the play.

What penetration beneath the nexus of roles discovers is not a lifelike personality but instead a different kind of role, the dramatic role, that which is dictated by the demands of the play. A glimpse of this kind of role can also be
seen in the 'characterization' that Antipholus of Syracuse provides for his
servant:

> A trusty villain, sir, that very oft,
> When I am dull with care and melancholy,
> Lightens my humour with his merry jests. (I.ii.19-21)

This passage, which prepares for Dromio's incidental comic routines, describes
only his function in the play, his dramatic role. It labels him the Comic Slave,
just as his master, at bottom, is no more nor less than the essentially neutral
figure that both tradition and necessity require for the role of victim in a farce
mechanism.

The notion of dramatic character underlying both of the definitions of
identity I have derived from *The Comedy of Errors* never finds full and unequivocal explicit articulation anywhere in the plays. But in one speech from *Much
Ado About Nothing* this notion of character does come nearer the surface
than usual. The speech is Claudio's account to Don Pedro of how his falling in
love with Hero has changed him utterly:

> O, my lord,
> When you went onward on this ended action,
> I look'd upon her with a soldier's eye,
> That lik'd, but had a rougher task in hand
> Than to drive liking to the name of love;
> But now I am return'd, and that war-thoughts
> Have left their places vacant, in their rooms
> Come thronging soft and delicate desires,
> All prompting me how fair young Hero is,
> Saying I lik'd her ere I went to wars. (I.i.258-67)

Claudio's description of how he became a lover implies that the 'soft
and delicate desires' which prompted him to dote on Hero thronged into his
consciousness *because* his prior 'war-thoughts' had already retreated, leaving
'vacant' places in their wake. This conceit pictures Claudio as being at bottom
an empty vessel without identity or personality until he assumes a particular
role. It suggests that he now assumes the lover's role only, or at least primarily,
because he is for the moment 'at liberty.' The war's end has deprived him of
his role as soldier, and he needs some other role - any role at all, according to
the implication - in order to have an identity, in order to be able to place him-

self in relation to the rest of reality. Aside from the tragedies, Shakespeare seldom focuses on such a moment of complete emptiness, of complete absence of 'character,' and therefore his doing so here introduces a particular implication about Claudio: the passive, almost accidental manner in which he assumes the role of lover is neatly consistent with his inability, throughout most of the play, to surrender himself fully to the part, to play it effectively. Nevertheless, the conceit of the empty vessel that derives its 'character' from the external role or roles it acquires is by no means out of keeping with the implications of *The Comedy of Errors* – or, indeed, of the other plays. The conceit can well serve as a metaphor not only for Claudio but for Shakespearian dramatic man in general.

The first of the two conceptions of identity I have extrapolated from *The Comedy of Errors* – that which regards identity as itself a role – does not, in its purest state, generate a great deal of impact in the plays as a whole. Shakespeare is not Brecht, nor do his characters much resemble a figure like Galy-Gay in *A Man's a Man*. Petruchio's Kate, it is true, does alter sharply from Shrew to Obedient Wife (with the ease of an actor changing parts, one could add – *if*, that is, the comparison presupposes an actor whose producer-director has energetically coerced him into making the change). But an alteration as thorough as Kate's is a rarity – one critical view on her play would deny even this case – and in Christopher Sly *The Taming of the Shrew* also dramatizes a counter-example, a character whose belief that he's been transformed clashes hilariously with his utter incapacity for change.

But this is not to say that this first conception of identity has no validity for the other plays. It expresses metaphorically the dramatic attitude towards identity which underlies and makes possible much of the action in them. One manifestation of this dramatic attitude – a manifestation that is most familiar in the comedies – is the capacity of the characters, when they assume disguises or adopt impersonations, to become *fully* what they become, to give the adopted identity convincing life, not only for their fellow characters (by fooling them) but often for the audience as well (through the thoroughness of their performance), and to do so even while maintaining – which means communicating to the audience – a sharp awareness of the identity behind the mask. Another manifestation of this dramatic attitude, one that cuts across all three dramatic genres, is the characters' capacity for abrupt and substantial change within a coherent identity: it can be seen, for example, in Proteus, Claudio, Richard III, Othello, Coriolanus, and Timon, all of whom undergo important transformations of one kind or another, though without experiencing, like Petruchio's Kate, a complete shift from one 'personality' to a totally different one. There is also, finally, a manifestation of this dramatic attitude which has its greatest significance for the tragedies, and which helps provide them with their characteristic action. This is the experience of the loss of identity – or, at least, of its felt loss – which occurs when the character has been deprived in some way of one or more crucial roles and can consequently no longer locate himself in relation to external reality.

It is not, however, for its validity that I find this conception of identity worth focusing upon but as an analogy for one of the two basic character types in Shakespeare. This is the type whose identity consists essentially of a single role, usually, though not always, of the dramatic variety. Pinch and the Duke of Ephesus are obvious examples of this type; so are the many nameless Knights, Attendants, and Gentlemen who help swell the population of the plays; and Jaques, far more considerable a figure than any of these, is a less obvious but equally valid example. For some of the characters of this type (e.g., Jaques), the role being played is recognizable as such because of the familiarity, the conventionality of its gestures and moves. For others (e.g., Pinch), the fact that it is a role is called attention to, either verbally or non-verbally. In the vast majority of cases, probably, the perception of a role exists in the spectators' response because the play as a whole has attuned them to the notion of role-playing, because they know that the character in question possesses a particular office or relationship or fulfils a particular dramatic function, and because his actions either live up to expectation (e.g., the Duke of Ephesus), or at least do not in any way violate it (e.g., most of the nameless attendants and similar figures).

This character type does not consist merely of such uncomplicated or relatively uncomplicated figures as those mentioned so far. It also includes characters for whom adherence to this type is a dramatic fact of some consequence, characters who possess more than one role but whose behaviour as a whole is governed by a single primary role, which retains dominance. Lucentio, in *The Taming of the Shrew*, provides a clear example: he plays a nonce-role, he is a lover, he is master to his servant Tranio, and he is a son, but the manner in which he performs each of these roles is the product of his consistent observance of the dictates of a role that for him is much more fundamental, the dramatic role of *amoroso*. Many 'major' or fairly 'major' Shakespearian characters, especially in the earlier plays, belong to the same category as Lucentio: further examples would include Shylock, Hotspur, and Prince Hal (if only the Prince Hal of *1 Henry IV*). The first character type is therefore more extensive than it might at first seem. In *The Tempest*, for instance (to select deliberately a late play as example), all the characters belong to this type except for Prospero and, perhaps, Caliban.

The other basic character type in Shakespeare corresponds to the second conception of identity I have extrapolated from *The Comedy of Errors*. This type is epitomized by the speech of Christopher Sly which introduces the chapter:

> Am not I Christopher Sly, old Sly's son of Burton Heath; by birth a
> pedlar, by education a cardmaker, by transmutation a bearherd, and
> now by present profession a tinker? Ask Marian Hacket, the fat ale-wife
> of Wincot, if she know me not. (*The Taming of the Shrew*, Ind.ii.16-19)

The speech does not provide much of a key to Sly's character as Shakespeare has rendered it dramatically, for existentially Sly consists almost entirely of two traits: his willingness to accept the new identity foisted upon him and his inability to coincide with its demands. Nevertheless, in defining the identity 'Christopher Sly' as a nexus of several roles, the speech articulates in brief the conception of identity Shakespeare has established for the two Antipholuses and some of the other characters in *The Comedy of Errors*. The roles that constitute the nexus, in Sly's speech as well as in *The Comedy of Errors*, are primarily social: Sly defines himself in terms of his various professions and his relationships to his father and to the woman who evidently supplies him with his beer and conceivably gives him the opportunity to play some variety of the lover's role. The nexus need not, however, have this sort of make-up. In Falstaff's case, it consists primarily (though not exclusively) of familiar dramatic roles, those Shakespeare has assigned to him – such as the *Miles Gloriosus*, the Morality Vice, and the Seducer of the Prodigal Son – as well as those he himself chooses to play – such as the Puritan religious fanatic and the melancholy penitent.

I use 'nexus' to denote a connected group in which all elements have substantive if not equivalent impact and in which the various elements interact simultaneously. The first of these criteria excludes characters like Lucentio from type two, while the second excludes another borderline figure, the character with more than one role whose roles tend to operate independently. One such borderline case is Titus Andronicus.

The talk in *Titus Andronicus* of plots and dumb shows and 'timeless tragedies,' the visual presence of Tamora and her sons disguised as Revenge attended by Rape and Murder and of Titus 'like a cook' resemble the other images of the play as well as its numerous repetitions and allusions because they suggest superimposition; they impress one as reflecting an effort to lend significance to an action intrinsically lacking it. At the same time, the histrionic imagery does encourage the spectators to perceive the two primary waves of action (Aaron's attack and Titus' ultimate response) as two familiar types of plays (from Titus' point of view, a tragedy of suffering followed by a tragedy of revenge) and Titus himself as passing through a series of appropriate roles.

The opening scene immediately introduces the theme of role-playing through the contention about who should play the role of Emperor. The choice goes to Titus, whose superior qualifications are stressed by his brother's praise of him and by his own review of his accomplishments, but because of his age

Titus refuses the office, thus demonstrating through his behaviour the legitimacy of his claim to be a man of perfect honour and once again establishing himself as the ideal actor for the role of Emperor. At Titus' request, Saturnine gains the part, but it is Titus who properly fulfils its demands. Titus' performance of this first role, that of the man of perfect honour, the Emperor by nature, is necessarily a brief one, because Aaron, acting on behalf of his mistress, Tamora, substitutes for the existing course of events a series of stratagems that soon form what Tamora calls the 'complot' of a 'timeless tragedy' (II.iii.265). Titus therefore becomes the grieving victim of Aaron's attack, a condition that Titus himself associates with the theatre by referring to the manifestations of his grief as 'dumb shows,' and by wishing to 'Plot some device of further misery / To make us wonder'd at in time to come' (III.i.131, 134-5); the new condition, he suggests, should also be regarded as a role, one that has replaced the first. But as his grief turns to frustration and despair, Titus moves into another distinct condition, the half-real, half-crafty madness of act IV, which resembles a role through its highly mannered speech and behaviour and through its similarity to what has already by the time of *Titus Andronicus* become a standard dramatic turn, a familiar phase in the progress of the revenge tragedy hero. Titus' next role, that of the revenger, is also familiar enough as a standard dramatic role, and in addition it is here explicitly defined as a role, partly because it is introduced by the playlet in which Tamora and her two sons appear as Revenge, Rape, and Murder, and partly because Titus himself appears in costume as the cook who has prepared Tamora a special banquet. Revenger is Titus' final role, although as the play closes there is an attempt – first by Titus when he compares himself to 'rash Virginius' (V.iii.36), then by Marcus and Lucius in their eulogies of Titus – to re-establish his first role, that of the man of perfect honour.

The separate stages that Titus passes through unquestionably accrue to a single figure; that they exist at all and that they come to exist in the order they do is perfectly understandable from the nature of the experiences this figure has been subjected to. Nevertheless, the impression of identity conveyed by Titus' progress is less that of a nexus, a group of interrelated roles with simultaneous impact, than that of a chain, a sequence of independent roles that happen to be connected. Titus is not, therefore, an example of the second basic character type. Nor, on the other hand, does he correspond to the Lucentio-type, the type whose behaviour as a whole can be attributed to the dominance of a single governing role. One can glimpse behind Titus' separate roles, as a further unifying factor, an additional more all-encompassing role whose progress conventionally forms itself into a sequence of this sort: the dramatic role of the revenge tragedy hero. But it is the concreteness of the individual roles, more than their underlying unity, that Shakespeare has dramatized. Titus belongs to the first basic character type, but he constitutes a highly unusual example of it, a character who exists not as a single dramatization of this type but as a series of such dramatizations.

The failure of Titus' separate roles to form a valid nexus can be seen even more clearly if Titus is contrasted with Henry v, whose composition appears at least superficially to be rather similar. Shakespeare explicitly associates Henry v with role-playing in iv.i, the scene that takes place on the eve of the battle of Agincourt. Here, after concealing himself with the cloak borrowed from Sir Thomas Erpingham, Henry comes upon Pistol in a confrontation between two counterfeits, the scoundrel who has been posing as a valiant, honourable soldier, and the monarch who now claims to be no more than 'a gentleman of a company' (iv.i.39), one 'Harry le Roy' by name (49). Henry then steps aside to become an unseen spectator while overhearing Gower and Fluellen, but within moments, after the appearance of Bates, Court, and Williams, Henry again takes part in the action, this time playing an even humbler role, that of a common soldier, one who loyally defends his king, 'his cause being just and his quarrel honourable' (126-7). When the three soldiers exit, the concern with role-playing in this scene shifts abruptly from the actual playing of counterfeit nonce-roles to the contemplation of the role-like qualities of the highest social office. While talking to Williams and the others, Henry had declared that the king, 'his ceremonies laid by, in his nakedness ... appears but a man' (104-5). Now, in soliloquy, he dwells on these 'ceremonies' that define *a* man as *the* king, such phenomena as the 'flexure and low bending' of others (251) as well as

> the balm, the sceptre, and the ball,
> The sword, the mace, the crown imperial,
> The intertissued robe of gold and pearl,
> The farced title running fore the king,
> The throne he sits on ... the tide of pomp
> That beats upon the high shore of this world. (256-61)

Henry's soliloquy is a lament. He dwells on this 'thrice gorgeous ceremony' (262) in order to claim that it constitutes the king's only reward – a worthless one, moreover, since it cannot provide the peace of mind the ordinary labourer enjoys nor compensate for its loss. Whatever his purpose, however, Henry also manages – especially after the emphasis on role-playing preceding this soliloquy – to call attention to the histrionic dimensions of the office of kingship. This is probably the most explicit dramatization in Shakespeare of the concept of kingship as a role. It indicates to the spectators that one thing *Henry v* is about is the office its hero possesses, and it should also prompt them to realize that this theme has affected the structure of the play in a significant way. For what shapes the diachronic design of *Henry v* is not only the chronology of history but also a sequence of demonstrations in which Henry manifests his ability to perform effectively the various kinds of action which occupancy of the royal office entails.

Canterbury's praise of Henry in the opening scene stresses his masterly knowledge of divinity, commonwealth affairs, and policy, and particularly his marvellous capacity for oratory. All of this, and more, is amply confirmed by the first two acts as a whole, which exhibit Henry not only as a shrewd, efficient, and righteous executive, but also, especially through the Scroop affair, as the embodiment and dispenser of justice. Acts III and IV, which centre upon the fighting in France, celebrate Henry's battlefield accomplishments, but these are overshadowed by his successful deployment of other skills. Act III features Henry the orator: the lion as orator in III.i, rousing his men, urging them on to their best efforts, and in III.iii the fox as orator, the clever negotiator, smoothly persuading a town to surrender without bloodshed. The orator returns in act IV scene iii, this time rousing his men to action under far more trying circumstances than before, but the primary emphasis in this act falls in its opening scene on the eve of the battle of Agincourt, the scene already examined, which presents Henry the *man*, first as he moves among and tries to share the experience of his soldiers – personally inspiring them, as the chorus would have it (IV.Prol.41-7) – then as in his loneliness he suffers the agonies of his office and his inheritance. In act V, with the war over, Shakespeare completes his portrayal of Henry by having him exhibit two final dimensions of himself – the magnanimous victor and the lover-wooer.

The office of kingship is a dramatic concern of much importance throughout the history plays, and in writing them Shakespeare has naturally been preoccupied in part with an effort to define this office. Prior to *Henry V*, however, his effort has consisted largely of negative means, the analysis of individual royal failures and their causes, while a more positive account of what the office requires has emerged only through retrospective portraits of former kings whose remembered greatness provides a standard of reference (such as Henry V at the beginning of *1 Henry VI* and Edward III in *Richard II*) and through the portrayals of those (such as Richard Duke of York, Faulconbridge, and Bolingbroke) who oppose, in conflict or contrast or both, the royal failures, and whose moral claim to the throne consists in the possession of a vaguely dramatized impression of suitability, or strength, or whatever it might be. In *Henry V*, Shakespeare takes on the difficult task of dramatizing the positive account, which he accomplishes by separating out the various functions of the office for individual examination and showing this time not how the role should not be played, but how it should.

The emphasis on Falstaff's death and the killing of the French prisoners introduce enough ambivalence into the portrayal of Henry to prevent one from seeing him as a wholly ideal figure, but he does not fall very far short, and his successful fulfilment of the demands of his office is demonstrated not only by his managing to perform most of its separate functions unusually well but also by the contrast Shakespeare establishes between him and two of the other characters. One of these is Pistol, whose main dramatic task is to exemplify the 'counterfeit' (III.vi.60), who cannot adequately perform the role with which he is associated, for, as Gower remarks, he is 'a gull, a fool, a rogue, that now and then goes to the wars to grace himself, at his return into London, under the form of a soldier' (66-8), and, as Fluellen adds, 'he is not the man that he would gladly make show to the world he is' (80-1); in the summation of Falstaff's ex-page, Pistol is 'this roaring devil i' th' old play' (IV.iv.68). The other character to provide a contrast for Henry is the Dauphin, whose role is much like Henry's own. His failure to fulfil its demands is defined less explicitly than Pistol's similar failure and accomplished without role-playing imagery, but Shakespeare implies his inadequacy – as well as his essential resemblance to the braggart Pistol – almost every time he appears and through almost every reference to him.

In its calculated plainness, the last dimension of himself Henry exhibits, that of lover-wooer, suggests a highly self-conscious performance. I am persuaded to call each of his dimensions, each of these individually defined functions of the kingly office a separate role, and not merely because it serves my argument. The opening words of the first chorus, in desiring 'A kingdom for a stage, princes to act, / And monarchs to behold the swelling scene!' (I.Prol.3-4), equate Henry's world with the theatre, his acts with acting. And this effect is enhanced as the chorus goes on to call attention to the specific theatre in which it now stands as well as to the fact that the spectators have gathered there in order to hear – and kindly judge – a play. By returning as often as it does, the chorus succeeds in keeping the spectators not just conscious of, but preoccupied with, this fact, and succeeds also in preserving a sufficient distance between them and Henry so that they are prompted to experience each of his appearances – and thus each new dimension of him – as itself a kind of separate playlet, especially since intervening scenes isolate Henry's appearances from each other. But it is IV.i that most effectively links Henry's separate dimensions with the concept of role, because in this scene one of these separate functions, that of the king as good if somewhat aloof mixer with his people, is accompanied by (actually accomplished through) Henry's literal role-playing in his impersonation as 'Harry le Roy.'

The relation between Henry's individual dimensions and his office as king suggests a similarity to the Lucentio-type. But Henry's case is not one in which one role governs and determines the actor's performance of any other roles he might also possess. In Henry's case, these other additional roles *constitute* the primary one; they supply it with specific substance; and together they imply its complexity. In Henry's case, the identity that the roles compose is less that of Henry himself than that of the King – though, obviously (and to England's good fortune) the two are virtually one and the same. Since the individual roles that compose the office of king are presented one after another in succession, the portrayal of Henry superficially resembles that of Titus Andronicus. Here, however, the sequence is merely a structural convenience. Henry's separate roles do not exist one at a time but simultaneously, even though only one or another of them may be appropriate at a given moment. Henry's identity, as well as that of the King, is genuinely a nexus of roles.

The portrayal of Henry v focuses on the separate roles that compose the nexus, but ordinarily in portraying a character of this second basic type Shakespeare dramatizes the nexus itself by focusing on the interplay of the separate roles. In the case of Julia, from *The Two Gentlemen of Verona*, the nexus combines two familiar social roles, the 'maid' and the lover.

The connection between being a 'maid' (in the sense of 'unmarried woman') and performing a role is articulated by the 'maid' herself, who spells out the role-like qualities of her maidhood in a careful analysis of her own behaviour. Julia has asked her servant, Lucetta, to indicate which of all her suitors seems worthiest of her love and has herself shown most interest in Proteus, but when Lucetta presents her with a letter recently sent by Proteus, she displays anger and orders Lucetta to leave. This outburst, as Julia's subsequent soliloquy reveals, is merely a bit of conscious play-acting that her circumstances have compelled her to adopt:

> What fool is she, that knows I am a maid
> And would not force the letter to my view!
> Since maids, in modesty, say 'No' to that
> Which they would have the profferer construe 'Ay.'
> ...
> How churlishly I chid Lucetta hence,
> When willingly I would have had her here!
> How angerly I taught my brow to frown,
> When inward joy enforc'd my heart to smile! (i.ii.53-6, 60-3)

According to this analysis, maidhood prescribes certain conventional gestures that every individual maid must adopt, even when they do not accurately express what she regards as her true feelings. And these gestures, like those of any other role, can be learned, just as Julia has 'taught' her brow to frown.

Julia also suggests, when she associates her love with 'inward joy,' that for her love is something different, something more genuine, the reality that lies behind the maidenly mask. The difference between her two conditions, however, is merely a matter of her conscious awareness. She recognizes the role-like qualities of her maidhood and can convey them to the spectators because her love for Proteus prompts her to behave immodestly, thereby turning what would otherwise be an instinctive performance into one requiring conscious effort. She does not demonstrate similar perception about her love simply because she has had no occasion to realize that love is as much a role as maidhood. But Shakespeare has assumed such a realization, and throughout the play, especially in depicting the efforts of Valentine and Proteus to observe the fixed 'ceremony' of love, he exploits the literary role of lover in order to assert the histrionic nature of its social counterpart.

Moreover – and it is here that the dramatization of the nexus itself can be glimpsed – the scene of Julia's soliloquy also makes it abundantly clear that her maidhood and her love have equivalent dramatic status, for her behaviour is governed not by one or the other but by the two together. Her love inspires such actions as her wish to say 'Ay,' her calling Lucetta back, and her restoration of Proteus' letter. But just as she is a lover, she is also a maid – her awareness of this, rather than altering the fact, actually calls attention to it – and just as her love determines certain actions, so does her maidhood; it forces her to feign anger and dismiss Lucetta, to say 'No' when she means 'Ay,' and to tear up the letter she will later restore. Her maidhood, then, is as substantial a fact of her nature as her love. Nor does she violate its dictates any more than she does those of her love; maidhood, after all, does not forbid her to love – on the contrary, it should encourage her – it merely requires that in the interests of modesty her love be concealed. Consequently, the labelling of her maidhood as a role, rather than indicating that it differs from her love, implies that her love can also be so labelled. Similarly, the self-consciousness in her performance of the gestures of maidhood, far from signifying the superficiality of the role, demonstrates instead the thoroughness with which she adheres to it. This integrity is entirely characteristic of her; throughout the play she continues to manifest it with regard to both her roles.

The primary expression of her dual integrity, and thus of the interplay between her two roles, is her adoption of a nonce-role, her disguising herself as Sebastian the page. Because she loves Proteus, she decides to follow him to Milan, but before she can carry out this decision she must also accommodate her maidhood. She appeals to Lucetta to 'lesson' her and tell her 'some good mean' how she can fulfil her intention and still retain her 'honour' (II.vii.5-7), by which she apparently means something much like the 'modesty' of maidhood that had governed her behaviour in I.ii, for a bit later she fears that her 'undertaking so unstaid a journey' will make her 'scandaliz'd' in the world's repute (59-61). Lucetta advises her to give up her idea, but Julia cannot: her love is too great. Nevertheless, she does not forget the demands of her other role. The costume she chooses for her journey, the costume that gives birth to Sebastian, is selected with her maidhood very much in mind:

LUCETTA But in what habit will you go along?
JULIA Not like a woman, for I would prevent
The loose encounters of lascivious men;
Gentle Lucetta, fit me with such weeds
As may beseem some well-reputed page. (39-43)

The role of Sebastian thus originates as a product of Julia's fidelity to her maidhood, and it remains throughout a symbol of this fidelity. At the same time, the subsequent history of the role also transforms it into a symbol of her fidelity to her role of lover. When Julia as Sebastian becomes Proteus' servant, she is, with regard to social interplay, altering her original relation to him, but symbolically she reaffirms it. In the courtly-love idiom of the play's romantic scenes, 'servant,' the term Silvia uses to address Valentine, is synonomous with 'lover.'

As Proteus' page, Julia acquires an additional nonce-role, that of his envoy to Silvia, which she reluctantly agrees to play but executes so poorly that, in effect, she rejects it. She cannot accommodate it to her other roles as she has managed to accommodate them one to another. To this limited extent, the portrayal of Julia veers towards the kind of dramatization which makes the nexus of the second character type especially conspicuous, that in which this nexus is a centre of conflict between wholly incompatible roles. This variety of the second character type is too common and important in Shakespeare to require much illustration. One good example is dramatized by the initial situation of Hermia, in *A Midsummer Night's Dream*. She loves Lysander, but she is also daughter of Egeus, and he, backed by Theseus' enforcement of Athens' rigid and arbitrary system of determining identity, insists that she can act only in accordance with his will. Even better among the early plays is the double example of Romeo and Juliet, who make the tragic error of believing that they can easily shed their familial roles in order to assume the leading parts in a concretely realized version of the Petrarchan love drama that Romeo has been mentally enacting.

These examples also point to a further quality of the second character type. Hermia, with Lysander, flees from her father's Athens, while Romeo and Juliet try to elude the consequences of the enmity between their families by entering into a secret marriage. Neither flight wholly succeeds, for just as that of Romeo and Juliet leads to their deaths, that of Hermia and Lysander opens the way to at least temporary difficulties in the confusion and pain they experience in fairyland. The results of the flight in each case stress the fact of the nexus, but the choice of flight rather than the suppression of the feelings of love in order to fulfil what the familial roles require indicates the greater importance of the role of lover. Similarly, Julia in the course of *The Two Gentlemen of Verona* as a whole clearly shows greater responsiveness to her role of lover than to her maidhood. As these examples suggest, for most characters of the second basic type identity has an additional determinant. It consists not only of the various roles that form the nexus but also of these various roles' relative impact.

The adherence of a character to one or more pre-formulated roles, his deriving his identity therefrom, by no means necessitates his being a lifeless stereotype, even if he is a character of type one and only a single role is involved. Some of the roles Shakespeare utilizes are themselves sufficiently fresh and new because they come into being, in effect, only through his work, through his supplying familiar social or literary categories (such as daughter, friend, fortune hunter) with gestures and moves so appropriate and convincing that they suggest the existence of a lengthy literary or dramatic tradition. Other roles achieve fresh-ness and newness as well as a sense of living vitality through the richness of their execution. Dogberry is more attractive and appealing than Shakespeare's two other versions of the malapropian constable, Dull and Elbow – especially Dull, whose name is so apt – but the reason for his greater appeal has little to do with his possessing a larger percentage of genuinely felt life. It is a matter partly of Shakespeare's having given him more stage time and partly of his having a clearer and more consequential involvement with the action of his play, but mostly, it seems to me, it results from his having better material and being a more thoroughly rendered version of the role than the others. A more significant example of richness of execution can be found in Jaques, whose portrayal evokes the feeling that one is observing not simply the reworking of a familiar literary-dramatic stereotype but its perfection.

But perhaps the chief reason why Shakespeare's characters avoid flatness and repetitiveness is his highly flexible conception of individual roles: often enough a given character is recognizably fulfilling a specific role while never-theless executing it in an unquestionably unique way. This flexibility can be glimpsed, for example, in the portrayal of the role of lover in the early come-dies (from *Love's Labour's Lost* to *Much Ado About Nothing*, say), not only in the way that the various lovers differ one from another but also in the many shifts in Shakespeare's attitude towards the conventional literary version. The flexibility can also be glimpsed, just as clearly and more conveniently, in the unusual portrayal this role receives in the second half of *As You Like It*.

Time and time again, in the second half of *As You Like It*, the forest landscape becomes the stage for clearly defined momentary playlets, like those referred to by Rosalind when she tells Celia 'I will speak to [Orlando] like a saucy lackey, and under that habit play the knave with him' (III.ii.278-80), and by both Rosalind and Corin when he, having found Silvius wooing Phebe, in-vites the others to 'see a pageant truly play'd' (III.iv.47) and Rosalind promises to 'prove a busy actor in their play' (54). In form, these playlets underscore the resemblance between the forest and a stage which is a central element in the play's contrast between forest and court. In content, however, the playlets utilize this stage as an arena for exploring one of the theatre's most familiar and popular roles, that of the lover. What takes place in the remarkably static second half of *As You Like It* – both in these playlets and elsewhere – is not action in the usual sense but, instead, an elaborate anatomy of the varieties of love.

The range of this anatomy is broad enough to include a 'Character' of the conventional stereotype (in Ganymede's account of its essential 'marks,' III.ii.346-55), several varieties of romantic love (Rosalind and Orlando, Celia and Oliver, Phebe and Silvius, Phebe and Ganymede), a parody of these relationships (in Touchstone's marrying the 'foul slut,' Audrey, in order to avoid living 'in bawdry,' III.iii.31, 84), and the outright rejection of love (by Jaques, whose only 'mistress' is the world he loathes so much, III.ii.262). Because of her dual role, Rosalind occupies a special position in the anatomy. In her own person she experiences and exhibits as intense a passion as anyone in the play. But as Ganymede, she is able to encompass as well the opposite extreme, to articulate for herself and the spectators the anti-love that Jaques for the most part can only enact.

Relationships like those linking Orlando and Adam and Rosalind and her father extend the range of the anatomy to include both friendship and familial love. But it is primarily the varieties of romantic love with which Shakespeare is concerned, and in the final act he underscores the importance of their portrayal for the meaning of the play through the three passages that juxtapose them rhetorically just as they have already been juxtaposed in the action (v.ii.76-115, v.iv.6-25, v.iv.110-34). These three passages thus call attention to the dramatic design of the second half of *As You Like It*. Also suggesting this design is a passage that has little to do with love, Jaques' and Rosalind's anatomy of melancholy:

JAQUES I have neither the scholar's melancholy, which is emulation; nor the musician's, which is fantastical; nor the courtier's, which is proud; nor the soldier's, which is ambitious; nor the lawyer's, which is politic; nor the lady's, which is nice; nor the lover's, which is all these; but it is a melancholy of mine own, compounded of many simples, extracted from many objects, and, indeed, the sundry contemplation of my travels; in which my often rumination wraps me in a most humorous sadness.

...

ROSALIND Farewell, Monsieur Traveller; look you lisp and wear strange suits, disable all the benefits of your own country, be out of love with your nativity, and almost chide God for making you that countenance you are; or I will scarce think you have swam in a gondola.

(IV.10-18, 30-6)

Rosalind corrects Jaques' attempt to claim uniqueness and originality for his melancholy by assuring him that it is as conventional a pose as any of those he mocks. She thus completes the partial awareness of the first half of his speech: there is not merely a single variety of melancholy, but several, and each of them is a role with specific dictates that its player must observe. Similarly, in the forest scenes as a whole, Shakespeare dramatizes an analogous awareness about the ceremony of love: that although falling in love means assuming a role, there is more than one way to 'play the lover.'

If the 'pageant of love' in *As You Like It* exhibits any ideal figure, that figure is Rosalind. She is ideal, however, not because of sweetness and charm but because she enjoys the capacity to play two contrasting roles simultaneously. This capacity spares her from falling victim to the tyranny of either role, from failing to use its gestures and moves expressively rather than mechanically. As Rosalind she can afford to sigh and swoon because her performance as Ganymede allows her to see this behaviour in ironic perspective. Unlike Jaques (for example), she knows that her behaviour is merely one possible role among many, she can recognize its limitations, and she understands exactly what it implies about herself. Rosalind emerges as the pageant of love's ideal figure because she possesses the two attributes required for all successful role-playing, both onstage and off: the insight to pick the right role and the ability to play it with creative detachment.

The example of Rosalind brings into focus a point that should in any case be self-evident, for it indicates that definition of the two basic character types does not tell the whole story about characterization in Shakespeare, and thus about character and identity. For one thing, identity can also consist in part of something that is independent of the character's roles but nevertheless measured by them. A character's choice of one role at the expense of another, the change in his identity brought about by the new circumstances such choices occasion, his loss of a role, the kind of response he makes to the resulting threat to his identity – all exemplify this additional factor of characterization. What the case of Rosalind especially emphasizes, however, is the individual character's particular acting style, the manner in which he plays his part. That the Duke of Ephesus should behave in a ducal fashion rouses little or no interest, but that a character like Lucentio, with more than one role to play, should act in a fashion that allows him, too, to be classified as an example of the first character type necessarily constitutes a significant factor of identity. So also does the more flexible playing of a character like Petruchio. A character may bungle his role (as Claudio does), wilfully violate it (like Antipholus of Ephesus), or evade it by assuming instead a self-conceived substitute (like most of the characters in *Twelfth Night*) – and each of these acts serves to express identity as surely as the roles themselves.

Many Shakespearian characters also manifest a further determinant of identity, one that has nothing to do with role-playing. Two speeches by Dogberry – selected in part to qualify and clarify my earlier remarks about him – exemplify this further determinant as well as any of the countless other passages that might be cited:

> Goodman Verges, sir, speaks a little off the matter – an old man, sir, and his wits are not so blunt as, God help, I would desire they were; but, in faith, honest as the skin between his brows.
>
> (*Much Ado About Nothing*, III.v.9-12)

> Dost thou not suspect my place? Dost thou not suspect my years? O that he were here to write me down an ass! But, masters, remember that I am an ass; though it be not written down, yet forget not that I am an ass. No, thou villain, thou art full of piety, as shall be prov'd upon thee by good witness. I am a wise fellow; and, which is more, an officer; and, which is more, a householder; and, which is more, as pretty a piece of flesh as any is in Messina; and one that knows the law, go to; and a rich fellow enough, go to; and a fellow that hath had losses; and one that hath two gowns, and everything handsome about him. Bring him away. O that I had been writ down an ass! (IV.ii.69-70)

Except for minor details like the misuse of 'suspect' and 'piety' and the confusion about whether the speaker is actually an ass or has merely been called one, these two passages cannot readily be accounted for by reference to the role of the bungling malapropian constable – certainly Elbow of *Measure for Measure* manages quite nicely without anything similar to their basic content – nor can one say they necessarily reflect Shakespeare's perfecting of the role. Some recourse might be had to an appeal to the second character type, for it might be claimed that these passages point to additional minor roles held by Dogberry which come into play only momentarily, and by and large only in these two passages. But this would be spinning the concept of role far too thinly and making it far too fragile to wear well.

What these passages actually reflect – and Dogberry is by no means the only character to exemplify it – is Shakespeare's tendency to fine excess in characterization. The identity of the Shakespearian character is a product not only of the character's role or roles and the manner in which he enacts them but also of those additional 'thickening' or complicating elements that arise from Shakespeare's allowing him his moments of improvisation, allowing him to do and say things that, while not violating his roles, have no recognizable origin in them.

Establishing the roles a character possesses, calculating their relative impact, and determining his skill in acting them will not, in other words, entirely account for him. Nonetheless, these attributes are the primary factors of his identity, and their discovery constitutes the first and most necessary step towards full understanding. For all his especially lifelike moments of condescending superiority and injured dignity, Dogberry is defined essentially by his possession of the role of bungling malapropian constable and by his capacity to play it to the hilt.

3 Role-playing and dramatic structure

ANTONIO I hold the world but as the world, Gratiano –
A stage, where every man must play a part,
And mine a sad one.
GRATIANO   Let me play the fool.
With mirth and laughter let old wrinkles come;
And let my liver rather heat with wine
Than my heart cool with mortifying groans.
                    (*The Merchant of Venice*, I.i.77-82)

The presence of the company of strolling players in the opening scene of *The Taming of the Shrew* points to an interesting difference between Shakespeare's first comedy and what is probably his second. Role-playing constitutes a central activity in *The Comedy of Errors*, but outside of a few scattered metaphors Shakespeare does not explicitly focus upon this theme. In *The Taming of the Shrew*, on the other hand, he introduces an explicit concern with role-playing as early as line 34 of the Induction, when the Lord, having decided to 'practise on this drunken man,' outlines the 'jest' that will convince Christopher Sly he's really 'a mighty lord' and sets it in motion by prescribing for his attendants the parts they must play, even supplying details of setting, props, costume, appropriate action, and sample dialogue. Throughout the play, moreover, this explicit concern with role-playing remains central to the action, with the result that in so far as *The Taming of the Shrew* can pass for an image of life, it characterizes life as a theatrical enterprise – an impression, by the way, that Shakespeare strengthens when he makes his main action a play-within-a-play performed by the company of actors that appears in the Induction.

One reason for the lack of explicitness in *The Comedy of Errors* is that its role-playing is primarily an unconscious activity. The characters cannot actually perceive the ubiquity of role-playing in themselves and their surroundings, however much their incidental metaphors may convey this notion to the spectators, because they engage in it only as a function of their familial and social ties or as a result of others having imposed alien identities on them. None of them indulges in a deliberate attempt to pass himself off as something he is not. *The Taming of the Shrew*, in contrast, fashions a vastly different world, one in which conscious role-playing predominates, in which play-acting and action are virtually synonomous.

The differences in this respect between the two plays are striking – so striking, in fact, as to suggest a particular relationship between them. It is as if Shakespeare has decided to take up in earnest a subject that he discovered through writing *The Comedy of Errors* (a discovery that was, to some extent, forced on him by the combined pressure of the Plautine material and his conception of human identity) and that he was also developing in his nearly concurrent work with the *Henry VI* plays and *Richard III* (where, among other things, he had to deal with one king who is a king in name only and with another who, as Machiavellian intriguer, already possesses a portion of the magnificent acting skill he fully acquires in Shakespeare's version of him). This hypothesis accounts for both the greater explicitness with which role-playing is established in *The Taming of the Shrew* and the tendency of its characters to engage in role-playing as a fully conscious activity. It also accounts for a third difference between *The Comedy of Errors* and this play, the fact that here Shakespeare shapes the material of role-playing into a coherent dramatic design.

One function of role-playing in *The Taming of the Shrew* is to help unite the three disparate actions contained in the Induction and in the two plots of the play-within-the-play. At the same time, because of the many and varied forms it assumes, the role-playing also creates a rich interaction of parallelism and contrast. Each of the three actions juxtaposes several kinds of role-playing, several motives for it, and several results. Together these actions thus provide an elaborate anatomy – not, as in *As You Like It*, of a specific part, but of role-playing itself.

The presence of the players in the first scene of the Induction allows Shakespeare to dramatize an example of role-playing in its purest state and thereby posit a norm that both highlights and sets off the numerous examples of more metaphorical role-playing. As professionals, the players' purpose is to 'offer service to your lordship' (Ind.i.76) – in other words, to entertain in return for a night's lodging and presumably a fee – and the result of their activity will be the pleasure provided by the skill of their performance. The players practise a variety of role-playing in which the discrepancy between the actor and his part is not only fully evident but also freely acknowledged, for they make a pact with their audience to accept them for what they claim to be only so long as the play they are performing lasts, and they do not attempt to suggest that the roles they have assumed in any way truly represent themselves. Nevertheless, proper fulfilment of their art necessitates a temporary concealing of the discrepancy, and so the players must also obey the fundamental requirements of all ideal role-playing, which the Lord makes explicit while praising one member of the professional troupe:

> This fellow I remember
> Since once he play'd a farmer's eldest son;
> 'Twas where you woo'd the gentlewoman so well.
> I have forgot your name; but, sure, that part
> Was aptly fitted and naturally perform'd. (81-5)

Only one of these requirements is met by the second kind of role-playing in the Induction, that which the Lord and his staff undertake. The Lord, who dreams up the trick to be played on Sly, instructs his staff in their contributory roles, and himself takes a part in the scheme, is an amateur playwright-director-actor who plays his roles for personal gratification – his scheme, he declares, is a 'jest' (43), which, if successful, will furnish 'pastime passing excellent' (65) – while the ultimate result of his role-playing, to which he gives little thought, will be to persuade another that an alien identity is his own and that his own identity is merely a mad delusion. The roles assumed by the Lord and his staff are 'naturally perform'd' (indeed, Sly, the audience, is completely fooled) but they are by no means 'aptly fitted.' The discrepancy is most extreme, of course, in the page's portrayal of Sly's 'lady,' but it exists in the other performances as well. The attendants are actually attendants, as they profess to be, but they are attendants of the Lord, not of Sly. The Lord is what his title implies, and thus in his case the discrepancy is measured by the incompatibility between his temporary role-playing and the decorum of his permanent role.

Shakespeare does not explore the moral issues implicit in this toying with another's sense of reality or in the Lord's violation of decorum; for him the real focus of the Induction is the fun arising from its third kind of role-playing, that performed by Christopher Sly. Sly's role-playing, like most of that in *The Comedy of Errors*, is fully unconscious; it is an enforced activity. He awakens from his drunken sleep to find himself in a particular setting, wearing a particular costume, and surrounded by numerous supporting players that address him as 'your lordship' and 'your honour.' These qualities of the established scene unequivocally assign its central figure a specific role, which Sly briefly resists, but only until one of his 'attendants' assures him that he really is 'a lord, and nothing but a lord' (Ind.ii.59):

> Am I a lord and have I such a lady?
> Or do I dream? Or have I dream'd till now?
> I do not sleep: I see, I hear, I speak;
> I smell sweet savours, and I feel soft things.
> Upon my life, I am a lord indeed,
> And not a tinker, nor Christopher Sly. (66-71)

From this point onward – for ever as far as the spectators are concerned, since no one ever disabuses Sly within the play – he continues to believe in his new role, and the extent to which he strives to make it 'naturally perform'd' is reflected in his adoption of blank verse, which he uses for the first time in the lines quoted above. But the chief joke of the Induction, of course, is that Sly is so *un*-aptly fitted for his role that he cannot avoid betraying the discrepancy:

> PAGE I am your wife in all obedience.
> SLY I know it well. What must I call her?
> LORD Madam.
> SLY Al'ce madam, or Joan madam? (105-8)

The performance of the rest of *The Taming of the Shrew* as a play-within-the-play before Sly and the other members of the onstage audience immediately defines its characters as theatrical figures, and most of them reinforce this impression by their failure to do or say anything that does not fall within the various provinces of the conventional comic roles whose destinies they fulfil. Gremio is identified as a 'pantaloon,' not only in the stage direction that records his entrance (I.i.45) but also explicitly in the dialogue (III.i.36). Tranio and Grumio embody the two standard servant types, the one a clever manipulator of people and situations in furthering his master's objectives, the other a 'zany.' Baptista is no more nor less than the typical comedic father of two marriageable daughters. All the characters of both plots are either purely functional and therefore colourless, or defined in broad strokes that leave little room for the evocation of 'felt life.'

Lucentio, the hero of the first of the two plots to be introduced, thoroughly conforms to this impression of character as dramatic role. Initially he is identified, through the way he talks as well as what he says, as a scholar, who has come to Padua to 'institute / A course of learning and ingenious studies' (I.i.8-9). But once he sees Bianca, he is overcome with love-at-first-sight, and when next he has an opportunity to speak alone to Tranio, his planned studies have been utterly forgotten. His language, too, has changed abruptly, becoming that of the anguished lover:

> Tranio, I burn, I pine, I perish, Tranio,
> If I achieve not this young modest girl.
> Counsel me, Tranio, for I know thou canst;
> Assist me, Tranio, for I know thou wilt. (150-3)

Lucentio has simply exchanged one role for another; no longer the scholar, he has become the *amoroso*, the young man in pursuit of a woman. Appropriately, he at once decides to employ one of the standard *amoroso* moves, the temporary adoption of a nonce-role that will enable him to get near and thus woo the object of his desire.

Like nearly every other element of *The Taming of the Shrew*, Lucentio's attempt to win Bianca from her other suitors by posing as Cambio, her schoolmaster, generates interest not through its own intrinsic emotional or intellectual profundity but through its contribution to the overall structure of the play. His stratagem helps produce dramatic unity by giving this plot of the play-within-the-play an action analogous to that of the Induction. Although his motives differ and there is less impropriety in his behaviour, Lucentio is another version of the Lord. Like the Lord, he devises the scheme, assigns subsidiary roles to his followers, and takes a leading part: he, too, is a playwright-director-actor. Even the results are similar, since Lucentio's scheme also involves transforming the identity of another – in this case, Bianca, who changes from Baptista's daughter to Lucentio's wife. Although Sly's transformation fails, Bianca's succeeds, not only because it is the kind of transformation that is humanly possible but also – judging from Petruchio's description of Bianca as essentially nothing more than a potential wife (IV.v.63-6) – because it is dramatically inevitable as well.

Lucentio's stratagem also has importance for the structure of the play through its participation in a role-playing triad that comprises the chief dramatic interest of the Lucentio-Bianca plot as a self-contained unit. Lucentio perfectly represents the fully adept *amoroso*. Not only is he able to play with complete success whatever nonce-roles the fulfilment of his objective might call for but he also possesses, in Tranio, the kind of ally no would-be *amoroso* can afford to do without, one that has the ability to act as an extension of himself, as Tranio does by impersonating his master in the negotiations with Baptista and, more important, by taking over from his master the functions of the playwright-director when an emergency arises and someone must be found to play the part of Lucentio's father. Lucentio's exact opposite is Gremio, who, despite his efforts to win Bianca, is in reality a Pantaloon and therefore totally unsuited for the role he tries so ineptly to play, and of whose standard moves he remains utterly innocent. The midpoint of the triad is occupied by Hortensio, who is distinguished from Gremio by his knowledge of at least one of the required moves and his successful fulfilment of it (in posing as Licio, Bianca's music teacher) and from Lucentio by the limited extent of his *amoroso* talents. Unlike Lucentio, he has not prepared for every eventuality, for there is a father to be won as well as a daughter, but Hortensio has no Tranio to take his part with Baptista while he himself is busy wooing Bianca. He also lacks the necessary perseverance: no true *amoroso* would ever abandon the chase as readily as he does when he discovers Bianca's affection for her schoolmaster – least of all in order to pursue a kind but not-so-beautiful widow.

The limitations of his rivals ensure smooth sailing for Lucentio right up to the unexpected arrival of his father. The near-disaster that this occasions seems for a moment to suggest a negative evaluation of the kind of role-playing Lucentio has been practising – but only for a moment. Lucentio is so thoroughgoing an *amoroso* that he also instinctively recognizes the moment when the jig is up and he must adopt the *amoroso*'s last strategic move, which is to drop to his knees, confess his 'wrongdoing,' and ask his father's forgiveness. He receives it, of course, and with it his father's blessing and a promise that the appropriate monetary arrangements will be made. Lucentio's role-playing has therefore succeeded completely, though the full extent of his success is not evident until later, in the final episode of the Kate-Petruchio plot.

The notion of character as dramatic role prevails in this plot as well, though with some difference. Kate, who enters with her family and Bianca's suitors in I.i, is rapidly and exclusively defined as a shrew (55-69), and until Petruchio's taming process is well under way she displays no other traits. Petruchio, who arrives in Padua in the next scene, defines himself as a fortune-hunter (I.ii.48-50). He has thrust himself 'into this maze,' he announces, 'Haply to wive and thrive as best I may' (53-4) – which means 'wealthily' (73) – and since 'wealth is burden of [his] wooing dance' (66), other factors are irrelevant; the woman he wives can be foul, old, curst, shrewd, or rough, it makes no difference, as long as she is 'rich enough to be Petruchio's wife' (65). Petruchio's manner and behaviour are in perfect accord with his self-announced identification: his roughness, the supremely confident abruptness with which he sets about completing his business, and the apparent love of adventure that compels him to pursue a notorious shrew – all proclaim the fortune-hunter. The difference here is that these roles ('shrew' and 'fortune-hunter') are not quite of the same order as the roles assigned to the other characters in the play-within-the-play. These other roles are recognized as such because they have been sanctioned by time and tradition; one has constantly met with them elsewhere in comedy. The shrew and the fortune-hunter, on the other hand, are not permanent members of the standard comic repertoire, though the shrew is familiar enough as the wife of the philandering husband in New Comedy and, in English tradition, as Mrs Noah. Nevertheless, Shakespeare has so contrived Kate and Petruchio that in the context of the play their original labels have the same force as do such labels as *amoroso* or Pantaloon. Before the taming process, Kate is not portrayed as a human being who happens to be shrewish; on the contrary, she is nothing but a shrew; her every gesture and move are the products of shrewishness. Petruchio puts forth a more complex impression, but not because he is a different kind of creature. His complexity, rather, springs from the particular way in which he plays his role.

Petruchio is as eager as the Lord or Lucentio to utilize conscious role-playing as a means of achieving his desires, though his first attempt at it would seem to indicate that he lacks their skill. This occurs during his opening confrontation with Kate, when he has already completed arrangements with Baptista and needs only to obtain her love in order to settle the match. He knows Kate is likely to resist his wooing, and so he also realizes that he must handle the interview with care; therefore, before she enters, he plans his part of their conversation in some detail:

> I'll attend her here,
> And woo her with some spirit when she comes.
> Say that she rail; why, then I'll tell her plain
> She sings as sweetly as a nightingale.
> Say that she frown; I'll say she looks as clear
> As morning roses newly wash'd with dew.
> Say she be mute, and will not speak a word;
> Then I'll commend her volubility,
> And say she uttereth piercing eloquence. (II.i.167-75)

Petruchio is unmistakably rehearsing a nonce-role which he will play for Kate as audience, and when he sees her entering, he concludes his rehearsal with a bit of self-direction: 'But here she comes; and now, Petruchio, speak' (180). Kate makes a poor audience, however. She refuses to respond properly to his performance and even commits the one unpardonable spectator-sin by deliberately calling attention to the performance's illusionary nature: 'Where did you study all this goodly speech?' (255). Petruchio has no choice but to drop his nonce-role, to set 'all this chat aside,' as he puts it, and resort to 'plain terms' (260-1) – in other words, to language more characteristic of his basic dramatic role. He assures Kate that 'will you, nill you, I will marry you' (263), tells her father that she has consented, and neutralizes her vociferous objections by insisting, ' 'Tis bargain'd 'twixt us twain, being alone, / That she shall still be curst in company' (296-7).

Petruchio's failure to employ conscious role-playing successfully in winning Kate and thus fulfilling the basic demand of his dramatic role suggests a contrast between him and Lucentio. This contrast is more apparent than real, however, and of far less significance to the dramatic design than the contrast that actually distinguishes the two. Each of them pursues the objective appropriate to his dramatic role – the one a wife, the other a rich wife – but where Lucentio cares only that his prize belong to the proper category, Petruchio, despite what he has said, requires more. Fulfilling his basic dramatic role is not his sole aim; he is equally concerned that the rich wife also have – or gain – other attributes: she must ultimately be a rich wife of a certain kind. Consequently, after he has named the wedding day, he tries his hand at conscious role-playing once again. And this time he succeeds.

The role he now adopts is the one that Kate has held throughout – the

shrew – and in performing it Petruchio is even 'curster' than she (III.ii.150).
His shrewishness obviously has an integral relation to his role of fortune-hunter, for it produces speeches such as this:

> I will be master of what is mine own –
> She is my goods, my chattels, she is my house,
> My household stuff, my field, my barn,
> My horse, my ox, my ass, my any thing. (225-8)

But it is nonetheless a deliberately chosen nonce-role, one that makes him, as
Tranio observes, 'so unlike' himself (100). In contrast to the Lord and Lucentio, who adopt entire false identities with appropriate changes in speech, costume, and (in Lucentio's case) name, Petruchio's more subtle play-acting is of
the sort that involves the adoption of an alien manner and behaviour without
any pretence of a corresponding change in identity, the sort that readily acknowledges *who* one is while deliberately misrepresenting *what* one is. Nevertheless, his performance as shrew includes not only the necessary changes in
speech and manner – both of which are far coarser and more brutal than before – but also a detail that especially defines the performance as a role, its
own appropriate costume (because so inappropriate for the wedding day):

> Why, Petruchio is coming – in a new hat and an old jerkin; a pair of old
> breeches thrice turn'd; a pair of boots that have been candle-cases, one
> buckled, another lac'd; an old rusty sword ta'en out of the town arm-
> oury, with a broken hilt, and chapeless; with two broken points ... (41-5)

Petruchio, as Gremio perceives, 'is Kated' (241), and this remark, by suggesting that playing the shrew is equivalent to playing Kate, underscores the fact
that Kate's single characteristic is her adherence to a specific role.

This role does not endure, however, for Petruchio – in this respect fully
mirroring the Lord and Lucentio – executes his stratagem in order to persuade
her to accept a new role, and he is successful. She vigorously resists his efforts
as long as she is able, but soon, like Sly in the Induction, she comes to experience the dream-like state of one who has lost his bearings (IV.i.168-70), and
by IV.v she has fully assumed her new role of obedient wife – as she reveals when,
again like Sly, she adopts a new voice, in her case one of resigned submission:

> Then, God be bless'd, it is the blessed sun;
> But sun it is not, when you say it is not:
> And the moon changes even as your mind.
> What you will have it nam'd, even that it is,
> And so it shall be so for Katherine. (18-22)

Filled out by labored summaries — predictable?

This time there is no comic discrepancy between the new role and its performer. Kate's transformation, unlike that of Sly, is thorough and utter; as her father later marvels, 'she is chang'd, as she had never been' (v.ii.115).

Petruchio's success is most fully demonstrated, of course, in the final scene, through the wager he makes with Lucentio and Hortensio, the winner of which is to be the one 'whose wife is most obedient, / To come at first when he doth send for her' (v.ii.67-8). Hortensio, who entreats rather than commands, never really has a chance; consequently, the match actually pits Petruchio against Lucentio in what becomes a final exhibition of the essential difference between them. Here both attempt to play the domineering husband, but only Petruchio can do so effectively because only Petruchio has fulfilled his basic role in an appropriate way. Lucentio has played the *amoroso* to perfection, but unimaginatively; fulfilment of this role guarantees him merely a wife, and he has done nothing to ensure that she shall have any attribute other than wifehood. Lucentio, in other words, has no reality beyond that of his role; he is, in fact, so thoroughgoing an *amoroso* that he has even fulfilled his original plea, 'And let me be a slave t'achieve that maid' (i.i.214). Petruchio, in contrast, is defined not only by his role but also by the creativity with which he has played it. Rather than just mechanically following its dictates, he has modified it in such a way that its fulfilment turns out to be ideal in every respect.

The wager episode is one of several narrative links connecting the two plots of the play-within-the-play. Such links engender only superficial unity, however; what really unifies not only these two plots but all three divisions of the play is the pattern of action common to each, the pattern in which one character operates as playwright-director-actor in order to persuade another to accept a new role. This pattern pervades the play so thoroughly that there is even a fourth, minor version of it forming a subsidiary action in the Lucentio-Bianca plot. This version occurs in iv.ii, when Tranio, already disguised as Lucentio, pretends concern for the welfare of the Pedant, falsely warns him that his life is in danger in Padua, and thus gets him to take on the identity of Lucentio's father. The ubiquity of this pattern gives the play a tight construction, while at the same time creating considerable dramatic interest. What ultimately delights the spectator of *The Taming of the Shrew* is the wide range of contrasts arising, on the one hand, from the many different uses, kinds, and results of role-playing and, on the other, from the varying degrees to which the many roles are 'aptly fitted and naturally perform'd.'

It is no denial of this interest to add that, in relation to most of the later plays, the structural technique of *The Taming of the Shrew* seems primitive. Although nearly all of them manifest Shakespeare's habit of linking individual characters and episodes through parallelism and contrast, thus giving a play inner cohesion as well as narrative unity, seldom again are the actions to be linked so disparate, and even more seldom is the process linking them so mech-anical. One exception, perhaps, is *Love's Labour's Lost* (also an early play), in which Don Armado and his fellow clowns serve as burlesque versions of the King and his Lords, while the show of the Nine Worthies, in its excessive ex-ploitation of the discrepancy between the clowns and the roles they try to play, provides a rather obvious analogy for the behaviour of the King and his Lords, both in their attempt to play the scholars and in their later bungling of the more appropriate role of lover.

Another early comedy, however, *The Two Gentlemen of Verona*, already exhibits a far more sophisticated handling of the process for achieving inner cohesion. Here, as in *The Taming of the Shrew*, the characters freely indulge in conscious role-playing – particularly of the sort Petruchio employed – and because the many instances of it spring from a variety of motives and lead to a variety of results, Shakespeare has once again built up an elaborate anatomy of his theme. In re-creating the structural panorama of *The Taming of the Shrew*, however, he improves on it in several ways. This time, rather than mechanically linking three basically simple actions, it simultaneously enriches and orders a single action of considerable complexity. This time the anatomy comprises fewer characters (Julia, Valentine, and Proteus primarily), and there-fore each of them is more fully realized and more fully knowable. Above all, this time the anatomy is made to serve as a vehicle for moral discriminations. The different kinds of conscious role-playing which Julia, Proteus, and Valen-tine indulge in, the different uses to which they put role-playing, and the vary-ing degrees of ease with which they bring it off provide for an abundance of juxtaposed parallelisms and contrasts, but in this play they are not important simply in themselves. They all contribute, as well, to the formation of precise distinctions of the sort that differentiate Petruchio and Lucentio, and this time, moreover, such distinctions do more than merely pave the way for a cli-mactic joke. Ultimately, Shakespeare is chiefly interested in the characters' re-lationships to their roles, and therefore the conscious role-playing has dramatic interest not for its sheer variety alone but also for what it reflects about the fidelity or lack of fidelity with which the characters perform the disciplines their lots as lovers, friends, maids, and gentlemen have obligated them to carry out.

What makes the structure of *The Taming of the Shrew* characteristic, then, is not its schematic quality but rather its reflection of Shakespeare's ten-dency to employ role-playing as a primary device in the process through which he effects inner cohesion. In this respect *The Taming of the Shrew* structurally anticipates nearly all the plays to follow it. *1 Henry IV* – in which the kind of role a character plays is as significant as his acting style – and *King Lear* – in which characters differentiate themselves from one another according to how they utilize Lear's sanction of play-acting as a valid mode of action – exemplify, along with *The Two Gentlemen of Verona*, a structural pattern which is weighted in the direction of contrast and uses role-playing as a means of aligning characters and incidents so that they may be more exactly discriminated. Other plays, while not lacking dramatically significant contrasts based on role-playing, exemplify a pattern leaning more towards parallelism, a pattern that uses a particular kind of role-playing, or some other aspect of histrionic activity, to link a number of otherwise dissimilar characters and thus establish a distinct and coherent world. The world of *Much Ado About Nothing* is characterized by its inhabitants' delight in amateur theatrics of all sorts. The world of *Twelfth Night*, as the name Illyria might well imply, provides a congenial setting for those who in their self-delusion strive to perform false and inappropriate roles of their own devising. Hamlet's world is a rich and varied one, with many distinguishing characteristics, but not the least important of these is the way in which acting is made especially difficult by the tendency of all to appoint themselves as directors – to see themselves as qualified to tell the others what roles they should play and how they should play them.

Fuller illustration of these comprehensive structural patterns is an inevitable by-product in many of the analyses that follow, both in this chapter and beyond. The primary focus of the rest of this chapter, however, is another widespread structural pattern based on role-playing. This pattern also appears in embryonic form in *The Taming of the Shrew* (in the contrast between Petruchio and Lucentio) and arises from the use of role-playing to fashion, or help fashion a broad spatial opposition at the heart of the play. I refer, for instance, to the contrast-conflict occurring often in Shakespeare's plays between two divergent worlds, one example of which – chronologically the first one of real significance – is the opposition in *A Midsummer Night's Dream* between Athens and fairyland.

Theseus' Athens, despite the initial focus on the coming marriage of Theseus and Hippolyta and the implications it conveys of ideal self-fulfilment, is a world of constriction and rigidity. Hermia's plight amply exemplifies the social order because of the arbitrary manner in which her father and Theseus insist that she has no identity other than that of daughter to Egeus and that therefore she must adapt her will to his. When Hermia, preferring Lysander to Demetrius, wishes that 'my father look'd but with my eyes,' Theseus retorts: 'Rather your eyes must with his judgment look' (I.i.56-7). Hermia, as a player of roles, is from Athens' point of view more a marionette than an actress. Theseus acknowledges that Lysander is fully 'worthy' (52-3) and he also 'must confess' that he has heard about Demetrius' prior obligation to Helena (111); but none of this makes the least difference. Should Hermia fail to perform her role of daughter properly, the laws of Athens dictate that she must either die or switch to a new and even more restrictive role; she will have to

endure the livery of a nun,
For aye to be in shady cloister mew'd,
To live a barren sister all [her] life,
Chanting faint hymns to the cold fruitless moon. (70-3)

Theseus is to use the categorical, 'either-or' rhetoric of this speech twice more before the scene ends (86-90, 117-21). Fully symptomatic, this rhetoric effectively epitomizes the inflexibility of both the laws of the state and their executors.

The plights of two other Athenians demonstrate that Athens' constricting rigidity also exists independently of its laws. Demetrius, who has won the love of Hermia's father but not that of Hermia herself, cannot successfully perform the role he desires because its fulfilment depends on the co-operation of another, and she refuses to respond in the necessary manner. But this is a condition that Shakespeare dramatizes more explicitly through Helena, whom Demetrius has rejected by transferring his affections to Hermia. Helena too, therefore, wants to play a role she is not allowed to play, though she confuses the role with its present performer, for what she actually expresses a desire to enact is nothing other than the identity of Hermia:

Sickness is catching; O, were favour so,
Yours would I catch, fair Hermia, ere I go!
My ear should catch your voice, my eye your eye,
My tongue should catch your tongue's sweet melody.
Were the world mine, Demetrius being bated,
The rest I'd give to be to you translated.
O, teach me how you look, and with what art
You sway the motion of Demetrius' heart! (186-93)

Hermia and Lysander decide to flee Athens and seek out Lysander's widowed aunt, who lives seven leagues away, where 'the sharp Athenian law / Cannot pursue us' (162-3). It is fitting that they should choose to flee during the night-time, 'a time that lovers' flights doth still conceal' (212), because this careful selection of a suitable time helps to signify the symbolic meaning of their flight. Athens has prevented them from playing their desired roles, and so they are seeking a different and more congenial setting, one that will render these roles dramatically appropriate.

Demetrius and Helena have other reasons for leaving Athens – he goes to follow Hermia, Helena to follow him – but all four of the lovers find within the woods what Hermia and Lysander are seeking, a setting that allows them to do what they cannot do in Athens. For apart from its charm and the ease with which its inhabitants practise magic, Oberon's fairyland is also characterized by a further quality of considerable relevance to the issues raised in the opening scene. One of Puck's chief traits, according to his boastful introduction of himself, is his capacity to be whatever he wishes to be:

> I jest to Oberon, and make him smile
> When I a fat and bean-fed horse beguile,
> Neighing in likeness of a filly foal;
> And sometime lurk I in a gossip's bowl
> In very likeness of a roasted crab,
> And, when she drinks, against her lips I bob,
> And on her withered dewlap pour the ale.
> The wisest aunt, telling the saddest tale,
> Sometime for three-foot stool mistaketh me;
> Then slip I from her bum, down topples she. (ii.i.44-53)

And later, when telling the audience how he intends to frighten Bottom's comrades away, he mentions other examples of his repertoire:

> Sometime a horse I'll be, sometime a hound,
> A hog, a headless bear, sometime a fire;
> And neigh, and bark, and grunt, and roar, and burn,
> Like horse, hound, hog, bear, fire, at every turn. (iii.i.98-101)

But if in these speeches Puck only boasts of his capacity for shape-changing, he amply demonstrates it in iii.i when he transforms Quince's rehearsal into a play and himself becomes an 'actor' in it (71) as well as towards the end of iii.ii when to prevent Lysander and Demetrius from fighting he assumes the role of first one and then the other so that he can lead them both astray. And Puck is not the only inhabitant of the woods who possesses this trait; Oberon, as Titania complains, has often

> stolen away from fairy land,
> And in the shape of Corin sat all day,
> Playing on pipes of corn, and versing love
> To amorous Phillida. (ii.i.65-8)

As the strife between Oberon and Titania indicates, fairyland is not entirely exempt from problems like those besetting the residents of Athens. But Puck's and Oberon's capacity to transform themselves at will suggests that fairyland, in contrast to Athens, is an area characterized by its general fluidity of roles. The experience of the four young lovers bears out this suggestion. In Athens they knew only a rigid reality that would not permit them to play any roles other than those their situations had imposed on them; in fairyland they continually improvise little playlets in which they assume alien roles as easily, if not always as gleefully, as Puck himself.

'This green plot shall be our stage, this hawthorn brake our tiring-house,' says Quince, as he and his fellows begin the rehearsal of their play (III.i.3-5), and with his remark he defines the fairyland setting as a kind of theatre; so do Puck and Oberon when they serve as onstage spectators to watch and enjoy the lovers' 'fond pageants' (cf. III.ii.114). But what especially makes playlets of the three fairyland episodes involving the lovers is the alien role-playing Puck's magic juice compels them to perform. Hermia and Helena virtually swap roles, while Lysander and Demetrius both transfer their allegiances as lovers from one woman to the other. As in *The Comedy of Errors*, the changes in identity become increasingly more frenzied, and by the climax of the third episode, Hermia and Helena, once the closest friends, have fallen to bitter quarrelling, and Lysander and Demetrius, once only rivals, have come to regard one another as 'villains' to be destroyed (III.ii.415).

Experience as the lovers knew it, although unsatisfactory, had at least been orderly, while the hectic transformations of the third playlet reduce this order to chaos. Lysander and Demetrius act out their part in the chaos without really being aware of what they are going through, but both Helena and Hermia feel a profound sensation of dislocated reality that is fully articulated in Hermia's bewildered 'Am not I Hermia? Are not you Lysander?' (273) and later in her 'I am amaz'd, and know not what to say' (344). She cannot know what to say because she, like the others, has been put beside her part. Fairyland's fluidity of roles has wholly dissolved the identities they formerly possessed.

But if fairyland's fluidity brings the lovers temporary chaos, its ultimate effect is beneficial. In dissolving their identities, it has sufficiently loosened the rigidity of the real world so that a new and more satisfactory order can emerge. When the lovers return to Athens, as Puck's song over their sleeping bodies indicates, the roles they play will be those that their situations had previously denied them:

> the country proverb known,
> That every man should take his own,
> In your waking shall be shown.
>   Jack shall have Jill;
>   Nought shall go ill;
> The man shall have his mare again, and all shall be well. (458-63)

The arrival of Theseus in IV.i restores the lovers to the real world and, as Shakespeare implies through Egeus, to their proper identities:

> My lord, this is my daughter here asleep,
> And this Lysander, this Demetrius is,
> This Helena, old Nedar's Helena. (125-7)

Thanks to Oberon and Puck, however, this 'Demetrius' is not the Demetrius of the beginning of the play but the one that of old had wooed Helena, and this difference is a measure of the change that fairyland has wrought in the identities of all four lovers.

But even though the lovers' situations have altered, and for a moment their surroundings seem to be transformed (184-96), the real world is no different from what it had been. It is still arbitrary, for Theseus now overrules Egeus as quickly as he had once supported him; and it is still as rigid as ever, for 'These couples shall eternally be knit' (178). The disappearance from the action at this point of Hermia's father – as if now that she is to become a wife she will no longer be a daughter – even suggests that identity must still be conceived of as equivalent to a single role. What really proclaims the rigidity of the real world, however, is its attitude towards the fluidity of fairyland. Theseus regards the lovers' narrative of their experiences as 'More strange than true' and ascribes it to the work of 'seething brains' (v.i.2, 4). Hippolyta is tempted to believe them, though she admits that what they say is 'strange and admirable' (27). The lovers themselves, according to the last word the spectators hear them devote to their experiences, look back on them as 'dreams' (iv.i.196). Oberon has, of course, arranged for this response (iii.ii.371), but it is clear enough that, for those enmeshed in the rigidity of the real world, fluidity like that of fairyland could exist only in a strange and wonderful dream.

Theseus, Hippolyta, and the young lovers have little opportunity to reflect on these matters, however, for most of what still remains of the play after their return to Athens is taken over by the performance of the 'tedious brief scene of young Pyramus / And his love Thisby' (v.i.56-7). From the time of its inception, one of the main points of the plot strand concerning the preparation of this 'very tragical mirth' (57) has been the obvious discrepancy between Quince's actors and the roles assigned them. Now that it is finally performed, it occasions, like the Show of the Nine Worthies in *Love's Labour's Lost*, numerous jokes that exploit this discrepancy for all it is worth and heighten the Lamentable Comedy's function as a metaphor to parallel and highlight the similar discrepancy between actors and roles exhibited during the lovers' Comedy of Errors in fairyland.

But the mechanicals' activity also has a more complicated relation to the rest of *A Midsummer Night's Dream*. The discrepancy they constantly betray pertains with equal relevance to Shakespeare's entire analysis of the real world. Just as Bottom and his comrades are all 'patches' and therefore cannot successfully portray tragic lovers – let alone lions, moons, and walls – so all men of the real world have fixed roles and cannot play others at the same time: as Hermia at the beginning of the play cannot simultaneously be both a dutiful daughter and the lover of Lysander; or as Egeus at the end of the play cannot be both tyrant father and obedient subject of Theseus. Bottom, of all the characters in the play, is the most explicit representation of this deficiency. Bottom longs to play all the roles in the Lamentable Comedy as well as others besides (cf. I.ii.20-4, 44-6, 62-5), but, as Quince tells him, he 'can play no part but Pyramus' (75), and, as he reveals by dropping out of character during the performance (v.i.182-5, 341-2), he cannot even manage to play this one successfully. Bottom is Puck's antithesis, and as Puck represents fairyland's fluidity, Bottom represents the real world's corresponding rigidity.

Bottom does achieve his heart's desire at one point: in fairyland. There he gets to play a variety of roles, and all at the same time. For in Titania's bower, while Oberson stands to one side as a spectator, Bottom is the Grand Signior:

> Give me your neaf, Mounsieur Mustardseed. Pray you, leave your curtsy, good mounsieur. (IV.i.18-19)

He is also an ass:

> I must to the barber's, mounsieur; for methinks I am marvellous hairy about the face; and I am such a tender ass, if my hair do but tickle me I must scratch. (21-4)

And, as the characteristic verbal blunder indicates, he also continues to be Nick Bottom:

> But, I pray you, let none of your people stir me; I have an exposition of sleep come upon me. (35-6)

But when the fairies have departed and, awakening, Bottom returns to the real world, the experience is for ever lost. Like the young lovers, he can recall it only as an unfathomable dream:

> I have had a most rare vision. I have had a dream, past the wit of man to say what dream it was ... It shall be call'd 'Bottom's Dream,' because it hath no bottom. (202-3, 210-11)

And evidently he cannot even allow himself to accept his experience in this form. He at first contemplates having Quince 'write a ballad of this dream,' which he can sing 'in the latter end of a play, before the Duke' (209-12), but he never mentions his dream again. He arouses the interest of his comrades by promising 'to discourse wonders' and to tell them 'everything, right as it fell out,' but ultimately they get 'not a word of' him (IV.ii.26-30).

The poignancy of Bottom's otherwise ludicrous experience arises from Shakespeare's awareness that, despite man's desires, the rigorous division remains. The freedom to play alien roles belongs only to fairyland, and man, on whom the real world has imposed fixed roles, can satisfy his yearnings only in his dreams. But, as Shakespeare suggests, there is more than one kind of dream, for man possesses the gift of imagination, through which 'airy nothing' and 'local habitation' merge, and one of the chief products of man's imagination is drama. At one point during the mechanicals' performance of The Lamentable Comedy, Hippolyta complains, 'This is the silliest stuff that ever I heard,' but Theseus replies:

> The best in this kind are but shadows; and the worst are no worse, if imagination amend them. (v.i.209-11)

Theseus' speech points to one more function of the mechanicals' activity, its participation in a contrast between their ineptness and the skill with which another theatrical venture is being simultaneously carried off. 'The best in this kind' are Shakespeare's own actors, who *have* been amended by imagination: their own and Shakespeare's. They too 'are but shadows,' merely players, but while they perform, the discrepancy between actor and role, though not forgotten, does not obtrude. Shakespeare's spectator does not suspend disbelief; he experiences belief and disbelief simultaneously. He sees Theseus, but he also sees Burbage; he sees, in fact, Burbage as Theseus, and some of his appreciation of the play stems from his witnessing Burbage's successful defiance – for himself and vicariously for the spectator – of the real world's prohibition against playing alien roles. Man escapes this prohibition only in his dreams, but the play itself – as the epilogue by the 'shadow' that portrayed Puck makes clear – is also a dream:

> If we shadows have offended,
> Think but this, and all is mended,
> That you have but slumb'red here
> While these visions did appear.
> And this weak and idle theme,
> No more yielding but a dream ...

The opposing of two divergent worlds whose differences depend in large measure upon the possibilities for role-playing that each has to offer constitutes a favourite structural pattern of Shakespeare's. He uses it again in *As You Like It*, in the contrast between the court's suppression of role-playing and the forest's encouragement of it, and also in *The Winter's Tale*, in the contrast between the mad, destructive play-acting of Leontes' Sicilia and the spontaneous, healthy, and ultimately restorative role-playing characteristic of the sheepshearing festival in Bohemia. Even more prevalent are the plays in which the broad spatial contrast opposes not divergent worlds but contrasting possibilities within a single world. This kind of structure is typical of the history plays, in which the Player-King who mechanically acts out the gestures and moves of a role for which he is not aptly fitted (Henry VI, Richard III, Richard II, John) must confront an opposite who aspires to this role, or who should, and who often helps his cause through the use of conscious role-playing (Richard Duke of York, Richard of Gloucester, Richmond, Bolingbroke, Faulconbridge). In *Othello*, this opposition arises from the conflict between Iago and Othello, whose contrasting uses of role-playing reflect two totally incompatible attitudes towards life. In *Much Ado About Nothing*, which consists almost entirely of its characters' amateur theatrics, the opposition involves the vitally necessary quality of histrionic sensibility, which Claudio unfortunately lacks but which Beatrice and Benedick possess in abundance. To illustrate this variation of the broad spatial contrast based on role-playing, I have chosen *The Merchant of Venice*, in which, it seems to me, the contrast between two divergent worlds – here, Venice and Belmont – is ultimately less interesting and less central than the role-playing opposition that helps to shape it.

Shakespeare introduces this opposition at the very outset of the play, in part through a speech that provides both an explicit focus on role-playing and a particular conception of character:

> I hold the world but as the world, Gratiano –
> A stage, where every man must play a part,
> And mind a sad one. (I.i.77-9)

Antonio voices this conception of character not as a casual remark but as an explanation of his own manner. He feels such acute depression that, as he says, 'I have much ado to know myself' (I.i.7); yet his sadness does not stem from worry about his business ventures, for these go well, nor is he in love. The only explanation he can offer is that he cannot keep from being sad because life has cast him in the role of the melancholy man, and he has no choice but to play it. Like every other human being, his nature is merely a part that he plays, an external pattern of experience with its own predetermined unity, and, moreover, it is a fixed part from which he can never escape.

This view of identity, which cannot embrace even all examples of the first basic character type, is usually no more true for Shakespearian characterization than it is for life outside his plays, and one would be inclined to regard Antonio's espousal of this view as *merely* a revelation of his own mood, his own present condition, were it not for the interesting fact that his speech echoes something Solanio has already expressed more abstractly:

> let us say you are sad
> Because you are not merry; and 'twere as easy
> For you to laugh and leap and say you are merry,
> Because you are not sad. Now, by two-headed Janus,
> Nature hath fram'd strange fellows in her time:
> Some that will evermore peep through their eyes,
> And laugh like parrots at a bag-piper;
> And other of such vinegar aspect
> That they'll not show their teeth in way of smile
> Though Nestor swear the jest be laughable. (47-56)

Antonio does not, then, simply introduce this view of character; by echoing something that the spectators have already heard and by rendering it in a more arresting form, he firmly establishes it as a dramatic element of some consequence.

No sooner has he done so, however, than Gratiano challenges it by arguing for a very different conception of character. If every man must play a specific part, Gratiano replies, then

> Let me play the fool.
> With mirth and laughter let old wrinkles come;
> And let my liver rather heat with wine
> Than my heart cool with mortifying groans. (79-82)

He then goes on to suggest – hesitantly, out of deference to his friend – that the role Antonio regards as an imposed one is perhaps instead wilfully assumed:

> I tell thee what, Antonio –
> I love thee, and 'tis my love that speaks –
> There are a sort of men whose visages
> Do cream and mantle like a standing pond,
> And do a wilful stillness entertain,
> With purpose to be dress'd in an opinion
> Of wisdom, gravity, profound conceit;
> As who should say 'I am Sir Oracle,
> And when I ope my lips let no dog bark.' (86-94)

This reply to Antonio and, indirectly, to Solanio does not dispute the notion that one's nature is a role, but Gratiano attributes far more flexibility to man the actor. The role that is one's nature, he insists, is not imposed but freely chosen. And since he advises Antonio to drop his melancholy manner – 'fish not with this melancholy bait / For this fool gudgeon, this opinion' (101-2) – he also implies that man can change his role at will.

The opposition introduced in this first scene between the two conceptions of character – the one arguing for rigidity, the other for flexibility – is the primary basis on which Shakespeare builds the play. The climax of the play, of course, is the trial in IV.i, and this scene forms the climax precisely because it juxtaposes, in Shylock and Portia, two characters whose contrasting contributions embody the two sides of the opposition. Shylock's behaviour at the trial, which is an extension of his previous behaviour, confirms his exemplification of Antonio's view of character. Portia, in contrast, symbolically exemplifies Gratiano's view, and in doing so she also sums up not only her own nature but that of most of Shylock's adversaries, whose representative she is and whose varied experiences she here draws together in a single expressive metaphor.

Throughout the trial scene Shylock is continually associated with images connoting his rigidity. The Duke calls him 'a stony adversary' (IV.i.4). Antonio speaks of his 'rigorous course' and adds, 'he stands obdurate' (8). Gratiano sees him as consisting wholly of some adamantine and impenetrable metal:

> Not on thy sole, but on thy soul, harsh Jew,
> Thou mak'st thy knife keen; but no metal can,
> No, not the hangman's axe, bear half the keenness
> Of thy sharp envy. Can no prayers pierce thee? (123-6).

The most forceful of these images occurs in a speech by Antonio which traces Shylock's rigidity to its ultimate source. Antonio reminds his advocates that they 'question with the Jew' (70) and proceeds to outline a series of impossible tasks that they 'may as well' attempt instead. He then concludes:

> You may as well do anything most hard
> As seek to soften that – than which what's harder? –
> His Jewish heart. (78-80)

According to Antonio, Shylock behaves as he does because he's 'the Jew.' Appeals for mercy and offers to double or triple the amount owed, which might influence an autonomous creature, can have no effect on Shylock, who is merely a specific incarnation of an unvarying pattern of behaviour over which he exercises no control. If Antonio is to be believed, Shylock is what Antonio has already labelled himself: an actor executing the predetermined gestures and moves of a particular role. And therefore his rigidity is not only, as Antonio claims, an attribute of his role but also a reflection of the persistence with which he adheres to its dictates.

Antonio's implication about Shylock warrants belief because it merely expresses with greater precision the view of Shylock already conveyed by his adversaries' habit of referring to him not by name but as 'the Jew.' Furthermore, Shakespeare has been careful to ensure that every detail in Shylock's characterization is perfectly consistent with the common Elizabethan stereotype of the Jew. Everything that Shylock is and does helps demonstrate his fulfilment of this single role. Shakespeare has, of course, categorized Shylock not only as Jew but also as usurer, as miser, and as one who is so exclusively devoted to business matters that for him 'good' has no other meaning than 'sufficient' – i.e., financially sound (I.iii.12-15). But from the point of view of Shakespeare's audience, these additional categories are not additional roles, they are specific functions of his Jewishness. His possession of them constitutes, in fact, the chief proof that he conforms to the one idea about character accepted by both Antonio and Gratiano – that, in other words, he is acting out a conventional role.

In terms of dramatic conflict, the most important attribute of this conventional role is its unmitigated evil, and, appropriately, Shylock's own dedication to evil is seen to have its roots in his Jewishness. Antonio's speech at the trial, which blames Shylock's 'Jewish heart' for the rigour with which he pursues his evil course, also implies that any Jew would necessarily have to be as evil as Shylock. This is a claim that Antonio has already advanced more directly, in his ironic comment on the conditions Shylock has fixed for the bond: 'The Hebrew will turn Christian: he grows kind' (I.iii.173). One may doubt Antonio's reliability with regard to Shylock or Jews in general, but it is probable that Shakespeare's audience would have agreed with him. At any rate, Shylock's dedication to evil is unequivocal. It becomes more obvious as the action progresses, but as early as Shylock's initial appearance it is already established through the emphasis on his unrelenting hatred, and Shakespeare is careful to show that the hatred stems directly from his role as Jew. Shylock's first uninhibited speech, the aside that runs from line 36 to line 47 of I.iii, uses the verb 'hate' twice. As usurer and miser, Shylock must hate Antonio because Antonio 'lends out money gratis, and brings down / The rate of usance here with us in Venice' (39-40). Shylock asserts that this motive for his hatred has more weight than the fact that Antonio is a Christian, for which he also hates him, but since Shylock's identities as usurer and miser are functions of his Jewishness, the distinction carries little meaning. Furthermore, the grudge he bears Antonio is an 'ancient' one (42), which suggests that, in its basic source at least, it antedates Shylock himself; and when he concludes, 'Cursed be my tribe / If I forgive him!' (46-7), the integral relation between his hatred and his role as Jew is no longer open to question.

To conform properly to Antonio's view of character, Shylock must not only be acting out a specific conventional role, he must also be incapable of separating himself from it. That he will not do so is also established as early as his first appearance. Shylock hates Antonio and probably Bassanio as well, since he too is a Christian. By coming to Shylock with their request for money, however, Bassanio and Antonio alter their existing relation to him, and, more important, they provide him with an opportunity to alter his relation to them. They make it possible for him at least to initiate a bond of friendship with them by performing an act of kindness and generosity. Shakespeare establishes this possibility by having Shylock profess that this is exactly what he has in mind:

> Why, look you, how you storm!
> I would be friends with you, and have your love,
> Forget the shames that you have stain'd me with,
> Supply your present wants, and take no doit
> Of usance for my moneys, and you'll not hear me.
> This is kind I offer. (132-7)

The point is, of course, that Shylock here performs not an act of kindness but a bit of conscious, artful role-playing, which he carries further, though with increasing irony, as he employs the phrase 'merry sport' to introduce the idea of taking a pound of Antonio's flesh, and in his mock display of misunderstood innocence:

> O father Abram, what these Christians are,
> Whose own hard dealings teaches them suspect
> The thoughts of others!
>   ...
>   I say,
> To buy his favour, I extend this friendship;
> If he will take it, so; if not, adieu;
> And, for my love, I pray you wrong me not. (155-7, 162-5)

That this is play-acting rather than sincerity is abundantly clear. Bassanio is momentarily taken in, but the terms of the bond soon disabuse him, and Antonio never seems to be in doubt. Shylock himself, moreover, cannot restrain the obvious irony that converts an effort to deceive into a sadistic joke. Shylock's attempt at play-acting ultimately has no effect on the action, therefore, but it does provide a convincing indication that any change in him is unthinkable. Its very transparency suggests that he is incapable of playing any role other than his given one, and the limited extent to which he tries to get away with his false performance merely demonstrates further his rigid adherence to all that his role as Jew implies. He can only be attempting to ensure Antonio's acceptance of his terms and, through this, a chance to catch Antonio 'upon the hip' (41).

No aspect of Shylock's subsequent conduct ever belies this original impression, but whether his failure to separate himself from his role results from unwillingness or, as Antonio's view of character would insist, from inability, Shakespeare does not specify. At the trial, however, where the failure is most conspicuous, Shylock himself hints that he will not yield because he cannot. He knows that his adversaries expect to hear some reason why he rather chooses 'to have / A weight of carrion flesh than to receive / Three thousand ducats,' and so he says 'it is my humour' (IV.i.40-3). Just as 'there is no firm reason' why some men 'cannot abide a gaping pig,' some 'a harmless necessary cat,' and others 'a woollen bagpipe,' so Shylock can give no reason for following a losing suit except 'a lodg'd hate and a certain loathing / I bear Antonio' (53-61). Shylock evidently subscribes to the same fatalistic notions as Antonio and Solanio, whose speech in I.i about nature's 'strange fellows' is paralleled by Shylock's, even to the extent of Shylock's also describing an unusual response to bagpipe music. Shylock's advocacy of such notions proves nothing, of course, not even that he genuinely espouses them, but it does allow Shakespeare to re-establish them at the exact moment when Shylock's rigid adherence to his role is most in evidence.

What makes Shylock's rigidity so conspicuous here is not only his adversaries' vigorous though fruitless efforts to placate him but also the presence of Portia, his chief adversary. Portia is Shylock's antithesis. Her celebration of mercy counterbalances his insistence on law, and her initial willingness to compromise exposes all the more clearly his adamancy. Above all, however, while Shylock exemplifies Antonio's view of character by continuing to play the role he has always held, Portia symbolically exemplifies Gratiano's contrasting view by performing the chief instance in the play of an entirely different kind of role-playing. Portia's confrontation of Shylock at the trial is a splendid stroke in terms of the standard criteria of dramatic criticism – it is both appropriate to her character and a boon to plot unity – but these criteria in no way require that she confront him in the guise of Balthasar, 'A young and learned doctor' (IV.i.144). Shakespeare is obviously working primarily in terms of dramatic contrast rather than plot and character, for Portia's role-playing has its justification not in her nature or her circumstances but in its own symbolic content. Her full-dress portrayal of Balthasar supplies an unusually incisive representation of man's capacity freely to assume new roles, and it thereby enables Shakespeare to oppose Shylock's rigidity with a striking symbol of flexibility.

It is, moreover, by no means merely an abstraction that is being opposed to Shylock, for in symbolizing flexibility Portia's role-playing also constitutes a metaphor for the flexibility that most of Shylock's adversaries exhibit as individuals. Portia herself has already, before coming to the trial, demonstrated her own flexibility by undergoing a change in identity which transforms her from her father's daughter – 'so is the will of a living daughter curb'd by the will of a dead father' (I.ii.21-2) – to Bassanio's wife:

> But now I was the lord
> Of this fair mansion, master of my servants,
> Queen o'er myself; and even now, but now,
> This house, these servants, and this same myself,
> Are yours – my lord's. (III.ii.168-72)

Bassanio, Gratiano, and Lorenzo alter their identities by assuming the new role of husband. Launcelot and Jessica also change, and their transformations are in part represented through theatrical imagery, for Launcelot's shift in allegiance from Shylock to Bassanio consists primarily of a change in costume – to one of Bassanio's 'rare new liveries' (II.ii.100) – and Jessica escapes from Shylock's house in a 'page's suit' (II.iv.32) while Lorenzo and his fellow masquers assist her by playing 'the thieves for wives' (II.vi.23). Jessica's transformation from Jew to Gentile – or 'gentle': in the prevailing idiom, the two words are interchangeable – underscores Shylock's failure to achieve a comparable transformation, a failure that Shakespeare specifically points to through the irony of Antonio's 'The Hebrew will turn Christian: he grows kind' (I iii.173). To a considerable extent, then, the contrast between Jessica's success and Shylock's failure epitomizes the entire action of the play.

But only to a considerable extent. Although the core of the action is this opposition between Shylock's fulfilment of Antonio's view of character and his adversaries' contrasting fulfilment of Gratiano's view, between his rigidity and their flexibility, Shakespeare complicates the dramatic core by adding two further criteria to the contrast that distinguishes Shylock from his adversaries. In keeping with the climactic nature of the confrontation in the trial scene, Portia's role-playing embodies not only the flexibility of Shylock's adversaries but also the additional ways in which they differ from him.

Portia assumes the role of Balthasar in order to save Antonio, who is her new husband's 'dearest friend' (III.ii.294) and therefore, she reasons, both her own friend and one that 'must needs be like my lord' (III.iv.18). She acts, then, out of friendship and love, and because of her motives her role-playing also embodies the warm responsiveness to one another that Shakespeare has shown to be a major characteristic of all of Shylock's adversaries. This responsiveness receives its fullest dramatization, of course, through the relationships that link Antonio and Bassanio, Bassanio and Portia, and Lorenzo and Jessica; but Shakespeare also stresses it in other ways as well: through the frequency with which the members of Antonio's circle explicitly call attention to their friendship for one another and their enjoyment of company, and, though less directly, through the characters' constant anticipations of dining together. These occur throughout the play and continually manifest the conviviality of Shylock's adversaries; ultimately, when Bassanio looks forward to his marriage feast (III.ii.213-14) and when Lorenzo and Jessica plan to let their feeling for each other 'serve for table-talk' (III.v.79), the constantly anticipated occasion even acquires implications of the love feast. In part, too, the delight that Shylock's adversaries take in their relationships with one another has already been established through activity similar to Portia's. The role-playing of the masquers, in itself an expression of their conviviality, also becomes, through the use to which it is put during the elopement of Lorenzo and Jessica, an emblem of both friendship and love.

Shylock's intense hatred of Antonio and of all Christians is not the only characteristic through which he provides a contrast to his adversaries' high valuation of love and friendship. Early in the play he tells Bassanio that although 'I will buy with you, sell with you, talk with you, walk with you, and so following' – in which the 'you' means Christians in general – 'I will not eat with you, drink with you, nor pray with you' (I.iii.30-3). The last clause indicates that Shylock is primarily concerned with religious differences between himself and his Christian adversaries, but his emphasis on eating and drinking also makes this speech an expression of his attitude towards one of his adversaries' chief delights. Later, indeed, he fully reveals his suspicion and loathing of conviviality in any form by ordering Jessica to lock his doors and shut his casements against the 'vile squealing' of the masquers' music: 'Let not the sound of shallow fopp'ry enter / My sober house' (II.v.29, 34-5). He is 'bid forth to supper' by the Christians, but, he says, 'I am not bid for love; they flatter me; / But yet I'll go in hate, to feed upon / The prodigal Christian' (11-15). This speech has an ominous ring considering his desire for a pound of Antonio's flesh. It associates Shylock not with the love feast but with cannibalism.

Furthermore, since Shylock himself believes his hatred of Antonio and the other Christians to be amply motivated, Shakespeare is careful to stress that hatred is the only feeling for his fellow man of which Shylock is capable. His play-acting in I.iii shows that while his adversaries act out of friendship he merely acts it out. His relationship with his daughter, whom he values lower than his ducats, shows that he is equally incapable of love. And it is also significant that, given the high regard his adversaries have for companionship, Shylock should be so much of a loner. His obvious evil and his hatred of all Christians pretty well guarantee his isolation in a play-world that is populated almost exclusively by good Christians, but Shakespeare both emphasizes his isolation and increases it by devoting two of the play's episodes to desertions of Shylock by his servant and his daughter. When Antonio's bond finally falls due, Shylock has no one with whom he can associate except Tubal, and even Tubal does not accompany him to the trial. Shylock's isolation reinforces the impression he gives of being totally out of place in the same world as his adversaries. He seems scarcely human, and, indeed, his humanity is called into question more than once. Shylock himself, in his most famous speech, contends that a Jew has the same human characteristics as a Christian, but he does so only in order to stress his dedication to revenge: 'And if you wrong us, shall we not revenge? If we are like you in the rest, we will resemble you in that ... The villainy you teach me I will execute; and it shall go hard but I will better the instruction' (III.i.56-7, 61-2). But it is the others that make this implication explicit: in III.ii, Salerio seems to be commenting on this very speech when he says, 'Never did I know / A creature that did bear the shape of man / So keen and greedy to confound a man' (276-8); and at the trial Shylock is called 'an inhuman wretch' by the Duke (IV.i.4) and an 'unfeeling man' by Bassanio (63). Shylock's rigid adherence to his role has cost him his claim to humanity; he is not a man but, as his adversaries insist again and again, a devil and an animal. As Gratiano puts it at the trial, he is a 'damn'd, inexecrable dog!' (128).

Shakespeare also complicates the basic opposition between Shylock and his adversaries through the theme of giving and hazarding all one has, which enters the play in the form of the test of the caskets. Portia's first suitors, those described in I.ii, are unwilling even to attempt this test. Morocco and Aragon attempt it, but pride prevents them from hazarding anything for lead, and so they end up losing all: they forfeit both Portia and any other wife. It is also suggested that they suffer a change in identity – for they have become 'deliberate fools' (II.ix.80) – and if so, this is a highly appropriate punishment because, as the emphasis upon their pride indicates, it is their identities that Morocco and Aragon actually refuse to risk: they are determined not to betray themselves by choosing basely. In this way, Morocco and Aragon provide analogies for Shylock, whose failure to separate himself from his role can be seen as the sign of a similar unwillingness to risk loss of identity. Shylock, in fact, glimpses an opportunity to realize his identity fully by achieving revenge against Antonio, and he refuses to let the opportunity slip. As a result, he too suffers a loss of identity, and in his case the loss is total.

It is otherwise with Shylock's adversaries, who exemplify the theme of hazarding and risking all one has in a positive manner. Bassanio, of course, successfully passes the test of the caskets, thereby winning both Portia and her wealth, while Jessica and Lorenzo, by temporarily assuming alien roles, win each other. The most important enactments of this theme, however, serve simultaneously as further evidence of the characters' deep concern for one another, for in these the risk of loss is entered into so that another may gain. This is the case, for example, with both Antonio's self-sacrificing assistance of Bassanio and Bassanio's own postponement of the consummation of his marriage in order to rush to the aid of his friend.

In claiming that Lorenzo and Jessica enact this theme, I am suggesting that the risk of loss which Shylock's adversaries undertake for themselves or each other involves the willing surrender of identity and therefore constitutes a form of role-playing. Gratiano's exemplification of the theme tends to confirm this. In II.ii, Bassanio consents to his accompanying him on his mission to Belmont only on the condition that Gratiano curb his 'skipping spirit,' 'lest through thy wild behaviour / I be misconst'red ... / And lose my hopes' (172-4). Gratiano would prefer to play the fool, as he has declared in I.i, but for his friend's sake he promises to assume an entirely different role:

> If I do not put on a sober habit,
> Talk with respect, and swear but now and then,
> Wear prayer-books in my pocket, look demurely,
> Nay more, while grace is saying hood mine eyes
> Thus with my hat, and sigh, and say amen,
> Use all the observance of civility
> Like one well studied in a sad ostent
> To please his grandam, never trust me more. (175-82)

Since Bassanio realizes his hopes in Belmont, Gratiano evidently keeps his promise, and in doing so he helps himself as well, for the trip to Belmont also provides him with a wife. Gratiano's role-playing thus anticipates that of Portia, which in addition to its other functions also embodies this final characteristic of Shylock's adversaries. She willingly surrenders her identity by becoming Balthasar, and in the process she gives Antonio his life. At the same time, moreover, her role-playing, like Gratiano's, also sums up every positive enactment of this theme, for by saving Antonio she symbolically saves herself as well:

> this Antonio,
> Being the bosom lover of my lord,
> Must needs be like my lord. If it be so,
> How little is the cost I have bestowed
> In purchasing the semblance of my soul
> From out the state of hellish cruelty! (III.iv.16-21)

To some extent the two further criteria distinguishing Shylock from his

Stylistic
clumsiness
! !

adversaries help develop the basic opposition between rigidity and flexibility. Shylock's resistance to the human action diagrammed by the theme of the willing surrender of identity helps measure the rigidity with which he adheres to his role, while his loathing of conviviality and his inability to respond favourably to others characterize this role more fully. His adversaries' ready willingness to hazard all they have is, of course, additional evidence of their flexibility, but their usual motive for this risk and the other signs of their constant concern with love and friendship do more than merely further define them: these signs also identify the source from which their flexibility in large measure derives. Nonetheless, despite such links as these, the further criteria are not implicit in the basic opposition, nor is their contribution limited to enriching its presentation. They are important dramatic elements in their own right, if only through the impact they have on the play's outcome.

Shylock's lack of human warmth and his refusal to hazard himself mean that his portrait is not just that of one who rigidly adheres to his role but rather that of one rigidly adhering to a role that is entirely inappropriate to the world in which he exists and disruptive of its harmony. Antonio's fatalistic adherence to his role of melancholy man causes him less disadvantage because this role does not preclude his also playing the role of friend; in fact, his conviction that he is 'a tainted wether of the flock, / Meetest for death' (IV.i.114-15) permits him to play this additional role with complete abandon. But Shylock possesses a role that disqualifies him for citizenship in a society founded like this one on intimate human relationships, and his stubborn refusal to separate himself from this role finally assigns him the ultimate dramatic role of the comic misfit, the social or moral monster who so deviates from the norm that he must be either converted or destroyed.

Shylock's defeat at the trial subjects him to both of these fates. His adversaries forcibly change his role by depriving him of his wealth and by demanding that he instantly become a Christian and acknowledge Lorenzo and Jessica as his son and daughter (IV.i.381-5). From Shylock's own point of view, he instead suffers the alternative fate of destruction. He sees the confiscation of his money as equivalent to a sentence of death:

> Nay, take my life and all, pardon not that.
> You take my house when you do take the prop
> That doth sustain my house; you take my life
> When you do take the means whereby I live. (369-72)

And when he learns the additional demands, he begs to be excused: 'I pray you, give me leave to go from hence; / I am not well' (390-1). As far as the audience is concerned, Shylock has correctly understood the situation: four lines later he silently exits and, though he is mentioned in the final act, he is never seen or heard again. The implication would seem to be that his failure to separate himself from his role was not wilful after all – that, indeed, the role of Jew was, in Antonio's terms, the part he must play, and he cannot survive its loss.

Shylock's adversaries likewise experience an appropriate outcome. Their victory over Shylock immediately – and inevitably, one would think – prompts two invitations to dinner, one by the Duke in the line following Shylock's exit (iv.i.396), and the other by Bassanio, which Gratiano delivers in the next scene (iv.ii.7-8). It also prompts, as antidote to the bond that Shylock conceived in hatred, explicit recognition of the true 'bond' of 'love and service' (iv.i.409; cf. iv.i.402, v.i.134-7). And in act v, all of Shylock's major adversaries – only the Duke, Solanio, and Salerio are missing – gather in Belmont, Portia's home, to participate in an elaborate celebration of peace and harmony and especially of their mutual love and friendship. In keeping with the characteristic flexibility of Shylock's adversaries, there is also deliberate role-playing here – as Portia and Nerissa tease their husbands about losing the rings – but this time the role-playing is nothing more than a good-natured joke, and along with almost everything else in the act it helps increase the general merriment. Only Antonio fails to seem entirely contented in Belmont, and his discomfort is to be expected: his part, which he must play, is a sad one; and since he *must* play it, he is too much like Shylock to be able to fit into his friends' world as fully as they do.

The ultimate association of Shylock's adversaries and all they stand for with Belmont brings into sharp focus a constant tendency of the play, its effort to shape itself into a central contrast between the world of Belmont and its antithesis, the world of Venice, which by the end of the play has become in effect a one-man domain and as such no longer exists. But Antonio, the merchant of Venice, who cannot find true sanctuary in Belmont despite his capacity for warmth and self-sacrifice, tends to obliterate this contrast, and his uncomfortable presence in the final scene ensures continued dramatization of the play's primary rendering of a broad spatial contrast: the opposition between rigidity and flexibility in the playing of roles. The similar opposition in *A Midsummer Night's Dream* eventuates in a direct focus on theatre, but Shakespeare uses this focus to extend his contrast between Athens and fairyland so that it can also embody the distinction between man's physical limitations and his unbounded imagination. In the focus on role-playing in *The Merchant of Venice*, Shakespeare is more concerned with dramatic form than with life. Here, ironically, although there is no direct focus on theatre, he creates not a statement about human experience but a juxtaposition of two kinds of dramatic man, the one always remaining what it was at the outset, the other bending and yielding in response to the action.

4 Role-playing as theme

I am not that I play. (*Twelfth Night*, I.v.173-4)

At the conclusion of *All's Well That Ends Well*, in a most unusual dramatic effect, Shakespeare has the actor who plays the King explicitly call attention to the fact that 'the King' is merely a role behind which is hidden someone else and, socially speaking, someone baser: 'The King's a beggar, now the play is done' (Epilogue, 1). Ostensibly a means of dismissing the play world and returning to the real world, this line in actuality keeps the play world very much in focus. The exposure of the false king echoes the fourth-act exposure of the *Miles Gloriosus*, Parolles, the pretender to heroism, and the parallel fifth-act exposure of his associate, the *Nobilis Honestissimus*, Bertram, a pretender to nobility. The play's central character, Helena, undergoes no similar exposure – and does not need to – but through its emphasis on discrepancy the Beggar-King's line also applies to her. She and Bertram participate in a broad spatial contrast in which the discrepancy she exemplifies balances his. Bertram possesses the role of nobleman, but he cannot perform its obligations. Helena has the native worth, but she lacks the nexus of roles through which such worth is formally and publicly embodied. The action of *All's Well* consists of Helena's gradual and successful effort to acquire these roles and thus eliminate her discrepancy, but it remains doubtful whether Bertram successfully emulates her. It is not at all doubtful, however, that the play as a whole is very much concerned with what has by the time of its writing become a theme of considerable importance to Shakespeare.

Actual discrepancies between characters and the parts they are called upon or choose to play already have some prominence in *The Comedy of Errors* and *The Taming of the Shrew* (where they serve as ready sources of laughs or as necessary plot devices) and in the earliest histories (where they help define both the Player-King and his opponent, the Pretender). But the discrepancy between the actor and his role assumes full thematic import only with *Richard III* (where the hero's play-acting forms the only real subject of at least the first three acts), *The Two Gentlemen of Verona* (where Proteus' inability to live up to the demands of friendship and love distinguish him from the extraordinarily faithful Julia and Valentine), and *Love's Labour's Lost* (where the Show of the Nine Worthies provides a metaphor for the histrionic failings of the King and his Lords, who first try to play the inappropriate role of book-man and then botch the more suitable role of lover by playing it false). In most of the subsequent plays, whether history, comedy, or tragedy, discrepancy continues to be either an important theme or sub-theme or a substantial source of action, and in at least five of the plays of Shakespeare's maturity it provides the dramatic core. One of these five is of course *All's Well That Ends Well*. Two others, *Julius Caesar* and *Troilus and Cressida*, I examine in chapter 7 because Shakespeare's exploitation of the theme in them has important bearing on the idea of the history play as a distinct genre. This leaves *Twelfth Night* and *Measure for Measure*, which develop their common theme in two interestingly differentiated ways.

Viola's 'I am not that I play' (i.v.173-4) might well be spoken by nearly any of her fellow characters, for with few exceptions all those who people *Twelfth Night* and define its world have obscured their true identities behind alien and inappropriate roles. In *Twelfth Night*, then, as in *Much Ado About Nothing*, a world emerges whose chief activity is histrionic in nature, though here there are few definable playlets because there is little recognition of any distinction between acting and play-acting, between fulfilling one's true identity and assuming a false one. And this fact of the play compels me to qualify what I have said about Viola's assertion: her words might well be spoken by nearly any of the characters only because of their validity; actually to speak them requires a self-awareness that by and large Viola alone possesses. For *Twelfth Night* not only dramatizes a spectrum of various kinds of discrepant role-playing; it also continually exploits a fundamental contrast between Viola's role-playing and that of the majority of her fellow characters.

Viola's portrayal of Cesario, like the similar impersonations by Julia in *The Two Gentlemen of Verona* and Rosalind in *As You Like It*, metaphorically embodies the kind of activity that the bulk of the characters, with varying degrees of overtness, engage in, but at the same time this metaphor also reflects the contrast that *differentiates* Viola from most of the others. She deliberately chooses to assume the role of Cesario because she finds herself in unfamiliar surroundings and wants to learn the lie of the land before revealing her true identity. Her disguise is thus a sign of her displacement from a setting in which the identity 'Viola' had assured meaning and a known function, a sign, that is, of an altered scene-agent ratio; but it is also, and more important, a sign of her innate shrewdness, of her wariness about external reality, and of her recognition that she had better comprehend it fully before submitting herself to it. Her disguise reflects, in other words, the same awareness of the possible discrepancy between appearance and reality that she expresses to the

Captain (i.ii.47-51) and the same need to locate herself with perfect clarity that she demonstrates when first visiting Olivia: 'I pray you tell me if this be the lady of the house, for I never saw her. I would be loath to cast away my speech ... ' (i.v.160-2).

For the others, however, Viola's disguise conveys a far different implication. In i.iv Duke Orsino observes to her that

> they shall yet belie thy happy years
> That say thou art a man: Diana's lip
> Is not more smooth and rubious; thy small pipe
> Is as the maiden's organ, shrill and sound,
> And all is semblative a woman's part. (29-33)

This speech ironically underscores Orsino's failure to penetrate her disguise. Like Olivia, he has 'made good view of' her (ii.ii.17), but, also like Olivia, he has nonetheless been 'charm'd' by her 'outside' (16). The similar failure of Malvolio, Sir Toby, Sir Andrew, and Maria may be more understandable, as well as less significant in terms of its consequences, but it has pretty much the same implication. In relation to her fellow characters, Viola's disguise comes to signify their inability to distinguish between appearance and reality. It becomes a sign of the moral blindness that informs their own very different kind of role-playing.

The clearest and in many ways the most interesting example of this other kind of role-playing consists of the career of Malvolio, whose self-miscasting gradually evolves from an internal and imaginative act to a public display that exposes him for what he really is. Malvolio's true identity corresponds to his social role as steward – as Sir Toby insists (ii.iii.108) – but, 'sick of self-love' (i.v.85), he sees himself as superior not only to his fellow servants but also to Sir Andrew and Sir Toby and equal if not superior to Olivia; in his own mind he is the darling of the gods – 'Jove, I thank thee' (ii.v.158; cf. iii.iv.71, 78) – and thus the proper determiner of values here on earth. Malvolio's blindness to reality betrays itself at once, when he mistakes Feste for a 'barren rascal' (i.v.78) and, to his cost, attempts to beat him at his own game (68-76). But at this point his discrepant role-playing manifests itself only through his attitudes: his contempt for Feste, his indignant loathing for Sir Toby's merry-making. And even here, though he speaks roundly to the malefactors (ii.iii.83-8), he carefully presents himself as no more than the agent of 'my lady' (91-6). As Maria knows, however, Malvolio is merely a 'time-pleaser; an affection'd ass that cons state without book and utters it by great swarths; the best persuaded of himself, so cramm'd, as he thinks, with excellencies that it is his grounds of faith that all that look on him love him' (138-42). Maria here associates Malvolio's self-love with a role-playing image, and in ii.v the scheme for revenge that she and the others have devised provides him with a stage upon which he can freely indulge his histrionic bent and initiate the process whereby it becomes increasingly public.

At the beginning of this scene Maria lays out the forged letter as if it were a prop, and Sir Toby, Sir Andrew, and Fabian hide in the 'box-tree' (13), where they form an audience to await the entrance of Malvolio, who has, according to Maria, 'been yonder i' the sun practising behaviour to his own shadow this half hour' (14-15). These acts effectively restore Olivia's garden walk to its original condition as the stage of Shakespeare's theatre and transform Malvolio the steward into an actor giving his part a final run-through just before 'going on.' Then Malvolio enters and begins the long soliloquy that constitutes his part of the scene. He is, from its inception, already engaged in role-playing, for he fancies himself admired by Olivia, he dreams of being 'Count Malvolio' (32), and he even manages to recall a precedent to convince himself that his dreams can easily come true. But it is not until line 41, when he shifts to present participles, that he gets 'deeply in': 'Having been three months married to her, sitting in my state – '

Malvolio now no longer merely dreams of being Count Malvolio; in his imagination, the role has become a reality. Consequently, he must give the stage an appropriate setting and himself the proper costume:

Calling my officers about me, in my branch'd velvet gown, having come from a day-bed – where I have left Olivia sleeping – (44-6)

And he must create a fitting dramatic situation:

And then to have the humour of state; and after a demure travel of regard, telling them I know my place as I would they should do theirs, to ask for my kinsman Toby ... Seven of my people, with an obedient start, make out for him. (49-51, 54-5)

Thus far Malvolio's little drama exists only in the theatre of his mind, but as he continues to embellish it with vivid and emblematic details, it moves outward from this private and imaginary stage to the solid public one on which he stands. Appropriate gestures come next, and these are no sooner conceived than actually executed:

I frown the while, and perchance wind up my watch, or play with my – some rich jewel. Toby approaches; curtsies there to me ... I extend my hand to him *thus*, quenching my familiar smile with an austere regard of control – (55-8, 61-3; my italics)

Now only the absence of dialogue prevents the playlet from being complete, and Malvolio at once supplies the missing ingredient, progressing, as he does so, from consciously creating appropriate speeches to merely delivering them:

> MALVOLIO Saying 'Cousin Toby, my fortunes having cast me on your niece give me this prerogative of speech' –
> SIR TOBY What, what?
> MALVOLIO 'You must amend your drunkenness' –
> SIR TOBY Out, scab!
> FABIAN Nay, patience, or we break the sinews of our plot.
> MALVOLIO 'Besides, you waste the treasure of your time with a foolish knight' –
> SIR ANDREW That's me, I warrant you.
> MALVOLIO 'One Sir Andrew.' (65-74)

With his last three lines, which the comments of his onstage audience isolate, Malvolio has dropped all spoken stage directions – such as 'I extend my hand to him thus' and 'Saying' – and with them all sense of any difference between himself and the starring role in his playlet. He has, as a result, fully theatricalized his role-playing. It is but a brief step from this playlet to the next (the dialogue between Malvolio and the planted letter), in which he freely enacts for the first time the more customary and less overt role for which the part of Count Malvolio provides a metaphor: his ludicrous misconception of himself.

But Malvolio's role-playing has not yet become sufficiently public. There still remains the playlet brought about by Maria's stratagem (III.iv), in which it acquires full-dress performance, complete with emblematic costume (yellow stockings and crossed garters), memorized dialogue (bits and pieces of the forged letter), and the best possible audience (Olivia). Here, in its outer form, Malvolio's role-playing has come to resemble that of Viola, but this playlet, especially since it has a second, unscheduled scene, also heavily underscores the crucial differences. Viola's role-playing is entirely successful, but Malvolio can fool no one into accepting his projected image of himself; even Olivia, the only one who witnesses his performance without foreknowledge, sees the episode for exactly what it is: an exhibition of Malvolio acting oddly. Viola's role-playing reflects her acute sensitivity to external reality, but Malvolio's, as the very existence of the second scene in his playlet proves, reflects his total obliviousness. For this addition occurs only because Malvolio has misinterpreted Olivia's clear response to his performance and her even clearer command, 'let this fellow be look'd to' (III.iv.57): he thinks he has pleased her and that she has sent for Sir Toby 'that I may appear stubborn to him' (63), and so he acts out before Sir Toby his share in the scene with him which he had earlier devised and rehearsed in the garden walk. Viola's role-playing is a sign of her shrewdness, but Malvolio's, chiefly because of the additional scene, is made to become a sign of madness. Sir Toby had looked forward with delight to this playlet because Maria's stratagem had put Malvolio 'in such a dream that when the image of it leaves him he must run mad' (II.v.173-4). To Olivia, however, the dream itself, or rather, the performance it provokes from Malvolio, is madness – in fact, 'very midsummer madness' (III.iv.53) – and during the additional scene of the playlet, the responses of Sir Toby, Maria, and Fabian assign Malvolio the appropriate role of madman. Finally, Viola's role-playing is the result of a calculated decision and is undertaken so that she can retain some control over her destiny; but Malvolio's stems from self-delusion, and the playlet in which he most publicly exhibits it is not only caused by others but is also the means by which he completely subjects himself to their power. Thus it is that he has one more engagement to fulfil, the dialogue between 'Sir Topas the curate' and 'Malvolio the lunatic' (IV.ii.21-2). Malvolio's role-playing may not constitute 'madness' in any medical or legal sense, but the long process of its externalization has made the term poetically apt. The dark prison cell is therefore a most fitting setting for the final playlet in which he appears.

Unlike Malvolio, Duke Orsino performs no formal playlets, and he can scarcely be accused of misvaluing himself, but he too has lost himself in a discrepant role, that of the despondent lover. It is not discrepant because of any inherent incongruity with his social role (after all, a duke has as much right to love, and be rejected, as a beggar) nor even because he plays it with the wrong woman in mind – though this, which betrays his blindness to external reality, is nearer the mark. What primarily creates the sense of discrepancy is that his projection of himself is so conventional, he so obviously enjoys playing it, and his performance of it constantly exposes him to ridicule. Such characteristics as the effort he goes through to provide an appropriate setting – either by surrounding himself with musicians or by deliberately seeking out 'sweet beds of flow'rs' (I.i.40) – make his projection of himself seem far too artificial and far too silly to constitute an expression of valid feelings. It is no wonder that he can talk about someone else acting his woes (I.iv.25), since the impression is that he is himself doing precisely the same thing. After such a display, in fact, all Shakespeare needs to do in order to confirm the sense of discrepancy is to suggest that behind this self-projection there exists another and different Orsino, the actor who has temporarily and misguidedly assumed the discrepant role. Thus it is that Shakespeare has the Captain remember Orsino as a 'noble duke, in nature as in name' (I.ii.25) and Olivia speak of him with such high praise:

> I suppose him virtuous, know him noble,
> Of great estate, of fresh and stainless youth;

> In voices well divulg'd, free, learn'd, and valiant,
> And in dimension and the shape of nature
> A gracious person. (I.v.242-6)

Not only do these passages describe a figure bearing little or no relation to the Orsino the audience has already observed; by focusing on those attributes that stress his eligibility, they also underscore a further important aspect of his role-playing: that it actually prevents him from playing the kind of lover a 'fresh and stainless youth' ought to play.

Like Malvolio, Orsino attempts to cast Olivia for a part in his private drama – that of the aloof and scornful object of his love – and although she seems to fulfil it, she does so only because she is acting out a private drama of her own. As I have already shown in the introduction, Olivia originally performs the role of cloistered mourner, and the discrepancy between this role and her basic identity as a beautiful and eligible young woman is stressed both by Feste the clown and by Viola. It is perfectly in keeping, therefore, that Olivia should fail to perceive the true identity not only of Viola, whose disguise she never penetrates, but also of Feste:

> CLOWN The lady bade take away the fool; therefore, I say again, take her away.
> OLIVIA Sir, I bade them take away you.
> CLOWN Misprision in the highest degree! (I.v.47-50)

Viola's arrival compels Olivia to discard this original role, but she continues to play the fool, for in its place she adopts the entirely fictitious part of Cesario's lover. Once again, moreover, the discrepancy is made explicit:

> OLIVIA I prithee tell me what thou think'st of me.
> VIOLA That you do think you are not what you are. (III.i.135-6)

Neither Orsino nor Olivia, however, approximate the pattern enacted by Malvolio as thoroughly as does Sir Andrew Aguecheek. Egged on by Sir Toby, this 'foolish knight' (I.iii.15) carries self-misconception and lack of awareness about what goes on around him to such an extreme that he forms a worthy low comic parody of Malvolio, an effect that is heightened by Sir Andrew's also pursuing – hesitantly, hopelessly, and from a distance – the Lady Olivia. Sir Andrew's role-playing, too, is explicitly seen in theatrical terms, in III.iv, just after Fabian sums up the nature of Malvolio's two-scene playlet by saying, 'If this were play'd upon a stage now, I could condemn it as an improbable fiction' (III.iv.121-2). When Sir Andrew enters with the challenge he has penned to Viola, Fabian's 'More matter for a May morning' (136) continues the theatrical imagery, this time applying it to the farce Sir Andrew is about to play on the duelling ground 'at the corner of the orchard' (167-8), the farce for which Sir Toby gives Sir Andrew the appropriate 'direction':

> So soon as ever thou seest him, draw; and as thou draw'st, swear horrible; for it comes to pass oft that a terrible oath, with a swaggering accent sharply twang'd off, gives manhood more approbation than ever proof itself would have earn'd him. (168-73)

The remaining inhabitants of Illyria, Maria, Fabian, Sir Toby, and Feste, also play discrepant roles, but they differ from Malvolio, Orsino, Olivia, and Sir Andrew in two important respects: they all share to some extent Viola's capacity to manipulate others and to expose or get them to expose the discrepancy inherent in their role-playing; and they are for various reasons largely exempt from the implicit charge of moral blindness. Maria and Fabian, for example, scarcely behave in a manner commensurate with their identities – certainly Maria's vicious treatment of Malvolio belies one sense of her title of 'gentlewoman' (I.v.154) – but Shakespeare does not emphasize this aspect of their behaviour. They function primarily not as characters of interest in themselves but as important instruments in the exposing of Malvolio, Sir Andrew, and even Sir Toby.

Sir Toby's refusal to observe the prescribed pattern of behaviour appropriate for the uncle of Olivia unquestionably involves him – as Malvolio insists (II.iii.83-90) – in a discrepancy between true identity and assumed role. And the resemblances between his experience and that of Malvolio are too numerous and too crucial to ignore. Sir Toby's drunkenness, the chief attribute of his role-playing, is, according to Olivia and Feste, a form of madness (I.v.100, 122-30). Like Malvolio, Sir Toby is made to play a role he neither expects nor desires, for Malvolio's daydreaming about him in the garden walk (in II.v) forces from him angry responses that inescapably put him into the playlet he had thought only to watch. Like Malvolio, he is symbolically punished by one he has sought to abuse, for his attempt to involve Viola in the farce with Sir Andrew gains him 'a bloody coxcomb' from Sebastian (v.i.170). And it is Sir Toby, rather than Malvolio, who receives from Olivia the sentence of banishment he and his confederates have designed for their enemy:

> Will it be ever thus? Ungracious wretch,
> Fit for the mountains and the barbarous caves,
> Where manners ne'er were preach'd! Out of my sight! (IV.i.46-8)

Sir Toby is also no more able than the others to penetrate Viola's disguise – he too thinks she's a 'gentleman' (I.v.111) – but this resemblance to Malvolio and the others is at the same time an indication of Sir Toby's uniqueness. For the others this failure signifies moral blindness, but for Sir Toby it is a sign of his complete indifference to identity, as he makes clear when he deflects Olivia's attention away from his drunkenness and back to the unexpected visitor:

> SIR TOBY There's one at the gate.
> OLIVIA Ay, marry; what is he?
> SIR TOBY Let him be the devil an he will, I care not; give me faith, say I. Well, it's all one. (118-21)

His indifference to Viola's identity suggests that what prompts his role-playing is not delusion but an equal indifference to his own identity. Whatever ultimate difficulties he may let himself in for, he seems on the whole to know perfectly well what he is doing – Shakespeare is careful to distinguish his 'fooling' from Sir Andrew's, for example (II.iii.77-80) – and thus the impression he conveys is that he has adopted the manner of a Falstaffian Lord of Misrule only because he finds it more congenial than the pattern of behaviour prescribed by his true identity. This is one reason why the bitter objections of Malvolio and Olivia do not greatly influence the spectators' attitude towards Sir Toby; the other is that the delusions of Malvolio, Olivia, and Orsino have created a world in which a performance like Sir Toby's is sorely needed in order to restore the proper balance.

Sir Toby thus enacts an important variation of the basic pattern in which all of Illyria's inhabitants participate; a different and equally important variation is enacted by Feste the clown. Although Feste's performance as Sir Topas in IV.ii is the clearest demonstration of his capacity for role-playing, he, like the others, has been playing a discrepant role from the beginning of the play. Part of his proof, in I.v, that Olivia is a fool consists of his arguing that *he* is not; thus he accuses Olivia of 'misprision': ' "Cucullus non facit monachum"'; that's as much to say as I wear not motley in my brain' (51-2). Evidently he is by no means merely 'fooling,' for when Olivia entered he had to prepare himself consciously for the ensuing scene:

> Wit, an't be thy will, put me into good fooling! Those wits that think they have thee do very oft prove fools; and I that am sure I lack thee may pass for a wise man. For what says Quinapalus? 'Better a witty fool than a foolish wit.' God bless thee, lady! (29-34)

This passage begins as an aside and then subtly blends into overt speech, so that even in its form it suggests a profound discrepancy between Feste's true identity and the role defined by his suit of motley.

The most significant fact about the discrepancy is that it is Feste him-self, and not any of the others, or Shakespeare through implication, who points out its existence. This self-awareness is fully in keeping with the sure sense of external reality that Feste also demonstrates. No one in Illyria sees through his fellow characters any better than he. Like Sir Toby and Maria, he has the full measure of Sir Andrew and Malvolio, but he can also define with complete ac-curacy the role-playing of Sir Toby, Olivia, and even Orsino, whose folly at one point he couples with that of Olivia:

> VIOLA I saw thee late at the Count Orsino's.
> CLOWN Foolery, sir, does walk about the orb like the sun – it shines everywhere. I would be sorry, sir, but the fool should be as oft with your master as with my mistress. (III.i.35-8)

Furthermore, he shares with Viola a realization of the virtual impossibility of fully knowing external reality because of the slipperiness and corruptibility of the words that embody it. He knows that, in Illyria, at least, where all abuse language through their role-playing, 'A sentence is but a chev'ril glove to a good wit. How quickly the wrong side may be turn'd outward!' (10-12); and he refuses to give the 'reason' for one of his witticisms because 'I can yield you none without words, and words are grown so false I am loath to prove reason with them' (21-3). Most of all, however, Feste even seems to succeed in doing what no one else in the play can do: penetrate the disguise of Viola. When she gives him a coin he thanks her by saying, 'Now Jove, in his next commodity of hair, send thee a beard!' (42-3). This remark may, of course, be only a comment on the youthful and feminine appearance of Cesario, but it suggests far greater perception, especially since, a few lines later, Feste point-edly adds, 'My lady is within, sir. I will construe to them whence you come; who you are and what you would are out of my welkin' (53-5). As Viola right-ly observes, 'This fellow is wise enough to play the fool' (57).

Feste, in other words, is in many respects Viola's symbolic twin. Like hers, his role-playing is a fully conscious and deliberate act, one that testifies to his acuteness of perception. And like hers, his role-playing is undertaken to guarantee his well-being. Through her portrayal of Cesario, Viola gains time and, she hopes, some control over her destiny; through his portrayal of 'the Lady Olivia's fool' (III.i.29), Feste gets his livelihood. He is, in effect, as much an outsider – an alien in Illyria – as Viola herself.

The contrasts of the play – between the conscious role-playing of Viola and Feste and the unconscious play-acting of the others; between Sir Toby and his fellow play-actors in terms of encouraged response – enrich the drama-tic design without obscuring its central pattern. Discrepant role-playing is the chief characteristic of the world depicted in *Twelfth Night*, and through most of those who participate in this activity it acquires a particular significance. Sir Andrew and Sir Toby, as I have shown, are carefully paralleled to Malvolio in various ways, and so also are Orsino and Olivia, both of whom match him in the desire for isolation he expresses in 'Go off; I discard you. Let me enjoy my private; go off' (III.iv.84-5). Since all four of them also indulge in the unconscious role-playing of which Malvolio's career furnishes the chief example, it follows that they likewise share his chief characteristic of madness, and the point is explicitly established not only for Sir Toby but also for Olivia: 'I am as mad as he, / If sad and merry madness equal be' (14-15). Viola and Feste are certainly not mad, but ultimately their sanity is of little avail, for although the madness that dominates the world of the play in no way originates from them, they are equally engulfed by it.

Thus far my analysis of the play has scarcely touched on any detail later than the first three acts, but this is entirely in keeping with its structure, which consists of two distinct parts. The first three acts, which are rather static, define the world of *Twelfth Night*, thus providing an appropriate context for the primary action, which occurs in the two final acts. The source of this action is Sebastian, who has already appeared in II.i and III.iii but does not fully enter the world of the play until IV.i. Once he arrives, however, his presence has a twofold significance. At first he provides, both by his comments and by the events that befall him, a neutral perspective that allows the world of the play to be seen with absolute clarity. Ultimately, in v.i, he becomes the means through which that world can finally achieve at least a partial purification.

The shocking (for him) triple reception that Sebastian experiences at Olivia's gate in IV.i focuses upon a quality of this world which has always been present but never with such force and clarity as it now acquires. Viola, struck by her discovery of Olivia's love for her, had seen as early as II.ii that 'Disguise' is 'a wickedness / Wherein the pregnant enemy does much' (25-6), and her later experience, despite Sir Andrew's cowardice and the opportune arrival of Antonio, has certainly demonstrated the potential danger inherent in role-playing when it reaches proportions of the sort it attains in *Twelfth Night*. Similarly, Antonio has insisted on accompanying Sebastian because he is 'skilless in these parts' – i.e., Illyria – and 'to a stranger' they 'often prove / Rough and unhospitable' (III.iii.9-11). In thus warning Sebastian about the danger he may face in Illyria, Antonio does not, of course, have the chief characteristic of the region in mind – or is 'parts' a pun? – but his own later taste of this danger (his arrest and imprisonment) has clearly resulted from role-playing, both the discrepant role-playing of Viola, Sir Andrew, and Sir Toby and his own attempt to fulfil the role of friend. In such a world, it is only natural that Sebastian's second reception at Olivia's gate should include a blow from Sir Andrew, seizure by Sir Toby, and a threatened 'action of battery' (IV.i.33).

But physical violence, especially here where it takes the form of rather harmless knock-about farce, is actually the lesser of the two dangers involved in the widespread role-playing. The other, more sinister one is the likelihood of being forced to play roles that others have imposed. This happens, as I have shown, to both Malvolio and Sir Toby. It also happens to Olivia, when she falls in love with the non-existent Cesario; to Viola, when she has to act as go-between for the man she loves and when Sir Toby decides to schedule a duel; and to Sir Andrew constantly. This danger, however, receives its clearest emphasis with the arrival of Sebastian. Each of those who meet him at the gate, Feste, Sir Toby and Sir Andrew, and Olivia, take him for Cesario and act accordingly, thereby determining how he must behave. With each reception, moreover, the consequences for him of this false attribution intensify, until at the end of the scene the beautiful, rich, and titled Olivia is virtually declaring her love for him. Eventually, this false attribution of identity leads to a real alteration in his identity as he accepts the new role of husband to Olivia. And it leads, as well, to one more occasion on which a character is compelled to play an alien role, for in V.i Antonio, Orsino, Olivia, the Priest, Sir Andrew, and Sir Toby all charge Viola with doing the things Sebastian has done – or is thought to have done.

Through his comments rather than his experience Sebastian helps stress the other 'wickedness' in the widespread role-playing of Illyria, its equivalence to madness. 'Are all the people mad?' he asks when struck by Sir Andrew (IV.i.26), and even though he is delighted by Olivia's reception, he regards it as further proof of madness, this time his own:

What relish is in this? How runs the stream?
Or I am mad, or else this is a dream.
Let fancy still my sense in Lethe steep;
If it be thus to dream, still let me sleep! (59-62)

Later on, after he has presumably had opportunity to reflect upon his situation, he delivers a long soliloquy (IV.iii.1-21) in which he tries to explain to his own satisfaction the exact nature of the situation in which he has become involved. He fails, of course, but in so doing, especially in his abrupt shifts of direction and his repetition of the contradicting 'yet,' he manages fully to articulate the ultimate result of Illyria's madness. Reality has become so thoroughly dislocated that, as Sebastian unwittingly reveals, it no longer possesses definable contours.

But even though Sebastian cannot fathom the dislocated world in which he now finds himself, his presence is nevertheless the means by which it finally acquires partial reordering. His entrance at v.i.200, which places him and Viola together onstage for the first time in the play, and his subsequent questions to her – 'Of charity, what kin are you to me? / What countryman, what name, what parentage?' (222-3) – initiate a sequence in which for four of the characters false and discrepant roles are discarded and true identities declared. Sebastian begins it by announcing his true identity for the first time in Illyria and thereby rejecting the false role the Illyrians have imposed on him (228-30). Viola then admits that Cesario – 'my masculine usurp'd attire' (242) – has been merely a disguise and promises, when restored to her proper costume, to prove 'that I am Viola' (245). Next, Sebastian points out that Olivia, now free of both her discrepant roles, at last can consciously play the role that the social order and the conventions of comedy have destined her for:

> So comes it, lady, you have been mistook;
> But nature to her bias drew in that.
> You would have been contracted to a maid;
> Nor are you therein, by my life, deceiv'd;
> You are betroth'd both to a maid and man. (251-5)

Finally, Duke Orsino, who opened *Twelfth Night* with his display of himself as the conventional melancholy lover, concludes the sequence by playing, for Viola's sake, a far different version of the lover's role:

> Your master quits you; and, for your service done him,
> So much against the mettle of your sex,
> So far beneath your soft and tender breeding,
> And since you call'd me master for so long,
> Here is my hand; you shall from this time be
> Your master's mistress. (308-13)

There is much deliberate ceremony in this speech, and the conceit of the 'master's mistress' suggests that Orsino may yet find good use for the stock of stereotyped images he has memorized. But the basic tone of simple eloquence is new to him, and he eludes any charge of verbal extravagance because everything he says is firmly anchored to an actual lady, the one he is addressing. If he still retains some traces of his former language, it is nevertheless clear that he now controls what once controlled him.

But the purification effected by Sebastian's entrance is by no means complete. The sequence I have just traced is followed, in fact, by another declaration of identity, and this one indicates not the discarding but the retention of a discrepant role. This declaration concerns Malvolio, who is spoken of as being 'distract' or a 'madman' by Olivia (272), Feste (278), and Orsino (314). Malvolio denies the allegation, and when Fabian confesses what he, Sir Toby, and Maria have done, the denial would seem to be confirmed. But it is Feste who has the last word on the subject, and he insinuates that Malvolio got no more than he deserved:

> I was one, sir, in this interlude – one Sir Topas, sir; but that's all one.
> 'By the Lord, fool, I am not mad!' But do you remember – 'Madam,
> why laugh you at such a barren rascal? An you smile not, he's gagg'd'?
> And thus the whirligig of time brings in his revenges. (357-63)

The significant word here is the 'But' introducing 'do you remember,' which Feste uses to prove that, no matter what the others have done, Malvolio has always been and continues to be a madman. Poetically, then, Malvolio remains a madman, and he does so because, as the tone of his accusation against Olivia (317-31) and his final speech show, he still entertains his misconception of himself. Furthermore, this emphasis on Malvolio's failure to abandon his discrepant role-playing should also serve as a reminder that at least two other inhabitants of Illyria – Sir Toby and Sir Andrew – likewise remain unchanged.

These three are not the first Shakespearian characters who fail to participate in the harmony marking the close of a comedy: a full list would include Shylock, Don John, Jaques, and even Egeus in *A Midsummer Night's Dream*. But the failure of these characters to participate in no way negates the impression of harmony because their dissent is advantageous in that it helps define (through contrast) exactly what the harmony consists of, and, more important, because their dissent has no force within the social order experiencing the harmony: Egeus and Shylock have already ceased to exist; Don John will be contained; Jaques agreeably decides to go elsewhere. Malvolio, Sir Andrew, and Sir Toby help to define the nature of the final harmony in *Twelfth Night* through their failure to know themselves and assume their proper identities, but they continue to be full-fledged members of the Illyrian society, and thus their failure to change seriously dilutes the impression of harmony. Some purification of the world of the play has been achieved, but not enough; although the once universal madness has retreated, it has by no means surrendered, and even the threat of physical violence persists, for Malvolio will 'be reveng'd on the whole pack of you' (364). Therefore the wry song sung by Feste, the only Illyrian always to retain a sure sense of reality, appropriately brings *Twelfth Night* to its close. As Shakespearian comedy reaches its full complexity, it also begins to take on some of the sombre colouring ordinarily associated only with the so-called dark comedies.

If Angelo, who dominates the first two acts of *Measure for Measure*, is typical of its world, and if the appraisals of him by Isabella and Duke Vincentio are to be believed, then the world of *Measure for Measure* suffers from the same flaw as that of the immediately preceding comedy, *All's Well That Ends Well*.

For Isabella and the duke see Angelo as a new version of Parolles; that is, as one whose behaviour provides an unequivocal example of hypocrisy, of deliberate feigning, of a discrepancy between the appearance he professes and the reality he lives; as Isabella puts it, 'This outward-sainted deputy ... is yet a devil' (III.i.90-3). Their appraisals do, of course, accurately assess Angelo's conduct after he has capitulated to Isabella's charms and also, perhaps, his past treatment of Mariana; but his fall, as Shakespeare dramatizes it, actually stresses a quite different implication.

The duke first expresses his suspicion of Angelo almost as an afterthought, as an additional 'reason' for his plan to hang around Vienna disguised as a friar (I.iii.53-4). Before this, significantly, in explaining why he has 'impos'd' his 'office' on Angelo, he has described him as 'A man of stricture and firm abstinence' (12), and, just before introducing the note of suspicion, he has added:

> Lord Angelo is precise;
> Stands at a guard with envy; scarce confesses
> That his blood flows, or that his appetite
> Is more to bread than stone. (50-3)

Lucio corroborates this evaluation – and without the innuendo of 'stands at a guard' and 'confesses' – when he speaks of Angelo as

> a man whose blood
> Is very snow-broth, one who never feels
> The wanton stings and motions of the sense,
> But doth rebate and blunt his natural edge
> With profits of the mind, study and fast. (I.iv.57-61)

And Angelo himself, in his first soliloquy, refers to his 'modesty' (II.ii.169), calls himself a 'saint' (180), and affirms that he now feels passion for the first time: 'Ever till now, / When men were fond, I smil'd and wond'red how' (186-7). Shakespeare does not focus on Angelo's 'firm abstinence' in his direct presentation of him, but he does emphasize Angelo's 'stricture,' his adamant refusal to compromise the laws, not only in his first interview with Isabella but also, before that, with Escalus (II.i.1-31) and with the Provost (II.ii.7-14).

The portrait of Angelo which emerges from these opening scenes, then, is not that of a conscious hypocrite but that of a man endeavouring to uphold a very rigorous ideal, both in his own conduct, with its abstinence, fasting, and study, and in his treatment of those whose actions place them under his control. This ideal, it is everywhere implied, is too rigorous, too severe, insufficiently responsive to the facts of human experience, and Shakespeare makes it perfectly clear that Angelo has been able to uphold it only by carefully evading these facts, by shutting himself off from experience in a kind of mental cloister. Isabella's visit forces him for the first time to confront the reality of his own flesh – or rather, as the play has it, his 'blood.' Previously he has acknowledged only 'form,' and now that his 'blood' asserts itself, he is unable to relate this new motivating force to the old. Thus, rather than attempting to work out some accommodation between 'form' and 'blood,' he abruptly shifts his allegiance from the one to the other:

> O place, O form,
> How often dost thou with thy case, thy habit,
> Wrench awe from fools, and tie the wiser souls
> To thy false seeming! Blood, thou art blood.
> Let's write 'good angel' on the devil's horn;
> 'Tis not the devil's crest. (II.iv.12-17)

And he soon vows to 'give my sensual race the rein' (160). Once fallen, as the passage about the 'devil's horn' indicates, Angelo shows his readiness, appropriately enough, to play the hypocrite, yet the fall itself has dramatized not hypocrisy but an unbridgeable gap between the ideal and the actual, between form and substance.

Numerous passages throughout the play express similar gaps and thereby suggest the central importance of the theme dramatized by Angelo's fall. The 'sanctimonious pirate that went to sea with the Ten Commandments,' Lucio points out, scraped 'Thou shalt not steal' from the table (I.ii.7-10). The proclamation directing that 'All houses' – i.e., bawdy-houses – 'in the suburbs of Vienna must be pluck'd down' does not apply to those in the city because 'a wise burgher put in for them' (89-95). 'The jury, passing on the prisoner's life, / May in the sworn twelve have a thief or two / Guiltier than him they try' (II.i.19-21). 'Some rise by sin, and some by virtue fall' (38). When Angelo would pray and think, he thinks and prays 'To several subjects':

> Heaven hath my empty words,
> Whilst my invention, hearing not my tongue,
> Anchors on Isabel. Heaven in my mouth,
> As if I did but only chew his name,
> And in my heart the strong and swelling evil
> Of my conception. (II.iv.1-7)

Men's natures and reputations may not coincide – as in Angelo's case after the fall (153-9). Vienna has 'strict statutes and most biting laws' (I.iii.19), but, according to the duke, since they have remained unenforced for fourteen years, 'quite athwart / Goes all decorum' (30-1), and, according to Lucio and Pompey, since these laws go against nature, they are in any event completely unenforceable.

The central importance of this theme is best seen, however, not through such passages as these, ubiquitous though they are, but through the aspect of Angelo's experience that links him to nearly every other character in the play. Another way of describing the Angelo that emerges from these opening scenes is to say that he has been playing a role for which he is not suited, that of the 'precise' man. And Shakespeare, as usual, has provided an overt instance of role-playing to call attention to this, its less overt equivalent. Angelo, in serving as the duke's deputy, 'bears' the 'figure' of the duke (i.i.17). The duke has 'Lent him our terror' and 'dress'd him with our love' (20). He has 'impos'd' on Angelo his own 'office' (i.iii.40). Thus, in being, as the duke puts it, 'at full ourself' (i.i.44), Angelo is playing a clearly defined role, that of the duke's 'office'; he indeed represents 'man ... *dress'd* in a little brief authority' (ii.ii.118; my italics). And this role, moreover, like that of the 'precise' man, is a discrepant one. Angelo believes he can perform it to perfection, but he cannot. His first confrontation with Isabella compels him to realize how thoroughly he has been miscast – 'O, let her brother live! / Thieves for their robbery have authority / When judges steal themselves' (ii.ii.175-7) – and from then on the discrepancy betrays itself in his every gesture and move.

It is this aspect of Angelo's experience which reverberates most extensively throughout *Measure for Measure*, because it is this which associates him with so many of the other characters, who act out the same discrepancy between themselves and the offices they profess. Elbow, Shakespeare's third rendering of the malapropian constable, supplies a farcical version of it. Far from being the 'wise officer' Escalus ironically calls him (ii.i.56), he is utterly incapable of performing the only constabulary function this play recognizes, that of reporting a crime, and his abuse of words, which amounts to violating their accepted offices, extends in an additional way the theme he enacts by his mere presence. In this same scene, Escalus manages a mild joke, reminiscent of the Show of the Nine Worthies from *Love's Labour's Lost*, about the discrepancy between Pompey, Elbow's prisoner, and the Worthy whose name he shares (206-7), but Pompey does not truly begin to participate in the basic theme of the play until iv.ii, when this bawd by normal occupation and humanitarian by instinct takes on the office of hangman despite Abhorson's complaint that 'He will discredit our mystery' (iv.ii.25). Nor is Pompey the only prison official who seems out of place in his appointed position. In ii.ii, the Provost protests so much about executing Claudio that Angelo must flatly tell him, 'Do you your office, or give up your place' (13). And in iv.ii, he shows so much pity for Claudio that the duke remarks, 'This is a gentle provost; seldom when / The steeled gaoler is the friend of men' (82-3).

Rather tired thematic
content without
asking anno...
9?

The chief manifestation of this widespread discrepancy, however – the one that gives all the others visual representation – is the constant presence of Duke Vincentio in his borrowed friar's habit. In this sense, therefore, the duke's function is much like that of Viola in her disguise as Cesario, and the similarity between the uses to which Shakespeare puts these two characters underscores the similarity between the two plays in which they appear: like *Twelfth Night*, *Measure for Measure* dramatizes a full-scale treatment of the discrepancy between the actor and his part by juxtaposing a number of variations upon this theme. But the parallel between the two plays is by no means complete, for where *Twelfth Night* focuses on the general idea of discrepant role-playing, *Measure for Measure*, in contrast, focuses on a specific version of this activity, and with quite different implications. The discrepant roles in *Twelfth Night*, which are distortions and falsifications of their players' true identities, have no basis in reality, and the play is concerned with how such roles prevent their players from fulfilling their true identities and how, until they are abandoned, they foster communal chaos. In *Measure for Measure*, however, the discrepant roles are fixed social 'offices': the forms that society has fashioned for the purpose of establishing and sustaining the tenuous order by means of which it struggles to ward off the chaos that constantly threatens. Here, then, the inappropriate member of the actor-part pairing is not the part but the actor. The dramatic focus is not the essentially comic one of what the actor does to himself by assuming a role that cannot set him off to best advantage but the far more sombre one (for the dramatist, at least) of what the miscast actor does to the role he wrongly assumes. The special kind of discrepant role-playing exemplified here makes *Measure for Measure* a play concerned with the ever-present undermining of the social order because of an unbridgeable gap between the ideal (the office) and the actual (its inappropriate holder).

This reading of the play is upheld with special force by the one major character I have not yet discussed. Isabella, as Lucio stresses when he inquires for her at her cloister, holds not one office but two: she is both

A novice of this place, and the fair sister
To her unhappy brother Claudio. (I.iv.19-20)

It is understandable that, as a novice striving to become a nun, Isabella should want to uphold law and justice, especially when the crime in question involves a sin of the flesh. And it is equally understandable that, as a sister, she would want to do everything in her power to help save her brother's life. Isabella's position, therefore, is one that could quite readily suspend her from the horns of a dilemma, and it is exactly this sense of herself which she conveys when she faces Angelo for the first time:

> There is a vice that most I do abhor,
> And most desire should meet the blow of justice;
> For which I would not plead, but that I must;
> For which I must not plead, but that I am
> At war 'twixt will and will not. (II.ii.29-33)

The surprising thing about Isabella is that she does not feel her dilemma as keenly as one expects her to. A single speech from Angelo (37-41) is sufficient to convince her that the issue is settled: 'O just but severe law! / I had a brother, then. Heaven keep your honour!' (41-2); and although she does eventually produce a vigorous and eloquent plea on her brother's behalf, she does so only because Lucio eggs her on. Furthermore, as soon as Angelo counters her plea by assuring her that her only hope of saving Claudio entails surrendering 'the treasures of your body' (II.iv.96), her response is immediate and unequivocal:

> Better it were a brother died at once
> Than that a sister, by redeeming him,
> Should die for ever. (106-8)

Isabella's unwillingness to go against the dictates of one of her offices thus forces her to violate those of the other: 'More than our brother is our chastity' (185). As Shakespeare makes clear in III.i, the scene in which Isabella visits Claudio in prison, her decision compels her to misplay the office of sister as surely as Angelo misplays that of the judge. Line after line of this scene – the Provost's 'Look, signior, here's your sister' (50), Claudio's 'Now, sister, what's the comfort?' (55), Isabella's 'Yes, brother, you may live' (65) – insists that Isabella is to be seen here in relation to her role as Claudio's sister and evaluated according to the manner in which she performs it. And she shows at once that it is not any kind of sisterly feeling she holds for her brother but suspicion that he lacks the moral courage she has demonstrated in making her own decision; she is reluctant to tell him Angelo's terms because

> I do fear thee, Claudio; and I quake,
> Lest thou a feverous life shouldst entertain,
> And six or seven winters more respect
> Than a perpetual honour. (75-8)

She also reveals that for her their relationship now has significance only for the obligations it imposes on Claudio. Thus when Claudio, still ignorant of Angelo's terms, expresses his readiness to die, she is quite willing to acknowledge their relationship: 'There spake my brother; there my father's grave / Did utter forth a voice' (87-8). But when Claudio learns what it is that Angelo has demanded and, reflecting upon it, finds it a less 'fearful thing' than death, she flatly rejects him. His plea for life emphasizes her sisterhood –

> Sweet sister, let me live.
> What sin you do to save a brother's life,
> Nature dispenses with the deed so far
> That it becomes a virtue – (134-7)

and he thereby helps to stress the full implication of her response:

> O you beast!
> O faithless coward! O dishonest wretch!
> Wilt thou be made a man out of my vice?
> Is't not a kind of incest to take life
> From thine own sister's shame? What should I think?
> Heaven shield my mother play'd my father fair!
> For such a warped slip of wilderness
> Ne'er issu'd from his blood. (137-44)

Isabella denies her brother not only by refusing to help him but also by the new titles with which she addresses him and by the insinuation about his paternity. Here and in the rest of this speech – with its 'Take my defiance; / Die; perish' (144-5) – she seems, in effect, to be trying to rid herself of a role that she finds only troublesome and that she has long since stopped making any effort to fulfil.

To say, however, that her unwillingness to violate one of her roles compels her to violate the other is not also to say that she keeps her preferred role inviolate. For Isabella, as the single title for her two roles might well imply, plays the office of religious 'sister' no more successfully than that of the familial. Her apparent easy compliance, at the end of the play, with the duke's proposal of marriage suggests in retrospect that she never took her role of votaress very seriously, but long before this ending, during the crucial scenes with Angelo and Claudio, the discrepancy between herself and this role is already fully evident. Her plea to Angelo may be prompted by her role as Claudio's sister (and by Lucio's urging), but since she is so obviously reluctant to violate her role of votaress, the arguments she advances while making her plea can be taken as an accurate reflection of what she understands this, her preferred role, to involve. Isabella herself thus offers some account of what it means to perform a religious office, and in so doing she provides a standard that she fails to live up to.

During her first interview with Angelo she emphasizes the importance of mercy:

> Well, believe this:
> No ceremony that to great ones longs,
> Not the king's crown nor the deputed sword,
> The marshal's truncheon nor the judge's robe,
> Become them with one half so good a grace
> As mercy does. (ii.ii.58-63)

> O, it is excellent
> To have a giant's strength! But it is tyrannous
> To use it like a giant. (107-9)

There is no evidence that Isabella regards herself as (potentially) one of the 'great ones,' that she equates the office of nun with the offices of king, marshal, and judge, that, in other words, she is also insisting her own office directs her to exercise mercy. But it is nevertheless clear that as votaress as well as sister she places great value on mercy, and thus her words, like some of those of Angelo, precondemn their speaker. For mercy is exactly what she does not exercise with Claudio; in the prison scene it is she that has, and uses, the giant's strength.

In her second interview with Angelo, she shifts her ground, but the result is the same. Here she affirms a belief that she and Angelo work out together. 'Which had you rather,' he asks,

> that the most just law
> Now took your brother's life; or, to redeem him,
> Give up your body to such sweet uncleanness
> As she that he hath stain'd?

And she replies: 'Sir, believe this: / I had rather give my body than my soul' (ii.iv.52-6). But Angelo, who 'talk[s] not of [her] soul' (57), has a different distinction in mind:

> Might there not be a charity in sin
> To save this brother's life?

And in responding Isabella falls into his trap more thoroughly than he thinks she has:

> ISABELLA Please you to do't,
> I'll take it as a peril to my soul
> It is no sin at all, but charity.
> ANGELO Pleas'd you to do't at peril of your soul,
> Were equal poise of sin and charity.

> ISABELLA That I do beg his life, if it be sin,
> Heaven let me bear it! You granting of my suit,
> If that be sin, I'll make it my morn prayer
> To have it added to the faults of mine,
> And nothing of your answer. (63-73)

To use these lines for evidence that Isabella fails to live up to the dictates of her office does not necessitate that one also assume the extremely difficult position that Isabella should have accepted Angelo's demand, however much Claudio's eloquent defence of this position in the prison scene renders it attractive. It is, instead, quite enough to say that her outraged response, once she understands exactly what Angelo proposes, includes no recognition whatever of her prior affirmation that there can 'be a charity in sin' or of the willingness she has expressed to take certain sins upon herself 'as a peril to my soul.' In insisting flatly that sin is sin and therefore to be shunned, she is violating her office as she has herself defined it.

Shakespeare incorporates into the first interview two passages that toy with the idea of the possible interchangeability of Isabella and Angelo. 'I would to heaven,' says Isabella, 'I had your potency, / And you were Isabel!' (II.ii.67-8). 'It is the law,' says Angelo, 'not I condemn your brother. / Were he my kinsman, brother, or my son, / It should be thus with him' (80-2). These passages encourage the spectators to consider Isabella's behaviour in the light of Angelo's, to look for a similarity between them, and in Isabella's outraged response of II.iv, the similarity emerges. Angelo's proposition is for Isabella what she has been for Angelo: the first real confrontation with experience. Like Angelo, she has devoted herself to an ideal that she can conform to only as long as it remains an ideal free from the test imposed by the concrete facts of experience. Just as Angelo can cling to his conception of himself as 'the precise' man only until Isabella's visit brings him his first real temptation, Isabella can cling to her notions of sin becoming charity and of self-sacrifice only until a specific sin is concretely proposed. The two cases are even parallel in their outcomes, for like Angelo, Isabella, instead of attempting to bridge the gap that suddenly opens between the ideal and the actual, abruptly leaps from one to the other. For her, notions about sin give way entirely to the immediate fact of sin.

It is also possible to see in Isabella's contribution to the play even a third example of the office-occupant discrepancy. As part of his effort to get her to accept his proposition, Angelo lures Isabella into talking of herself not as a votaress or a sister but as a woman. He then presses his advantage:

> Be that you are,
> That is, a woman; if you be more, you're none;

If you be one, as you are well express'd
By all external warrants, show it now
By putting on the destin'd livery. (II.iv.134-8)

The image of his final line defines her womanhood as one more role – indeed, the word 'livery' makes it a further office – and the whole speech insinuates that in rejecting his proposition she is violating not only the two offices that most concern her but also a third and even more fundamental office. Angelo scarcely qualifies at this point as a dramatist's spokesman, nor, surely, does the office of woman dictate losing virginity under the circumstances he has in mind. But his general point cannot be disputed, for she is a woman who has decided not to wear the costume appropriate to her, and it must be significant that at the end of the play it is her womanhood to which she evidently pays her ultimate allegiance.

However a spectator may respond to the focus on Isabella's womanhood, it is clear that in any event her contribution to the play amplifies its basic theme. Her twofold, if not threefold, demonstration of the discrepancy between office and occupant, between the ideal and the actual, helps put beyond question the proposition that *Measure for Measure* dramatizes a world whose inhabitants simply cannot live up to the forms they are expected to fulfil. This is, however, not all that the play dramatizes, for *Measure for Measure* utilizes the same two-part structure as *Twelfth Night*, and therefore it does not initiate its central action until it has finished establishing the conditions of its world. The first half of the play – to III.i.153 – focuses on Claudio, Angelo, and Isabella in order to establish the widespread gap between the ideal and the actual. Only then does the duke abandon his stance as observer and occasional commentator and take over the management of the play. 'To the love I have in doing good a remedy presents itself' (194-5), he says, and thereby initiates a sequence that runs continuously from this point until the end and sets the world of the play to rights. His soliloquy at the end of act III explains what has happened. 'He who the sword of heaven will bear / Should be as holy as severe,' the duke says in this soliloquy; but his period of observing has taught him 'what ... man' may 'within him hide, / Though angel on the outward side,' and so, he now realizes, 'Craft against vice I must apply' (III.ii.243-4, 253-4, 259). The duke has seen what the audience has seen, that this world lies on the verge of chaos and lacks the means to heal itself. If it is to survive, it needs external aid, and so he decides to intervene.

The incongruity between form and content in this curious, jingly soliloquy serves as an invitation to give the resulting action careful scrutiny, and although its general course is clear enough, its implications deserve analysis. For the man who controls this action is by far the most interesting character in the play. There is, from the beginning, an element of mystery or caprice in his behaviour. His departure is sudden 'and leaves unquestion'd / Matters of needful value' (I.i.55-6). Escalus, he states, knows all the 'properties' of the ideal governor (3-7), and Escalus is 'first in question' (47), yet it is Angelo to whom he surrenders his authority. He is leaving, it turns out (I.iii), so that someone other than himself can perform the task of putting teeth back into Vienna's laws, but he is also sticking around in disguise because the man he has chosen over Escalus is a man that bears watching. There are also, he adds, 'Moe reasons for this action' (I.iii.48), but these he does not care to go into at this time. The duke's 'givings-out,' Lucio observes, are 'of an infinite distance / From this true-meant design' (I.iv.54-5), and the speech would seem to cover far more than his having 'strew'd it in the common ear' that he travels to Poland (I.iii.14-16).

All this tends to be rather odd behaviour for a duke, and for this reason it is perfectly in keeping with the rest of Shakespeare's presentation of Vincentio in these early scenes. Part of this presentation has to do with a close similarity between him and Angelo. It is the duke's 'figure' that Angelo will 'bear,' his 'absence' he will 'supply,' his 'terror' and 'love' he will be 'lent' and 'dress'd' in (I.i.17-20). The duke need not praise Angelo any further than he does because, as he knows, 'I do bend my speech / To one that can my part in him advertise' (41-2) – one, that is, who is well suited to play Vincentio because he readily exhibits in his own behaviour a remarkably similar life-style. And, like Angelo, the duke denies the potency of his 'blood':

No, holy father; throw away that thought;
Believe not that the dribbling dart of love
Can pierce a complete bosom. (I.iii.1-3)

As in the case of Isabella, the duke's similarity to Angelo is a sign of his also being like Angelo in embodying the basic theme of the play. The duke has 'ever lov'd the life removed,' he reminds Friar Thomas (I.iii.7-8), and in the first scene he has already suggested as much while explaining why he takes his departure secretly:

I love the people,
But do not like to stage me to their eyes;
Though it do well, I do not relish well
Their loud applause and Aves vehement. (I.i.68-71)

The theatrical imagery reinforces the duke's distaste by expressing his feeling of an incongruity between himself and this kind of display; it is not something that he can perform naturally or spontaneously but something that involves him in play-acting. Nevertheless, this imagery also defines it as a valid part of his office as duke: he dislikes, in other words, the important public function of his office, a function whose value he is well aware of. Nor is this the only function of his office for which he feels distaste. As Friar Thomas, abandoning his usual deference, points out, his scheme to have Angelo revive the laws that he has let slip constitutes a clear evasion of his ducal responsibilities:

> It rested in your Grace
> To unloose this tied-up justice when you pleas'd;
> And it in you more dreadful would have seem'd
> Than in Lord Angelo. (i.iii.31-4)

The duke's reply is scarcely a defence:

> I do fear, too dreadful.
> Sith 'twas my fault to give the people scope,
> 'Twould be my tyranny to strike and gall them
> For what I bid them do. (34-7)

Even if, as he here implies, he truly fears that his office might be corrupted and its efficacy thus reduced, his refusal to act still constitutes a mishandling of his responsibilities, for this is a risk he must take. But he soon reveals that it is not his office at all for which he fears, but himself; he refuses to act in order to protect his image:

> I have on Angelo impos'd the office;
> Who may, in th' ambush of my name, strike home,
> And yet my nature never in the fight
> To do in slander. (40-3)

It is, then, the duke, and not Angelo, who first exemplifies the discrepancy between office and occupant; and, significantly, it is at this very point that he introduces his intention of going about in the habit and manner of a friar. His disguise thus makes visual not only the condition of the other characters but his own as well.

When Vincentio takes command of the action, Shakespeare does nothing to mitigate this initial questionable impression; on the contrary, he intensifies it. Vincentio need not, for example, insist so vehemently on the validity of the discrepant role he now plays; he need not, that is, continually threaten to perform certain important functions of the friar's office. It is one thing for him to gain entry to the prison by claiming that he wants to 'minister' to the prisoners (ii.iii.7-8), but it is quite another to vindicate the killing of Barnardine – a step in his plan – by promising to 'give him a present shrift, and advise him for a better place' (IV.ii.194-5). The unpleasant feeling this evokes has nothing to do with the possible effect of the promised action, for Barnardine, who has consistently refused to listen to religious counsel, seems to be a 'man that apprehends death no more dreadfully but as a drunken sleep; careless, reckless, and fearless, of what's past, present, or to come' (135-7), and even if he should not prove to be incorrigible, Vincentio's action could only work to his benefit. What does disturb, therefore, is Vincentio's arrogant assumption that he is somehow entitled to take upon himself the solemn rites reserved for those who wear his costume legitimately. As Lucio, echoing Feste, will later remark, 'Cucullus non facit monachum' (V.i.261).

Furthermore, the scene in which Vincentio first takes command of the action is immediately followed by the curious sequence with Lucio. No spectator can believe Lucio's half-jocular malicious slanders of the duke because Shakespeare expends considerable effort here to discredit their source: he that in the beginning of the play was so kind and helpful now refuses to go bail for Pompey, betrays Mistress Overdone, and turns out to have formerly deserted the pregnant Kate Keepdown. The weight of this sequence thus falls not on Lucio's charges but on Vincentio's excessive response to them. Rather than taking them in his stride as the worthless slanders he knows them to be, he insists on refuting them, insists even on setting the record straight by substituting for them his own more positive account:

> LUCIO ... the greater file of the subject held the Duke to be wise.
> DUKE Wise? Why, no question but he was.
> LUCIO A very superficial, ignorant, unweighing fellow.
> DUKE Either this is envy in you, folly, or mistaking; the very stream of his life, and the business he hath helmed, must, upon a warranted need, give him a better proclamation. Let him be but testimonied in his own bringings-forth, and he shall appear to the envious a scholar, a statesman, and a soldier. (III.ii.128-36)

If any reply to Lucio is necessary, this one, surely, does the job; but Vincentio is far from through. There is also his soliloquy following Lucio's exit:

> No might nor greatness in mortality
> Can censure scape; back-wounding calumny
> The whitest virtue strikes. What king so strong
> Can tie the gall up in the slanderous tongue? (173-6);

his wholly gratuitous and (considering what will happen to Lucio) threatening examination of Escalus:

DUKE I pray you, sir, of what disposition was the Duke?
ESCALUS One that, above all other strifes, contended especially to know himself.
DUKE What pleasure was he given to?
ESCALUS Rather rejoicing to see another merry than merry at anything which profess'd to make him rejoice; a gentleman of all temperance; (217-23)

and even the quite unexpected soliloquy he recites while waiting for Isabella to settle with Mariana:

O place and greatness! Millions of false eyes
Are stuck upon thee. Volumes of report
Run with these false, and most contrarious quest
Upon thy doings. Thousand escapes of wit
Make thee the father of their idle dream,
And rack thee in their fancies. (IV.i.58-63)

There can be only one explanation for such excess: Vincentio, despite the errand of mercy in which he is now engaged, still cares about his own image above all else.

His next run-in with Lucio occasions a rather obvious contrast which suggests that at any rate he is totally indifferent to the feelings of those he is trying to help. Just as the fortuitous death of Ragozine has solved Vincentio's problem of finding a head to substitute for Claudio's, Isabella returns, but instead of telling her that her brother will be saved, he pointedly decides to do just the opposite:

She's come to know
If yet her brother's pardon be come hither;
But I will keep her ignorant of her good,
To make her heavenly comforts of despair
When it is least expected. (IV.iii.103-7)

And in response to her grief about Claudio and her rage against Angelo, he offers her only the cold comfort of a likely revenge. Then Lucio enters and at once speaks in a strikingly different vein:

O pretty Isabella, I am pale at mine heart to see thine eyes so red. Thou must be patient. I am fain to dine and sup with water and bran; I dare not for my head fill my belly; one fruitful meal would set me to't. But they say the Duke will be here to-morrow. By my troth, Isabel, I lov'd

> thy brother. If the old fantastical Duke of dark corners had been at
> home, he had lived. (148-54)

This speech does something to help redeem the now debased impression of
Lucio, but its primary function lies in the way its humaneness – and, since it
is so inept, its *humanness* – sets off and underscores the cold and indifferent
voice of 'the old fantastical Duke of dark corners.'

    The contrast is an extremely important one, not only for what it direct-
ly implies about Vincentio but also because it and such related effects as his
peculiar use of 'heavenly' in the soliloquy I have just quoted prepare the spectators to fully appreciate his most outrageous achievement, his management
of the fifth act. Unlike any other fifth act in Shakespeare, this one forces from
its spectators a series of puzzling questions. The prolonged concealing of the
crucial fact that Claudio still lives can, perhaps, be partially explained. It is part
of Vincentio's plan to keep Isabella 'ignorant of her good' so that she will experience 'heavenly comforts of despair' – whatever that exactly means – 'When
it is least expected'; it puts Angelo in a position where he can most acutely
feel remorse; and it creates a situation in which Isabella, by pleading for the
life of the man she considers responsible for her brother's death, can show
that she has genuinely learned how to be merciful. Yet it is curious that Isabella never does experience the 'heavenly comforts of despair' – or if she does,
she remains strangely silent about her experience, for no word ever escapes
her lips after Vincentio finally undeceives her. And it is equally curious that
she couches her plea for Angelo's life in a clever legalism which suggests she
may not really have learned about mercy after all:

>   I partly think
> A due sincerity govern'd his deeds
> Till he did look on me; since it is so,
> Let him not die. My brother had but justice,
> In that he did the thing for which he died;
> For Angelo,
> His act did not o'ertake his bad intent,
> And must be buried but as an intent
> That perish'd by the way. Thoughts are no subjects;
> Intents but merely thoughts. (v.i.443-52)

    But even if these explanations were fully satisfactory they would still
leave unanswered the more important questions raised by the fifth act. Why
has Vincentio chosen this particular method of bringing things to a head? Why
has he elected to carry it out at the city gate with Vienna's citizens looking
on? Why does he delay so long before revealing that he knows all? Why does

he once again assume the disguise of the friar, and, having done so, why does
he proceed to attack the duke and the state? Why does he torture Isabella and
Mariana by leading them to believe that their statements, statements he has
told them to make, will get them into serious difficulty? Why, before finally
pardoning Angelo, does he first insist that he must die? Why does he toy with
Lucio, if, ultimately, all he intends for him is a fate he evidently merits?

Once again, there can be only one explanation, and this is suggested by
Vincentio's reference to what he plans for the fifth act as 'our plot' (IV.v.2),
by Isabella's calling Mariana's anticipated contribution her 'part' (IV.vi.3), and,
above all, by Vincentio's first fifth-act exchange with Lucio:

> DUKE You were not bid to speak.
> LUCIO   No, my good lord;
> Nor wish'd to hold my peace.
> DUKE   I wish you now, then;
> Pray you take note of it; and when you have
> A business for yourself, pray heaven you then
> Be perfect.
> LUCIO I warrant your honour.
> DUKE The warrant's for yourself; take heed to't.
> ISABELLA This gentleman told somewhat of my tale.
> LUCIO Right.
> DUKE It may be right; but you are i' the wrong
> To speak before your time. (v.i.78-87)

The voice Vincentio adopts here is that of the director controlling an over-
eager actor, and it points to what he is doing throughout this scene. The man
who once expressed his dislike of 'staging' himself to his people's eyes is now
doing nothing else but – and in a carefully devised playlet that he has written,
produced, and directed, and in which, like some film star more interested in
his own virtuosity than ideal representation of the script, he plays two of the
featured roles. Vincentio's choice of this most public of all possible resolutions
and the suspenseful way in which he executes it are obviously designed to add
lustre to his public image. But what primarily motivates him is the sheer delight he can derive from successfully bringing off his multiple theatrical
achievement.

The climax of Vincentio's playlet is of course the moment when the
friar's cowl is torn off and his full achievement both in his own play and in
Shakespeare's becomes suddenly known. Ironically, however, no incident
could more perfectly dramatize the discrepancy between role and actor, and
therefore this climax also underscores the point Shakespeare is making in having Vincentio resolve things in the manner he has chosen. The widespread dis-

crepancy between office and occupant has created a situation for which, given its cause, there is no internal remedy. Vincentio has rightly seen that external intervention is mandatory, but he has not seen that, even while setting things to rights, he will simultaneously act out the most startling example of the existing discrepancy. Shakespeare has him reassume his disguise as friar because once again it is metaphorically apt. This time the office-occupant discrepancy it visually embodies is that which distinguishes Vincentio the man from the office he now plays with such flagrant theatricality and with so little of the appropriate compassion: the office of the intervener, the outsider who steps in to help those who cannot help themselves.

Vincentio's intervention has resolved the specific difficulties within the play, but his manner of accomplishing this shows that the condition causing them remains unchanged. The discrepancy between office and occupant continues to exist, and so also, therefore, does the more abstract discrepancy that this one symbolizes: the gap between the ideal and the actual. One of Vincentio's specific accomplishments, in fact, suggests as much. This is the set of marriages in which he has had either an entire hand or at least a main finger. To be rightly understood these marriages must be seen in relation to the significance that the marriages concluding a comedy normally have, the significance, for example, of those that conclude *As You Like It* and *Twelfth Night*. The marriages of these plays, and in this they are typical, express the attainment or restoration of a valid harmony; they symbolize the coming together of two beings who discover in each other both their complement and their completion; they testify to the existence of the local order on which the social order as a whole depends. In relation to this ideal conception of marriage, none of the specific marriages focused on in the final lines of *Measure for Measure* comes off very well. That of Claudio and Juliet could and should, but it is spoken of only as a grim necessity, as a kind of expiation for guilt (v.i.523). That of Angelo and Mariana is a forced marriage, which unites Angelo with a woman he once rejected and about whom he has just said extremely unkind things (214-20) – nor, despite his remorse about the rest of his behaviour, does he ever suggest that his attitude towards her has changed. That of Vincentio and Isabella consists only of his twice-offered proposal and her utter silence in response; but should it take, it will link a man whose chief interest is his public image with a woman who not long before had a far different marriage in mind and who has claimed to value her chastity even above her brother's life. That of Lucio, the last of the set, could inspire no better comment than he has already given it: 'Marrying a punk, my lord, is pressing to death, whipping, and hanging' (520-1).

5 The comic pattern

Come, Lady, die to live. (*Much Ado About Nothing*, IV.i.253)

Shakespearian comedy is nothing if not various. The earliest comedies, up to and including *The Merchant of Venice*, seem consciously experimental in their tendency simultaneously to backtrack and break away, to repeat each other with or without variation even as they abruptly try on new shapes. If role-playing constitutes the primary material of Shakespeare's comedies, as I believe it does, the impression these earliest comedies create is that Shakespeare is constantly searching for the specific aspect of role-playing which might serve him as comic subject, or, perhaps, that he is systematically attempting to exhaust every possibility implicit in his basic theme. The later comedies, from *Much Ado About Nothing* to *Measure for Measure*, show signs of settling down, for in terms of form at least they tend to comprise a coherent group. But they also display a great range in mood – from *Much Ado* and *As You Like It* at the one extreme to *All's Well That Ends Well* and *Measure for Measure* at the other – and they include as one of their number *The Merry Wives of Windsor*, a play that in its lack of subtlety and complex design harks back to the days of *The Taming of the Shrew*.

One cannot, therefore, speak of a Shakespearian comic pattern, if by 'pattern' something like a formula is meant. Unlike many successful writers of comedy, Shakespeare never evolved – and evidently did not wish to – an elaborate vehicle that could constantly be readied for reuse with a little minor retooling. In keeping with this flexibility, I use 'pattern' – in the following chapters as well as this one – not to refer to a specific formal and thematic design that recurs in play after play, but in a much looser sense, as a means of designating the particular ways of using role-playing which a body of plays happen to have in common and which help give them their shape without imposing any rigid restrictions or requirements. With respect to comedy, my term 'pattern' is intended to designate a small number of formal characteristics and, far more important, a formal-thematic sequence that is virtually ubiquitous in the comedies and can well be said to constitute *the* Shakespearian comic theme.

Two of the formal characteristics have been examined, both explicitly and implicitly, in the two preceding chapters. Beginning with the fairly primitive and schematic structural anatomy of *The Taming of the Shrew*, Shakespeare's tendency to juxtapose characters and events in terms of role-playing soon develops in complexity and subtlety in the comedies, while at the same time undergoing a shift in emphasis from contrasts to parallels. From *The Merchant of Venice* to *Measure for Measure*, with one or two exceptions, each of Shakespeare's comedies is in large part valuable for the rich, highly distinctive, and coherent world it presents, and in every case this world is defined by the particular involvement with role-playing that its otherwise dissimilar inhabitants share. Also originating with *The Taming of the Shrew* but not becoming truly distinctive until *A Midsummer Night's Dream* is the use of the materials of role-playing to fashion broad spatial contrasts like those that distinguish Athens from fairyland and the Forest of Arden from Duke Frederick's court. Among the more impressive of the mature comedies only *Measure for Measure* lacks a contrast of this sort, and the absence is of considerable dramatic significance, for it underscores the degree to which the world of the play is all of one piece and its dark vision both unredeemed and irredeemable.

Role-playing also contributes to the diachronic design of most of these plays. *Love's Labour's Lost, A Midsummer Night's Dream*, and *The Merchant of Venice* all move towards a play-within-the-play or internal playlet which provides an emblematic version of the central dramatic issues. *Much Ado About Nothing* and subsequent comedies derive even firmer structuring through means of a pattern of action that Shakespeare revives from *The Taming of the Shrew:* the sequence in which a playwright-director-actor puts on a clearly defined playlet in order to alter the identity of one who is not privy to the plot. *Much Ado, Twelfth Night, All's Well That Ends Well*, and *Measure for Measure* all utilize this pattern of action as one significant element of their designs, while in *The Merry Wives of Windsor* it forms the core of the play. The Falstaff of this play – or rather, judging from his imperfect resemblance to the Falstaff of *Henry IV*, the impostor that has usurped his identity – persists in fancying himself a great lover, and beginning with III.iii, Shakespeare devotes the bulk of the action to the planning and execution of three playlets by Mistress Ford and Mistress Page, who devise the playlets in order to punish Falstaff for his arrogant assumptions about the ease with which he can seduce them; as Mistress Ford puts it, they want to teach 'this unwholesome humidity, this gross wat'ry pumpion ... to know turtles from jays' (III.iii.33-5). Falstaff is so stubborn or so dense that it takes three playlets to get him to give up his discrepant notion of himself, and therefore the full pattern in which a character is transformed through the amateur theatrics of others occurs only once and is extended throughout the action. It is, nevertheless, the same pattern as that which repeats itself with such frequency in the Messina of Beatrice and Benedick and less often, though still prominently, in Illyria, the France of *All's Well*, and Duke Vincentio's Vienna.

Not that the device always has the same implications; these shift from play to play, and like so many other characteristics of the comedies from *Much Ado About Nothing* to *Measure for Measure*, in shifting they help trace the increasingly darkening mood. The contrast in this respect between *Much Ado* and *All's Well That Ends Well* is especially instructive. The playlets of *Much Ado* which are not simply the product of villainy (as are those of Don John) or temporary delusion (as is Claudio's performance in the church) stem from a notion that with a little help the victim of the playlet will improve and that, as a result, both he and the others will be much better off. There is, of course, no question that the 'dialogue between the Fool and the Soldier' in *All's Well That Ends Well* (IV.iii.92-3) improves Parolles, for, having been exposed by its means, he resolves to give up his pretensions and become 'simply the thing' he is (310). In doing so, however, he is not actually responding to the intentions of the Lords who have planned this playlet. Their motive is not to change Parolles but to force Bertram to open his eyes to 'this counterfeit module' (94). They assume that Bertram can improve and are striving to bring this improvement about, but as far as their victim is concerned, the playlet has the same function as those that Maria directs against Malvolio – in other words, the function of providing 'sport royal' and food for 'mockery' and 'jesting' (*Twelfth Night*, II.iii.161, II.v.16, 18). Towards their victim, the Lords are acting ignobly. Their intention is not to cure, but to shame and destroy, and, simultaneously, to enjoy the sport of his exposure.

The behaviour of these Lords – which is not dissimilar to that of the less vicious but equally unfeeling Vincentio of *Measure for Measure* – suggests the kind of world in which the final and most important characteristic of the comic pattern would seem to be incapable of realizing itself. This characteristic is a formal-thematic sequence which combines role-playing with the religious idea of losing oneself to find oneself, and which, as I have claimed, can be said to constitute *the* Shakespearian comic theme. Almost all the comedies, despite their differences, dramatize this sequence in one way or another, though with varying degrees of emphasis in the overall design, and with varying degrees of explicit reference.

In *The Comedy of Errors*, as Antipholus of Syracuse is about to enter both the centre of Ephesus and the farcical portion of the play, he announces, 'I will go lose myself, / And wander up and down to view the city' (I.ii.30-1). And he soon does 'lose' himself, as he suffers all the errors that ensue. But his words point to much more than the mere temporary loss of identity brought about by the mistakes of others. They also point to the end of the play, where he truly loses his original self through the modification of his identity caused by winning Luciana and being reunited with his father, mother, and brother. And they point as well to related passages that offer some justification for his ultimate good fortune. The only reason why Antipholus is in Ephesus at all is that he has willingly risked his own contentment, if not his life, in an effort to find his relatives:

> I to the world am like a drop of water
> That in the ocean seeks another drop,
> Who, falling there to find his fellow forth,
> Unseen, inquisitive, confounds himself.
> So I, to find a mother and a brother,
> In quest of them, unhappy, lose myself. (I.ii.35-40)

This passage gains added weight because it echoes some expressions from the first important focal point of the play, Aegeon's tale of how his wife and son were lost to him, how he 'hazarded the loss' of the remaining son, 'whom I lov'd,' in an attempt to find the lost one (I.i.131-2), and how he himself now faces loss of life because he 'came to Ephesus; / Hopeless to find, yet loath to leave unsought / Or that or any place that harbours men' (135-7). The love Antipholus and his father feel for others has compelled them to risk losing themselves in the fullest possible sense, and therefore, it could be said, the final happy reunion, in which they fully find themselves as well as finding those they sought, is not something that merely happens but something they have *earned*.

The theme of losing oneself to find oneself is operative only during the romantic frame in *The Comedy of Errors*, but in the later comedies, most of which are touched by romance throughout, the theme becomes more truly central to the entire action as well as more thoroughly dramatized as a function of the characters' role-playing. This is to some extent even the case with the unromantic *Taming of the Shrew*. Lucentio's attempt to win Bianca from her other suitors by posing as Cambio, her schoolmaster, exemplifies a version of the theme of losing oneself to find oneself that is familiar in all comedy, the version in which a stock character – a villain, say, or, as here, an *amoroso* – temporarily loses himself (plays a nonce-role) in order to find himself (fulfil his dramatic role by gaining the ends that it prescribes). Much the same thing can be said of Petruchio's performance as shrew, even though the self he deliberately sets about finding is his own revised conception of a stock role. Despite the differences between Petruchio and Lucentio, however, both exemplifications of the theme in *The Taming of the Shrew* seem fairly crude and mechanical. Neither of them possesses any nuance of the sort already evident in the less fully dramatized version of the theme in *The Comedy of Errors*, where the references to it evoke implications of deep human feeling and an abiding faith in the worth of familial and social bonds.

I suspect that Shakespeare's work with *The Taming of the Shrew* contributed to his own developing sense of the theme and thus had a considerable effect on the later comedies, but I doubt that a spectator actually experiences the actions of Lucentio and Petruchio in such a way that he is aware of their losing themselves to find themselves. *The Two Gentlemen of Verona* and *Love's Labour's Lost* therefore represent significant advances, for in them the theme is not only central to the action but also carefully articulated in the characters' speeches.

In *The Two Gentlemen of Verona* Julia assumes the fictitious role of Sebastian in order to follow Proteus, and in the process she demonstrates her fidelity to her basic roles of maid and lover. She provides, in other words, an exemplification of the comic theme which resembles Lucentio's in form while restoring a focus on implications of the sort *The Taming of the Shrew* had ignored. But even though Julia's performance is a central element of *The Two Gentlemen of Verona*, it is nonetheless Proteus with whom Shakespeare here most strongly associates the theme. Proteus' discrepant role-playing is motivated by notions pertinent to the theme, and his progress establishes the thematic pattern as a whole by enacting its opposite.

Proteus' interview with his father in I.iii, which occasions his first conscious role-playing, serves as a preview of the central action. In order to conceal his love for Julia from his father, Proteus pretends that the letter his father has caught him with is from Valentine in Milan, who among other things urges Proteus to join him. Antonio has already decided to send his son to Milan so that he, like Valentine, might acquire the graces of a courtier, and he asks Proteus how he feels about Valentine's supposed request. Proteus' reply perfectly befits the dutiful son his father takes him to be: 'As one relying on your lordship's will, / And not depending on his [i.e., Valentine's] friendly wish' (I.iii.61-2). The fact is, of course, that Proteus here consciously play-acts a role he ought to perform instinctively, and he thereby violates it. He sacrifices his role of son in order, he hopes, to preserve his other role of lover. But he soon realizes, to his great dismay, that his scheme has backfired. His perfidy has cost him what he had hoped to gain, for his father, accepting his claims at face value, orders him to leave for Milan at once. And this means full separation from Julia.

Proteus clearly realizes his error on this occasion, but the experience teaches him nothing, and almost as soon as he reaches Milan he treats his other roles no better than he had treated his role of son. His motive, moreover, is the same. He wants to preserve his role of lover as he now comprehends it, with Silvia now the object of his love, and so he must sacrifice both his role as Valentine's friend and his other role as lover to Julia:

> Julia I lose, and Valentine I lose;
> If I keep them, I needs must lose myself;
> If I lose them, thus find I by their loss:
> For Valentine, myself; for Julia, Silvia. (II.vi.19-22)

This soliloquy demonstrates that Proteus entirely misunderstands the significance of one's roles, for he fails to perceive that his identity is inseparable
from those he already possesses. And although he knows the language of the
comic theme, he is utterly confused about its workings. He regards losing and
finding as alternative states rather than as stages in a process requiring them
both. Unlike Julia and Valentine – as well as the other successful characters of
Shakespearian comedy – Proteus is therefore unwilling to have anything to do
with loss. He seeks to find himself directly and immediately, and thereby he
risks losing himself altogether. He regards his decision as a discovery of his true
identity, but what stands out most forcefully in this soliloquy is the realization
expressed in its first three lines, the importance of which Shakespeare emphasizes through the repetition:

> To leave my Julia, shall I be forsworn;
> To love fair Silvia, shall I be forsworn;
> To wrong my friend, I shall be much forsworn. (II.vi.1-3)

Proteus' loss of himself acquires dramatic representation through his behaviour from this point until the final scene of the play. He no longer behaves
instinctively but instead acts out the strategy through which he hopes to bring
about Valentine's banishment, 'blunt Thurio's dull proceeding' (41), and thus
have Silvia all to himself. He is, to use Julia's words, playing false, both in the
sense of mismanaging his original roles – particularly in the way he play-acts
the role of Valentine's friend – and also in the further sense that 'play false'
often has in Shakespeare of 'cheat' and, by extension, 'do evil.' Julia's words
thus not only describe what Proteus has done, they also define the ultimate result of his actions. By violating his original roles, Proteus has cast himself in an
entirely new one. Initially a gentleman according to the title, he has transformed himself into – as Silvia expresses it – a 'subtle, perjur'd, false, disloyal
man' (IV.ii.91), or – as Launce puts it more succinctly – 'a knave' (III.i.262).
And he would remain a knave except for the help of Valentine and Julia. Their
unfailing fidelity to their roles and their glad willingness to lose themselves
eventually create the conditions through which Proteus can at last once more
find himself. Or, given Proteus' imperfect role-playing from the beginning, it
might perhaps be more accurate to say that they create the conditions through
which he can fully find himself for the first time.

The spokesman for the comic theme in *Love's Labour's Lost* seems to
understand its workings better than Proteus does, but his application of it also
involves much confusion. This spokesman is Berowne, who introduces the
terms of the theme in IV.iii as part of his attempt to justify his and his companions' change from book-men to lovers. The others, not wholly satisfied
with Berowne's claim that they had to forsake their vows because these were

in conflict with the natural impulses of their true selves as young men, beseech him to provide 'some salve for perjury' (iv.iii.285). He answers with a long, knotty discourse in which he argues that true learning comes only through love. Women's eyes, he declares, 'are the books, the arts, the academes' (348), and therefore the violation of the vows he and the others have spoken is not only excusable but necessary – the one means through which they can actually attain the end they originally sought. As men they must love because being attracted by women is natural to them. As individuals wanting to become wise men they must love because love is the only source of wisdom. Thus, he concludes, the change from hermit-scholars to lovers can be regarded only as the discovery of their true selves:

> For wisdom's sake, a word that all men love;
> Or for Love's sake, a word that loves all men;
> Or for men's sake, the authors of these women;
> Or women's sake, by whom we men are men –
> Let us once lose our oaths to find ourselves,
> Or else we lose ourselves to keep our oaths. (353-8)

Berowne is, of course, mistaken. Although they indeed give up a false role, and although this act might well be construed as the losing of a particular self (a self that is defined by the need to try out the false role of book-man), the King and his Lords by no means find themselves. Instead of giving up a false role for reality, they shift from one discrepant role to another, from the hermit-scholar to the stage-lover. And in the process they acquire a further role, one they would much rather avoid. As part of his attempt to justify the abandoning of their vows, Berowne had declared, 'Then fools you were these women to forswear; / Or, keeping what is sworn, you will prove fools' (351-2). Earlier in the same scene, however, he had used the term 'fool' eight times – nine, counting 'scenes of fool'ry' – to refer to himself and his comrades in their new condition of lovers, and this same term is used over and over in v.ii, mostly by the ladies, to denote what the King and his Lords make of themselves through the performance of their masque; as Rosaline says, 'fools were here, / Disguis'd like Muscovites' (302-3). Contrary to Berowne's argument, it is the decision to play the lover in earnest that causes them to 'prove fools.' Instead of finding themselves, they lose themselves more thoroughly by becoming the very thing they tried to avoid becoming. The change from their first discrepant role to their second thus finds its ideal label in the Princess' phrase, 'wit turn'd fool' (70).

Berowne, who had seen their initial folly, also finally perceives the folly of their subsequent behaviour. He admits that he and his comrades have in a sense duplicated the inept performance of the clowns, donning in the process a kind of fool's motley, the 'parti-coated presence of loose love' (754). He has already realized, moreover, that he richly deserves the mockery Rosaline directs his way because he sees that in trying to be lovers he and his companions have managed only to play a highly artificial version of the lover's role. And he has already abjured his previous performance, vowing that in the future his 'wooing mind shall be express'd / In russet yeas, and honest kersey noes' (412-13). In discarding the 'ostentation' (409) characterizing his previous performance, Berowne also discards the role of fool for which this ostentation had suited him. But this act only restores him (and by implication his comrades) to the self he possessed before making his initial vows. The process enacting the comic theme has not really occurred. For Berowne and the King, however, this process will occur in the future, during the year-long penance in which they must perform the roles assigned them by their ladies. This time they will not, as before, simply be losing themselves; by demonstrating a capacity to perform effectively *some* role before once again trying to play the lover, they will also be helping to ensure that finding themselves can some day genuinely occur.

In the comedies of Shakespeare's early maturity – from *A Midsummer Night's Dream* to *Twelfth Night* – the comic theme becomes even more surely central, as it constantly finds positive, full, and direct dramatization. The loss of self in *A Midsummer Night's Dream* is experienced by the four lovers during the hectic night in fairyland that deprives them of any firm sense of identity, but this loss, which for a while seems so devastating to them, soon proves to be only a necessary prelude to their finding themselves in the new circumstances created when the rigidity of Athens has been momentarily slackened. In *The Merchant of Venice*, the comic theme manifests itself in the motif of giving and hazarding all one has and in the numerous cases in which Shylock's adversaries assume new roles in order to win fulfilment for themselves and others. Beatrice and Benedick of *Much Ado About Nothing*, having been compelled by Don Pedro's amateur theatrics to lose abruptly the selves they had presented to the world and each other, gradually find full realization in their new roles as mutual lovers. But it is the Friar that engineers *Much Ado*'s primary dramatization of the comic theme, for his stratagem enables Hero and Claudio both to 'die to live' (IV.i.253), she by losing herself in pretended death and the false identity of her cousin, he by successfully fulfilling the role of penitent and thus acquiring at least some measure of the histrionic sensibility he had lacked.

The central metaphor embodying the representation of the comic theme in *As You Like It* is Rosalind's temporary portrayal of Ganymede, but all the characters originating in the court world pursue virtually the same course of action, in which they lose themselves by suffering exile and thereby, whether instantaneously or gradually, win the opportunity to act out or develop the selves they could not, while at court, freely perform. In *Twelfth Night*, as in

As You Like It, the assumption of proper roles and true identities near the end of the play also constitutes the final stage of the comic theme. Both Viola and Sebastian have enacted it in full, and although Orsino and Olivia have not (they start out as lost souls and find themselves only through the pressure of events) their experiences nevertheless reinforce the theme, giving it a more universal scope. Far less universal than usual, however: Malvolio, Sir Toby, and Sir Andrew are too deeply immersed in their private worlds ever to emerge – so deeply that for them losing *is* finding – and Feste, for whatever reason, cannot come out from behind his mask to dramatize the identity he conceals not only from the others but even (almost) from himself.

In *All's Well That Ends Well*, Shakespeare seems even more preoccupied with his theme than usual. Its key terms can already be heard in the opening lines, which focus on Bertram's imminent departure for court and on the health of the King. The Countess associates her son's departure with the loss of her husband, and Bertram 'weep[s] o'er [his] father's death anew,' but Lafeu assures them, 'You shall find of the King a husband, madam; you, sir, a father.' This emphasis on losing and finding recurs in Lafeu's answer to the Countess' inquiry about the health of the King: 'He hath abandon'd his physicians, madam; under whose practices he hath persecuted time with hope, and finds no other advantage in the process but only the losing of hope by time' (i.i.12-15). Somewhat later in the scene, these same terms figure prominently – and rather surprisingly – in Parolles' advice to Helena about virginity: 'Loss of virginity is rational increase; and there was never virgin got till virginity was first lost. That you were made of is metal to make virgins. Virginity by being once lost may be ten times found; by being ever kept, it is ever lost' (120-4).

The repetition of these familiar terms suggests that *All's Well*, like most of Shakespeare's comedies, will dramatize a version of the comic theme, and in the process through which Helena finally acquires all the roles necessary formally to embody her native worth, the theme is fully realized. By leaving France so that Bertram can allow himself to return, Helena also abandons the roles she has gained through her service to the King; like Shylock's adversaries in *The Merchant of Venice*, she voluntarily loses herself – the stage metaphor for this is her adoption of 'the dress of a pilgrim' (s.d., iii.v.26) – so that another may find himself. But it is she that does the finding: first Diana, and then – after once more losing herself by temporarily playing the part of Diana – the identity she has sought since the beginning of the play. The involvement in this process of the loss of her virginity gives the words of the unwitting Parolles a retrospectively prophetic ring.

What especially distinguishes this dramatization of the comic theme from those in the earlier comedies is that in *All's Well That Ends Well* Shakespeare attempts for the first time to name explicitly the source from which the pattern of losing to find derives its energy. The previous comedies imply that successful self-realization springs from love and selflessness; they convey the impression that the character's own actions trigger the comic pattern. In the first scene of *All's Well*, Helena espouses this notion when she asserts:

> Our remedies oft in ourselves do lie,
> Which we ascribe to heaven. The fated sky
> Gives us free scope; only doth backward pull
> Our slow designs when we ourselves are dull. (I.i.202-5)

And she decides, in keeping with her assertion, to try her hand at curing the King, even though 'my project may deceive me' (214). She also realizes, however, that at least one 'remedy' – her father's medicine – has 'something in't / More than my father's skill' (I.iii.233-4): her art surpasses that of other physicians, she assures the King in II.i, because it flows from God, who 'of greatest works is finisher' (135) and whose help often reverses expectation, 'Where hope is coldest, and despair most fits' (143). Helena's emphasis in this scene on 'the help of heaven' (151) guarantees that the ensuing action is played out within a context defined in part as an arena in which God exercises his beneficent power. Her decision to leave France so that Bertram might return is unquestionably an act of her own will – or, more exactly, her satisfactory fulfilment of the proper move here dictated by her ultimate dramatic role – but the fortuitous meeting with Diana and her mother is an event over which she has no control. Consequently, after she has used this piece of good fortune to her best advantage, she attributes her overall success to its only possible source:

> Doubt not but heaven
> Hath brought me up to be your daughter's dower,
> As it hath fated her to be my motive
> And helper to a husband. (IV.iv.18-21)

The contrast between this speech and her assertion in I.i shows that she has come to accept fully her own words of wisdom to the King: 'But most it is presumption in us when / The help of heaven we count the act of men' (II.i.150-1).

But the title of the play is bitterly ironic. All does not end well despite appearances, despite the seeming fulfilment of conventional comic form – the probable falsity of appearance and form is, of course, the central concern of the play – and thus there is a further irony in the fact that it should be just this particular rendering of the comic theme that accompanies the focus upon providence as its motivating force. The preceding comedies have characters like Proteus and Berowne who temporarily distort the comic theme and others like Shylock who remain always impervious to it, but generally speaking these comedies dramatize a world in which the pattern of losing to find is natural, prominent, and consistently beneficial in its effects. It is equally prominent (if not more so) in *All's Well That Ends Well*, and its association with providence gives it its firmest testimonial yet as a valid phenomenon of experience. Or does it? Shakespeare has obviously begun to wonder about a theme he has heretofore simply dramatized, and in suggesting that the pattern may not after all have a beneficial result, he so steeps it in irony as even to cast doubt on its validity. It is not surprising that the next, and darkest, comedy, *Measure for Measure*, offers no dramatization whatever of the comic theme, not even a parodistic one of the sort that Helena has undergone.

Shakespeare's next three comedies after *Measure for Measure* (the three romances) form a recognizable group, which distinguishes itself not only by an abrupt change from the dominant tone of *All's Well* and *Measure for Measure* but also by the development of a new comic pattern. *Cymbeline* and *The Winter's Tale*, at least, are every bit as theatrical as their predecessors – probably even more so. Shakespeare constantly and deliberately insists on the artificiality of the romances, in order, evidently, to get closer to the miraculous, especially the miracle of art. But the theatricality of these plays is of a different order from that which had prevailed. Examples of discrepancy between the actor and his part continue to appear, but discrepancy itself no longer has the great thematic importance it had in *Twelfth Night, All's Well That Ends Well*, and *Measure for Measure. The Winter's Tale* makes crucial use of the familiar sequence in which amateur theatrics transform their victim, but this use is special and unusual, and the other romances ignore the sequence. Broad spatial contrasts are no longer conspicuous, and while one can still speak of coherent worlds when discussing the romances, in shaping them Shakespeare seems less concerned with establishing such worlds than with the adventures his characters experience; or, perhaps, what should be said is that these plays all dramatize a single world whose nature is defined by the kinds of adventures occurring within its boundaries.

These adventures make the new comic pattern more reminiscent of *The Comedy of Errors* frame than the intervening comedies had been. The romances play down, for the most part, literary and dramatic roles and the nonceroles concocted by deluded imaginations. Important social offices tend to retain prominence, but only those acquired by birth; for Shakespeare now seems to equate identity with what his characters are through birth and through the social roles that affect them most intimately. He thus emphasizes familial roles before all others; he is interested in his characters as husbands, wives, parents, children, brothers, and sisters. He is, moreover, less interested in these roles as fixed patterns of behaviour to be performed or misperformed than as valuable possessions whose loss is the source of profound grief as well as the cause of a dissolution of identity, and whose reacquisition is the source of an even profounder joy. The action sequence common to the romances, as a result, is one that traces in the experience of one or more of the central characters the loss and ultimate reacquisition of roles of this kind.

This action sequence is, of course, closely related to the lose-to-find motif that runs throughout the comedies. It results, one might say, from the stripping away of all extraneous actions in a search for the essential action of comedy. There are also, however, some significant differences. For now the self that is lost is invariably defined in terms of the deepest layers of identity. And, oddly, in becoming the primary action of comedy the motif no longer dramatizes a continuous, strict cause-and-effect patterning. I use the term 'reacquisition' to refer to what the romances end with because what is found is essentially a set of relationships which would have existed had the loss never occurred – and sometimes even less is found, as in *The Winter's Tale*, where the death of Mamillius and the ageing of Hermione and Leontes constitute irreversible elements of the loss. In other words, although the profound joy of the reacquisition could not exist without the prior pain of the loss, the loss itself is no longer a blessing in disguise, the only way of finding (or *founding*) a potential identity, but an evil, the immediate source of considerable and longlasting pain. In the earlier comedies the phase of losing oneself was necessary so that one could find oneself; in the romances the finding has become necessary because the loss has already happened. To define through analogy this difference between the lose-to-find motif and the pattern of action in the romances, it is as if Shakespeare had shifted his focus from an exploration of the continuous but complex action through which the individual Christian finds his true self as one of the Blessed to a dramatization of the fundamental action that has made such a discovery possible: the action encompassing both the fall of Adam, through which man cuts himself off from heaven, and the sacrifice of Christ, which provides man with a way back.

What makes this analogy particularly appropriate is that throughout the romances the reacquisition is consistently seen to be the product of divine intervention. Pericles can at the end of his career assure the gods that their 'present kindness / Makes [his] past miseries sports' (v.iii.41-2). Jupiter, in *Cymbeline*, declares that he 'crosses' those he loves best, that he oppresses only in order to make his 'gift, / The more delay'd, delighted' (v.iv.101-2); and he tells the spirits of Posthumus' parents that their son shall be 'happier much by his affliction made' (108). The gods also look down on the action of *The Winter's Tale*, and if Leontes' losses result in part because the 'heavens ... / Do strike at [his] injustice' (iii.ii.143-4), at least one of the factors constituting the reacquisition – the union of Perdita and Florizel – has come about through the heavens' 'directing' (v.iii.149-51). The claims of *All's Well That Ends Well* are thus established anew, but the irony that helped to darken Helena's world has been dispelled. Heaven's 'magic' is genuine, and it is responded to with 'wonder.'

This unequivocal insistence on the divine source of the comic climax does not mean, however, that Shakespeare has entirely abandoned his earlier tendency to attribute the magic to the willing decisions of the individual. It is also characteristic of the romances that, despite the loss, at least one of those involved in the action demonstrates a strict fidelity to his (actually, it is ordinarily *her*) true identity, and this suggests that the magic depends in part on some sort of collaboration between divine intervention and human behaviour, that, perhaps, the fideltiy in some way 'earns' the divine intervention.

In *Pericles* the character who fulfils this function is Marina. *Pericles* differs from the other romances in that it contains no explicit imagery of role-playing, either verbal or in the form of conspicuous stage metaphors, and this is a quality that makes the play unique among the comedies. Antiochus, his daughter, and Dionyza all publicly misrepresent themselves, but, unusually for Shakespearian comedy, the performance itself acquires no significance. The only thing in the play that even begins to focus directly on the idea of role-playing, then, is the emphasis Shakespeare gives to the 'profession' of whore through the Bawd's futile efforts to make Marina worth the money paid for her. The Bawd's accounts of what Marina must do and should have done (IV.ii.117-22, IV.vi.5-10) show that, like other public figures, the whore also has an 'office' with its prescribed pattern of behaviour. But the most significant factor of this attempt to isolate and define the role of whore is that it should in large measure consist of Marina's refusal to play the role – indeed, of her failure even to comprehend the Bawd's instructions. Marina will not play this role because it is an improper one for 'an honest woman' (IV.ii.84). Her resistance, as the effect she had on her clients especially makes clear, thus dramatizes her strict fidelity to her true identity as the daughter of a king and queen – one, moreover, who has had 'princely training, that she may / Be manner'd as she is born' (III.iii.16-17). Her father and mother and her proper setting are lost to her, but Marina remains true to herself by continuing to act as if the losses had not occurred. What effect the fidelity she demonstrates has on the climax cannot be exactly pinpointed, but she does demonstrate it, and the gods eventually do turn all the miseries to sports.

The absence of explicit role-playing imagery in *Pericles* is but one indication that, despite their common form, the romances also exhibit important differences among themselves. *Pericles* also differs from the others by dramatizing the basic pattern of action not once but twice. The first version, which gives form to acts I and II, is almost a new rendering of the motif of losing oneself to find oneself, for although in fleeing Antiochus' wrath Pericles becomes 'a prince ... bereft ... of all his fortunes' (II.ii.9), he does not acutely feel his loss, and the 'stars of heaven' (II.i.1) or 'Fortune' (119) soon fashion it into the means by which he wins as his wife not Antiochus' corrupt daughter but the pure Thaisa. Their marriage, moreover, is crowned by Thaisa's pregnancy and by the news of Antiochus' death, which means that Pericles can safely return to Tyre and resume his lost kingship. This first version of the basic action thus rounds out for Pericles the identity as king, husband, and father that makes possible the second and more important version, which constitutes the primary interest of the play.

Pericles' shipwreck during the first version of the pattern had caused him to experience the sensation of identity loss: 'What I have been I have forgot to know; / But what I am want teaches me to think on: / A man throng'd up with cold' (II.i.71-3). This was, however, only a sensation, and it is not until he has lost both his wife and daughter that his identity genuinely suffers the destruction symbolized by his condition on board his ship off Mytilene, where Helicanus can say of him, 'This was a goodly person / Till the disaster that, one mortal night, / Drove him to this' (v.i.35-7). This time the loss is deeply felt and long-lasting, remaining in effect until the gods, working through the winds that direct his ship, through their agent Cerimon, and through direct contact in the vision of Diana show their 'present kindness' by restoring to Pericles first Marina and then Thaisa and thus himself to himself. Much of his full reacquisition of identity already occurs with the restoration of Marina, for to Pericles she is 'Thou that beget'st him that did thee beget' (194), 'another life / To Pericles thy father' (206-7), and the cause prompting him to command, 'Give me fresh garments. Mine own, Helicanus' (212). But the process of reacquisition is not finally complete until Pericles arrives at Ephesus (where he is to be reunited with his wife), declares himself 'the King of Tyre' (v.iii.2), and then outlines the full history of his adventures (3-13). To focus on Pericles alone, however, is to miss the full 'wonder' of the climax. Marina and Thaisa also reacquire the roles from which they had been separated, and Marina, for whom Lysimachus turns out to be a worthy husband, even gains a new one.

The obvious similarities between *The Tempest* and the three preceding comedies suggest that it should be regarded as a fourth romance. The same sort of roles are emphasized, the issue of fidelity has considerable prominence (though in *The Tempest* the fidelity seems to be of a different kind) and, above all, much of the action suggests the romance sequence of loss and reacquisition. Despite these similarities, however, *The Tempest* does not ultimately resemble the three romances. In particular, something has happened to the sequence of loss and reacquisition. The outward shape of Prospero's career, it is true, has followed this sequence closely, and he himself attributes his good fortune to 'Providence divine' (I.ii.159). But the loss he suffers, which consists only of the loss of a social office he has already abandoned and of his exile from a land that no longer commands his interest, is even less significant than Pericles' first loss: Miranda is the only one with whom Prospero has a meaningful relationship, and she accompanies him in his exile. More important, although Prospero's whole career figures prominently in the *story* told by *The Tempest*, his career does not form the diachronic design of the action. What does form this design is a second version of the romance sequence – the adventures of the group that Prospero, through his art, has brought under his control – and this version also conforms more exactly to the usual representation of the loss. But it is Prospero that causes this loss, and it is he that, when he is ready, resolves it. These effects make it impossible to regard *The Tempest* as simply a fourth play in the mode of *Pericles, Cymbeline,* and *The Winter's Tale.* For not only is the energizing force of the romance sequence here identified as a human being rather than providence, but, even more important, the dramatic focus is less the experience traced by this sequence than Prospero's manipulation of it. Prospero's art shapes a new version of the romance sequence, through which he and others who have in one way or another lost themselves can find themselves, but what actually gets emphasized in *The Tempest* is the shaping process itself, the drama Prospero creates in using his art to control Ferdinand, Alonso, and the rest as if they were his characters rather than Shakespeare's.

6 The pattern of the histories

As in a theatre the eyes of men
After a well-grac'd actor leaves the stage
Are idly bent on him that enters next,
Thinking his prattle to be tedious;
Even so, or with much more contempt, men's eyes
Did scowl on gentle Richard. (*Richard II*, V.ii.23-8)

The opening scene of *Richard II* quickly establishes a highly distinctive language. One senses it from the very first words, and within a few lines its ring has become unmistakable. Here, for example, is Richard's third speech:

Then call them to our presence: face to face
And frowning brow to brow, ourselves will hear
The accuser and the accused freely speak.
High-stomach'd are they both and full of ire,
In rage, deaf as the sea, hasty as fire. (I.i.15-19)

The royal plural does not ordinarily call attention to itself, but it does here – partly because of the rare 'ourselves,' more so because it is accompanied by such clearly rhetorical devices as the balanced phrasing and the rhyme. The comparisons, abrupt and conventional, have come not from the heart but from a handbook, and there can be no doubt that it is Richard rather than Shakespeare who has looked them up. The speech as a whole has a decidedly studied effect. Bolingbroke and Mowbray easily sustain this effect, because, contrary to Richard's claim, they do not 'freely speak.' They may very well get said what they wish to say, or at least what can safely be said under the circumstances, but the words they use nearly all form themselves into obvious formulas as they pronounce the required speeches of royal flattery and cast their accusations and counter-accusations in quasi-legal terminology. Soon, as they throw down their gages, ritualistic speech finds a counterpart in ritualistic action. No one in the scene can unequivocally be convicted of play-acting – even though Mowbray and Bolingbroke charge each other with lying – but the established milieu is undeniably histrionic and theatrical.

The next scene reveals that Richard is primarily guilty of the major crime with which Bolingbroke has charged Mowbray, and this reinforces the effect of the opening scene by implying that Richard, at least, *was* play-acting. Scene iii increases the theatrical aura of Richard's milieu by more direct means, by multiplying the effects that suggest the theatre. The trial-by-combat in the lists at Coventry occasions an abundance of spectacle and pageantry. Trumpets sound frequently. A large number of splendidly costumed figures fill the stage. Patterned, ritual-like movements and the careful assumption of precise stations – visually attesting to the long tradition behind the trial – provide a recognizable choreography. Whole speeches echo each other nearly verbatim, as not just the Marshal and the Heralds but all the characters involved employ a purely formulaic language. It is all a grand show, and it is suddenly made to seem even more show-like when Richard cuts it short just as the main event is about to begin, the event that would make the ritual newly meaningful by suffusing it with fresh action. Richard himself becomes the centre of attraction as he substitutes for this event his pronouncing of the sentences on Bolingbroke and Mowbray which, it soon becomes clear, he and his council have decided on *ahead of time*. This renders the preceding ritual entirely purposeless; it has been nothing but empty show, and one can explain its existence only by surmising that Richard has let things go thus far for the sake of the show itself. Evidently he enjoys a good show – especially one in which he can take a leading and impressive part.

Richard II stands at the midpoint, numerically as well as chronologically, of the sequence of nine history plays that Shakespeare devoted so much effort to during the 1590s. The central focus of these histories is a specific role, the social office of king, and these details from the first three scenes of *Richard II* constitute Shakespeare's first concerted attempt to bring out the role-like qualities of the kingly office by emphasizing its ritualistic, spectacular, and showy attributes, and by trying to associate with it a distinctive language (with its own vocabulary, rhetorical characteristics, and store of ready-made sentences and phrases), which can sound to some extent like a permanent attribute of the office, something that every occupant of the office must learn as the commedia dell'arte actor learns the language belonging to his role. Occasional moments in the *Henry VI* plays and *Richard III* anticipate in a minor way this direct dramatization of the gestures – the external histrionic attributes – of the kingly office, but by and large in the earlier plays Shakespeare works more by implication to define kingship as a role. He stresses the current king's inadequacy, his failure to be a *good* king, and this necessarily indicates that the office which he holds and which so many others aspire to consists of more than just a title, a crown, and an undefined amount of power.

Richard II also carries over this technique. Scene iv gives the spectators their first glimpse of Richard out of the public eye, in company with only those he trusts, and it becomes apparent at once that Richard is no more 'apt-ly fitted' for the kingship than the kings Shakespeare has previously created. Richard has no intention of keeping his word by letting Bolingbroke return at the end of his period of exile. He has squandered the wealth of his country and now intends to lease it out for profiteers to exploit. He prays for the immedi-ate death of John of Gaunt, his wise, loyal councillor and his uncle, so that he can plunder the wealth that by law and custom should pass on to Bolingbroke. Richard's misbehaviour as king is also the principal theme of the scene that follows (II.i), in which it is developed through the accusations that his uncles, Gaunt and York, direct at him. Richard may look like a king – he does, as York points out, physically resemble his father, the Black Prince, who would have made a perfect king (II.i.176-83) – but in no other respect can he be said to qualify for the office he holds, which, according to Gaunt, he has so abused that he has transformed it into a base parody of itself: 'Landlord of England art thou now, not King' (113). The insistent implication of these two scenes is that Richard's behaviour is wrong not only because it is evil but also because it violates his office. The stress on his misbehaviour thus keeps in focus a role-like quality of this office that is far more important, though less conspicuous, than its gestures. This quality is the accumulated repertory of moves proper to kingship and obligatory for every occupant of the office. The string of crimes and other failings accruing to Richard helps provide through contrast some sense of what this repertory consists of.

In using Richard's bad performance to define kingship as a role, these scenes also, of course, simultaneously establish a far more significant dramatic fact: Richard's own situation. The relation between Richard and the role his birth has assigned him, which perfectly exemplifies the theme of the discrep-ancy between the actor and his part, has more than one dimension. Richard's actions violate his role by conflicting with, and often inverting, the moves proper to it, but at the same time Richard publicly pretends to play what James I called 'the wise King's part.' Scene iv also establishes this dimension of Richard's discrepant role-playing, because the wrongs this scene attributes to him not only brand him as unkingly, they also expose the falsity of specific public representations of himself he has projected in preceding scenes. The first focal point of scene iv, moreover, Aumerle's proud account of the show of 'counterfeit' grief with which he responded to Bolingbroke's farewell, pro-vides an analogy for seeing more clearly Richard's performance as king.

These two dimensions of Richard's tenure as player-king liken him to the immediately preceding king from Shakespeare's histories, Richard III. But in the case of Richard II, 'player-king' has also a third dimension, which makes Richard II unique among Shakespeare's kings and gives him much of his drama-tic interest. He cannot play his role by fulfilling its proper moves, but he can play to perfection its external histrionic characteristics. He not only, as York observes, looks the way a king should look, but he can also stand, move, wear his costume, and speak in the best kingly manner. He loves the showy attributes of his role, as his handling of the trial-by-combat demonstrates, and he has completely mastered them – too well, perhaps, for this mastery also contributes to the impression of discrepancy. It does so partly because it emphasizes Richard's simultaneous failure to master the proper moves of his role, but mostly it is a matter of the same kind of overacting to which Claudio in *Much Ado About Nothing* and the King and his Lords in *Love's Labour's Lost* subject the role of lover. Like them, Richard theatricalizes his role, turns it into nothing but a part.

In III.ii, the scene of the return from Ireland, the tendency to theatricalize has become the dominant element in Shakespeare's presentation of Richard. It manifests itself in the exaggeration and excessive self-dramatization of individual moments, such as Richard's regreeting of his kingdom's earth. And it manifests itself in the ease and rapidity with which he shifts from one mood to another on cue, as if he were proving his ability to represent in proper rhetorical style each of the various passions. There is almost an impression of fakery in Richard's performance during this scene, but of course he is not faking. It is simply that his world is so completely a stage that only outward show truly exists for him. His feelings are genuine, but if he is to experience them fully, they must find expression in appropriate speech and mime. Richard, this scene implies, fails to be a good king because, like the characters of *Twelfth Night*, he devotes all his energies to a fictitious role of his own devising. It may be that he cannot properly fulfil the kingly office because he is already entirely taken up with the role of King Richard.

The performance of III.ii should in no way surprise a spectator who has seen the show at Coventry in I.iii, but Richard has never before seemed quite this histrionic, nor has his prior role-playing involved displays so likely to detract from the image of a strong and self-sufficient king. Performances like the one at Coventry may lead to suspicion or doubt, but it is clear that Richard intends them as a means of enhancing himself in the eyes of his audience: he has always before sought admiration or awe rather than, as now, pity. The performance of III.ii is noticeably different, then, and one is tempted to ask why this should be the case. The answer lies, I believe, in a further effect recorded by the scene, Richard's discovery that he can no longer feel secure about the role he has been playing so flamboyantly.

Richard begins III.ii by insisting that his being king is in itself enough to protect him from any dangers Bolingbroke's return might signify:

Not all the water in the rough rude sea
Can wash the balm off from an anointed king;

> The breath of worldly men cannot depose
> The deputy elected by the Lord. (III.ii.54-7)

There is more of the same – much more. It too sounds excessive, as well it should: despite this insistence, Richard has been deeply affected by news of Bolingbroke's successes, and he continues to be shocked by further reports – almost as much so as his extreme reactions indicate. He tries to mislead himself as well as others, but he can evidently see with perfect clarity that he stands in jeopardy of having his power and position violently wrenched from him. At least he has unquestionably come to a related realization, one that he expresses in the central speech of the scene (144-77). His self-dramatization of every mood and every reaction has led him from an exclusive awareness of himself as *the* king to a consideration of 'the death of *kings*' (156; italics supplied). He has discovered that it is Death who actually 'Keeps ... his court ... within the hollow crown / That rounds the mortal temples of a king' (160-2). It is Death that does the ruling, mockingly allowing the king 'a little scene, / To monarchize' (164-5).

The theatrical image epitomizes Richard's new perception of himself. He can die and someone else can become king in his place, and since this is so, he cannot really regard himself as king. The kingship is not, as he seems to have assumed, a dimension of himself, but an external role that he as actor has been allowed to perform for a certain (short) length of time. And now, he suggests to his followers, the performance has come to an end:

> Cover your heads, and mock not flesh and blood
> With solemn reverence; throw away respect,
> Tradition, form, and ceremonious duty;
> For you have but mistook me all this while.
> I live with bread like you, feel want,
> Taste grief, need friends; subjected thus,
> How can you say to me I am a king? (171-7)

Richard here suggests that his followers should stop playing their subordinate roles because he, the leading actor, has already abandoned his part. His discovery that he, like all monarchs, is merely a player-king in one crucial respect is evidently *by itself* sufficient to bring about his deposition.

The following scene, at Flint Castle, where Richard has gone to 'pine away' (III.ii.209), certainly bears out this implication. Bolingbroke, Northumberland, and York are surprised to learn that Flint Castle contains a king, but once they know it, they act accordingly. Bolingbroke's charge to Northumberland about what he shall say to Richard vigorously indicates that Bolingbroke will not yield one inch with regard to what he considers his just demands, but otherwise his speech thoroughly reflects a sense of Richard's royalty and of the proper ceremony due him as king. York notes that 'Yet looks he like a king' (III.iii.68). Northumberland forgets or refuses to kneel to Richard, but in speaking to him he too manifests the proper ceremony. Richard responds to the occasion with a splendid speech in which he expresses with unusual force a sense of both the reality and the invulnerability of his kingship (72-100). It is, however, a farewell performance. He must accept Bolingbroke's demands, and, as he reveals to Aumerle, this necessity painfully convinces him that despite the single splendid speech he now sadly misperforms his role:

> We do debase ourselves, cousin, do we not,
> To look so poorly and to speak so fair?
> Shall we call back Northumberland, and send
> Defiance to the traitor, and so die? (127-30)

He can no longer play his role, and so he surrenders it. It is Richard that suggests deposition (143-6), and, after having come down from the castle walls to the 'base court' at Bolingbroke's request, it is Richard that makes Bolingbroke – 'King Bolingbroke,' as Richard already calls him (173) – stop showing him the ceremony due a king. The deposition in London will merely embody formally an event that has already taken place.

Richard's abdication occasions several new moments of self-dramatization as Richard recites speeches far more studied than any he has yet pronounced. Two of these occur before he has left Flint Castle. 'What must the King do now?' he asks (III.iii.143), like an actor seeking guidance for a role he does not know how to play, and then answers his own question by verbally divesting himself, one by one, of all the trappings accompanying his role, until all he has left for himself is 'A little little grave, an obscure grave' (154). He sees his descent to the courtyard as a fall like that of 'glist'ring Phaethon' (178), and through repetition and other rhetorical devices tries to make his listeners also see it that way.

At London, Richard is the central figure in what the Abbott of Westminster will ultimately call 'a woeful pageant' (IV.i.321). He tries to involve Bolingbroke in a tug of war for the crown and indulges in further wordplay in the speech with the nine repetitions of the word 'care' (IV.i.195-9) and in the carefully wrought 'Ay, no; no, ay' with its multitude of meanings (201). He repeats and improves upon one of his moments at Flint Castle, for this time in verbally divesting himself of his kingly attributes he actually removes and surrenders his crown and sceptre. And he provides a brilliant climax for the whole performance by calling for the looking-glass, which he then smashes. Bolingbroke may object when Richard defines the smashed mirror as his own face, which his sorrow has destroyed, but Richard could scarcely have selected a better symbol to summarize his experience. He has existed, as it were, only at some removes from himself. Richard has been, first of all, a series of gestures; either those belonging to his social office or, as now, those arising from his own dramatization of losing that office. And he has also been a series of responses by others, who – like mirrors – have let him see reflected by them the success of his performance.

More than once the self-dramatization of Richard's abdication scenes involves an attempt to select and play a new role as a replacement for the one that has been lost. Already in III.ii, even before he had fully articulated – and thus really experienced – his awareness of himself as player-king, Richard's misunderstanding about the fate of Bushy, Green, and the Earl of Wiltshire had prompted him to call them 'Three Judases, each one thrice worse than Judas!' (III.ii.132), but it is not until the scene at London that he fully assumes the role of another Christ (IV.i.169-71, 239-42). Other roles with which he associates himself include the hermit, 'almsman,' or 'palmer' whose circumstances he will, he says, exchange his kingly trappings for (III.iii.147-54), 'glist'ring Phaethon,' whose fall he imitates (178), both the priest who intones 'God save the King!' and the clerk required for the response of 'amen' (IV.i.172-4), 'a mockery king of snow' (260), and a damned soul, crying out to Northumberland, 'Fiend, thou torments me ere I come to hell' (270).

All these roles, as well as the excessive overdramatizations, constitute attempts by Richard to lend substance to the nebulous condition he has entered into in losing his role as king and to provide gestures for what he perceives as a new role, the role he designates when he opposes to Bolingbroke's title of 'King Henry' his own new one of 'unking'd Richard' (220). He describes some characteristics of his new role when he tells Bolingbroke, 'I hardly yet have learn'd / To insinuate, flatter, bow, and bend my knee. / Give sorrow leave awhile to tutor me / To this submission' (164-7). But most of the gestures of this new role cannot be so easily acquired because they are far less clearly known. They must first be discovered, and Richard's self-dramatizations represent his attempt to make this discovery, to shape the experience of losing the kingship in such a way that it can seem to be, for himself and others, a role as traditional and familiar as the kingship itself.

Richard's efforts to shape a new role for himself have a desperate quality about them which suggests that they spring from profound need. There can, moreover, be no doubt about the source of this need because Richard refers to it more than once. At Flint Castle, after he has tasted the failure of his last effort to play the king and just before asking for Bolingbroke's direction with 'What must the King do now?' Richard expresses the heartfelt wish, 'that I could forget what I have been! / Or not remember what I must be now!' (III.iii.138-9). From one point of view this wish might be said simply to convey regret about the loss he is experiencing: how terrible it must be to stop being king after having once enjoyed the splendours and glories of the office. But the speech does not focus just on that which is lost, it also emphasizes the new – and obviously unpleasant – state that will follow upon the loss. Richard cannot or will not define the new state any further at this point, but in London he has evidently become even more sharply aware of what lies in store for him. When Bolingbroke asks him if he is contented to resign the crown, Richard seems to reply that he is not because if he does he then 'must nothing be' (IV.i.201), but his words here are too cryptic to paraphrase with any certainty. There is, however, no doubt at all about his sense of what he has become once he finally does resign the crown:

> I have no name, no title –
> No, not that name was given me at the font –
> But 'tis usurp'd. Alack the heavy day,
> That I have worn so many winters out,
> And know not now what name to call myself!
> O that I were a mockery king of snow,
> Standing before the sun of Bolingbroke
> To melt myself away in water drops! (255-62)

The first half of this speech apparently derives from the attempts by contemporaries of the historical Richard to brand him a bastard, but the background has certainly not been dramatized. What the lines do dramatize is the agonized feeling of Shakespeare's character that he has indeed become nothing, that in losing his role of king he has wholly lost his identity. And thus, in the lines that follow, he expresses his desire for a new role to replace the old, in this case a role especially suited to the actor who will play it. The speech explains and sums up a great deal. Richard's constant self-dramatizations and frequent attempts to cast himself in new roles have sprung from the awareness recorded here. His identity has consisted wholly of his role as king, and therefore losing the kingship also means losing everything. It leaves him without identity, without any bearings, without any structure by means of which he can relate himself to the rest of reality. He must find or create some kind of role to play, any kind at all, in order to stave off the alternative of sheer emptiness, and in keeping with the peculiar nature of Richard's histrionic sensibility, the new role, like the old, must incorporate a high degree of conspicuous theatricality.

Richard's prison soliloquy of V.v re-enacts the experience he has gone through, while giving it further clarification. His effort to 'beget / A generation of still-breeding thoughts' with which to 'people this little world' of his prison (V.v.7-9) involves him, as he realizes, in further role-playing, and because he realizes it, he is able to provide an explicit statement that pertains not only to the present moment but also, at least in its opening words and its basic drift, to his whole career:

> Thus play I in one person many people,
> And none contented. Sometimes am I king;
> Then treasons make me wish myself a beggar,
> And so I am. Then crushing penury
> Persuades me I was better when a king;
> Then am I king'd again; and by and by
> Think that I am unking'd by Bolingbroke,
> And straight am nothing. (31-8)

He also realizes *why* his role-playing is and has been necessary to him:

> But whate'er I be,
> Nor I, nor any man that but man is,
> With nothing shall be pleas'd till he be eas'd
> With being nothing. (38-41)

Without a role or roles to give him identity man is nothing; yet nothingness is a state that can be borne only by the dead. The man who lives must attain an identity of some kind, even if he has to 'hammer it out' (5) from his own imagination.

Richard finally gains the nothingness of death that he has longed for ever since fully tasting the nothingness of life. Before this, however, he gets one more opportunity to play the kingly office, and seems to carry it off with greater success than ever before. The reverence of the Groom restores the sense of Richard's kingliness, which Richard then himself helps solidify through the way he behaves, both physically and verbally, towards his murderers: Exton must confess that his dead victim was 'As full of valour as of royal blood' (113). These final moments in Richard's career – his death and his last-minute fulfilment of kingliness – are of minor dramatic importance, however, as is his realization that he has misplayed the kingly office by concentrating all his talents on its external histrionic attributes (cf. 45-9): as this realization satisfies a spectator's moral instincts, the end given Richard's career satisfies the instinct for form. What does have dramatic importance is the experience preceding these minor aspects of its ending, the experience of loss and, especially, the glimpse of horrible emptiness this loss leads to.

Richard's association of himself with 'any man that but man is' (V.i.39) argues that in the need he has shown for some kind of role he is typical rather than unique, and the action of the play helps confirm this implication by centring in part on another career with important parallels to Richard's. This other career, of course, is that of Bolingbroke, whose role loss has two phases, the one occasioned by his exile, the other by Richard's decision to seize the dead Gaunt's valuables and property and prevent Bolingbroke's inheritance of his father's title. Gaunt's death should make Bolingbroke the Duke of Lancaster but he gains this position 'Barely in title, not in revenues' (II.i.226). Having lost one role and being prevented from playing another he knows to be his due, Bolingbroke has ample reason to feel the sense of deprivation and outrage he expresses to York in II.iii:

> I ... stand condemn'd
> A wandering vagabond; my rights and royalties
> Pluck'd from my arms perforce, and given away
> To upstart unthrifts. (II.iii.119-22)

Bolingbroke gives no more decisive expression of how the loss he has experienced actually feels to him, because although he parallels Richard in suffering the loss of role that threatens loss of identity, he by no means resembles Richard in other respects. He is, in contrast to Richard, a man of action. He acts while Richard plays, or, better, he acts while Richard *merely* acts. And, as he insists when saying farewell to his father, he lacks completely the kind of imagination Richard possesses in such abundance, for he cannot find any satisfaction in substituting mental images for concrete actuality, cannot, for example, 'cloy the hungry edge of appetite / By bare imagination of a feast' (I.iii.296-7). Both Bolingbroke's obvious affinity for action and his lack of Richard's verbal imagination are thoroughly reflected in the language he speaks when he is most himself. His language, in sharp contrast to Richard's, is without noticeable rhetorical flourishes; it is sparse in images, terse, conditioned to the needs of argument. Also, evidently, it can convey the most significant statements in the fewest possible words; what Sir Pierce Exton interprets as the command to kill Richard consists of no more than the twice-urged 'Have I no friend will rid me of this living fear?' and a highly expressive look:

> And, speaking it, he wishtly look'd on me,
> As who should say 'I would thou wert the man
> That would divorce this terror from my heart';
> Meaning the king at Pomfret. (V.iv.2, 7-10)

Bolingbroke, one is tempted to say, speaks a totally different language from Richard's, and nowhere is the contrast-conflict between the two more effectively epitomized than in the speeches they exchange during the formal deposition at London.

Bolingbroke's nature prevents him from responding to his loss of role in Richard's manner: he cannot and would not try to cling to an identity by dramatizing his situation or by acting out imaginary self-reassuring roles. But he does, obviously, feel the loss as acutely as Richard and experience a similar need to secure a substitute role, because he also emulates Richard in satisfying this need. He does it, however, in his own manner – by seizing a role that already exists. The role of Duke of Lancaster, which belongs to him and which he has returned to England in order to claim, is no longer really there; Bushy, Green, and Richard's other favourites, says Bolingbroke, have

Dispark'd my parks and fell'd my forest woods,
From my own windows torn my household coat,
Raz'd out my imprese, leaving me no sign
Save men's opinions and my living blood
To show the world I am a gentleman. (III.i.23-7)

Bolingbroke needs a role with valid, concrete signs; when Richard's role as king becomes available through its present occupant's own willing abdication, Bolingbroke, who fits the part admirably, makes it his own.

Richard claims at the time of Bolingbroke's exile that Bolingbroke has been wooing the common people, 'As were our England in reversion his, / And he our subjects' next degree in hope' (I.iv.35-6), but prior to the deposition Bolingbroke himself never directly reveals even the slightest aspiration towards the role he eventually seizes, and this extreme reticence means that a spectator tends to experience him simply as the actions he performs. There is no self-dramatization to call undue attention to the performer, and the gestures of the performance are too inconspicuous, too thoroughly untheatrical to suggest that a part of any kind is being played. One cannot even acquire an impression of the performer as an autonomous agent by thinking about what he does, by contemplating, for example, its morality; he acts too rapidly and, if not without forethought, at least without foretalk. This perfect equivalence between the performer and his performance suggests that Bolingbroke will readily become the ideal king Richard failed to be. But this promise is not fulfilled, and Bolingbroke's performance *as king* is accompanied by almost as many images of discrepant role-playing as was Richard's.

To the extent that Bolingbroke's assumption of the kingship can be pinpointed in time, it occurs when York proclaims, 'long live Henry, fourth of that name!' and Bolingbroke replies, 'In God's name, I'll ascend the regal throne' (IV.i.112-13). The next words, however, come from the Bishop of Carlisle, who sounds the first strong note of discrepancy: 'My Lord of Hereford here, whom you call king, / Is a foul traitor to proud Hereford's king' (134-5). York's attitude towards the new king, whom he intends to serve loyally, differs sharply from Carlisle's, yet he too contributes to the sense of discrepancy when, in a later scene, he describes the impression Richard made while following Boling-broke into London:

> As in a theatre the eyes of men
> After a well-grac'd actor leaves the stage
> Are idly bent on him that enters next,
> Thinking his prattle to be tedious;
> Even so, or with much more contempt, men's eyes
> Did scowl on gentle Richard (V.ii.23-8)

There is no criticism here of the better-grac'd Bolingbroke, and no insinuation – even in the preceding account of Bolingbroke's behaviour during the entry – that he, as Richard had done, exaggerates his performance of the more con-spicuously histrionic attributes of kingship. There is nothing more than the image of Bolingbroke as an actor on the stage and the parallel in this respect between him and Richard. But this is in itself quite sufficient to evoke the no-tion of discrepancy and associate it with the new king as well as the old.

In assuming the kingship, Bolingbroke has, moreover, become involved in something much like a play. The first half of IV.i occurs before York's pro-clamation, but Bolingbroke has in effect become king already, and here he is confronted by a situation paralleling the one Richard found himself facing in the opening scene. The public quarrel between Aumerle and his opponents, with its charges and counter-charges, is actually far more serious a conflict than the one Richard had to cope with, because this new quarrel involves more nobles: it seems to imply an even greater breach in the fabric of the kingdom's order than did the conflict that has already brought about a change in kings through something approximating civil war. Bolingbroke avoids duplicating Richard's performance (he does not use the occasion for self-dramatization and self-glorification) but he can do no more than Richard did to resolve things on the spot; he too must simply postpone final action until a later date. The occasion is thus not one that Bolingbroke controls but one that controls him. And because it is virtually the same sort of occasion as Richard had ex-perienced, it assigns to the kingship a further role-like attribute. The kingship, this scene implies, resembles a role not only because of its gestures and moves but also because of the characteristic episodes it requires each of its occupants to act out.

It is, nevertheless, a later scene that most fully defines Bolingbroke's new life as unusually play-like, the scene in which York tries to persuade King Henry to kill his treasonous son, Aumerle, while Aumerle and his mother plead for his life. The basic situation is theatrical in itself, as King Henry notes when the Duchess arrives: 'Our scene is alt'red from a serious thing, / And now chang'd to "The Beggar and the King" ' (V.iii.79-80). Shakespeare has, more-over, greatly exaggerated the theatrical effect with all the locking and unlock-ing of doors, the kneeling, and above all the extremely artificial language. In the strained rhetorical effects and the constant rhyme of this scene, the lang-uage of the beginning of the play is heard once more. It is as if nothing has happened, as if someone with a new way of speaking had not taken over the kingship. The point is, of course, that it is the kingship that has done the tak-ing over. Bolingbroke speaks as he does here not because it is his kind of lang-uage but because he is trying to achieve the speech of kingship. Bolingbroke sounds neither like himself nor like Richard when he was king; he merely sounds strained and uncomfortable. He is quite obviously playing something quite other than himself, a part that does not wholly suit him.

Richard II thus ends as it had begun, by stressing that kingship is a kind of role. Once again, however, the more significant dramatic consequence of this emphasis pertains to the actor possessing this role, for the emphasis nec-essarily occurs at his expense: it insists on his failure, his inability to fulfil the role well enough to deflect attention away from the notion of a player playing a part. Richard II rightly closes with Bolingbroke's feelings of guilt for the mur-der of Richard – and for whatever else has contributed to the feelings – be-cause the action as a whole has dramatized a change-over not from a bad king to a good one but from one player-king to another. Richard's birth and blood entitle him to play the role, but (in the terminology of The Taming of the Shrew) he is not aptly fitted for it, and therefore he is incapable of natural performance, of properly observing the gestures and moves of kingship and acting out its characteristic episodes in the best manner possible. Bolingbroke seems quite aptly fitted, seems entirely capable of giving a natural perform-ance, but he can never achieve it because he lacks the one qualification Richard has possessed. His failure to achieve the role in the proper manner means at the very least that he must devote most of his energy simply to holding on to it. If Richard has reduced the role to a parody of its gestures, Bolingbroke looks as if he will reduce it to a vehicle for intrigue.

Two elements of the action of Richard II – the two that have most to do with forming the structure of the play – are well worth isolating and emphasizing. Spatially, the play takes its shape from a conflict-contrast between Richard and Bolingbroke, between, that is, a player-king and a would-be-king. Linearly, it takes its shape from the contrasting progresses of its two central figures, the one rising while the other falls – although Shakespeare places the greater weight on Richard's progress, and a spectator is likely to experience the diachronic design of the play as consisting primarily of Richard's gradual fall, of his grad-ual loss of the role that provides him with an identity. These two elements of the action are significant because it is through them that Richard II most fully coincides with the other history plays. Both the spatial opposition between the unkingly king and the pretender-usurper and the diachronic design of the fall from a highly desirable role capable of providing identity already exist in substantial development in the *Henry VI* plays, and these two thematic-structural motifs, with greater or lesser emphasis and in one variation or another, continue to help shape the histories up to and including *Henry V*. Together these two motifs constitute the basic pattern of the histories.

The *Henry VI* trilogy, as the theatrical pun in its opening line implies ('Hung be the heavens with black') and several of its characters assert, constitues one long, unrelieved tragedy. The tragedy is that of England, of its collapse into civil war and anarchy following the loss of its ideal ruler. It is also the collective tragedy of the many characters experiencing the individual falls that give the action its moment-to-moment form and substance. And, above all, it is a tragedy about a role that no one can fill. 'England ne'er lost a king of so much worth,' Bedford says about the dead Henry V, and Gloucester echoes him with 'England ne'er had a king until his time' (Part I, I.i.7-8). Henry's kingship was an ideal union between role and performer, and with his death this ideal union has ceased to exist. There is, of course, a son to succeed to the throne and become king in name, but he is entirely inadequate for the office. And there are as well a number of would-be kings, who seem or who see themselves as far more fit for the office than Henry VI, but they, of course, are effectively barred from it by his occupancy. The situation is obviously ripe for dramatization of the opposition between the unkingly king and the pretender-usurper, and Shakespeare seizes the opportunity. A preliminary version of this opposition is acted out early in Part I by Charles the Dauphin, unkingly in his frivolity, and La Pucelle, who must fight and win his wars for him. But throughout the trilogy as a whole, it is Henry VI who consistently exemplifies the unkingly king (although Edward briefly supplants him in this respect during Part III) while the place of the pretender-usurper is taken not by one but by several candidates.

Henry's inadequacy for his office is perhaps *the* central dramatic fact of the trilogy, but Shakespeare dramatizes it far less carefully and concretely than he was later to dramatize the similar performance as player-king by Richard II. Part I stresses Henry's youth (' 'Tis much when sceptres are in children's hands,' IV.i.192), his utter ineffectuality on the few occasions when he does try to act ('Can you, my Lord of Winchester, behold / My sighs and tears and will not once relent?' III.i.107-8), his bookishness, and his meek-and-mild pastel-saintliness –

> Marriage, uncle! Alas, my years are young!
> And fitter is my study and my books
> Than wanton dalliance with a paramour; (V.i.21-3)

- and, perhaps of greatest importance, the necessity that his kingly functions be carried out for him by agents, by the Protector and others at home, by Talbot on the battlefield in France, and by Suffolk, who seemingly must not only woo and win Henry's queen for him but even serve her as consort.

Parts II and III then more or less assume this background, and Shakespeare does little further to define specific instances of Henry's inadequacy. It can, of course, still be seen reflected in a variety of ways. Almost no one will speak to Henry as a king should be spoken to. Others - first Gloucester and then Margaret - still perform his functions for him. Henry himself does nothing to contradict the impression already established by Part I, and more and more he seems to withdraw from his role by ceasing even to try to fulfil its demands. Henry does become a figure of considerable prominence and importance in Part III, but not as king, or at least not by virtue of playing that part as it ought to be played.

Part I establishes a number of applicants for the role of pretender-usurper: Gloucester, whom Winchester accuses of seeking more power than is appropriate to the office of Protector; Winchester himself, whose refusal to remain 'Jack out of office' (I.i.175) provides the role with an expressive image; Talbot, who qualifies through having the stuff of kingship but lacks the ambitions of the others; and Suffolk. Part I also introduces the chief embodiment in the trilogy of the pretender-usurper figure, Richard Duke of York, who retains this role until his death in Part III. In II.v of Part I, York learns from Mortimer that he inherits Mortimer's own not easily dismissed claim to the throne, but when Mortimer dies and the scene ends, York deliberately suppresses or postpones any interest he may have in appropriating the kingship: 'Well, I will lock his counsel in my breast; / And what I do imagine, let that rest' (II.v.118-19). York seems at this point interested only in winning for himself the title of York and the honour his father has lost, and not until the opening scene of Part II does he, in a context rich in role-playing imagery, express his intention of becoming king in Henry's place. The occasion is the splendid soliloquy at the end of the scene, in which York, by contrasting Henry with himself, also makes fully explicit Shakespeare's concern in the trilogy with the opposition between the unkingly king and the pretender-usurper. Henry, 'whose church-like humours fits not for a crown' though he holds 'the sceptre in his childish fist,' has, York feels, usurped *his* 'right' (I.i.239-42), but 'A day will come when York shall claim his own' (234).

York's tenure as pretender-usurper continues well into Part III. In the second half of Part II, while he is absent in Ireland, Jack Cade assumes this function, but as York's soliloquy of III.i informs the spectators, Cade is his agent, virtually created by him for the purpose of temporarily taking his place (367-73), and that Cade does, in effect, play York's identity Shakespeare suggests through Cade's parody, in IV.ii, of York's pedigree. York's death in the first act of Part III occasions the rise of a new pretender. Edward, York's oldest son, inherits his titles and his claim to the throne, but there can be no question that it is his third son, Richard, who inherits his drive along with his dramatic function as Henry's opposite – and, when it becomes appropriate, Edward's opposite.

Richard's acquisition of the role his father has left vacant becomes fully explicit in III.ii of Part III, in the long, self-explanatory soliloquy that parallels dramatically York's soliloquy in the first scene of Part II. Like his father before him, Richard also yearns for the crown, but while his father sought it at least in part because of his conviction that he could play the role of king far more effectively than the impotent Henry, Richard's motive for seeking the role is quite different and quite simple: he is unfit for any other. A lover he cannot be because of his deformity, which, he adds in what may well be an amplifying pun, disproportions him 'in every part' (III.ii.160). Richard doesn't catch this pun himself, obviously, because while it defines him as unfit for any role, he sees his inadequacy for other possible roles as the determining factor in his decision to seek the role of king:

> Then, since this earth affords no joy to me
> But to command, to check, to o'erbear such
> As are of better person than myself,
> I'll make my heaven to dream upon the crown. (III.ii.165-8)

And he *can* become king, he decides, because of his marvellous capacity for deceit, because, despite his inability to play the lover, he is the superb, accomplished actor none of his predecessors in the trilogy has managed to be:

> Why, I can smile, and murder whiles I smile,
> And cry 'Content!' to that which grieves my heart,
> And wet my cheeks with artificial tears,
> And frame my face to all occasions. (182-5)

Richard's purely selfish motivation and his unmitigated evil indicate that he is far less fit for the kingship than Henry, no matter how inept *he* has proved, but so also does Richard's transformation of Shakespeare's idea of the kingship as role. Shakespeare sees it as a role with special demands and special requirements which call for an actor with particular talents. For Richard, on the other hand, although it is the best possible role (the 'fattest' part), it is simply a role, and as such the only requirement for possessing it is a superior capacity to act. But here, too, a pun is involved, for given such a view, Richard as king would feel no compulsion whatever to restrict or modify his own actions, or even examine them. Richard's view of the kingship, like all else about him, demonstrates that he is truly qualified for only one role, the one he mentions in the final act of the trilogy, just after murdering Henry:

> The midwife wonder'd; and the women cried
> 'O, Jesus bless us, he is born with teeth!'
> And so I was, which plainly signified
> That I should snarl, and bite, and play the dog. (V.vi.74-7)

The only crown York ever acquires is the paper one Queen Margaret forces on his head during the playlet in which she compels him to perform as mock-king. The episode makes much the same point as the scenes of Bolingbroke's kingship in *Richard II*. It implies that however superior York may be to the unkingly Henry, he nevertheless remains ultimately unfit to play the kingly office. Like other pretender-usurpers, he remains himself merely a mock-king. In the case of Cade, who 'rules' briefly during *2 Henry VI*, and Richard of Gloucester when he becomes king in *Richard III*, the superiority of the pretender-usurper consists only of a capacity to act decisively, and since there exists no barrier of any kind to prevent the decisiveness from exploding into irresponsibility or recklessness – since, indeed, the evil nature of the actor virtually guarantees this explosion – the usurper converts the bad situation created by the unkingly king into a situation of sheer horror.

The failure of the pretender to succeed any better than the incumbent probably has many causes: the restrictions imposed by the historical nature of the material, Shakespeare's high esteem for the office of king, the standard political-philosophical-religious-ethical-social views of his time. At any rate, Shakespeare found it extremely difficult to vary the pattern of *Henry VI* and *Richard II* in any significant way, though his attempts in the other histories suggest how much he wished to. Richmond, the pretender-usurper of the second half of *Richard III*, wins total victory over his unkingly adversary, Richard, because not only does he replace him on the throne but he also will without doubt prove to be an ideal king. The cost is high, however: Richmond's adversary must lack all redeeming qualities, and he himself must be too perfect to seem real or compel interest – even though his own pedigree for the kingship is declared to be more valid than that of the monster he ousts. *King John*'s version of the opposition pits John against Faulconbridge the Bastard, who has all the qualities John lacks. Faulconbridge would make a perfect king and does, in fact, perfectly play the role when he substitutes for John, as John's agent, late in the play. But Faulconbridge is so ideally qualified for the kingship that his actually assuming the role can never become an issue: like Talbot, he is too correct ethically ever to act as usurper, or even to think of so doing. The opposition exists in *King John*, but only as contrast, not as conflict, and the play suffers accordingly.

In the three plays about Prince Hal-Henry V, Shakespeare manages far more successfully to vary the basic pattern he follows in *Henry VI* and *Richard II*. Henry IV is the unkingly king of the two plays bearing his name, while Hotspur and Falstaff, who inherit some of the superiorities of the pretender figure, also inherit all of his unacceptability as usurper. But Hal himself is a new version of the pretender-usurper, especially in Part II, when he 'seizes' his father's crown before his death. Hotspur and Falstaff – and to some extent Hal's brother John in Part II – serve Hal as lightning rods, by withdrawing from him and absorbing into themselves the guilt and resulting discredit accruing to the usurper figure. He, in return, absorbs from them, through conquest or contact, his valour, wit, humanity, and flexibility – and his wiliness. Hal therefore possesses all the talents and more that qualified his father for the role of king, and in addition he assumes that role legitimately. His accession to the throne eliminates the figure of unkingly king by fusing the king and pretender into a new unity. *Henry V* sustains this achievement. Henry is legally king through the validity of his claim and morally so because of his performance, which demonstrates his possession of all the talents usually held, actually or supposedly, only by the pretender. The opposition of the histories continues to help shape this play, too, but here the inadequacy of the unkingly king, the discrepancy he exhibits between his role and himself as actor, has been transferred to Henry's opponents – to the symbolic usurpers, Pistol and the Dauphin.

The *Henry VI* trilogy also establishes the diachronic design of the fall that is a fall out of a role – and not merely in the sense of its being a fall from high place, though this, of course, obviously contributes. The fall of Joan la Pucelle, for example (which is a high point of Part I) consists not only of her capture and execution but also of her being exposed as a fraud. The image of herself she has projected as the 'holy maid' (I.ii.51), the heroic saint whom heaven and the Virgin Mary have singled out for special blessing, turns out to be a false role to which she had no valid claim whatsoever, and she loses through the exposure the identity she has had in the eyes of the spectators. Part I also celebrates the fall of the heroic Talbot, but it is in Part II that Shakespeare really begins to use the action of the fall as the chief means of giving form to his dramatic action. Part II consists of a series of falls as one after another – though in their entirety the actions often overlap – a number of characters experience defeat and death. And each of them, as it were, engages in a little drama, whose nature is perfectly characterized by the shift in tone distinguishing Eleanor's theatrical metaphor for experience from the one her husband later employs. From Eleanor's standpoint as one who is about to begin this drama, it seems like 'Fortune's pageant,' in which the actor eagerly seeks to play his part (I.ii.66-7). But as the drama nears its conclusion, it ultimately becomes the 'plotted tragedy' of Gloucester's lament (III.i.153).

Eleanor, the Duchess of Gloucester, enacts the first version of this drama in Part II, and her career provides a paradigm allowing the spectators to experience the full impact of later and sometimes less fully presented versions. She cannot persuade her husband, Good Duke Humphrey, to make the crown his own, but she can, in a soliloquy dramatically echoing York's important one of the preceding scene, resolve to find herself some means of removing 'these tedious stumbling-blocks' (I.ii.64). She already affects the role of queen in her behaviour, as Queen Margaret jealously notes (I.iii.75-7), and now she seeks to win the role in earnest. Thus she dabbles in black magic, gets caught and sentenced to banishment, and must endure the scene of her public penance (II.iv). Her failure to gain the role she sought as well as the loss of the role she had held is symbolized in this scene by the costume and trappings of the role she now is forced to play: *'Enter* [the Duchess of Gloucester] *bare-foote, and a white sheet about her, with a waxe candle in her hand, and verses written on her backe and pind on ...'* (II.iv; stage direction from *The First Part of the Contention*, the quarto version of *2 Henry VI*). She enacts her penance defiantly, however, for since she can neither be what she has longed to be nor endure the shame she is now subjected to, she yearns for non-existence: 'Ah, Gloucester, teach me to forget myself!' (II.iv.27).

The other characters of Part II whose careers shape similar dramas include Gloucester (though in his case without the sense of guilt, of a fall triggered by the tragic victim's own inordinate ambition), Suffolk, Winchester, and (especially) Jack Cade. York's corresponding fall is not complete until the first act of Part III, but it is well on its way in Part II and thoroughly predicted by the falls of Eleanor and Cade, both of whom serve as evaluative parallels of York.

The chief fall of the trilogy is Henry's, which thematically extends throughout all three parts but which Shakespeare does not dramatize until Part III, where, like that of Richard II, it has a heavy flavour of abdication. The *Henry VI* trilogy thus initiates not only the diachronic design of the fall but also the specific form it tends to have throughout the histories, where, more often than not, a play, or a good part of it, takes its shape from the gradual fall of the king whose name has given it its title. The second half of *Richard III* defines in clearly marked stages the defeat and destruction of the usurping Richard. King John is initially a strong, secure monarch, an unkingly king only in the minds and words of his enemies, but in trying to handle the threat posed by Arthur he stops acting as a king should; his two new coronations (of IV.ii and V.i), which symbolize a discrepancy between him and the kingship, also cost him the support of his nobles, and he ends up sick and dying, helpless to act either for his country or for himself. The revisions in the opposition between unkingly king and pretender-usurper which Shakespeare effected for the three plays about Henry V pretty well hinder an unaltered continuation of the diachronic design so prevalent up to this time. Nonetheless, the falls of Hotspur and Falstaff are prominent in *Henry IV*, and, more important, so is the fall of Henry IV himself, whose decline and final loss of a role he never fully attained form a substantial motif if not a valid shaping element in Part II. *Henry V*, as my analysis in chapter 2 indicates, has a quite different linear design and a king who – in his own play, at least – is incapable of falling, but the motif of the fall still exists even here, in the exposure, discomfiting, and demoralizing of Pistol.

The fall of Henry VI in the third part of his trilogy reaches its obvious conclusion when he is murdered by Richard of Gloucester. But in so far as the fall consists of full separation from the role that has conferred identity, it can also conclude with the assumption of a new role, as Eleanor, in Part II, became the defiant penitent. In II.v of Part III, Henry seeks one such new role and finds another. He had refused to leave the field of battle when ordered away by Margaret and Clifford in II.ii, but now he does so, to seat himself on a molehill – like York's molehill in I.iv, a stage for enacting the loss of a crown – and let the victory go to whom it will. He welcomes, momentarily, the idea of death (II.v.19-20), but then hits on a quite different cure for the 'grief and woe' he feels: the creation in imagination of a substitute role, that of the 'homely swain' (22). The lines that follow (23-54) constitute his attempt to give this role substance by listing some of its likely elements (especially its superiority to his old role, the kingship) and by employing the heavy rhetorical apparatus with which he welds these elements together. Henry cannot finally possess this role, however, no matter how desirable it seems. For one thing, his characterization of it is no sooner complete than another 'alarum' forcibly returns his attention to his true situation. But even in the very act of defining the role, he has kept himself apart from it through his conscious, deliberate focus on it as a desirable alternative, through the subjunctive mood, and through the overly conspicuous rhetoric. The role remains something he contemplates; unlike the roles Richard II shapes for himself, it never becomes something he enacts.

Henry does, however, acquire a new role in this scene, and, ironically, it is the forcible return of his attention to the battle which gives it to him. Shakespeare's most consistent metaphor for what happens in the trilogy characterizes Henry's world as a vast stage on which an unrelieved tragedy plays itself out, not just for those who experience the recurring falls but for all its actors, whatever their social rank or dramatic importance. Henry, on his molehill, is made to realize this acutely when two instances of the collective tragedy are presented before him like two scenes of a playlet – or, as Henry himself calls it, a 'piteous spectacle' (73). His hearing and seeing the 'Son that hath kill'd his Father' and the 'Father that hath kill'd his Son' inspires Henry to adopt, spontaneously and without distancing calculation, his new role. He cannot escape from England's woe into his pastoral idyll, but he can and does detach himself from it by becoming simultaneously the spectator who observes and the presenter who interprets the tragedy. He becomes at last what he has for some time unwittingly sought to be, a choral voice lamenting and formally proclaiming the 'bloody times,' the 'Woe above woe,' and 'grief more than common grief' (73, 94) which suffering England must endure.

Henry's seeking and finding a new role to replace the one he is losing makes him something of a prototype of Richard II, not only in being an unkingly king and in undergoing the appropriate fall but also in that dimension of Richard's career which most compels attention and ultimately constitutes the primary motif of *Richard II*. And this motif can also be glimpsed elsewhere in the histories – for example, in Henry IV's half-sincere, half-politic dream of dying in Jerusalem as Christ's soldier. Nevertheless, the desperate search for a new role, for any new role at all, is not actually a prominent motif in the histories as a whole. Outside of *Richard II* and *3 Henry VI*, it is scarcely more than a thought a character might toy with. In *3 Henry VI*, moreover, it gives shape to a single scene only, and the character who participates in the search, unlike Richard II, never manages to articulate its most important element, the profound fear of full loss of identity which makes the search necessary. The motif of the desperate search for a new role is therefore not – like the opposition between the unkingly king and the pretender-usurper and the diachronic design of the fall – an essential element in the pattern of the histories. It is, rather, in its full development a motif that, in so far as the histories are concerned, is unique to *Richard II*, a motif linking that play less with the other histories than with the tragedies.

The technique of fulfilling the pattern of the histories while at the same time developing a unique, independent focus is one Shakespeare had already tried out in *Richard III*. Its unique focus consists in the special nature of Richard's career during the first half of the play and is well epitomized by one of Richard's boasts:

> And thus I clothe my naked villainy
> With odd old ends stol'n forth of holy writ,
> And seem a saint when most I play the devil. (I.iii.336-8)

In expanding his presentation of Richard, Shakespeare has chosen to emphasize his capacity to act through acting. The promise Richard made in III.ii of *3 Henry VI* but did not fulfil there is at last fulfilled. One of the chief signs of the remarkable advance that *Richard III* shows in relation to the plays of the trilogy is Shakespeare's movement from a purely verbal representation of the motif of play-acting to a visual and highly dramatic one. Richard's boast also reveals, moreover, that the notion of dramatic man as a role-playing animal has taken on firmer contours. The idea that a character's primary activity con-

No Goffman

sists of role-playing (or an attempt at it), that, in fact, he thereby attains an identity, is something that the *Henry VI* plays project but vaguely, usually by such negative examples as Henry's obvious failure adequately to perform something (which thereby becomes a role) or the others' striving to attain a position they feel themselves suited for. But here, in Richard's boast, in the distinction between himself as saint and himself as villain, is an unequivocal statement of the basic notion. What Richard *plays* is not, as might be expected, his pretended saintliness: the governing verb for this is 'seem.' What he *plays* is that which, at bottom, he essentially is: his 'naked villainy.' His role – which he splendidly performs – is that of a 'devil.'

In delivering this boast, as in doing what it refers to, Richard is fulfilling a role he has already selected for himself in his opening soliloquy. He begins this soliloquy by describing and then ridiculing the order that has resulted in England with his brother's final, uncontested accession to the throne – and ridicule it he must, since it provides such an incongruous setting for his own 'rudely stamp'd,' 'Deform'd, unfinish'd,' 'scarce half made up' condition. The setting demands a lover, and since Richard is 'not shap'd for sportive tricks, / Nor made to court an amorous looking-glass,' he cannot help but 'hate the idle pleasures of these days.' His only hope for contentment, since the given setting fails to suit him, is to change it, to furnish himself with a new and more appropriate one. And this he has already begun to do by so manipulating the situation as to set his brother 'Clarence and the King / In deadly hate the one against the other.'

This soliloquy obviously resembles Richard's soliloquy from III.ii of *3 Henry VI*, but there are important differences, and these are highly instructive. For one thing, Richard's deformity, that which makes him out of place, is no longer merely something that prevents him from being 'a man to be belov'd' (*3 Henry VI*, III.ii.163): in *Richard III*, it has truly become what he said it was in the earlier play, 'Like to a chaos' (ibid, 161). Through the way it is dramatically and poetically defined in this soliloquy, Richard's deformity makes him not just a misshapen man, nor even just a monster, but to some extent the very spirit of disorder. For another thing, in this soliloquy Richard does not explicitly refer to his capacity or plans to indulge in play-acting; play-acting has become, in Shakespeare's mind (as well as Richard's own), so much a fundamental element of Richard that it is assumed: it is not something he need talk about beforehand but rather something he simply enters into when the occasion dictates it – as when Clarence's entrance brings the soliloquy to a close. The explicit theatrical imagery that the soliloquy does contain thus relates not to his acting but to the capacity for the manipulation of others he possesses by virtue of his talents as playwright and stage manager: 'Plots have I laid, inductions dangerous ... '

The most significant, and quite shocking, difference lies in what Richard does not say in this soliloquy. The Richard of *3 Henry VI* has in mind a specific, clear-cut goal, which he keeps in focus throughout his soliloquy: he wants the crown. But the Richard of *Richard III* never mentions, in his opening soliloquy or anywhere else, any desire for the crown or any intention of acquiring it. Unlike the Richard of *3 Henry VI*, he does *not* assume the role of Pretender. Rather, he assumes, and explicitly tells the spectators so, a quite different and far more consequential role, one that is highly appropriate both to what Shakespeare has already suggested about his embodiment of disorder and to the ultimate context in which he finds himself:

> therefore, since I cannot prove a lover
> To entertain these fair well-spoken days,
> I am determined to prove a villain
> And hate the idle pleasures of these days. (I.i.28-31)

The role he selects is the dramatic role of villain of the piece, which, it is implied, he will strive to perform not because doing so will help him attain the kingship but because this is the role for which he is most aptly suited.

Proving a villain involves more than simply hating 'the idle pleasures of these days.' It also involves carrying out all the activities traditionally associated with the villain in drama: such things as oppressing the weak and helpless, undermining the efforts of the hero (here identified by Richard – for lack of a better candidate, obviously – with King Edward), and constantly devising and executing crimes of an increasingly hideous nature. Richard adds to the role a further dimension – more accurately put, he elaborates upon a standard routine of the most familiar dramatic villains of Shakespeare's time, the evil figures of the morality play – by making his principal activity as villain the theatrical endeavours through which he successfully seeks to 'clothe' his 'naked villainy' and 'seem a saint' while at the same time discomfiting and destroying his victims.

With the exception of the scene of Clarence's death (I.iv) and occasional scenes and part scenes presenting the lamentations of Richard's female victims, the first three acts consist almost entirely of Richard's staged playlets. Already in I.i, as his soliloquy ends, Richard is playing for Clarence's benefit the role of devoted brother, promising, ambiguously, that if he has anything to do with it Clarence's imprisonment will not last long. In I.ii, he plays for Anne the dual roles of lover and penitent. In I.iii, he presents a highly complex representation of himself as open and frank (and therefore an easy victim), incapable of dissembling and loathing such behaviour in others, filled with moral indignation at the evil around him, bitterly conscious of unjust treatment and of the lack of the sort of reward his virtue deserves, but at the same time duly humble and properly repentant for any crimes he may have committed inadvertently. II.i contains the brief but devastatingly effective playlet in which Richard, at the king's urging, amicably promises peace and friendship to Queen Elizabeth's followers before suddenly and almost casually revealing the fact of Clarence's death and implying his belief that they have caused it. III.iv, in the Tower, contains the odd playlet that finishes with the decree of Hastings' execution. And, of course, III.v and III.vii dramatize the splendid little two-act comedy that might well be called Richard's Crowning Performance. Here, indeed, Richard himself once or twice becomes the comic butt, but all's well that ends well, and for Richard the ending could not be better as, flanked by his two Bishops (his 'Two props of virtue for a Christian prince,' III.vii.96), he wins the king-ship by deciding, as Buckingham puts it, to 'Play the maid's part: still answer nay, and take it' (51).

Each of these playlets propels Richard further on his way towards that which he formally attains in IV.ii, the crown of England, but as I have said, Richard never explicitly defines the kingship as his goal, nor, regardless of what Buckingham seems to know early on, does Richard himself ever evince any interest in it (either to his fellow characters or the spectators) until the comedy of III.v and III.vii. What Richard expresses when he talks about his playlets is not his awareness of any practical advantages they may furnish him but, on the contrary, the enjoyment he derives from them, the sheer fun of putting them on. His long self-congratulatory soliloquy after conquering Anne, for example, in no way touches on what he may have gained by winning her; instead, his whole focus celebrates the audacity of his achievement:

> Was ever woman in this humour woo'd?
> Was ever woman in this humour won?
> ...
> What! I that kill'd her husband and his father –
> To take her in her heart's extremest hate,
> With curses in her mouth, tears in her eyes,
> The bleeding witness of my hatred by;
> Having God, her conscience, and these bars against me,
> And I no friends to back my suit at all
> But the plain devil and dissembling looks,
> And yet to win her, all the world to nothing! (I.ii.227-37)

What he stresses here is his histrionic skill, a skill so rich that he has even man-aged, he sarcastically suggests, to make her believe in his physical beauty:

> I do mistake my person all this while.
> Upon my life, she finds, although I cannot,
> Myself to be a marv'llous proper man. (252-4)

He follows up his complex representation of himself in I.iii by recapitulating in detail how he has duped the 'many simple gulls' (I.iii.328) who are his adversaries, and the only accurate way to describe this speech (the one about playing the devil) is to call it a highly favourable review of a good performance. In III.i, while duping Edward's son and heir, he makes the notion of himself as actor even more explicit by comparing his language to that of a well-known stage figure, 'the formal vice, Iniquity' of the morality plays (III.i.82-3). But perhaps the chief indication of Richard's whole-hearted commitment to playacting is the odd little playlet that accompanies the fall of Hastings (III.iv), which, so far as I can see, is totally unnecessary – unless, of course, one's purpose is not what the show may accomplish but the show itself.

As spectator one admires and enjoys Richard rather than loathes him, and this happens because of the interest, vitality, and attractiveness he acquires in contrast to the drab background of figures – especially his female victims – each of whom relentlessly and unimaginatively carries out the dictates of a single conventional role. They can speak but a single language, the language of conventional morality, which they studiously adhere to, while Richard, in contrast, can boast of considerable flexibility in language. He has, as in his opening soliloquy, his own language of disorder and anarchy. He can, when necessary, also adopt that of the others, speaking it flawlessly as a means of deceiving them. And he can, at times, combine his language with theirs by forming from theirs delightfully amusing parodies, such as the one that follows Clarence's exit in the opening scene:

Simple, plain Clarence, I do love thee so
That I will shortly send thy soul to heaven,
If heaven will take the present at our hands. (I.i.118-20)

Each of the others steadily plays a single role assigned him by his circumstances, but Richard constantly creates for himself new roles, each of which he brings off with equal success – and the spectator is both attracted by his facility and entertained by the resulting variety. Richard's parodies of his opponents' language ridicule it so effectively that it becomes impossible to take a moral stance with regard to him. Nor would one if one could. For what the spectator witnesses in the first three acts of the play is not the criminal activity of an evil monster but – because of the constant emphasis on Richard's playacting – a series of brilliant performances by a charming entertainer at the peak of his career. Significantly, even his plan to dispose of the princes and Clarence's children, which, sentimentally speaking, could be considered his blackest deed, first comes up in the same speech in which he sends Lovell and Catesby for his bishops (III.v.106-9), and thus, initially at any rate, this plan seems no more than an adjunct to the comedy he and Buckingham are currently engaged in.

I have specified 'the first three acts' quite purposefully, because, despite what is true of them, one is by the end of the play entirely prepared to accept Richmond's wholly moral summary of Richard as 'God's enemy' (V.iii.252) and as 'A bloody tyrant and a homicide' (246) who, once he has been disposed of, deserves the utter disregard accorded him in the final speeches of the play. The spectator manages the required shift in attitude because of a decisive change in tone and mood beginning with the first scene of act IV. To some extent this change results from the spectator's being carefully separated from Richard. IV.ii ends with a soliloquy by Buckingham and IV.iii begins with one by Tyrell, and although Tyrell emphasizes the horror of murdering the young princes, it is perhaps even more significant that he, like Buckingham, adopts Richard's own favourite speech-form and uses it in such a way as to encourage the spectators to see Richard from a point of view other than his own. A further important source of the separation from Richard is the increased prominence – in frequency and stage time – Shakespeare extends to the scenes of lamentation by Richard's female victims, and this also contributes another effect, which itself helps bring about the shift in tone and mood. Earlier the women had tried to characterize their experience as a tragedy (II.ii.38-9), but at that time Richard still monopolized the stage and determined what kind of shows took place there. Now Margaret's voice is added to the public lamentation, and her similar attempts to so characterize their experience (IV.iv.5-7, 83-91) manage to acquire far greater weight.

Mostly, however, it is Richard himself who effects the change, specifically by the manner in which he performs the new role he has gained at the end of act III. His speech acknowledging formal acquisition of the throne simultaneously reflects a heretofore nonexistent sense of uneasiness and a lack of full self-confidence. 'Give me thy hand,' he says to Buckingham:

> Thus high, by thy advice
> And thy assistance, is King Richard seated.
> But shall we wear these glories for a day;
> Or shall they last, and we rejoice in them? (IV.ii.3-6)

As he adds, he 'would be King' (12, my italics), for plainly, in his own mind, he is not yet so. And the feeling of uneasiness betrays itself in other ways as well. Before, things that needed to be done were simply done (performed) but now they first become deeply felt necessities inducing anxiety. Richard frets about the fact that Edward's sons still live, and about Clarence's daughter. The thought of securing his position by marrying Edward's daughter is something that strikes him not as a clever idea but as a dire necessity: 'I must be married to my brother's daughter, / Or else my kingdom stands on brittle glass' (62-3). Buckingham's hesitancy when directed to supervise the elimination of Edward's sons prompts Richard, uncharacteristically, to betray his feelings to others by gnawing his lip (27). Mention of Richmond compels Richard to remember that 'Henry the Sixth / Did prophesy that Richmond should be King' and that a 'bard of Ireland' had told him once he should not live long after he saw Richmond (99-100, 110-11). The next scene suggests that the feeling of uneasiness is clearly warranted, for things now happen on their own, free from Richard's manipulation. Richard has begun to function again, to act in response to the needs so strongly felt in IV.i, and once again he feels his old confidence. But he has scarcely started expressing this mood before Ratcliff interrupts him with 'Bad news':

> Morton is fled to Richmond;
> And Buckingham, back'd with the hardy Welshmen,
> Is in the field, and still his power increaseth. (IV.iii.46-8)

Accompanying Richard's sense of not fully possessing his new role is the refusal on the part of Margaret, his mother, and Edward's widow to recognize him as king and speak to him as a king is spoken to; instead, as he complains without his usual irony, 'these tell-tale women / Rail on the Lord's anointed' (IV.iv.149-50). Queen Elizabeth is the most insistent in her refusal, the most effective in articulating this verbal deposition. She calls him 'villain slave' (144); she wonders, when he offers to make her daughter queen, 'who dost thou mean shall be her king?' (264); and, as he urges her to win her daughter for him, with mounting defiance she asks:

> What were I best to say? Her father's brother
> Would be her lord? Or shall I say her uncle?
> Or he that slew her brothers and her uncles?
> Under what title shall I woo for thee
> That God, the law, my honour, and her love
> Can make seem pleasing to her tender years? (337-42)

She gives in to his demands finally – or seems to – but even then it is not a king she yields to but 'the devil' (418).

Richard's uneasiness and the response of his female victims define him as the unkingly king. These effects establish a sense of discrepancy between him and his role which Shakespeare renders even more emphatic by once again regarding Richard as actor. After he finally wins over Queen Elizabeth – and celebrates his victory with a brief restoration of his sense of superiority: 'Relenting fool, and shallow, changing woman!' (431) – he is suddenly confronted by more bad news, which requires a quick response, for Richmond approaches England's shores at the head of 'a puissant navy' (434). At once Richard be-

gins to act. He orders Catesby to 'fly' to the Duke of Norfolk and Ratcliff to
'Post to Salisbury' (441-3). Then he notices that Catesby has not moved:

> Dull, unmindful villain,
> Why stay'st thou here, and go'st not to the Duke?
> CATESBY First, mighty liege, tell me your Highness' pleasure,
> What from your Grace I shall deliver to him.
> RICHARD O, true, good Catesby. (444-8)

And so he gives Catesby his instructions, but when Catesby goes, Ratcliff still
remains:

> RATCLIFF What, may it please you, shall I do at Salisbury?
> RICHARD Why, what wouldst thou do there before I go?
> RATCLIFF Your Highness told me I should post before.
> RICHARD My mind is chang'd. (452-5)

Richard has clearly lost control of himself, and, significantly, Shakespeare has
so represented the loss of control as to suggest an actor who has forgotten his
lines.

   This passage, which implies Richard's inability to play the part he now
holds, follows soon after a much longer episode suggesting that Richard no
longer has any histrionic ability at all. Queen Elizabeth makes the point by devising a test of acting which not even the Richard of the first half of the play
could have successfully passed, for she tells him there is no reasonable way for
him to win her daughter, 'Unless thou couldst put on some other shape / And
not be Richard that hath done all this' (286-7). But the point is also made by
the episode as a whole. Richard's struggle with Queen Elizabeth is a revival of
his successful playlet of I.ii, The Wooing of Anne, and this time he miserably
fails. No matter what ruses he employs, what arguments he advances, or what
misrepresentations of himself he projects, his audience of one remains uncon-
vinced. She knows who he is, as she frequently assures him, and he clearly has
lost the capacity he once had to convince others through his play-acting that
he is someone or something else. He does eventually seem to win her over, but
not through deluding her. The only way he can secure even her feigned acqui-
escence is through naked threats of the dire consequences that will ensue if
she continues to refuse him her daughter:

> In her consists my happiness and thine;
> Without her, follows to myself and thee,
> Herself, the land, and many a Christian soul,
> Death, desolation, ruin, and decay.

> It cannot be avoided but by this;
> It will not be avoided but by this. (406-11)

Act IV scene ii, the first scene of Richard's kingship, begins with a sennet, after which Richard enters 'in pomp' and dressed as king, accompanied by his chief followers, other courtiers, and pages, and then, to a second blast of trumpets, ascends the throne. This important stage imagery calls attention to the role-like qualities of kingship by emphasizing its external histrionic characteristics (in one of the few moments of the histories to do so before *Richard II*), and for spectators who have watched Richard assume one part after another the effect must surely suggest that he now takes on one more. Almost at once, however, Richard the magnificent actor has become the unkingly king and has begun enacting his fall. This role is one that he cannot play, and his failure has much to say about both the kingship and himself.

One reason, surely, for his failure is that this role is different in kind from those he has successfully performed. Although he can readily utilize minor actors like Buckingham as extensions of himself, Richard is, essentially, a one-man show, a wholly self-sufficient artist who creates his own roles as well as performs them, who perhaps requires such freedom from external control if he is to succeed. But, as Shakespeare partly suggests by the stage imagery of IV.ii and partly expects his audience to realize spontaneously, the kingship is a role established by tradition and convention. Richard's roles constitute a peculiar form of self-expression, while the kingship is a role demanding that its performer define himself by adapting himself to an ideal. To use the terms of the opening soliloquy, the kingship embodies order while Richard thrives on anarchy.

Another explanation for Richard's failure – or perhaps the same one put in a different way – is that in becoming king, Richard enters into a moral structure for the first time in the play. That he has unquestionably entered such a structure Shakespeare establishes not only through what now happens to him but also through a decisive change in his language. In the opening scene, Richard anticipated the wooing and winning of Anne with the kind of glee the audacity of his intention merits:

> What though I kill'd her husband and her father?
> The readiest way to make the wench amends
> Is to become her husband and her father. (I.i.154-6)

Within minutes after his accession to the throne, however, he contemplates a similar intention in a far different spirit:

> I must be married to my brother's daughter,
> Or else my kingdom stands on brittle glass.

Murder her brothers, and then marry her!
Uncertain way of gain! (IV.ii.62-5)

He is, quite clearly, already thinking in terms of the unequivocally moral language that rushes to the surface in his next line-and-a-half: 'But I am in / So far in blood that sin will pluck on sin' (65-6). There is no glee in this speech. Richard, it might be said, shows signs of having acquired a conscience. More important, by adopting this kind of language without irony, he cancels the conditions of response established for the first half of the play. He recognizes, and thus certifies, the existence of a moral order.

Richard traps and ultimately destroys himself by becoming king, because he has already elected to become a villain. This means, first of all, that it is impossible for him to perform successfully the role of king because he is already playing another part of a far different nature. Yet this consequence of his initial choice is as nothing compared to the – for Richard – far more devastating fact that becoming king places him within a moral structure where his self-chosen role of villain can acquire its full meaning. Becoming king thus allows him to perform the role of villain with total success. And this includes, as central to the action the role entails, not only oppressing the forces of good but also finally capitulating to them. It includes engaging the hero in battle and being destroyed by him, and therefore one further important sign that becoming king puts Richard within a moral structure is the fact that, dramatically speaking, his acquisition of the crown occasions the coming into existence of the hero of the play. It is not until IV.i, between Richard's winning the crown in III.vii and his enthroning in IV.ii, that Queen Elizabeth advises Dorset to 'cross the seas, / And live with Richmond, from the reach of hell' (IV.i.42-3) and thus introduces the first mention in the entire play of Richard's future adversary.

An interesting link between the first three acts and the final two involves the spectator's experience of Richard as actor. Richard is admired only for his histrionic skill; it is as a spectacular performer that he is applauded; and thus when he botches the role of king and reveals that his skill is more limited than first seemed to be the case, he naturally declines in the spectator's esteem. In other words, the new experience of Richard as actor facilitates the acceptance of the moral judgment Shakespeare now urges his audience to assume. Nevertheless, it is the moral emphasis that is uppermost in the final two acts, and this is shown especially by Richard's last important attempt to act, in his soliloquy of V.iii. Terrified by the accusing ghosts of his dream and seeking to resteel his nerves, Richard tries to revive a tactic that has worked for him so well in the past: establishing his own superior integrity by opposing himself to an adversary he can readily mould into a reflection of his own skill. The trouble is that most of his adversaries from the past have now, as ghosts, banded together in support of his only current adversary. There is no one else he can effectively oppose, and thus in this soliloquy Richard opposes himself:

> What do I fear? Myself? There's none else by.
> Richard loves Richard; that is, I am I.
> Is there a murderer here? No – yes, I am.
> Then fly. What, from myself? Great reason why –
> Lest I revenge. What, myself upon myself!
> Alack, I love myself. Wherefore? For any good
> That I myself have done unto myself?
> O, no! Alas, I rather hate myself
> For hateful deeds committed by myself!
> I am a villain; yet I lie, I am not.
> Fool, of thyself speak well. Fool, do not flatter.
> My conscience hath a thousand several tongues,
> And every tongue brings in a several tale,
> And every tale condemns me for a villain. (V.iii.182-95)

Richard's last nonce-role is that of his own accuser, his conscience; and the success of this performance – of its having attained the same end as the performance directed against Anne, say – is marked by his finally explicitly establishing that he has succeeded in his original determination of proving a villain. Richard has doomed himself in his opening soliloquy by making this determination. And although this final soliloquy, with its focus on a divided self, obviously reaches after a tragic effect, Richard's original determination has also ensured that his play must instead be a melodrama, the genre appropriate to the dramatic role he so brilliantly fulfils.

Despite the performances of the two Richards or Henry V's ideal fulfilment of his office, the most impressive and most interesting instance of role-playing in the histories takes place in Mistress Quickly's tavern in II.iv of *1 Henry IV*. The 'play extempore' in which Hal and Falstaff 'practise an answer' for Hal to use when facing his father the following day is, indeed, one of the most impressive moments in Shakespeare. Few other moments, with or without role-playing, epitomize so effectively and concisely so many of the basic issues of the play in which they occur.

The 'play extempore' impresses, first of all, through its peculiar appropriateness. It forms the climax of a long scene (531 lines) which has consisted largely of 'excellent sport' (II.iv.379), particularly sport with a histrionic aura. Hal has begun it by getting Poins to help him tease Francis, while Falstaff has contributed his marvellous portrayal of the brave and heroic defender overcome by superior numbers. The idea of acting out a play is introduced early, by Hal, who says to Poins, 'I prithee call in Falstaff; I'll play Percy, and that damn'd brawn shall play Dame Mortimer his wife' (104-6); and the idea is kept alive by Falstaff, whose suggestion about having a 'play extempore' (271) is not acted upon for some time. When this play-within-the-play does begin, therefore, it seems inevitable, the most natural thing in the world – at least the most natural thing in *this* world. It rounds off a series of effects which tend to define the world of the tavern as a domain where one form of role-playing – that which is undertaken for the pleasure it can provide – constitutes a primary, distinguishing characteristic.

This is not to say, of course, that the two participants in the 'play extempore' use it in exactly the same way. Falstaff's role-playing is more in the true spirit of the occasion than Hal's. There is, to be sure, a serious undercurrent to Falstaff's role-playing. He is trying, here as well as otherwise, to control Hal's more permanent role-playing, to determine what kind of king he shall be. His pleading demand, 'Play out the play: I have much to say in the behalf of that Falstaff' (467-8), expresses therefore a desperate need to revoke Hal's resolute 'I do, I will' (464). But at the same time Falstaff's speech is also simply a demand for more stage time, so that he can continue to participate in something that gives him the high degree of pleasure he obviously derives from shaping and executing the two different parts he gets a chance to play. The serious undercurrent may dominate by the end of the 'play extempore,' but Falstaff's unabashed playing to his audience and particularly the energy he throws into his parody of the king indicate that the original impulse behind his contribution to the performance has been a purely histrionic one. And this histrionic impulse continues to manifest itself right up to the end. For Falstaff, the 'play extempore' is to a high degree an extension and formalization of the same impulse he is constantly demonstrating through his more incidental role-playing. The king and the prince become two further portrayals in a repertory that has already included not only the heroic defender from earlier in the scene but also such figures as the saintly puritan, the innocent who has been led astray by bad companions, and the youth who turns to highway robbery only out of sheer need.

Hal's participation differs markedly. That he takes part at all suggests he must feel the histrionic impulse to some extent, but it obviously is not very powerful in him. Unlike Falstaff, Hal does not really do any acting. Both of Falstaff's roles compel him to play alien figures, at least to shape fictional versions of them that he can fit comfortably to himself. Hal, on the other hand, first plays himself and then his father, the king he is already practising to become. His performance involves little or no attempt at characterization: as himself, he scarcely speaks; as king, he simply adopts the voice he usually employs when jestingly insulting Falstaff. Hal addresses himself almost exclusively, moreover, to the serious undercurrent of the playlet, and his chief contribution, which occurs after he has taken over the role of king, is to accomplish symbolically the rejection of Falstaff he has promised in I.ii and will actually execute at the end of the second part of *Henry IV*. Falstaff concludes his participation in the 'play extempore' by demanding more stage time: with equal appropriateness, Hal ends his by moving abruptly but comfortably from Falstaff's world into the more ordered and heroic world of the sheriff, who enters at this point, and by exchanging Falstaff's prose for the blank verse spoken by Hotspur and his father.

Hal's failure to use the occasion histrionically suggests that he is not fully at home in a world where such activities are characteristic, and in this respect his participation in the 'play extempore' accurately reflects his entire relation to this world. Hal can usually hold his own in the witty duels with Falstaff, but he makes no attempt to equal or outdo Falstaff in his constant incidental role-playing. And, apparently, without Falstaff he cannot operate effectively in the mode of action distinctive to this world – such, at least, is the implication of the odd, unpleasant episode with Francis, which obviously does not come off as it is supposed to. The most telling effect of the episode is Poins' bewildered question when it is over, 'But hark ye: what cunning match have you made with this jest of the drawer? Come, what's the issue?' (86-8). Hal can supply only a lame answer, but this matters far less than the fact that Poins felt compelled to ask: he would never ask Falstaff a similar question. Falstaff's jests do not imply hidden motives and some sort of complicated intrigue.

Hal can play-act, and he does so while in Falstaff's world, but his play-acting is radically different in kind from Falstaff's role-playing. It does not consist of gaily shifting from one mask to another for the entertainment of oneself and one's audience but of wearing a single mask with such care that the audience never realizes a performance is going on. Hal tells Shakespeare's audience almost at once (as soon, one might say, as he gets the opportunity) that his whole presentation of himself in Falstaff's world is a false role sharply contrasting with his true kingly self. His 'loose behaviour' is a disguise he will 'throw off,' like an ill-fitting cloak, when the time is ripe (I.ii.201). Falstaff's role-playing shows that he is a natural denizen of the world of the tavern. Hal's play-acting allows him to be in this world without being of it. 'The true prince' – to alter only slightly one of Falstaff's speeches – proves 'a false thief' (148-9).

The kind of role-playing Hal indulges in places him securely in a far different world. It is of exactly the same sort his father, King Henry, claims for himself when he tells Hal how he won the allegiance of the people during the days of Richard's kingship (III.ii.39-59) and that he thoroughly demonstrates in the opening scene of the play by managing the news about the troubles in the west and north in such a way that he can place himself in the best possible light as a Christian monarch who yearns to lead a crusade but cannot do so because he is beset by rebels at home. Henry feels that Hal is not playing his role as prince properly, but his account in III.ii of how it ought to be played indicates that he is mistaken. Hal and his father are two of a kind in this respect: one requirement of kingship is emulation of the fox, and both Henry and Hal fulfil this requirement perfectly. Hal cannot play roles in Falstaff's manner because all his energy goes into playing what to him is the only role worth playing, that of king.

The histrionic differences between Falstaff and Hal point to one basic element of the central contrast between the world of the tavern – the world of prose and life – and the world of Hotspur and Henry IV – the world of verse and history. As in *A Midsummer Night's Dream* and *As You Like It*, one of the chief differences between the two worlds consists of the contrasting kinds of role-playing they permit or encourage. Falstaff's is a world for playing roles for pleasure, as many as possible, and the more innovative the better; the emphasis falls on the skill of the playwright-actor. In the heroic world, however, such role-playing would be unequivocally evil. There the ideal consists of finding one's proper role from an approved list of existing possibilities and striving to fulfil it satisfactorily by obeying its dictates. In Falstaff's world, all roles are possible because none is crucial. In the heroic world, only certain roles can be tolerated, and one of them, that of king, matters more than all the others.

The heroic world eventually comes to dominate in *1 Henry IV*, and the crucial importance to this world of the role of king gives the 'play extempore' a further significance. As an action, it dramatizes a struggle between Falstaff and Hal, one strand of which consists of Hal's deposing Falstaff and taking his place: 'Dost thou speak like a king? Do thou stand for me, and I'll play my father' (II.iv.418-19). The drama enacted here is one that could aptly be entitled 'Who Shall Play the King?' and a drama of the same sort is going on throughout *1 Henry IV* as a whole. The climax of the larger drama takes place on the battlefield in act V, where the basic theme is underscored not only by the exertions of the many pretenders seeking to unseat Henry but also, and especially, by the role-playing image Sir Walter Blunt projects in wearing the king's armour in order to serve as a decoy. There are many pretenders here – Hotspur, Worcester, Falstaff, Douglas in a way – but only one of them, Prince Hal, is aptly fitted for taking over the role that Henry himself cannot properly play because of the manner in which he came into possession of it. Hal proves his suitability during the battle by showing that the fox is also a lion, as he repeats his action from the 'play extempore' of deposing and replacing a dangerous pretender. Hal has, however, already established his suitability in a variety of ways, not the least of which occurs in the first six lines of act V, where he demonstrates his mastery of kingly speech. He picks up where his father leaves off and mimicks him so perfectly that it is impossible to tell from the words alone when one stops speaking and the other begins:

> How bloodily the sun begins to peer
> Above yon busky hill! The day looks pale
> At his distemp'rature. The southern wind
> Doth play the trumpet to his purposes,
> And by his hollow whistling in the leaves
> Foretells a tempest and a blust'ring day. (V.i.1-6)

Role-playing and role-playing imagery are also prevalent in the second part of *Henry IV*, which has for its climax Hal the usurper's premature assumption of the crown that possesses his father more than he possesses it. In this scene Hal's denunciation of the crown as a 'polish'd perturbation! golden care!' that 'Hast eat thy bearer up' (IV.v.23, 165) helps bring to the surface an important implication dramatized by the action as a whole: the player who takes the part of king must possess youth, health, and vigour in addition to any other requirements. *2 Henry IV* thus adds another detail to the portrait in the histories of the ideal king, the portrait that it is the business of *Henry V* to articulate fully.

I have already examined *Henry V* from this point of view in an earlier chapter, and all that needs to be added here is that it appropriately closes Shakespeare's writing of the plays normally known as histories. No one can know exactly why Shakespeare stopped writing such plays after *Henry V*. The reasons are no doubt both many and complex, and include, among others, the fact that he had already covered the most likely periods of English history. Nevertheless, it seems clear to me that a substantial part of the cause was his awareness of having pretty well exhausted the form he had devised in order to make possible the dramatization of English chronology. *1* and *2 Henry IV* and *Henry V* are less history plays (in any formal sense that term has acquired) than the plays preceding them. Each goes its own way; each constitutes an attempt to shape a new form – if only one that might fill the needs of the immediate material. The pattern that has given shape to the histories becomes gradually less central in these three plays, and although it is still recognizable in *Henry V*, it is barely so; it has had to be considerably revised in order to survive at all, and it obviously no longer serves any valid purpose. Apart from this pattern, moreover, the only other significant recurring formal element in the histories is the focus on kingship, the definition of it as role, and the definition of what it, as role, constitutes. And it could well be argued that *Henry V* makes any further attempt to define the kingship quite superfluous.

7 Two plays about history

CASSIUS   How many ages hence
Shall this our lofty scene be acted over
In states unborn and accents yet unknown!
BRUTUS How many times shall Caesar bleed in sport,
That now on Pompey's basis lies along
No worthier than the dust!
CASSIUS   So oft as that shall be,
So often shall the knot of us be call'd
The men that gave their country liberty. (*Julius Caesar*, III.i.112-19)

This trio of speeches is surely meant to be highly ironic. *Julius Caesar* is itself one of the dramatizations of the murder of Caesar which Cassius prophesies for 'states unborn and accents yet unknown,' and thus his excited and joyful vision of these future dramatizations suddenly defines Shakespeare's play as a play. The effect is calculated to make the spectators keenly self-conscious about themselves and their responses, to get them to note consciously how much their responses differ from Cassius' prediction about them. Few members of Shakespeare's original audience would have been sufficiently uninformed to regard Cassius and his fellow conspirators as 'men that gave their country liberty,' and those who were this uninformed had only to wait until the end of the play to realize how inaccurate and inappropriate the designation is. Some spectators undoubtedly agreed that the assassination was a 'lofty' act, but it is highly probable that a far greater number would have subscribed to the view of the assassination reflected in *The Divine Comedy* and regarded Cassius' 'lofty scene' more as the 'savage spectacle' later referred to by Brutus (224). Those spectators who let their responses be determined less by their own attitudes towards the historical events and more by Shakespeare's dramatization of these events would at the very least have felt that the assassination and the people involved in it are far more complicated than Cassius would allow. These speeches by Cassius and Brutus record therefore (and in a role-playing image) an ironic discrepancy between, on the one hand, the characters' assumptions about their activity and, on the other, its true nature – i.e., those views of it held by Shakespeare and by all those spectators who for whatever reason cannot agree with Cassius and Brutus.

Cassius' anticipation of future plays dramatizing the conspirators' act is the most striking of the explicit allusions to role-playing in *Julius Caesar*, but there are several such allusions, and all of them evoke the notion of discrepancy. Casca regards Caesar's rejection of the crown Antony offers him on the Lupercal as a piece of fakery, and it prompts him to see the whole occasion in theatrical terms: 'If the tag-rag people did not clap him and hiss him, according as he pleas'd and displeas'd them, as they use to do the players in the theatre, I am no true man' (I.ii.257-60). Brutus uses similar imagery in advising his fellow conspirators to 'look fresh and merrily':

> Let not our looks put on our purposes,
> But bear it as our Roman actors do,
> With untir'd spirits and formal constancy. (II.i.224-7)

The conspirators' successful carrying-out of this advice on the morning of the assassination provides an explicit non-verbal image of discrepant role-playing, Antony's later use of the conspirators' own technique against them provides another, and a third occurs on the battlefield in act V when Lucilius poses as Brutus in order to protect him. Shakespeare has, moreover, already established the motif of discrepant role-playing before introducing this explicit development of it. For when the commoners are milling about the streets of Rome at the beginning of the play, what at first seems most to disturb the tribunes Flavius and Marullus is that these commoners are out of costume and failing to observe the decorum proper to their lots (I.i.1-8) – that, in other words, they are misplaying their social roles.

These evocations of role-playing, like Viola's impersonation of Sebastian in *Twelfth Night*, are merely the outer, explicit dimension of a dramatic design that embraces the entire action of the play. Almost every character in *Julius Caesar* becomes a sort of 'Roman actor' through his participation in discrepant role-playing, and most of them practise the specific form of it embodied in Cassius' anticipation of future dramas. Cassius gives the murder of Caesar a more favourable interpretation than Shakespeare or most of his spectators can accept. He glorifies it, and in so doing, he defines himself as better than he is. This element of self-glorification is absent from most of the explicit evocations of role-playing, but the *act* of projecting a representation of the self which is superior to the reality is entirely typical. It is without doubt the most characteristic act of the play.

Shakespeare's version of the actual striking down of Caesar, for example, is as much as anything else a moment of sardonic humour ironically exposing the absurd pretensions of a self-deluded fraud. Caesar cannot be persuaded to change a decision, he assures Brutus and the others, because he is as 'constant as the northern star, / Of whose true-fix'd and resting quality / There is no fellow in the firmament' (III.i.60-2). The world, he continues, is

> furnish'd well with men,
> And men are flesh and blood, and apprehensive;
> Yet in the number I do know but one
> That unassailable holds on his rank,
> Unshak'd of motion; and that I am he,
> Let me a little show it, even in this – (66-71)

The appeals persist, however, and Caesar must make himself more emphatically clear: 'Hence! Wilt thou lift up Olympus?' (74). There can be no doubt how this imperfect human regards himself, despite his age and infirmity, his partial deafness, and his epilepsy. In his own eyes, as Cassius has perceived, Caesar is not only the most perfect of men but even more: a god, a true resident of Olympus. And so, naturally, he speaks and acts accordingly. But although he strives constantly to play the god, he continually betrays his human frailty. 'Wilt thou lift up Olympus?' he cries out; and yet he is about to be struck down by the knives of his assailants, about to perform the most characteristically human (or 'mortal') act possible, that of dying. This final view of Caesar is in perfect keeping with Shakespeare's entire presentation of him. While Cassius' account of Caesar's physical deficiencies (I.ii.93-131) is a complex speech that says perhaps even more about Cassius than about Caesar, it does explicitly establish the theme of Caesar's incongruous assumption of godlikeness ('this god did shake,' 121), and each of Caesar's subsequent appearances keep this incongruity in the forefront. Shakespeare's Caesar has scarcely any reality apart from his highly ironic attempt to play a role for which he is utterly unfitted.

Cassius is a more complex and in many ways a more self-aware character than Caesar, but he also suffers from self-delusion, as is revealed by his motive for the assassination. His eventual characterization of himself and the other conspirators as 'men that gave their country liberty' rings oddly coming from him because he has clearly held, and all but expressed, a far more personal motive for killing Caesar. 'I cannot tell what you and other men / Think of this life,' he says to Brutus, in broaching the subject of doing *something* about Caesar, 'but, for my single self, / I had as lief not be as live to be / In awe of such a thing as I myself' (I.ii.93-6).

Cassius at once enlarges the ranks of those equalling Caesar to include Brutus, and in his next speech he removes himself even further from the centre of attention through his sarcastic talk of '*we* petty men,' his assurance, 'The fault, dear Brutus, is not in our stars, / But in ourselves, that *we* are underlings' (136, 140-1; italics added) and, especially, his insistence that the name *Brutus* is as fair as Caesar's (142-7). Nevertheless, Cassius obviously thinks primarily of himself rather than Brutus or some collective 'we.' In his speech on Caesar's infirmities, he measures Caesar and finds him wanting, not in relation to all men but to himself, and, in keeping with the feeling of superiority this gives him, he views Caesar's political success not as a public scandal but as a personal injustice: 'And this man / Is now become a god; and Cassius is / A wretched creature, and must bend his body / If Caesar carelessly but nod on him' (115-18). Furthermore, although Cassius needs Brutus and the others to help him correct this injustice, he certainly does not regard them as his equals in worth. He assumes naturally the role of leader in relation to most of them, and although he flatters Brutus in order to ensure his participation, he considers him as nothing more than a useful tool. This, his true view of Brutus, is amply conveyed by his soliloquy concluding I.ii and by his later remark to Casca: 'Three parts of him / Is ours already, and the man entire / Upon the next encounter yields him ours' (I.iii. 154-6).

Cassius sees himself as the true Caesar; he already plays this role in his imagination, and he seeks, through the conspiracy, to set the stage so that he can also play it in reality. His discrepant role-playing is less advanced than Caesar's but quite clearly a valid and central fact of his identity. His career also differs from Caesar's in that its irony is less explicit, less insistent than the irony of the mortal immortal. But the irony of Cassius' career is fully evident. It is writ large in the failure of the conspiracy and Cassius' consequent death. It is also, moreover, implicit in Cassius' actual position in relation to the two figures that most frustrate his hopes. Despite his feeling of injustice, the fact remains that it *is* Caesar, not Cassius, who has achieved such a high state of success. And although Cassius conceives the conspiracy and seduces Brutus into joining it, it is Brutus, not Cassius, who ends up as the actual leader of the conspiracy. Cassius sees himself as the true Caesar, but in reality he always remains (wherever the fault may lie, in the stars or in himself) an 'underling.' One is almost tempted to say, an 'understudy.'

The role Brutus claims and plays but cannot really fulfil is the one Antony refers to again and again in his funeral oration. Brutus is, or so he believes, an 'honourable man.' He thinks only of 'the general good' (I.ii.85), can be provoked to act against Caesar only to prevent tyranny, wants the conspirators to 'be sacrificers, but not butchers' (II.i.166), and wishes they 'could come by Caesar's spirit, / And not dismember Caesar' (169-70). He and Cassius both use the word 'honour,' but while Cassius is thinking of personal glory, Brutus means moral purity and integrity, that which compels the good man to act uprightly and to do so in a positive way – that is, by actively making sure that things which should be done get done.

One dramatic fact casting a good deal of ironic light upon Brutus' presentation of himself is Cassius' manipulation of him. Brutus' complete ignorance about what Cassius is doing to him (or, for that matter, about the true state of his entire relationship with Cassius) is in itself sufficient to make him look rather naive and thus cast doubt on any favourable self-impression he might project. Cassius, moreover, deliberately heightens the effect by mocking in his soliloquy Brutus' pretensions to nobleness and honour:

> Well, Brutus, thou art noble; yet, I see,
> Thy honourable metal may be wrought
> From that it is dispos'd. Therefore it is meet
> That noble minds keep ever with their likes;
> For who so firm that cannot be seduc'd? (I.ii.307-11)

But Brutus' own soliloquy in II.i is even more destructive. Here he expresses more clearly than ever his refusal to act in such a consequential and questionable business as the assassination without just, public motives, and yet, at the same time, he resolves to so act while revealing his utter unfamiliarity with any such motives. This man of perfect honour resolves to kill Caesar because Caesar *may* become dangerous to 'the base degrees / By which he did ascend':

> Then, lest he may, prevent. And since the quarrel
> Will bear no colour for the thing he is,
> Fashion it thus – that what he is, augmented,
> Would run to these and these extremities;
> And therefore think him as a serpent's egg,
> Which, hatch'd, would as his kind grow mischievous,
> And kill him in the shell. (II.i.28-34)

The decision to take such an important step purely on the basis of possibilities and virtually manufactured suppositions ('Fashion it thus') suggests that Antony may well be right when he later implies that 'honour' is merely an empty word for Brutus. Certainly, it is not a word that Brutus gives thought to, in order that it may have concrete meaning, but one he uses as a substitute for thought, apparently believing that since *he* is 'honourable' whatever he fancies doing must also be honourable. Brutus is perfectly capable of deliberately creating a fraudulent impression, as his behaviour to Caesar demonstrates and as the odd double account of Portia's death may also exemplify, but it seems clear that in playing the fraudulent role of the honourable man he deceives himself as well as others. Like Caesar and Cassius, he holds a distorted conception of his own nature.

Brutus' discrepant role-playing has a further dimension, and his desire to be honourable contributes to this one in a different way. Both the decision to preserve Antony and other followers of Caesar despite the objections of Cassius

and the decision to let Antony address the Romans indicate that Brutus can
actually manage to devise and carry out concrete acts of honour. But there is
also irony here, of course, for these acts as much as anything else cause the ultimate downfall of the conspirators. To the extent that Brutus does manage to
behave honourably, then, he cripples himself for successful action in the realm
of practical affairs. This is why, I believe, Shakespeare puts so much emphasis
on Brutus' relations with Portia and with Lucius his servant-boy – and why of
all the characters in the play, only Brutus is allowed to be seen in other than his
public manifestations. Brutus views himself as the true heir of the ancestor who
drove 'The Tarquin' from the streets of Rome (II.i.53-4) and therefore as qualified to fill the public role of Rome's saviour now that conditions make this role
necessary once more. In Shakespeare's eyes, however – and thus in those of the
spectators – Brutus shows himself to be far more suited to the roles of private
life.

Antony's discrepant role-playing occurs during the second half of the
play and closely resembles that of Cassius. His soliloquy near the end of III.i,
just after the assassination, is entirely concerned with the horrid revenge he
vows to wreak against 'these butchers' (256); and this, it seems, is the only intention the death of Caesar has occasioned for him. In IV.i, however, as he and
Octavius and Lepidus make plans for the future, revenge is not once mentioned. The three triumvirs concern themselves with the political power they
will hold once they defeat Brutus and Cassius, and they show that they intend
to hang on to it. Antony, moreover, indicates that he regards this power primarily as his own personal possession. He contemptuously dismisses Lepidus
as 'a slight unmeritable man / Meet to be sent on errands' (IV.i.12-13), he reminds Octavius, 'I have seen more days than you' (18), and, essentially, it is
he that makes the primary decisions in the scene. Antony has clearly assumed
the leadership of the triumvirate and regards himself, evidently, as Caesar's
heir. But just as Cassius is destined to remain an underling, so is Antony. His
reign is short. The next time he appears (v.i), Octavius has already assumed
control, though Shakespeare also manages to represent the shift in power within the scene:

> ANTONY Octavius, lead your battle softly on,
> Upon the left hand of the even field.
> OCTAVIUS Upon the right hand I: keep thou the left.
> ANTONY Why do you cross me in this exigent?
> OCTAVIUS I do not cross you; but I will do so. (v.i.16-20)

Four lines later Antony calls Octavius 'Caesar' for the first time in the play,
and by the end of the play the only function he still retains seems to be that
of saying nice things about the fallen enemy. The final speech belongs to the

new Caesar. It deals with practical arrangements for Brutus' funeral, the disposition of the troops now that the battles have ended, and the dividing of the
spoils. It is intrinsically a far less interesting speech than the one by Antony
just before it, but it prevents any doubt about who finally guides the destiny
of Rome.

The three other characters that participate in discrepant role-playing are
much less central to the action, but they help substantially in amplifying its
primary theme. Casca's coarse, cynical manner, according to Cassius, is a 'tardy
form' that he deliberately 'puts on' (I.ii.298). Cassius thinks that this exterior
conceals a genuine enthusiasm for any 'bold or noble enterprise' (297), but the
fearful, superstitious attitude Casca reveals towards the storm in I.iii suggests
that his tough-guy pose may well be intended to conceal something a little less
praiseworthy. Portia believes that her identity as daughter of Cato and wife of
Brutus renders her worthy enough for Brutus to take her into his confidence,
to share with her the secrets of such obvious import which trouble him, but
Brutus has not treated her as she deserves, and this makes her 'Brutus' harlot,
not his wife' (II.i.287). Since Brutus agrees to share his secrets with her, and
her anguish in II.iv indicates that he has done so, Portia actually becomes what
she considers herself to be, but Shakespeare gives far more emphasis to her original expression of failure than he does to her ultimate success – it is the first
of these motifs that is the fully dramatized one – and Portia is, moreover, the
only one participating in the discrepant role-playing who manages to eliminate
the discrepancy. Cinna the poet certainly does not. He has as much right as
Portia to actually be what he takes himself to be – he really is, after all, Cinna
the poet – but the wild mob of III.iii nonetheless determines that he shall for
all practical purposes possess a different and less desirable identity: if not that
of Cinna the conspirator, at least that of Cinna the victim of their vengeance.

The examples of Portia and Cinna differ slightly from the others, but all
these characters, without exception, exemplify a discrepancy between what
they esteem themselves to be and what they really are – by nature, by the circumstances others force on them, or by a combination of the two. The characters of *Julius Caesar*, in other words, are remarkably similar to the characters
of *Twelfth Night*, especially Malvolio and Sir Andrew Aguecheek. And this resemblance is appropriate enough. *Julius Caesar* was written at pretty much the
same time as *Twelfth Night*, at the start of the brief span of years during which
discrepant role-playing was the dramatic theme (and act) that interested
Shakespeare the most.

There are, however, some important differences between the two plays.
In *Twelfth Night*, Shakespeare establishes his characters' true selves quickly,
perfunctorily, and for the most part indirectly: he is here fascinated by the distorted self-conceptions and the characters' efforts at playing them. In *Julius
Caesar*, it is almost the reverse: he gives much more attention to the true, in-

ferior selves, and he exposes them – along with the great breadth of the gap separating them from the distorted self-conceptions – with emphasis and even violence. *Julius Caesar* thus dramatizes human failure by stressing the unsatisfactory reality man experiences despite his grandiose dreams. The more important difference between the two plays is that while in *Twelfth Night* the contrast between the two selves, the false and the true, is essentially a spatial phenomenon (for example, Malvolio's discrepant role-playing consists at any given moment of the steward's inappropriate assumption of the role of count), in *Julius Caesar* the contrast is both spatial and temporal. What the characters of *Julius Caesar* exemplify can be described as a contrast between what they esteem themselves to be and what they really are, between their false and their true selves, between dream and reality. The action of the play, however, is such that the condition its characters exemplify is more accurately described as a contrast involving not only the opposition between what they esteem themselves to be and what they really are but also the additional and more prominent opposition between their aspirations and what really happens to them. The 'unsatisfactory reality' man experiences despite his grandiose dreams has also another and perhaps better name: it is 'history.'

Julius Caesar, with its notorious clock, may not always *be* good history, but it is very much about history, and almost explicitly so. Cassius' anticipation of future plays on the assassination, for example, is a challenge to the spectators to compare his assumptions with the facts and attitudes they have acquired through their familiarity with history, and most of them will necessarily realize that while Cassius represents things one way, history has represented them in quite another. More important, however, is the fact that Cassius' challenge prompts the spectators to become aware of the phenomenon of history in itself, so that it becomes a valid, almost conscious element of their experience of the play. Much the same thing occurs on each of the numerous occasions when a character prophesies about the future, which for the audience is the past, something that history has already settled, usually in such a way that the character is proven wrong. And, given this context, much the same thing probably occurs every time one of the characters whose historical career is especially familiar conveys any assumption about himself that does not coincide with the way things have actually turned out, any time he plays the role conceived by his own self-esteem rather than the role written for him by history.

Cassius, who began with the belief that man has full control over his destiny, eventually comes to realize that 'the affairs of men rest still incertain' (v. i.95). A few minutes later, as the battle of Philippi is about to begin, Brutus expresses his anxiety about the outcome:

> O that a man might know
> The end of this day's business ere it come!

> But it sufficeth that the day will end,
> And then the end is known. (122-5)

Cassius' change of mind and Brutus' suggestion that the outcome of an event is somehow autonomous record their partial realizations that history is an active force operating independently of the wills of individual men. Shakespeare dramatizes this idea of history by constantly keeping his spectators aware of history as a phenomenon while they watch his play. He also manages to embody the force of history in one of the concrete elements of the action. The last character to gain prominence in *Julius Caesar* is the only important character not participating in the discrepant role-playing. Octavius Caesar remains exempt from the ironic contrast between dream and reality because he has no imagined conception of himself which the reality of history can mock. He does not, like Caesar or Brutus, assume a manner foreign to his true nature, nor does he, like Cassius, betray aspirations not in harmony with his accomplishments. Even more than Bolingbroke on his way to the kingship in *Richard II*, Octavius Caesar simply acts: he exists only in and as his accomplishment, which is the accomplishment of the historical Octavius Caesar. He is therefore less a character than an embodiment of history. As an agent in the narrative design, he prevents Antony from fulfilling his aspirations; as an element of the symbolic design he represents the force that trips up all the others.

Julius Caesar could be described as a play about the difficulty of producing historical drama. For Shakespeare, in focusing on the imperviousness of history to the human will, dramatizes not only the plight of his historical characters but also his own as a writer of historical drama. He can, he knows, fiddle with the incidental details of history to his heart's content – Hotspur's real age or the lack of clocks in ancient Rome do not ultimately matter – but he cannot alter or ignore the major familiar facts of the historical record. And he must, he believes, express through his play the basic truth these major facts embody. He is therefore, in a way, in much the same position as his characters; he too is to some extent a victim of history, though not quite to the same extent. For them the clash between imagination and the reality of history has an unequivocal and consistent outcome: history denies their dreams. But history is by no means total victor in its clash with Shakespeare's imagination. The play itself is one proof of this, in its successful moulding of the details of history in order to shape forth more clearly the truth they tend to obscure – here, ironically, the truth about the indifference of history to imagination. And there is also within the play a more immediately conspicuous, more spectacular sign of the refusal of Shakespeare's imagination wholly to yield to history. This sign is Shakespeare's deliberately restoring to some of his characters the dream that history has denied them.

What prevents the characters from converting their dreams into reality is their human limitations: their individual weaknesses and their common inability to force history to shape itself in accordance with their aspirations. Their mortality is the chief cause for several of the characters, for with them the primary weapon of history is death. Yet these are the same characters to whom Shakespeare can restore the dream that history denies. Death mocks the characters' discrepant role-playing, but it also frees them from the tyranny of history. Caesar alive cannot be the god he dreams of being because he is a man. But in death he exists only through Antony's verbal account of him. There is no human – and therefore limited – figure to contradict the supernatural image Antony projects when he speaks of Caesar as 'the heart of' the world (III.i.209), as a 'bleeding piece of earth' (255), and as a non-pareil: 'O, what a fall was there, my countrymen!' (III.ii.190); 'Here was a Caesar! When comes such another?' (253).

Cassius dreams of himself as the true Caesar but in life can be no better than an 'underling.' When he dies, however, he becomes in Brutus' words exactly what he had hoped to be:

The last of all the Romans, fare thee well!
It is impossible that ever Rome
Should breed thy fellow. (v.iii.99-101)

Brutus' primary conception of himself as a public figure of merit unalterably governed by allegiance to strict principles of honour is belied by his actions and by the full reality of his situation. With his death, his contradictory actions cease and his situation loses its relevance. He becomes, as it were, the appropriate subject of Antony's eulogy. As he had himself imagined, he 'was the noblest Roman of them all':

His life was gentle; and the elements
So mix'd in him that Nature might stand up
And say to all the world 'This was a man!' (v.v.68, 73-5)

Shakespeare does not finally, however, allow this victory of imagination to deny or even obscure the basic truth dramatized throughout the play: the last speech, properly enough, goes to Octavius Caesar. *Julius Caesar*, as a result, though categorized as a tragedy, proves to be more truly a history play than those ordinarily so designated. They are history plays chiefly in the sense that they take their subjects from English history, but they would more accurately be described as plays about kingship. *Julius Caesar*, on the other hand, takes history itself as subject by dramatizing it as an active force. Unlike most history plays, by Shakespeare or others, *Julius Caesar* is actually a play *about* history.

The only other play by Shakespeare that could be called a history play in this sense is *Troilus and Cressida*, which also compels its audience to respond to the characters and events on the stage through the perspective of history, even though, of course, these characters and events actually derive from legend.

The vows of Troilus, Cressida, and Pandarus in iii.ii parallel Cassius' anticipation of future dramas on the assassination, fulfilling the same sort of function even more openly and with even heavier irony. Troilus vows his eternal constancy to Cressida by saying that 'True swains in love shall in the world to come / Approve their truth by Troilus' and that in 'their rhymes,' when all the trite similes about truth have been sounded in vain, ' "As true as Troilus" shall crown up the verse / And sanctify the numbers.' Cressida vows her constancy by devising a curse to which she will be subject should she 'be false, or swerve a hair from truth'; if so, she says, 'When time is old' and Troy and other mighty cities 'grated

> To dusty nothing – yet let memory
> From false to false, among false maids in love,
> Upbraid my falsehood when th' have said 'As false
> As air, as water, wind, or sandy earth,
> As fox to lamb, or wolf to heifer's calf,
> Pard to the hind, or stepdame to her son' –
> Yea, let them say, to stick the heart of falsehood,
> 'As false as Cressid.'

'Go to, a bargain made,' Pandarus concludes: 'If ever you prove false one to another, since I have taken such pains to bring you together, let all pitiful goers-between be call'd to the world's end after my name – call them all Pandars; let all constant men be Troiluses, all false women Cressids, and all brokers between Pandars. Say "Amen" ' (iii.ii.169-200).

By playing on his audience's knowledge that the vows have all come true as expressed, Shakespeare juxtaposes the speakers' historical moment to the moment the play is being performed, a moment he gives additional dramatic focus to a few seconds later by having Pandarus step forward and speak to the audience directly:

> And Cupid grant all tongue-tied maidens here,
> Bed, chamber, pander, to provide this gear! (206-7)

The characters view themselves at a point within their history, but the audience, reminded that it exists 'when time is old,' must view them from 'the world to come,' from a point when the characters' history is finished, decided, and perpetually frozen. The audience is made to experience not just the characters'

dreams but also the mockery of these dreams by history, made to realize the
truth of Troilus' fear (expressed later on) that 'something may be done that we
will not' (IV.iv.93). Cressida would be true, faithful, constant, but history –
her nature in combination with her circumstances – turns her into the most
famous symbol of inconstancy of all time. Pandarus sees himself as a sort of
whimsical and jolly old fellow whose only concern is to derive pleasure from
helping to bring about the lovers' happiness, but history, the course events take,
redefines him as a pimp and, at least in name, the father of all future pimps.
The contrast between dream and reality is less immediately apparent in Troilus'
case, for his name *has*, as he hopes, become a byword for constancy. Nonetheless, the Troilus-the-true of history is by no means quite the same as the fate
Troilus here envisions for himself. He imagines not only his constancy but also,
as an apt reward, eternal happiness as Cressida's lover. The Troilus-the-true of
history, on the other hand, is much more the naive victim suggested by Troilus'
later answer to Cressida's question about whether he will remain true:

> Who, I? Alas, it is my vice, my fault!
> Whiles others fish with craft for great opinion,
> I with great truth catch mere simplicity. (IV.iv.101-3)

The visions of themselves which Cressida, Troilus, and Pandarus project
and which history has already mocked resemble the false self-conceptions held
by the characters of *Julius Caesar*. Shakespeare does not, during the recital of
the vows, explicitly associate the ironic contrast involving Cressida, Troilus, and
Pandarus with the idea of role-playing, but the association is clearly implicit in
the action as a whole. Prior to III.ii, Troilus and Cressida have both engaged in
discrepant role-playing in some form. Troilus is introduced in the opening scene
playing a rather conventional version of the lover, and this role is made to seem
inappropriate not only because of its artificial character but also because it unmans him: it makes Troilus the warrior perform the 'womanish' act (I.i.106)
of shunning his proper arena, the field of battle. Cressida, in the following scene,
struggles bravely to convince Pandarus of her lack of interest in Troilus, of her
indifference to love; she conceals her true feelings behind this mask in order to
build up Troilus' desire: 'Men prize the thing ungain'd more than it is,' she
knows, while 'Things won are done' (I.ii.279, 281).

Whether or not a spectator will associate the discrepant role-playing of
these initial glimpses of Troilus and Cressida with the ironic contrast evoked
by the vows of III.ii cannot, of course, be said. This particular association is unnecessary, however, for act V contains more substantial images of role-playing
which pertain directly to the vows and involve all three characters. In v.ii, Cressida entertains Diomedes at her father's tent, while Troilus and Ulysses watch
from a distance and are in turn observed by Thersites. This careful positioning

of onstage spectators creates the effect of placing both Cressida and Troilus on a stage, thus defining them as actors playing parts and doing so in a context directly connected with the vows because it dramatizes the extent to which these vows have held up. The parts Cressida and Troilus play on this temporary stage-upon-the-stage are not the misconceptions of themselves and their lots which they have been improperly acting out but instead the parts written for them by history. Cressida's response to Diomedes demonstrates her infidelity, Thersites underscores it with his nasty comments, and Troilus draws the appropriate conclusion:

> O Cressid! O false Cressid! false, false, false!
> Let all untruths stand by thy stained name,
> And they'll seem glorious. (v.ii.176-8)

Troilus himself, despite this ultimate response, spends most of the scene acting out the role history has written for him of naive constancy, first through the patience he strives to retain, primarily through his rationalization that it is 'Diomed's Cressida' he observes (135), not his own. 'Will 'a swagger himself out on's own eyes?' asks the incredulous Thersites (134), and Troilus makes the same point about his performance in less contemptuous terminology: 'Never did young man fancy / With so eternal and so fix'd a soul' (163-4). Pandarus is absent during this scene, but he gets his opportunity to play his true role – the role history has cast him in – openly and unequivocally at the end of the play when, with the stage to himself, he steps forward to chat with the audience as the pimp that Troilus has just declared him to be. Pandarus' speech also frees the audience from the obligation assigned it by the opening line of the Prologue to regard the scene as Troy. The only moment any longer having dramatic validity is the moment in time of the performance. The victory of history is now entirely complete.

This victory also includes the conquest of history with regard to another set of characters in the play, the Greek and Trojan heroes providing the 'war' side of Thersites' 'still wars and lechery' (v.ii.192). Shakespeare introduces this dimension of his action through the Greek council meeting of i.iii, and the initial impression is an odd one indeed. The scene contains the famous speech on 'degree' which has served commentators so well, but *dramatically* the scene arouses interest through what Shakespeare reveals about its speakers, Agamemnon, Nestor, and Ulysses, all of whom indulge extensively in bombast, inflated rhetoric, over-elaborate and over-extended but essentially empty ceremony, and in strained, obscure, learned diction of a type rare in Shakespeare: several of the words used here and in other passages by the Greek and Trojan heroes do not occur elsewhere in Shakespeare's plays. Ulysses may have something impressive to say, but it seems quite unnecessary to the occasion, and for the

most part the effect of the council meeting is to make these great figures seem
rather pathetically ludicrous.

This scene follows immediately after the introductions of Troilus and
Cressida, both of whom perform discrepant role-playing, and the notion of
discrepant role-playing is also made explicit within the scene when Ulysses describes the unacceptable behaviour of Achilles, who has been lying in his tent,
mocking their designs:

> with him Patroclus
> Upon a lazy bed the livelong day
> Breaks scurril jests;
> And with ridiculous and awkward action –
> Which, slanderer, he imitation calls –
> He pageants us. Sometime, great Agamemnon,
> Thy topless deputation he puts on;
> And like a strutting player ...
> ...
> He acts thy greatness in; and when he speaks
> 'Tis like a chime a-mending; with terms unsquar'd,
> Which, from the tongue of roaring Typhon dropp'd,
> Would seem hyperboles. At this fusty stuff
> The large Achilles, on his press'd bed lolling,
> From his deep chest laughs out a loud applause;
> Cries 'Excellent! 'tis Agamemnon just.
> Now play me Nestor; hem, and stroke thy beard
> As he being drest to some oration.' (I.iii.146-53, 158-66)

Ulysses continues in the same vein for several more lines, and in III.iii what he
here describes becomes dramatized when Thersites (the foul and nasty Thersites) assumes the title role in his 'pageant of Ajax' (III.iii.269), thus further
mocking a hero that Shakespeare has already transformed to such an extent
that he seems less Á-jax the Greek warrior than A-jáx the Elizabethan convenience of such puns as 'Ajáx employ'd plucks down Achilles' plumes' (I.iii.386).

Ulysses' long account of Patroclus' dramatic activity, both in its sum and
in its details, easily serves as a commentary on the ludicrous impression he,
Agamemnon, and Nestor are in the process of creating. It is as if Ulysses were
trying to explain this version of the Greek heroes by suggesting to the spectators that instead of seeing the real thing they are watching bad imitations produced by malicious actors – or, perhaps, by grossly inept ones. Aeneas reinforces this suggestion upon his entry through his inability to pick out Agamemnon, even though, surely, a 'god in office,' someone so 'high and mighty'
and possessing 'most imperial looks' (I.iii.224, 231, 232) ought to be easy

enough to spot. As further Greek heroes (especially Ajax and Achilles) appear, and as Thersites' pageant echoes and reasserts the suggestion of Ulysses, the action involving these famous heroes comes more and more to evoke the sense of a large-scale 'Show of the Nine Worthies.' This one does not, however, mock the inept actors, for they do not genuinely exist. It mocks, instead, the heroes themselves by equating them with the impression of inept acting that can be felt in their performances. It cuts them down, debases them, insists that they are in reality far inferior to their historical reputations, no matter how strenuously they try to create an appropriate projection of themselves.

The Trojan heroes are not so severely subjected to mockery and ridicule as the Greeks, but they by no means evade it entirely. The Trojan council meeting of II.ii seems more rational than that of the Greeks as well as being devoid of gross ludicrous effects, but ultimately these characteristics serve most to heighten the shock of Hector's sudden and highly irrational capitulation. Even more in the same vein as the treatment of the Greeks is the portrayal in III.i of Paris and Helen as a couple of jaded sophisticate lovers seeking cheap thrills in order to keep themselves titillated. Shakespeare seems frequently tempted to accept Hector as a true worthy and dramatize him accordingly, but there is nonetheless Hector's performance in the council meeting, as mentioned, and when he arrives at the Greek camp in IV.v Shakespeare cannot resist having him sound as if he had been taking lessons in rhetoric from his enemies.

By and large, therefore – although there are exceptions and the impression is not constantly maintained with its usual vigour – these famous heroes of legend demonstrate a sharp contrast between their real worth and the inflated conceptions of themselves they perform so badly. As it happens, these inflated self-conceptions correspond to the reputations they have acquired and which have become an integral part of the history passed on to the spectators watching Shakespeare's play. These reputations, Shakespeare implies, are a supreme example of the over-prizing with which *Troilus and Cressida* is so much concerned. And they constitute as well a supplement to the lesson conveyed by the careers of Troilus, Cressida, and Pandarus, a further demonstration of the might of history. For despite the ineptness of these mediocre figures, the impossibility of their ever living up to the version of them handed on by Homer and others, it is this version that has survived – survived so well, in fact, that although the spectators of *Troilus and Cressida* may enjoy Shakespeare's witty exposure of these fraudulent heroes, the attitude they hold towards them after leaving the theatre will most likely, as Shakespeare certainly knew, continue to resemble the one they held before they came. History can build up as well as tear down. Some of the roles it writes for the individuals whose memory it preserves may destroy the dream, but history can also invent the dream, can make it the substance of the roles its actors must play through all time.

Troilus and Cressida has prompted much debate about whether it is a tragedy or a comedy. I would suggest that it is neither and that, moreover, though called a 'History' on its original title-page, it is also not a history play in the term's usual sense. Like *Julius Caesar*, which it closely resembles thematically, it belongs to a fourth genre consisting of plays *about* history as opposed to plays simply based on it. *Troilus and Cressida* seems to have been written as much as two years after *Julius Caesar*, and the difference in tone and mood between the two plays suggests the difference in these respects between *Twelfth Night* and *All's Well that Ends Well* – or even *Measure for Measure.* Nevertheless, *Troilus and Cressida* and *Julius Caesar* fit well together. Because of its considerable amount of comedy, *Troilus and Cressida* might well be regarded as the comic subplot *Julius Caesar* otherwise lacks.

8 The tragic pattern

> Poor Turlygod! poor Tom!
> That's something yet. Edgar I nothing am. (*King Lear*, II.iii.20-1)

Shakespeare's creation of a special kind of history play in writing *Julius Caesar* cannot, very probably, be attributed to a conscious intention of enlarging the existing dramatic types. *Julius Caesar* is obviously an attempt to write tragedy, and if it has become something else, this is only because of the special development Shakespeare has given certain characteristics typical of the early tragedies, *Titus Andronicus, Romeo and Juliet*, and *Hamlet*. These differ from one another in many significant respects, either because Shakespeare is experimenting as he searches for a tragic pattern, or because he simply brings to full realization the patterns inherent in his sources; but all three have at least two important characteristics in common. The death of the hero closes the action, and while his death signifies great loss, it is at the same time partially redeemed through equally sure implications of triumph. These early tragedies are also characterized by an attempt to provide the hero with an appropriate tragic setting. His world is defined as one in which action produces reaction, in which initiated actions do not necessarily end as planned but frequently must give way to other, superior actions that cut through and thus cut off the original ones.

In the earliest tragedy, curiously enough, it is the hero himself who instigates the reaction. The 'timeless tragedy' (II.iii.265) to which Tamora and Aaron subject Titus during the first half of *Titus Andronicus* is motivated by Tamora's desire to wreak revenge on her enemy, but Shakespeare dramatizes it from Titus' point of view, so that the spectators perceive it as a tragedy of suffering, a series of increasingly agonized responses to increasingly vicious horrors. Titus complicates the action during the second half by taking command of it and reversing its direction. For the tragedy of suffering that Tamora and Aaron have initiated, he substitutes a genuine revenge tragedy, which ends with their destruction. It also ends, of course, with his own destruction, as it must. In making himself a revenge tragedy hero, he has necessarily also guaranteed his own death.

One could say that Titus' own play has had to yield to the superior action represented by the entire revenge tragedy pattern, that no matter what he may have intended when initiating the action of revenge, once he has done so, the progress of this action no longer lies in his control but must follow its stereotyped course and conclude with a climax that encompasses both the successful fulfilment of the revenge and the death of the revenger. Shakespeare does not fully dramatize this effect, however, because he establishes no clear distinction between the revenge tragedy as Titus plans it and the course it finally takes. As a result, the tragic setting of action-producing-reaction depends for its existence almost exclusively on the one sure instance in which the first wave of the play yields to the second. In *Romeo and Juliet*, on the other hand, the thwarting of one course of action by another, the turning of one kind of play into another, is constant. Here, moreover, the tragic setting is more clearly tragic from the hero's point of view, because it is the hero – in this case, both Romeo and Juliet – at whom the various reactions tend to be directed.

Romeo mentally enacts from the beginning of the play a Petrarchan love drama, which he tries to impose on external reality as soon as he has met and fallen in love with Juliet. Their familial identities, however, make them liable to a different kind of action, that of the feud between the Montagues and the Capulets, and prevent them from fully acting out the roles they seek to play in the drama of love. They must try to satisfy themselves with a secret marriage, but the opposing action intrudes almost immediately. The assault by Tybalt, the killing of Mercutio and Tybalt, the banishment of Romeo – these incidents not only temporarily force the love drama off Shakespeare's stage, they also alter its shape and give it new plot twists. And they completely transform the mood of *Romeo and Juliet* as a whole from the light, gay, comic one that has prevailed throughout the first two acts to the desperately urgent, sombre, threatening – and therefore 'tragic' – one that governs the rest of the play almost entirely.

It is, however, the next phase of the opposing action which more effectively suggests the notion of another *play* competing with the one Romeo and Juliet have sought to enact. Tybalt's attack is a single, sudden, and immediately consequential incident, but Capulet's contribution to the counter-action (his decision that Juliet must obey him and wed the County Paris on the following Thursday) promises, like a play, a specific, devised action extending through a certain amount of time and prescribed roles that its various actors – principally Juliet – must assume and fulfil. Juliet herself heightens this impression of play and counter-play by seeking help from the friar, who concocts his desperate scheme with the potion to serve both as a playlet to counter Capulet's and as the final act in the love drama, which will thereby end triumphantly. The Friar's playlet will free her from 'this present shame,' he assures Juliet, 'If no inconstant toy nor womanish fear / Abate thy valour in the acting it' (IV.i.118-20), and on the eve of her 'acting' in his playlet, she picks up his histrionic image in order to give it full development:

> I have a faint cold fear thrills through my veins,
> That almost freezes up the heat of life;
> I'll call them back again to comfort me.
> Nurse! – What should she do here?
> My dismal scene I needs must act alone. (IV.iii.15-19)

These words explicitly characterize the friar's scheme as a playlet. Juliet's next words, in which she anticipates in gruesome detail the horrors of the vault should she wake too soon, endows this playlet with an atmosphere that mocks the friar's good intentions and any hopes his scheme may have aroused. These words virtually promise that the friar's playlet, like *Romeo and Juliet* as a whole, will transform itself into a tragedy. Primarily because of the plague and the impossibility of the friar's letter getting through to Romeo, the promise of Juliet's words is fulfilled. Once more, and with finality, another, counter-action cuts across to thwart an action initiated by, or at least on behalf of, the tragic hero and heroine. This final counter-action also characterizes itself as a kind of play (because of the great emphasis on coincidence) and this play issues not from one of the characters but (as its nature implies) from the dramatist himself. He now intrudes and interferes with the plans and hopes of Romeo and Juliet so that they can finally play their assigned roles in the drama of sacrifice and redemption anticipated in the prologue.

The contribution Romeo and Juliet make to ending the family feud is not the only element of triumph in their deaths. Titus Andronicus' death derives its triumphant qualities from the same source that renders it necessary: the conventions of the revenge tragedy pattern. Romeo and Juliet rise above the drama requiring their deaths, however. They almost manage to counteract even this final thwarting force because they endow their deaths with a personal significance that is neither inherent in nor necessary to the drama of sacrifice and redemption. Romeo and Juliet have acted otherwise, but they possess complicated identities: they are members of their respective families as well as lovers. They have been unable to relate the familial role with the role of lover except by preferring the one to the other or, when forced to acknowledge the equal validity of both, by employing the oxymorons through which they express their sense of the incompatibility between the two roles. Both devices constitute denials of their identities, and death results. But death also forces upon them something they can no longer dismiss. They must try to find a way of coping with death, of reconciling it with the longing they feel for each other. The means they find is the richly complex language of their final speeches, in which artificial oxymorons have yielded to more spontaneous, closely packed figures that fuse the opposites rather than hold them apart be-hind the walls formed by frozen verbal patterns. They finally discover, in other words, a vehicle allowing them to experience for both themselves and the spec-tators the complexity which their identities have always implied but which for so long they strove to deny.

The images of role-playing in *Hamlet*, which are numerous and constant, include the travelling players and their performance of 'The Murder of Gon-zago,' acts of spying which transform other occasions into further plays-within-the-play, countless evocations of discrepancy as existing roles are violated, misperformed, and miscast, and various attempts by the characters of the play to become its dramatist. What may well be the chief sign of the concern with role-playing, however – as well as the most unusual and interesting one – is the steady recurrence of a particular type of speech that is employed at one time or another by nearly all the major characters. The three speeches at the beginning of III.ii in which Hamlet not only explains to the travelling players the theoretical basis of their art but also directs them in its practical appli-cation – in which, that is, he tells them how to play their parts – call attention to and emphasize his and his fellow characters' preoccupation with the type of speech whose form and content he here makes explicit. The giving of ad-vice on how to behave for the moment or for ever – in effect, the defining for another of how he should play his part – is one of the most characteristic acts of the play, perhaps its *most* characteristic act.

Act I scene iii, with Laertes' warning to his sister, Polonius' 'few pre-cepts,' and his repetition, with emphasis, of Laertes' warning, scarcely contains anything other than speeches of advice, but although the characters' tendency to address each other only for this purpose is probably most noticeable in I.iii, it has been well established before this scene and continues to manifest itself throughout the play. Horatio's attempts to get the Ghost to respond as desired probably reflect the tendency, but it is first clearly established in I.ii, in the speeches of Gertrude and Claudius requesting Hamlet to 'cast [his] nighted colour off' (I.ii.68) and to 'throw to earth / This unprevailing woe, and think of us / As of a father' (106-8). Other prominent directorial speeches include those that Claudius addresses to Rosencrantz and Guildenstern (II.ii.10-18) and Laertes (IV.v.136-45, 199-208, IV.vii.1-5, 128-39); those of Polonius to Reynaldo (II.i.1-73), Ophelia (III.i.43-9), and Gertrude (III.iv.1-5); Horatio's two warnings to Hamlet (I.iv.62-81, V.ii.201-10); and the Ghost's commands of I.v. Hamlet himself contributes not only his advice to the players but also his insistence to Horatio and Marcellus that they not give him away should he 'think meet / To put an antic disposition on' (I.v.169-80) and his various pleas to his mother in III.iv. In their attentiveness to details of speech, gesture, and even costume, Hamlet's speeches especially illustrate the extent to which the speech of advice more often than not transcends simple command to evoke genuinely the notion of a full-scale role whose specific attributes the speaker is carefully outlining.

The characters' delight in advising one another can be coupled with another widespread trait: the confident assurance of Hamlet's fellow characters that they can understand and explain him. These traits suggest that the characters generally hold a rather naive view of experience. They see it, evidently, as elementarily simple, easily defined and categorized, and readily translatable into clear and precise patterns of behaviour which are evident to anyone (except, of course, the uncomprehending recipients of their advice). They seem to feel that experience is capable of being mastered and that they hold the necessary key.

This view of experience is a naive one under any circumstances, and it comes to appear especially odd and mistaken in the world of *Hamlet*, where experience has been rendered even more complicated than usual through the breakdown of the basic units by means of which man holds on to at least partial and tentative order in the universe. Claudius doubly embodies the theme of discrepancy because his duplicity, the contrast between his true self and the mask he exhibits publicly, reflects the further and even more important contrast he acts out: the discrepancy between his qualifications and the social office he has obtained through murder. Claudius as king symbolizes the state of roles generally in Denmark, for the basic units of order in society, the standard familial and social roles, have all had, or are in the process of having, their validity cancelled out because of violation, misappropriation, or some form of interference preventing proper, effective performance.

Claudius' act of murder also violates the role of brother, leads to corruption of the marital roles – it is, of course, Hamlet who especially urges this view – and makes it impossible for Hamlet to play his roles in relation to both his father and mother. The familial relationships linking Polonius, Laertes, and Ophelia are, on the evidence of I.iii, obviously corrupt, and Polonius scarcely improves things by sending Reynaldo to Paris to spy on his son, an act that also involves corruption of the master-servant relationship. Laertes and Polonius work successfully to hinder Hamlet's and Ophelia's fulfilment of the lover's role; Rosencrantz and Guildenstern contribute their eager, flagrant, self-interested violation of friendship; and in act IV, as if to provide a suitable climax, the king and one of his courtiers plot the murder of the prince. The perfect commentary on this thorough corruption and cancellation of the standard roles comes from Hamlet, in his creation of the freakish hybrids, 'uncle-father and aunt-mother' (II.ii.372), and in his calling Claudius 'dear mother' (IV.iii.49).

The characters' naive assurance that they can master experience with ease is made to seem even more ironic through what ultimately happens to them. Their assumption about experience makes it possible for most of them to decide quickly and decisively how they wish to behave, but the results almost never prove satisfactory. Many of the speeches of advice, such as Polonius' precepts and Horatio's warnings, advocate a policy of playing it safe and not asserting oneself. Ophelia, who decides to obey her father, follows this policy and goes mad. The majority of the characters, including some who have advocated the policy of playing it safe, ignore it in order to follow more active courses, and most of them lose their lives. Claudius, Polonius, Laertes, Rosencrantz, Guildenstern, and Gertrude can each be said to have been in one way or another 'Hoist with his own petar' (III.iv.207), and in most of these cases something of the sort actually *is* said. They all experience, in other words, something very much like the thwarting reaction felt by the characters of *Julius Caesar, Troilus and Cressida, Titus Andronicus*, and *Romeo and Juliet.*

Claudius, with Laertes' help, brings *Hamlet* even more in line with *Titus Andronicus* and *Romeo and Juliet* by acting as amateur dramatist. In IV.vii, he and Laertes define the forthcoming duel as a playlet through the care with which they plot it out. Hamlet's somewhat cryptic remark to Horatio about the 'they' that 'had begun the play' before he 'could make a prologue to [his] brains' (v.ii.30-1) pertains to Claudius' manoeuvre of sending him to England to be disposed of, so that this plan, too, becomes defined as a play of sorts. Hamlet's remark is part of a context in which he describes how he has revised this manoeuvre of Claudius' by giving it his own ending, one that contains his resolution definitely to kill Claudius now that he has been able to return safely. Hamlet also thwarts Claudius' playlet of the duel. When it has ended, Hamlet addresses those on the stage who have not participated in it as 'You that look pale and tremble at this chance, / That are but mutes or audience to this act' (326-7). His theatrical imagery applies equally to both of Claudius' play-like actions, the England manoeuvre and the duel, each of which has just played out, at the same moment, its final scene. Hamlet's words underscore Claudius' attempt to master experience through dramatizing it; and they occur at a time when the sight of Claudius' dead body vividly demonstrates the totality of his failure.

It is, as I have noted, Hamlet's speeches to the players which especially call attention to the pervasiveness of directorial advice, and Hamlet also contributes a number of further, more blameworthy speeches of this sort. His whole involvement with role-playing differs significantly from that of the others, however, because it reflects an intelligence and sensibility more in tune with the real nature of his world. His involvement with role-playing is established almost at once, when he assures his mother, and, of course, all other members of the court, that although the external signs of his mourning are indeed 'actions that a man might play' (I.ii.84), he is not at all merely playing. He has 'that within which passes show' (85), and this means that the role of the public mourner, however theatrical and showy it may be, provides a legitimate vehicle for the expression of his feelings. Unlike the others, however,

Hamlet has not fully surrendered himself to his role. His awareness of it as something histrionic indicates that he feels at least a partial separation between it and himself, as if it did not – as it cannot – fully express all dimensions of his nature.

Hamlet's first soliloquy reveals his lack of any role that might serve such a purpose. The loss of his father through death and the loss of his mother through her transformation into something other than the conception he has held of her have deprived him of his roles in relation to them, and he has, as a result, experienced the loss of his identity. Consequently, he no longer feels at home in the world. He has become a mere object, a body without any coherent non-material dimension, and so, like Richard II, he yearns for the appropriate state of non-existence which death brings. It may, that is, indeed be the solidity of his flesh with which he is concerned rather than its having been 'sullied.'

Despite Hamlet's initial lack of any role except that of the mourner, one of the most noticeable characteristics of his behaviour is his refusal to play the parts others outline for him. This is observable at once in I.ii, when Gertrude and Claudius try to get him to end his mourning as the other, sensible members of the court have done, and, like them, freely go along with 'this affair' (I.ii.15-16) – that is, with the death of old Hamlet, Gertrude's remarriage to Claudius, and Claudius' assumption of the throne. Hamlet cannot and will not accept this attempt to mould his behaviour. He resists it as decisively, if not as explicitly, as he later rejects the efforts of Rosencrantz and Guildenstern to define him and to play upon him as on a pipe (III.ii.354-63). This rejection provides an especially clear symbol for all of Hamlet's similar acts of resistance, but long before it occurs he has already been performing the steadiest and most remarkable act of this sort, his failure to perform the role of revenger assigned him by his father's ghost, despite his initial declaration that he will assume the role at once and immediately carry out its demands.

Hamlet's stubborn resistance to the directorial efforts of others suggests his independence from them with regard to assumptions about experience. He does not, obviously, share their naive confidence about the ease with which experience can be formulated – at any rate, he certainly does not value the particular formulations they have come up with. But since he also resists the Ghost's attempt to impose on him a role he should want to play, his resistance suggests even more. Hamlet has apparently been able to perceive the condition of the standard roles in his world, to realize how they have all been rendered empty of meaning. For he behaves as if all roles have become suspect for him and he can no longer accept any role as a potentially valid expression of himself or entrust himself to any role with a sense of security.

Other aspects of Hamlet's involvement with role-playing help confirm these implications of his resistance. As a playmaker, for example, he is quite unlike Claudius, Polonius, or Laertes. They, with their certainty about themselves and the world, try to manipulate experience by moulding large chunks of it into closely plotted playlets. Hamlet, who cannot do this, acts spontaneously or not at all; his playmaking, therefore, must consist of his involvement with an actual play, 'The Murder of Gonzago,' which he takes a hand in partly to have something to do, partly to try to establish for himself at least one bit of certainty. But Hamlet's realization about the state of roles in his world is perhaps most strikingly demonstrated by the last version he supplies of the most pervasive type of speech in the play. Hamlet often uses this speech-type unquestioningly. He tells Horatio and Marcellus how to conduct themselves should he ever put on an antic disposition, he advises the players on their art, and, especially, he urges his mother to adopt a pattern of behaviour designed to purge and save her soul (III.iv.144-70). Suddenly, however, when she asks, 'What shall I do?' he shatters the form that he and the others have so often endorsed:

> Not this, by no means, that I bid you do:
> Let the bloat King tempt you again to bed;
> Pinch wanton on your cheek; call you his mouse;
> And let him, for a pair of reechy kisses,
> Or paddling in your neck with his damn'd fingers,
> Make you to ravel all this matter out,
> That I essentially am not in madness,
> But mad in craft. (180-8)

The speech continues for a few more lines in the same vein, and while all of it urgently communicates the need Hamlet feels to direct his mother's actions, the inversion and consequent rejection of the form through which such direction must be given also communicates, and just as urgently, Hamlet's profound doubts about the legitimacy of what he wants so much to do.

Hamlet resists the efforts of others to impose roles on him because no role seems valid any more. Nevertheless, he obviously feels the need for some kind of role through which he can once again acquire an identity, or he would not be constantly grasping at substitute roles, at makeshift sets of gestures and moves that can serve him as vehicles of expression without his having to commit himself wholly to them. The first of these is the role of mourner, but it cannot fully express him, and in any case it cannot last long: already the pressure on him to abandon it is keen. He replaces it with the far more flexible 'antic disposition,' with its wide variety of effects and especially the dimension of madness that serves so well as an outlet for his anguish and uncertainties and as an appropriate response to his perceptions about the world. At times, especially in III.ii before, after, and even during 'The Murder of Gonzago,' he expands the framework of the antic disposition so that it can include brief and rapid performances, one after the other, of his fellow characters' various notions about him. And in III.iii and III.iv, as he busies himself with the damnation of Claudius and the salvation of his mother, he suspends performance of the antic disposition in order to try to play God.

Ultimately, Hamlet can cease playing – or play-acting – these substitute roles because he finds at last a role seemingly imposed from outside which he can accept and willingly submit to. The experiences of his sea-voyage convince him that there is, after all, 'a divinity that shapes our ends' (v.ii.10), and that this divinity watches over him in the same way that 'there is a special providence in the fall of a sparrow' (211-12). He knows that this divinity has saved him from the fate Claudius had planned for him and also made it possible for him to return to Denmark. Now that he has come back, he talks of his revenge as 'perfect conscience' (67) and asks 'is't not to be damn'd / To let this canker of our nature come / In further evil?' (68-70). The 'interim,' he believes, is his (73), yet instead of acting, he waits patiently, and when, in the form of the duel, an occasion for acting presents itself, he accepts it despite his own misgivings and Horatio's attempt to stop him. Hamlet has obviously submitted his will to that of the divinity he has perceived. He has assumed in earnest the role he was playing while attempting to substitute for God: he has become the 'scourge and minister' of heaven. He finds, as a result, for the first time in the play a clear-cut pattern of action to follow, a pattern that permits him to act with firmness and certainty at last.

It is difficult to speak with full confidence about what happens finally in *Hamlet*. Hamlet seemingly purges Denmark of evil, himself dying in the process as a necessary sacrifice; his loss is great, but his death is also made glorious and triumphant through what he has accomplished by it. There are, however, other ways of regarding Hamlet's death. His acquiring the capacity to act with firmness and certainty because he has accepted a role as valid puts him in much the same position as that in which most of his fellow characters began. One is tempted to say that Hamlet's tragedy lies in his losing the power to resist, that like the others he has naively accepted an over-simplified version of experience and must, like them, pay the price. And although in becoming the scourge and minister of the heavens he thwarts Claudius' plays, it might also be said that Claudius and Laertes equally thwart his, or at least give to the play in which he has accepted a role an ending different from the one he has expected. It is not, of course, entirely clear what sort of ending Hamlet expects. His promise, associated with the 'scourge and minister' speech, to 'answer well / The death' he gave Polonius (III.iv.176-7) suggests he may indeed expect the ending that occurs, but certainly he also assumes that the ending will somehow 'report [him] and [his] cause aright' (v.ii.331) – which never happens. To this extent Hamlet unequivocally is thwarted, and perhaps even more so. Laertes' insistence, at the time of Hamlet's death, that he and Claudius have both been hoist with their own petars suggests that much the same may also be true of Hamlet. Perhaps, as well, the two opposing internal dramas – Claudius' and the one Hamlet acts in – should be seen not as simply having thwarted each other but instead as having combined to produce the counter-action that thwarts them both.

This view of the ending of *Hamlet* links the play closely with *Romeo and Juliet*. But *Romeo and Juliet* is clear-cut and definite in a way that *Hamlet* cannot equal. In *Romeo and Juliet* Shakespeare defines experience as tragic by confidently viewing it as a process of action and reaction: actions are thwarted because those who plan them provide them with too narrow a compass – as when Romeo and Juliet try to ignore their familial roles and act only on the basis of their roles as lovers. *Hamlet* uses many of the same devices and motifs as *Romeo and Juliet* to suggest that experience, even the portion of it which the play has carefully shaped, is too uncertain to be defined, and that it is *this* which makes it tragic. No action can succeed as planned because experience is too uncertain, too unfathomable to allow confident reliance upon any formulated pattern for ordering one's behaviour – even though such an ordering is apparently at least a psychological necessity.

It seems incongruous to classify *Hamlet* among the 'early tragedies,' to link it with *Romeo and Juliet* and *Titus Andronicus* instead of with the later masterpieces that share its complexity, but I have made this classification because of the centrality in *Hamlet*, as theme and dramatic design, of the action-reaction pattern. Certain prominent elements of *Hamlet* nevertheless bring it more in line with the later plays. Hamlet's feeling of being out of place in the world, his expression of the suffering he experiences because he has lost his identity, is one of these elements. The other consists of his enthusiastic playing of nonce-roles, as if he were compelled to assume some kind of role and, lacking more adequate and appropriate vehicles of expression, had to content himself with makeshift substitutes. These two dramatic motifs, with a greater causal relationship than this description of them indicates or, indeed, than is clearly dramatized in *Hamlet* form Shakespeare's primary tragic pattern, the pattern that shapes decisively, though in different ways, *Othello*, *Macbeth*, *King Lear*, *Coriolanus*, and *Timon of Athens*.

The beginnings of this pattern, oddly enough, lie in a comedy, *The Comedy of Errors*, whose characters are constantly threatened with loss of identity, since every attribution of false identity in the play simultaneously denies the identity the character thinks he possesses. This side effect of the false attributions need not have had any dramatic importance, but Shakespeare gives it importance by emphasizing his characters' responses to the threat of loss. As the action develops, these responses tend to become increasingly extreme and cataclysmic, both for the character whose identity is threatened and for those who threaten him.

Antipholus of Syracuse, the visiting Antipholus, is the first to be threatened, when he mistakenly believes Dromio of Ephesus to be *his* Dromio and therefore interprets Dromio's untimely jesting as mockery of his role as master. But Antipholus readily averts the potential disaster by beating Dromio and thereby re-establishing both his role as master and his threatened identity. The local Antipholus also overcomes with comparative ease the first threat to his identity. When his wife denies him, his immediate impulse is to reassert himself by breaking down his door – thus emulating his twin from Syracuse – and although his friends restrain him from acting upon this impulse, he nevertheless manages to preserve his identity by quickly adopting a different stratagem. He activates one of the other roles forming his identity, the role he possesses by virtue of his relationship with the Courtesan:

> You have prevail'd. I will depart in quiet,
> And in despite of mirth mean to be merry.
> I know a wench of excellent discourse,
> Pretty and witty; wild, and yet, too, gentle;
> There will we dine ...
> ...
> Since mine own doors refuse to entertain me,
> I'll knock elsewhere, to see if they'll disdain me. (III.i.107-11, 120-1)

But the threats continue, and soon both Antipholuses find themselves in situations they cannot cope with as readily. The subsequent errors confronting the visiting Antipholus and Dromio prompt them to begin to doubt their own identities and suspect that they have stumbled into some 'fairy land' (II. ii.188) inhabited by 'goblins, owls, and sprites' (189), 'witches' (III.ii.154), 'Lapland sorcerers' (IV.iii.11), and 'fiends' (60). They feel, in other words, a profound sense of dislocated reality, especially Antipholus, who comes to look upon his present existence as an illusion or a dream:

> Am I in earth, in heaven, or in hell?
> Sleeping or waking, mad or well-advis'd?
> Known unto these, and to myself disguis'd! (II.ii.211-13)

He has wholly lost his bearings and can conceive of no other response than to adopt what can be regarded as, in dramatic terms, a highly promising version of the local Antipholus' first expedient. Antipholus of Ephesus, when one of his roles is denied, immediately assumes another in its place. The visiting Antipholus, whose whole identity is denied, must instead take on a discrepant role. Since he cannot be what he always has been, he decides to play along with those who define him as someone else; he decides to 'say as they say, and persever so, / And in this mist at all adventures go' (214-15).

The local Antipholus, whose predicament becomes even more cataclysmic, eventually reaches a point where the only remedy he can still perceive for holding on to his proper identity is outright violence of a sort far more severe than a simple beating like that which the visiting Antipholus administered. 'Dissembling harlot,' says the local Antipholus to his wife,

> thou art false in all,
> And art confederate with a damned pack
> To make a loathsome abject scorn of me;
> But with these nails I'll pluck out these false eyes
> That would behold in me this shameful sport. (iv.iv.98-102)

His wife and others threaten his identity by imposing a false one on him, and he is nearly ready to try preserving himself by destroying them and thereby also destroying the false identity that they impose. His condition is by no means very far removed from the madness attributed to him by his wife, the Courtesan, and others. The visiting Antipholus has already associated madness with identity loss by wondering about this own sanity (ii.ii.212), and the adversaries of the local Antipholus reinforce this association when they charge the local Antipholus with madness simply because in their eyes he no longer acts in conformance with his original identity. No one in the play actually goes mad because of identity loss, but the connection between the two has obviously already begun to interest Shakespeare a good deal.

This linking of identity loss with the sense of dislocated reality and madness indicates that Shakespeare already conceives of the nexus of roles which form a character's identity as the source of his bearings, the means by which he locates himself within and orders himself in relation to the wilderness of the universe. The character's roles equip him with the gestures and moves he needs in order to act precisely and securely, both for the particular moment and throughout a whole career. Conflicting roles can complicate an identity and create uncomfortable or destructive collisions, as the case of the local Antipholus shows (not to mention the more decisive case of Romeo and Juliet), but judging from both *The Comedy of Errors* and the great tragedies, Shakespeare sees the loss of identity as the far greater problem – as, in effect, the tragic problem par excellence. This loss destroys the character's bearings and instantly deprives him of order, so that necessarily his surroundings seem altered, less appealing, even threatening and sinister, while he himself stands on the verge of madness (which, after all, constitutes an extreme form of lost bearings). The character who has lost his identity or is threatened with such a loss thus occupies a position of high dramatic potential. He must respond to the loss or threatened loss in some decisive and appropriate way – again judging from both *The Comedy of Errors* and the great tragedies, by going mad, resorting to violence, finding new roles to play, or perhaps, by some combination of all these expediencies.

Shakespeare's comedies make little use of the element of *The Comedy of Errors* just outlined; as I argue in chapter 5, they derive from another element of *The Comedy of Errors* and dramatize the pattern of losing oneself to find oneself. In the great tragedies, on the other hand, this early and highly tentative investigation of identity loss finds its natural territory for fruitful development. In the tragedies, losing oneself is not a necessary and ultimately beneficial stage in the progress towards final happiness. It is to lose all, to be torn loose and cast adrift in a void without dimensions. It is to be exposed to an experience that no one can survive.

Despite the high dramatic potential of the pattern and the relative fullness with which its basic lines have already been worked out in *The Comedy of Errors*, Shakespeare does not begin to exploit it for several years. Christopher Sly, Kate, Valentine, and Hermia all experience an identity crisis of some sort, and all respond by expressing a sense of dislocated reality, a perception of life as a dream (Sly and Kate) or as hell (Hermia) or as an emptiness devoid of light, joy, music (Valentine). Valentine and Henry vi both tend, moreover, to exemplify with more or less clarity the attempt to compensate for identity loss by finding new roles through which the self might be preserved and expressed. And undoubtedly there are also other moments in the early plays which exemplify elements of the pattern. In every case, however, these exemplifications merely *are* moments; they constitute unemphasized, even incidental, details of the plays in which they occur. Most of the characters in the early histories suffer a fall that is in part represented by the loss of an important (and obviously definitive) role, but the dramatic focus tends to be the fall itself as a fact of action far more than the effect this fall has as identity loss for the character experiencing it. *Titus Andronicus* and *Romeo and Juliet* offer ample opportunity for exploiting the pattern, but, despite Titus' madness, Shakespeare is in both plays preoccupied with a different notion of tragedy.

Shakespeare's true exploitation of the pattern does not begin, therefore, until *Richard II*, but in this play (as my analysis in chapter 6 should demonstrate) the pattern has attained full and central representation and has given the action its most significant and compelling dimension. *Richard II*, which effectively exemplifies the history play pattern, is thus also Shakespeare's first tragedy in his primary mode. The second, despite the relative prominence the pattern achieves in *Hamlet*, is *Othello*.

Othello's involvement with role-playing is explicitly signalled quite early, in the first scene he appears in, when he prevents the battle between Brabantio's men and his own:

> Hold your hands,
> Both you of my inclining and the rest.
> Were it my cue to fight, I should have known it
> Without a prompter. (I.ii.81-4)

The imagery of cue and prompter, which the role-playing of Iago in the opening scene should help to stress, identifies Othello as an actor whose part is that
of the warrior. But the imagery has more importance for the service it provides
in helping the spectator to perceive and place certain prominent qualities in
the language of Othello's other speeches from this and, especially, the following scene. Othello is very much aware of his merits – 'My parts, my title, and
my perfect soul' (31) – and does not hesitate to talk about them, to celebrate
them even. There is, moreover, an extreme carefulness in his manner, which
manifests itself most noticeably in his speech to the Duke and the Senators in
I.iii.

Unlike Brabantio, Othello does not simply speak but delivers an oration.
Brabantio is governed by the emotional upset he feels, while Othello seems excessively attentive to his audience – 'Most potent, grave, and reverend si-
gniors, / My very noble and approv'd good masters' (I.iii.76-7) – and excessively concerned with constructing a specific impression of himself as one too
'rude' of speech to defend himself effectively because he has spent most of his
life 'in the tented field':

> And little of this great world can I speak
> More than pertains to feats of broil and battle;
> And therefore little shall I grace my cause
> In speaking for myself. Yet, by your gracious patience,
> I will a round unvarnish'd tale deliver
> Of my whole course of love. (81-91)

This is, of course, a standard trick of the clever orator (Antony uses it in
Julius Caesar), and therefore a more important indication of Othello's attempt
to control his audience's impression of him is the shrewd way he manages to
dramatize his heroic, exotic, and moving life while reporting that he had won
Desdemona by dramatizing it.

One other detail of Othello's performance should also be mentioned –
his flair for unusual words, the ease with which he glides from the 'antres vast'
of his autobiographical narrative (140) to the 'agnize' that he uses in dealing
with the more abstract subject of his personality (231). Othello leans towards
words of the sort Agamemnon, Nestor, and Ulysses are guilty of in *Troilus and
Cressida*, yet while this tendency in them helps put them in a ludicrous light,
Othello has established a stature that can sustain his words – and be enhanced

by them. His words enlarge the sense of dignity surrounding him, but their rarity nonetheless calls attention to them and makes it clear that it is a sense of dignity carefully and deliberately cultivated. The speaker of 'Keep up your bright swords, for the dew will rust them' (I.ii.59) can also be heard in these peculiarities of diction.

Othello's careful, controlled presentation of himself as meritorious is neither play-acting nor discrepant role-playing, but it is touched by both. His position in Venice and the Duke's response to him indicate that his dignity is deserved, yet he wears it in a highly histrionic fashion. He consciously plays himself by acting out his dignity and meritoriousness. There is, of course, a clearly recognizable explanation for this behaviour in his immediate situation. He feels defensive from the very beginning, knowing, even before Iago warns him, that he will have to cope with Brabantio's attempts to undo his marriage and perhaps destroy his career. Nevertheless, this Othello is the one Shakespeare introduces the spectators to; they may very well perceive a reason for the histrionic manner, but they cannot think of Othello apart from it. The tendency to theatricalize thus seems a fundamental part of his nature, one that his immediate situation does not create but merely renders especially visible.

Othello's tendency to act his own identity suggests his particular enjoyment of it. It is as if he were especially pleased with himself, not only for having won Desdemona from all the curled dandies of Venice but also because of his social position and the importance it lends him. There is also, however, another possible explanation for his tendency. By playing his own identity, he evokes the notion of a felt discrepancy, of a felt lack of full equivalence between this identity and himself. The impression conveyed is that he harbours doubts about whether he actually deserves this identity or whether it genuinely expresses him; and he overplays it, apparently, in order to help convince himself and others of its validity.

I am suggesting, in other words, that Othello's defensiveness does not pertain only to his worry about Brabantio but colours his entire relationship with the world outside himself. He is, as it were, unsteady on his own feet and in need of strong supports to keep him from toppling, supports like the Duke and, especially, Desdemona. The fact that he has won her provides him with his surest justification, not only because of what she signifies but because he is so certain of her love. He knows he can rely on her, and so he comes to depend on this reliance, to depend wholly upon it: 'My life upon her faith!' (I.iii.294); 'Excellent wretch! Perdition catch my soul / But I do love thee; and when I love thee not / Chaos is come again' (III.iii.91-3). She is, he says, the place

> where I have garner'd up my heart,
> Where either I must live or bear no life,

> The fountain from the which my current runs,
> Or else dries up. (iv.ii.58-61)

His 'Chaos is come again' is especially suggestive because although he apparently means the primeval chaos, his words can also denote a more personal chaos whose recurrence – or perhaps first encroachment – he deeply fears. His love for Desdemona, at any rate, is his guarantee of personal order. Should anything cause him to stop loving her, all his supports will collapse along with this supreme one, and his location in the universe will be utterly eliminated.

Othello's somewhat precarious situation, despite the histrionic aura he gives it, scarcely qualifies as a play of the sort Romeo and Juliet or Claudius devise, but he too must confront a counter-action consisting of a play engineered by another. The extreme contrast between Othello and Iago also extends to their histrionic activity, for where Othello's play-acting is moderate, perhaps not fully conscious, and designed to preserve, Iago's is destructive in intention, highly calculated, and constantly operative whenever he is in the presence of another. Iago, whose credo reads 'I am not what I am' (i.i.66), is a worthy successor of Richard III, and only in his soliloquies or under the cover of darkness does he say or do anything not suiting his fictitious role of 'honest Iago.' Like Richard, he is also an accomplished play-maker, as he demonstrates at once in the opening scene by shaping, with Roderigo's carefully coached assistance, the scene of disorder that sends Brabantio in search of Othello. This episode also serves as a prologue or opening scene for the primary play Iago directs against Othello. This one, which the spectators can see gradually taking shape in Iago's mind from soliloquy to soliloquy, betrays its play-like qualities most obviously in iv.i, when Iago manipulates Cassio and Bianca like puppets while Othello forms an audience of one as well as an unsuspecting participant.

This play has overtones of the revenge tragedy, with Iago taking the part of the just avenger, and further overtones of a comedy of cuckoldry, in which Iago as clever servant helps his master Roderigo-Cassio cuckold the *senex* with the young and beautiful wife. Primarily, however, what Iago seeks to shape is a melodrama of Mediterranean passion with Othello taking the lead role while Iago himself, as he says, assumes the part of the 'villain' (cf. ii.iii.325, 337). It is difficult to say what ending Iago has devised for his play, if, indeed, with his extemporaneous methods, he has actually planned that far ahead. But Cassio eludes him, and he himself is caught after trying desperately to silence Emilia, and therefore it seems clear that Iago, like the play-makers of the earlier tragedies, suffers the typical fate of having his own action thwarted by a counter-action. This does not occur, however, before he succeeds in getting Othello to destroy Desdemona and himself.

Iago's manipulation of Othello includes persuading him to avenge the crime Desdemona has, he thinks, committed against him, but the success of Iago's play is already assured before that, as soon as he manages to dislodge Othello from the identity he has worked so hard to keep. In addition to persuading Othello to accept the role of cuckold, Iago also, with uncanny perceptiveness, seeks to increase the sense of dislocation Othello has betrayed. He helps Othello build his feeling of being a man out of place, a Moor *in* Venice, by suggesting that Othello trusts his wife only because he does not, like Iago, sufficiently know 'our country disposition' (III.iii.205) and by reminding Othello how much he differs in appearance from the native Venetians. Minutes later, after Iago has left him alone, Othello seizes upon these insinuations and adds to them, shaping the whole into a declaration of his unfitness for the role of lover:

> Haply, for I am black
> And have not those soft parts of conversation
> That chamberers have, or for I am declin'd
> Into the vale of years – yet that's not much –
> She's gone. (267-71)

Othello's acceptance of himself as cuckold destroys for him the role he has selected for his main one, that of the lover, and because he has come to depend so much on his relation to Desdemona, he loses as well his other roles, primarily his role of Venice's highly valued general. His discovery that his wife has cuckolded him becomes his cue for bidding 'Farewell' not only to 'the tranquil mind' and 'content' – and thereby further showing his increasing sense of dislocation – but also to 'the plumed troops, and the big wars / That makes ambition virtue': 'Othello's occupation's gone' (352-4, 361). For one brief moment, moreover, Othello even has an inkling of being cast adrift in a universe without meaning and clarity. He rapidly approaches full belief in Iago's lies and insinuations, but at one point he can still cry out, 'I think my wife be honest, and think she is not; / I think that thou art just, and think thou art not' (388-9).

Two moments in IV.i mark the climax of Othello's complete loss of identity. The more verbally explicit of these is Lodovico's expression of shock after seeing Othello strike Desdemona:

> Is this the noble Moor whom our full Senate
> Call all in all sufficient? Is this the nature
> Whom passion could not shake, whose solid virtue
> The shot of accident nor dart of chance
> Could neither graze nor pierce?

'He is much chang'd,' Iago replies (iv.i.261-5). The true climax has already occurred, however, and consists of what Iago calls Othello's 'fit': the momentary
total collapse marked by Othello's almost incoherent 'Lie with her – lie on
her?' speech (37-44), which reflects the incoherence of his now crumbled self,
and by his falling into a trance. This speech is far more than a jealous rage. It
proves that Othello has seen the utter nothingness also seen by Richard II, the
void without bearings into which loss of identity precipitately leads. Othello
does not, like Richard, try to describe or even name it, but he enacts his contact with it through his speech, and the impact it has on him is amply testified
to by his loss of consciousness.

Othello can bear the glimpse of nothingness no better than Richard
could. He, too, must recoil from it and find some form of response to protect
himself from it. Encouraged by Iago, one of the responses he adopts is that of
violence. He decides to kill the woman who has undermined his identity by
making his role of lover impossible to play. He seeks to preserve himself by
destroying what threatens him. He also adopts, however, another response, one
with greater dramatic potential because of the abundance and variety of episodes it promises, and with richer tragic significance because it constantly
dramatizes the nearness of the void and the greatness of the effort required to
elude it. This other response is one that he shares with Richard, whose desperate search for substitute roles he soon begins to emulate.

Lines like 'I have a pain upon my forehead here' (iii.iii.288) and pieces
of business like the examination of Desdemona's 'moist' hand (iii.iv.30-44)
reflect Othello's attempt to play the role of cuckold, to turn it into a vehicle
for preserving an ordered relationship with his surroundings. Simply adopting
some of the appropriate gestures of this role does not prove entirely satisfying
to him, however; his histrionic nature in conjunction with his feeling of desperate need prompts him to seek further roles and thus to shape the great role-
playing episode of iv.ii, in which he tries to restore certainty to his existence
by concretely dramatizing the version of it that Iago has depicted for him.

Despite Emilia's insistence that Desdemona is 'honest, chaste, and true'
(iv.ii.17), Othello must think of her as a 'subtle whore' (21) and of Emilia, accordingly, as a 'bawd' (20). Consequently, when Emilia returns with Desdemona, he addresses to Emilia a speech that assigns all three of them their appropriate roles in his little playlet:

> Some of your function, mistress:
> Leave procreants alone, and shut the door;
> Cough, or cry hem, if any body come.
> Your mystery, your mystery; nay, dispatch. (27-30)

His own role quickly alters, for with Emilia gone he plays Desdemona's accuser rather than her client. He is too grieved and angry, too outraged over what has been done to him, to be able to keep his mind focused on the *artistic* elaboration of his fiction, and so his dramatization of her as 'whore' consists for the most part merely of his frequent uses of the title (73, 87, 90) or of variations like 'public commoner' (74) and 'strumpet' (83). But as he brings the episode to a close, he resumes full dramatization, introducing this time a new twist designed to give his domestic tragedy cosmic dimensions.

As a whore protesting her innocence, Desdemona is in Othello's eyes 'double-damn'd' (38), as 'false as hell' (40). He therefore appropriately comes to experience her setting, the space she occupies, not only as brothel but also as hell itself. The two conceptions receive simultaneous dramatization when Othello ends the episode by calling Emilia back:

> You, mistress,
> That have the office opposite to Saint Peter
> And keeps the gate of hell! You, you, ay you!
> We ha done our course; there's money for your pains.
> I pray you turn the key, and keep our counsel. (91-5).

His fantasy about visiting hell has probably also an important overtone in his mind. Desdemona the whore has not merely damned herself, she has wrecked his paradise and destroyed the order of his universe; of course her location is hell because she herself is Satan. And Othello, in consequence, is a retreating, defeated Christ whose new effort to harrow hell has proved to be in vain.

Othello's need for substitute roles also prompts him to give appropriate dramatic expression to his decision to kill Desdemona. The highly ritualistic ceremony in which he vows revenge characterizes his decision as the assumption of a role. He adopts the language proper to the role of avenger when he calls upon 'black vengeance' to arise 'from the hollow hell' (iii.iii.451) and when he sounds his cry of 'blood, blood, blood!' (455). His declaration that his 'bloody thoughts, with violent pace, / Shall ne'er look back, ne'er ebb to humble love, / Till that a capable and wide revenge / Swallow them up' (461-4) recalls Hamlet's vow to 'sweep' to his revenge – though not, I think, because Shakespeare wants his spectators to recall *Hamlet* specifically at this point, but for the reason that he regards such a claim as an example of the kind of speech that the role of avenger appropriately calls for.

Othello assumes this role, but he does not remain satisfied with its conventional formulation. Perhaps its primary move, that of delaying, of biding one's time while awaiting an almost heaven-sent opportunity, strikes him as undesirable. Perhaps he regards the standard version of the revenger's role as beneath his dignity. At any rate, with Iago's prompting, he hastens the moment of consummating his revenge, and when he approaches Desdemona's bed, he comes not as the outraged husband or the honour-offended revenger but in a new role, that of sacrificing priest, or of the God of vengeance himself. Prompted by 'the cause' (v.ii.1, 3) and knowing that 'she must die, else she'll betray more men' (6), he sees himself as figuratively wielding a sword of justice (17). He cannot emulate the God of creation by re-illuming Desdemona's light once he has put it out, but he is at least god-like in his grief: 'This sorrow's heavenly; / It strikes where it doth love' (21-2). And again and again, before he kills her, he plays the priest by urging her to pray, to think on her sins, to prepare her spirit for death.

The murder of Desdemona constitutes an appropriate act for the victim of the whore-devil as well as a necessary one for the avenging god-priest, but even though the murder thus helps Othello fulfil his substitute roles, it by no means gives him peace of mind. Almost immediately, he experiences his most acute sensation of dislocated reality yet:

> My wife! my wife! what wife? I have no wife.
> O insupportable! O heavy hour!
> Methinks it should be now a huge eclipse
> Of sun and moon, and that th' affrighted globe
> Did yawn at alteration. (v.ii.100-4)

The slight glimpse he once had of a disordered universe has now developed into a full, terrifying vision. And when he learns that he has fallen for Iago's lies, that it is not Desdemona but Iago and (far worse) himself who must bear the blame for destroying the perfect situation he once enjoyed, the vision takes full hold of him. More than once, he fears his own damnation, but he cannot constantly remain sure even of this horrible certainty, and his prevailing sense of the universe he now inhabits is more accurately reflected when he wonders why something so evil as Iago has not been destroyed – 'Are there no stones in heaven but what serves for the thunder?' (237-8) – when he searches in vain for Iago's cloven hooves – 'I look down towards his feet – but that's a fable' (289) – and when he asks the supremely tragic question his experience as a whole has forced to his lips: 'Who can control his fate?' (268). The man who had once felt out of place in his local environment, who had known what it means to be a Moor *in* Venice, now experiences the sense of dislocation appropriate to all men, which comes from inhabiting an alien universe, whose dimensions, if any, are utterly imperceptible.

Thus deprived of the most important bearings of all, Othello must necessarily be more concerned with what has happened to him than with what he has done. He feels remorse for having killed Desdemona and some grief because she is dead, but mainly he dwells on the vulnerability he has acquired by his crime. Not only has he lost Desdemona for all eternity, but through this act he has also cancelled out for ever the other pillar of his identity, his original role as Othello the valiant hero:

> I am not valiant neither –
> But every puny whipster gets my sword.
> But why should honour outlive honesty?
> Let it go all. (246-9)

Desperately, he tries to hang on to this role, by mentioning, even though alone, the special nature of the sword he still has access to:

> I have another weapon in this chamber;
> It was a sword of Spain, the ice-brook's temper. (255-6)

And he continues to develop this theme when Gratiano returns:

> Behold, I have a weapon;
> A better never did itself sustain
> Upon a soldier's thigh. I have seen the day
> That with this little arm and this good sword
> I have made my way through more impediments
> Than twenty times your stop. (262-7)

He cannot, however, sustain his effort but must again confess, and now more thoroughly, how utterly inappropriate this role has become:

> 'Tis not so now.
> Be not afraid though you do see me weapon'd;
> Here is my journey's end, here is my butt,
> And very sea-mark of my utmost sail.
> Do you go back dismay'd? 'Tis a lost fear;
> Man but a rush against Othello's breast,
> And he retires. (268-74)

The seemingly excessive egotism Othello manifests in this scene, as well as earlier, is not, I think, primarily a quality of his own individuality; as Macbeth's apparent indifference to the news of his wife's death also suggests, the great self-concern may well be inevitable in the basic Shakespearian tragic situation. Loss of identity means that the ties linking one to others have already been severed; there remains, in effect, no one for the victim of identity loss to be concerned with outside himself. And even if there were, the state of identity loss – or, more accurately, the consciousness of this loss and of the abyss that opens before one – creates such a desperate need to struggle for self-preservation that thought of anyone or anything else borders on the impossible.

Othello's final act affirms once more and decisively the kind of need the tragic situation produces. The speech beginning 'Soft you; a word or two before you go' (341) shows once again the oratorical grace and the careful, studied presentation of a self Othello had exhibited in his speech to the Duke and Senators. Then he felt his identity threatened and sought to solidify it through his performance; now he seeks to re-create an identity where none any longer exists and thus preserve himself from the encroaching nothingness. The identity Othello here acts out is his old one. He is once again the valiant hero who has 'done the state some service' (342), and he is also the lover, albeit one that 'lov'd not wisely, but too well' (347) and that, as a result, must accustom his eyes to 'the melting mood' (352). His earlier efforts to re-establish his role as Othello the hero failed because he could not effectively supplement his words with the proper gestures and moves. Now, however, he validates his words through two highly appropriate emblematic gestures (the sword thrust and the kiss); and through his death, he makes sure that contradictory external circumstances cannot mock his performance. Othello the murderer has been absorbed into the 'malignant' Turk, which is only one of the roles Othello now plays. He dies as the malignant Turk, but he also dies as the hero who smote him; and as Desdemona's true and faithful lover, he dies 'upon a kiss' (362). The three roles of malignant Turk, hero, and lover all validly represent aspects of Othello's experience; the necessity of their being maintained through histrionic effort and the fact that this effort constitutes a willed alternative to the perception of nothingness bespeak the thoroughness with which this experience has been a tragic one.

The form of *Othello* is by no means totally different from that of *Hamlet,* as my analyses of the two plays have demonstrated. Both plays are shaped in part by the clash of action and reaction, which I have defined as the chief characteristic of *early* Shakespearian tragedy, and both focus to some extent on what I call the primary tragic situation in Shakespeare. My basis for separating *Hamlet* from *Othello,* therefore, is the difference in emphasis these two formal characteristics acquire in the plays. *Othello* utilizes the action-reaction pattern as a useful dramatic frame (so also do *Macbeth* and *King Lear*), but the spectator of *Othello* is scarcely made to experience this clash as the core of the play. Hamlet undergoes a loss of identity and suffers deeply as a result, but the most forceful expression of this suffering comes too early and too abruptly (rather than as the culmination of an action) to impress itself as dramatically central. And although Hamlet plays substitute roles in response to his loss, this is a factor of the action the spectator must infer; in this play, Shakespeare stresses the role-playing itself rather than its psychological origins. There is, in any case, such an abundance to *Hamlet* that the tragic sequence of

identity loss followed by some kind of appropriate response cannot fully assume control of the action. In *Othello*, of course, it does so. And in *Macbeth*
and *King Lear.*

Three speeches by Macbeth (one of his first, one of his last, and one from the
midpoint of his career) effectively chart out his involvement with role-playing.
In I.iii, with reference to the witches' hailing of him, he observes in an aside
that 'Two truths are told, / As happy prologues to the swelling act / Of the
imperial theme' (I.iii.127-9). In the soliloquy triggered by news of his wife's
death, he defines life as 'but a walking shadow, a poor player, / That struts and
frets his hour upon the stage, / And then is heard no more,' and as 'a tale / Told
by an idiot, full of sound and fury, / Signifying nothing' (v.v.24-8). In III.iv,
he promises the guests at his banquet that he 'will mingle with society / And
play the humble host' (III.iv.3-4).

Before he utters the first of these speeches, Macbeth has already called
the witches 'imperfect speakers' (I.iii.70), as if they were actors who had forgotten their lines or pronounced them indistinctly and thus prevented him
from acquiring the exposition he wants so much to hear ('tell me more,' 70).
His talk of prologues, acts, and themes then defines his encounter with the
witches even more precisely as a theatrical occasion, as the prologue or opening scene of the play he enters into by listening to the witches' hailing of him
and letting their greetings influence his behaviour. His costume for this play
consists of the 'borrowed robes' he accuses Ross of dressing him in (108-9)
and the 'False face' he must wear to 'hide what the false heart doth know' (I.
vii.82). His performance begins almost at once, as he helps strengthen the impression of a play through his play-acting, through his concealing of his true
feelings and intentions either by simply keeping quiet or by professing other
feelings and intentions. The invocations to night and darkness which he initiates in I.iv constitute requests for a setting suitable to the play, and, as Ross
indicates in II.iv, the request is granted. Darkness at noon and other unnatural
phenomena transform Scotland into a domain in keeping with 'the deed that's
done' (II.iv.11) – the murder of King Duncan – and 'the heavens, as troubled
with man's act, / Threatens his bloody stage' (5-6).

The play enacted upon this bloody stage has been set in motion by the
witches and soon comes under the direction of Lady Macbeth, whose efforts
to shape her husband's performance are prominent in I.vii and II.ii. But if his
killing of Duncan is an act others have plotted for him, Macbeth soon reveals
a desire to take over control of the play himself, to make it his play rather than
merely one in which he must act. His decision to kill Banquo and Fleance is
oddly motivated. He begins the soliloquy in which he explains it to himself by
indicating his wish to have the kingship 'safely,' and he mentions the fears
about Banquo that 'stick deep' in him (III.i.47-9), but he never explains how

Banquo and Fleance threaten his safety, and the rest of the soliloquy would suggest that this issue is of minor importance. Far stronger, evidently, are Macbeth's feelings of envy and jealousy and, with regard to his having won the kingship, not fear but disappointment and frustration. He dwells on the idea that he has sinned horribly and forfeited salvation only for the benefit of Banquo's descendants. By killing Banquo and Fleance, he will ensure that Banquo's descendants never wear his crown and thus provide himself with the minor satisfaction of knowing that if he cannot enjoy the kingship neither can they. More important (although this is something he does not seem at all aware of consciously), by killing them he will ensure that the witches' prophecy to Banquo can never be fulfilled. Macbeth will therefore, as a result, be performing an act of his own, one that not only is in no way anticipated by the witches' prophecies but even runs counter to them. He will have seized control of the play.

The escape of Fleance thwarts this attempt by Macbeth to fulfil his apparently unconscious intention and prompts him to seek other means. In IV.i he returns to the witches, demanding that they tell him everything else they know, that they answer all his questions about the future, even if he is to learn the worst. He wants to know how the play will turn out, to possess it by that means since he does not seem able to take an active, collaborative part in the plotting. The witches' series of apparitions provide him with a (mistaken) feeling of security about his own individual future, about the remainder of his part in the play, but then they add a 'Show of eight kings' (IV.i.111,s.d.), which stars Banquo and his descendants and obviously previews the final scene of the internal drama. The show grieves and angers Macbeth, who immediately thereafter – and therefore? – resolves:

> From this moment
> The very firstlings of my heart shall be
> The firstlings of my hand. (146-8)

No longer will he think before acting, either to plan out something in detail or simply to decide upon it; from now on he will merely act. His attempts to possess the play by altering its plot or learning its outcome have led to failure; now it is as if he has decided to try the opposite tactic of wholly extemporaneous action, of possessing the play by eliminating all effects that in any way separate him from spontaneous participation in its inner world.

This tactic succeeds no better than the prior ones, of course. The scene prompted by Macbeth's hideous resolve, the killing of Lady Macduff and her son, is less significant for Macbeth's experience than for its contribution to a further dimension of the inner drama. This is a dimension that Macbeth not only cannot control but also has no knowledge of and, most significant of all, cannot even act in, properly speaking, since the part it calls upon him to play requires only his death. This further dimension of the play is the counter-movement directed against Macbeth of the restoration of Scotland, which ultimately culminates in Malcolm's invasion. It becomes identified as a play, or at least a segment of a play, in IV.iii through Malcolm's play-acting (his pretending to possess all imaginable vices and to lack entirely 'The king-becoming graces,' IV.iii.91) and even more explicitly through the role-playing imagery Macduff uses to transform the slaughter of his family into the first act of a revenge tragedy:

> O, I could play the woman with mine eyes
> And braggart with my tongue! But, gentle heavens,
> Cut short all intermission; front to front
> Bring thou this fiend of Scotland and myself;
> Within my sword's length set him; if he scape,
> Heaven forgive him too! (230-5)

When Birnam Wood comes to Dunsinane and Macduff describes his unnatural birth, Macbeth learns how the witches have equivocated with him. He realizes the absurdity of his desire to possess the play in which he has starred. He has, contrary to his belief, not even known its outcome, and all he has accomplished through his attempt to give this outcome a favourable turn is to help ensure that the inner drama shall shape itself into his tragedy – or, worse yet from his point of view, a kind of morality play in which he gets only the role of 'this fiend of Scotland.' Macbeth's experience thus redramatizes the symbolic action of *Hamlet* and the other early tragedies (as well as, less centrally, *Othello*), the symbolic action that expresses the impossibility of attempts to determine the future, the futility of efforts to become a playwright of experience. For this reason, Macbeth appropriately echoes the prominent theme in *Hamlet* of ironic reversal, of the engineer's being hoist with his own petar (I.vii.7-12). He could with equal appropriateness also have asked Othello's question: 'Who can control his fate?'

Macbeth's assessment of life as a 'poor player' fits effectively into this sequence of action and counter-action, for it helps express the sense of futility instilled in him by his failure to take possession of the play-within-the-play. As in *Othello*, however, the sequence of action and counter-action is secondary, and the speech about life as a 'poor player' is even more expressive as a climax to the central focus of *Macbeth:* its hero's enactment of the primary tragic pattern of identity loss. The third speech by Macbeth that I have singled out, his promise to 'play the humble host,' helps indicate the specific shape Macbeth's enactment of the pattern takes.

Macbeth's original identity is essentially equivalent to a single role. He

begins as 'brave' and 'noble' Macbeth (I.ii.16, 69), the heroic and loyal follower of his king, who acknowledges his perfect fulfilment of his role in calling him, 'O valiant cousin! worthy gentleman!' (24) and later, 'O worthiest
cousin!' (I.iv.14). Both of Macbeth's first two titles, the one he already has and
the other that he earns at the beginning of the play, belong to this role, and
their common element of 'Thane' provides it with an appropriate name. Macbeth's ideal performance of this role is also indirectly testified to by his wife,
when she protests that he 'is too full o' th' milk of human kindness':

> Thou wouldst be great;
> Art not without ambition, but without
> The illness should attend it. What thou wouldst highly,
> That wouldst thou holily. (I.v.14-18)

Macbeth's adherence to his original role is not so perfect, however, that
it prevents him from being disturbed, and tempted, by the witches' apparent
prophecy of his future kingship. He becomes interested in the idea of having
a different, better role to play, and he does not wholly reject the possibility
of seizing this role, and thereby making it a role he cannot in any way be entitled to have. Even this much interest in the new role is enough to dislodge
him from his old one, for almost at once he stops simply fulfilling the part of
the loyal Thane and, as his many asides indicate, begins to play it as if it were
a fictitious role. Lady Macbeth, who persuades him to move from simple interest in the kingship to a full-blown intention of getting the office by murdering its present occupant, helps him separate himself even further from his old
role by transforming it into a mask, the false face he speaks of at the end of
act I. When he has killed Duncan and thus performed the most inappropriate
act a loyal Thane could perform, he loses the ability even to feign his former
role. He can no longer speak the kind of lines that are characteristic of it:

> I could not say 'Amen'
> When they did say 'God bless us!'
> ...
> ... wherefore could not I pronounce 'Amen'?
> I had most need of blessing, and 'Amen'
> Stuck in my throat. (II.ii.28-33)

The role of loyal Thane exists no more, and so, through the histrionic activity
of the Porter, its proper setting, Macbeth's castle, is transformed into the depths
of hell.

The role of king becomes available with Duncan's death, and Macbeth
soon acquires the title. But he does not really thereby gain a new role to re-

place the one he has lost. He must continue to play-act, both before and after his coronation, and the sense of discrepancy this evokes helps characterize his attempt to play the king. News of his coronation, moreover, prompts Macduff to reintroduce the costume imagery and associate Macbeth's occupancy of the kingly office with robes that not only are new but also, quite possibly, ill-fitting (II.iv.38).

The loss of his old role and his failure fully to assume the new one would remain essentially neutral facts, however, if Macbeth himself did not make them dramatically central through his increasing preoccupation with his condition. His coronation is followed almost immediately by his cry, 'To be thus is nothing, / But to be safely thus – ' (III.i.47-8), in which 'safely' is a word chosen virtually at random, as a substitute for the seemingly absurd 'really' that should stand in its place. Banquo's existence troubles him, though not primarily because of fear, or even envy; the trouble with Banquo, according to Macbeth's assessment of him here, is that he seems so perfectly qualified for the role Macbeth now holds: Macbeth uses Banquo, so to speak, as a means of expressing his feeling of his own failure to fulfil the role adequately. Macbeth suffers from sleeplessness, though he also experiences 'these terrible dreams / That shake [him] nightly' (III.ii.18-19). He envies Duncan, sleeping peacefully in his grave, free from 'life's fitful fever' (23). He calls once more on night and darkness and evil, this time as if seeking to make disorder the order of the universe, so that his own internal disorder can become bearable. Macbeth's state is that of the felt dislocation, the sense of existing in chaos, which is experienced by those who have lost their identities.

The banquet scene epitomizes what Macbeth has done. Here he promises to 'mingle with society / And play the humble host' (III.iv.3-4), but as Banquo's murderer, he is totally unsuited to the conviviality and ordered ceremoniousness called for by the part. Despite one or two abortive attempts to keep his promise, he is mainly preoccupied with Banquo's ghost and the terror it causes him. He cannot control himself or conceal his fear and horror and even nearly gives away his guilt. The upshot of his performance at the banquet, therefore, is as Lady Macbeth describes it to him: 'You have displac'd the mirth, broke the good meeting, / With most admir'd disorder' (109-10). Similarly, Macbeth's attempt to play the king – another role he is in no way qualified for – produces disorder on a larger scale, for Scotland and, tragically, for himself.

Through its concern with the issue of Macbeth's manhood, the banquet scene also elaborates the theme of identity loss. Shakespeare has already introduced the issue of manhood in I.vii, when, in reply to his wife's charge that his hesitation about murdering Duncan betokens cowardice, Macbeth insists, 'I dare do all that may become a man; / Who dares do more is none' (I.vii.46-7). He thus associates being a man with properly fulfilling his original role of loyal Thane, and this role tends therefore to become less a role in its own right than an aspect of a far more fundamental role (that of man in the sense of human being) whose loss would be even more crucial. Lady Macbeth disputes her husband's association; she equates being a man with boldly seizing the kingship, and evidently he accepts her new definition because the issue does not come up again until the banquet scene. What counts here, moreover, is not the definition of manhood, but Macbeth's loss of his. The ghost's presence, as his wife implies more than once and as he himself admits, 'quite unmans' him (cf. III.iv.73). Under ordinary circumstances, he claims, he dares do all a man dare do, but the confrontation with the ghost transforms him into 'The baby of a girl' (106). Macbeth's loss of identity also consists, therefore, of his being dislodged from his most fundamental role, and although the ghost's exit prompts Macbeth to feel that he has become 'a man again' (108), Shakespeare's subsequent uses of the term 'man' quite discredit this feeling. Macduff, who assumes the role of avenger against Macbeth, also defines himself as a 'man' (cf. IV.iii.220-1, 230-5), thereby paralleling Malcolm, who has just helped establish Macbeth's unfitness for the kingship by demonstrating himself to be the proper aspirant for the role. When Macbeth learns about Macduff's unnatural birth he as much as admits defeat: the news, he says, 'hath cow'd my better part of man' (v.viii.18). Another parallel involving Malcolm then follows almost immediately: while the title of king passes over to Malcolm, Macbeth's other vacant title is given to Siward's dead son, who 'only liv'd but till he was a man ... / But like a man he died' (40, 43).

The version of the tragic pattern enacted in *Macbeth* dramatizes several of the possible responses to identity loss. One of these is performed not by Macbeth himself but by his wife – and appropriately enough, since she has undergone a parallel experience as well as having had so much to do with his. She has matched his loss of his original roles (and thereby helped give his loss increased dramatic significance) through her more wilful rejection of her role as woman. And although she tries to give him strength as his sense of well-being crumbles, she herself has also felt that 'nought's had, all's spent' (III.ii.4). Her final appearance demonstrates that she too ultimately undergoes full loss of identity even while it simultaneously dramatizes her means of coping with the void that has thus opened before her. Her sleep-walking episode is quite aptly known as a 'scene' in popular parlance because it is exactly that. It is watched by an onstage audience consisting of her doctor and her gentlewoman (who speak of it as one of her 'performances,' v.i.12), and it consists of play-like elements: a ritualistic, repeated gesture stemming from the night of Duncan's murder, and remembered scraps of dialogue, some from herself, the rest from her husband. Her experience has deprived her of her identity by transforming her from herself into a theatrical parody of herself, which she must continue to perform until she dies. She has evidently glimpsed the void and been unable to bear it, for she has hit on a kind of substitute identity whose quality of pastiche characterizes it less as a coherent role than as a form of protective madness.

Lady Macbeth's sleep-walking episode acquires most of its impact through its association with her husband's experience, rather than because her own has been carefully dramatized, and, naturally, it is her husband's various responses to the void that constitute the centre of interest in act v. Macbeth's return to the witches in the preceding act had as one of its purposes the acquiring of some kind of certainty about his future as king so that he might at last feel secure with the role and thus actually possess a role once more. The witches seem to satisfy him on this score, and early in act v he boasts of his assurance that he has nothing to fear. Nevertheless, he must 'feel his title / Hang loose about him, like a giant's robe / Upon a dwarfish thief' (v.ii.20-2), because he also speaks of his withered, empty, lonely life and of how, having 'supp'd full with horrors' (v.v.13), he has lost the capacity to feel strongly, to know fear or, apparently, any other emotion. Despite his boasts, he is obviously experiencing the state of emptiness that accompanies full loss of identity, and in the great 'To-morrow, and to-morrow, and to-morrow' speech (19-28), he produces his first clear response. He acknowledges the emptiness by describing it, by articulating it, and in a voice whose tonelessness dramatizes its possession of him. With no role to play, the 'shadow' in the sense of actor becomes a 'shadow' in the sense of nothingness; he of necessity is a 'poor player' who cannot do otherwise than 'strut and fret his hour upon the stage' in a drama that is not a proper drama but a performance so devoid of meaning as to have become a 'tale / Told by an idiot.'

Macbeth is more able than any other Shakespearian tragic hero to see the nothingness steadily and whole, to see it clearly enough to provide the most discursive account of it to appear in Shakespearian tragedy, but he too is ultimately unable to continue confronting it without recoiling. When Birnam Wood comes to Dunsinane, thus inspiring additional conscious awareness of what he already knows thoroughly otherwise, his response to the threatening nothingness alters from that of merely passively recording it. He begins 'to be aweary of the sun' (49), to yearn for the oblivion that Richard II said constituted the only means of contenting those who had themselves already become nothing. But Macbeth also recoils in yet another way, which is strengthened when Macduff appears and produces final assurance, assurance doubly sure. In resolving to fight his attackers, Macbeth to some extent emulates Othello in his revenge against Desdemona: should he overcome all odds and win, he will destroy those who contribute to his identity loss by making sure the role of king can never be fully his. This resolution makes Macbeth parallel to Othello even more certainly, however, in a more important fashion. It also constitutes an attempt to shape a role for himself where none really exists. He turns down one possible substitute role when he says, 'Why should I play the Roman fool, and die / On mine own sword? Whiles I see lives, the gashes / Do better upon them' (v.viii.1-3). He will not kill himself but will instead attack his enemies; like Othello at the very end, he too will attempt to reassume his original identity. The attempt is not successful. He who had once been brave and noble Macbeth, the heroic warrior, can now manage only a 'valiant fury' (v.ii.14). His effort does gain him the oblivion he also seeks, however, and no longer need he envy Duncan sleeping peacefully in his grave. Macbeth's own fitful fever of life has come to an end.

The brief prologue opening *King Lear* has for one of its functions the task of instructing the spectators how to respond to the crucial scene in which Lear divests himself of his kingdom and exiles the two people who most wish him well. Kent and Gloucester make it clear that Lear's 'darker purpose' is already known. They are aware of his plan to divide the kingdom and have learned enough of the details of the plan to be able to express surprise that the Dukes of Albany and Cornwall will be allotted equal shares. What is about to occur, this prologue points out, is merely a formal ceremony sanctioning a *fait accompli* by giving it public representation.

It does not seem strange, therefore, that so many of the speeches in the scene sound as if they had been written to order and carefully rehearsed. Such is the case, obviously, with the extravagant claims of Goneril and Regan, but the impression also owes a great deal to the highly artificial rhetoric of Lear's speeches, especially when he indulges an apparent tendency for formal balance and excessive amplification:

> Of all these bounds, even from this line to this,
> With shadowy forests and with champains rich'd,
> With plenteous rivers and wide-skirted meads,
> We make thee lady. (I.i.62-5)

Moreover, it is as if all these speeches have been written specifically to Lear's order, for although Goneril and Regan have certainly supplied their own words, they speak in response to formal cues from Lear – 'Goneril, / Our eldest-born, speak first' (52-3); 'What says our second daughter, / Our dearest Regan' (66-7) – and his replies, because they ignore the content of what has been said and go directly to the business of pronouncing rewards, define these speeches as having successfully measured up to some preconception of what they ought to have been.

Cordelia's contribution to the ceremony underscores its dominant manner in two ways. The simplicity and directness of her language, both in her asides and in her speeches to Lear, offer a sharp contrast to the high-flown rhetoric of the other members of her family. And her refusal to say what she knows is expected of her occasions the most forceful indication that what is occurring is a kind of play-within-the-play. When Regan has finished and received her reward, the third of Lear's formal cues can be heard:

> Now, our joy,
> Although our last and least ...
> ...
> ... what can you say to draw
> A third more opulent than your sisters? Speak. (81-2, 84-5)

The urge to regard Lear's repeated requests for speech as formal cues becomes irresistible in the lines that follow. Cordelia has 'Nothing' to say, but Lear insists, 'Nothing will come of nothing. Speak again,' and when she still fails to satisfy him, he adds, 'How, how, Cordelia! Mend your speech a little, / Lest you may mar your fortunes' (88-94). Lear means 'a lot,' of course, because he treats Cordelia like an actress who has forgotten her lines. He is obviously waiting to hear a particular speech, or at least a speech of a particular kind, one that will surpass in its assertions of love even the speeches already recited by Goneril and Regan. But Cordelia continues her refusal to say what is expected of her, and this initiates a rapid-fire sequence of events which no one onstage could have anticipated. Her refusal thus strikingly highlights the contrived and artificial quality of all that has preceded it. Through her lack of co-operation the beginning of the scene stands fully revealed as a little playlet that its chief actor, director, and virtual author has staged evidently for the sole purpose of publicly glorifying himself.

This playlet forms a complex metaphor charged with several important implications. First, it helps characterize Lear's own condition, for by originating the playlet he defines himself as the inhabitant of a world of unreality. He is, in fact, so fully immersed in the play-world he has devised that he cannot penetrate beyond its limits. The real world is abundantly present on Shakespeare's stage, by implication in the true feelings held but concealed by Goneril and Regan, more concretely in the asides spoken by Cordelia. But Lear is blind to these hints and glimpses of alternative possibilities; for him they do not exist. Cordelia soon compels him to recognize the existence of some of them, it is true, but his response merely confirms his allegiance to his own world of unreality: instead of altering his vision so that it will conform to the facts before him, he tries to destroy the facts and make the real world coincide with his own.

Second, Lear's playlet calls to the spectators' attention another kind of role-playing with which the role-playing in his playlet interferes. Cordelia refuses to play the role Lear has assigned for her because it conflicts with other roles that she feels to be more valid. As a daughter, she is obliged through her bond to obey, love, and honour her father (though not to indulge him by practising a 'glib and oily art,' 224), and as a wife, which she is soon to become, she is obliged to surrender to her husband 'Half my love ... half my care and duty' (101). Cordelia seems already to realize what *King Lear* as a whole so powerfully demonstrates – that social and familial roles must be faithfully adhered to because it is through them that both society and the individual find their only possibility of order. More than any of the other histories and tragedies (including *Hamlet*) *King Lear* is concerned with the violation or loss of roles of this type and with the chaos that necessarily follows. This emphasis, despite Cordelia's resistance, begins with the opening scene and is initiated by Lear's playlet. Lear's plan to divest himself partially of his role as king – that is, to shed its responsibilities and retain only its rights and privileges – clearly involves him in a violation of the demands of his role. But as the playlet indicates, Lear, like Richard II, has already violated its demands by becoming a player-king. Instead of role-playing, he has been play-acting; for the fixed pattern of behaviour belonging to the office of king ('the wise King's part') he has substituted an imaginary role, his distorted conception of himself as king. *King Lear* begins, then, with Lear's double violation of the most important social role of them all, and his act simultaneously causes and signifies a complete disruption of order for his kingdom.

Cordelia's breaking off of Lear's playlet introduces a symbolic action by means of which the disruption of order can be given concrete representation, and the events set in motion by her act provide further evidence of the full significance of her father's errors. Once order *per se* has crumbled, evidently, its individual constituents rapidly fall as well, for Shakespeare immediately shows more roles being subjected to violation or nullification. Through his treatment of Cordelia, Lear, as France suggests (213-23), violates his role as father; his ultimate mistreatment of her, of course, is his attempt to nullify her role as daughter:

> Here I disclaim all my paternal care,
> Propinquity and property of blood,
> And as a stranger to my heart and me
> Hold thee from this for ever. The barbarous Scythian,
> Or he that makes his generation messes
> To gorge his appetite, shall to my bosom
> Be as well neighbour'd, pitied, and reliev'd,
> As thou my sometime daughter. (112-19)

Obviously Cordelia continues to be Lear's daughter and still strives to fulfil the demands of her role to the extent of her ability; but although Lear cannot literally separate her from her role (in contrast to his ability to un-king himself, or Edmund's ability to separate both his father and his brother from their socially created and sanctioned roles), he does manage to deprive her of both the material circumstances appropriate to her role and the responsiveness from himself necessary for its wholly satisfactory performance. Kent suffers a similar loss almost at once. His one and only role is that of Lear's loyal follower, which he emphasizes even as he voices his objections to Lear's behaviour:

> Royal Lear,
> Whom I have ever honour'd as my king,
> Lov'd as my father, as my master follow'd,
> As my great patron thought on in my prayers – (138-41)

Lear symbolically deprives Kent of his role the moment he acts in such a way that he compels Kent to become 'unmannerly'; then, in pronouncing Kent's banishment, he converts symbol to reality. Kent's response of 'Freedom lives hence, and banishment is here' (181) is for him the most telling way possible of evoking a topsy-turvy world. And it forms a fitting climax to the rapid series of events through which Lear's initial disruption of order is confirmed.

Probably the most important significance of Lear's playlet, however, is the way it ensures continued disorder because of the precedent it establishes. By introducing play-acting into his world, Lear sanctions a mode of action that can favour only masters of deceit like Goneril, Regan, and Edmund, who, because they lack any sense of the integrity of social and familial roles, are capable, both psychologically and morally, of making what Lear has introduced a truly viable mode of action. This result of Lear's playlet is clear enough already in the opening scene, where only Goneril and Regan succeed in fulfilling their ends, but it becomes even clearer in the two following scenes, where, as if deliberately going Lear one better, first Edmund and then Goneril create playlets of their own.

Lear's nullification of the roles upon which order depends creates an ideal setting for Edmund. As bastard he possesses fairly specific roles, both dramatically and socially, but he is cut off from the kinds of social and familial offices the play stresses in its opening scenes. In these terms, he is virtually role-less, so that although his condition has previously made him unable to function, he is the one character in the play wholly suited to operate in a context where roles have lost their meaning. His role-less condition also makes him the one character most able to thrive in a context where play-acting has become the primary mode of action; like liquid, which takes its form from its surroundings, Edmund is free to assume whatever role he needs at the moment. This is why he is able to bring off so successfully the complicated sequence of play-acting which begins in I.ii and concludes in II.i. In I.ii he plays for Gloucester's benefit the part of a son so loyal that he is compelled to bring to his father's attention the possible villainy of the brother to whom he is also loyal. Later in the same scene he plays for Edgar's benefit the part of a brother so loyal that he must warn him of the danger threatening him, even though that danger would seem to stem from their father. And in both episodes he is carefully laying plans for the playlet he will stage in II.i, in which the father as spectator will be made to behold the versions of his two sons that Edmund wishes to convey. Like Richard III before him, Edmund is quite conscious of himself as playwright-actor. He sees Edgar in terms of the 'catastrophe of the old comedy' (I.ii.128); he knows that his own 'cue is villainous melancholy, with a sigh like Tom o' Bedlam' (129-30); and just before he is about to begin the playlet of II.i, he refers to it as 'one thing, of a queasy question, / Which I must act' (II.i.17-18).

The playlet produced by Goneril (or 'Vanity the puppet,' as Kent will later call her, II.ii.33) involves fewer complications than Edmund's sequence, but it admirably fulfils its purpose. Goneril begins not as actor but as playwright-director, working through her agent, Oswald. She will not speak to Lear when he returns from hunting, she informs Oswald, and Oswald is to say that she is sick. Moreover, he and his fellow servants are to 'Put on what weary negligence' they please with Lear (I.iii.13) and to 'let his knights have colder looks' (23). In this way, she feels, Lear will be taught to accept the new status he has created for himself by giving away his kingdom:

> Idle old man,
> That still would manage those authorities
> That he hath given away! Now, by my life,
> Old fools are babes again, and must be us'd
> With checks as flatteries, when they are seen abus'd. (17-21)

Goneril's playlet extends into the following scene (I.iv), where Oswald, playing the role his mistress has coached him in, refuses to 'entertain' Lear with 'that ceremonious affection' (I.iv.57-8) which Lear expects. Lear still considers himself *King* Lear, but Oswald will address him as no more than 'My lady's father' (78), while his treatment of Lear defines him as no better than an equal. Goneril's playlet reaches its climax when the lady herself, like a matador confronting the victim his picadors have carefully prepared, enters to administer the *coup de grâce*. Her performance is so effective that Lear can no longer distinguish the actress from the part. He first wonders, 'Are you our daughter?' (217), and then concludes she is not: 'Your name, fair gentlewoman?' (235).

Edmund and Goneril are the most accomplished practitioners of amateur theatrics, but almost every character engages in play-acting of one kind or another, and the character's skill or lack of skill in play-acting is a crucial factor in determining the nature of his experience. Three relevant categories quickly emerge. The first consists of those characters who find play-acting to be a congenial mode and employ it either (like Goneril) to enhance their social roles or (like Edmund) to enhance their identities by seizing roles not rightly theirs. The paradigm for this category is the rapid rise of Edmund, who becomes, in quick succession, Gloucester's favourite son and promised heir (II.i.83-5), Cornwall's trusted follower (II.i.112-16), Earl of Gloucester in his father's place (III.v.16), lover of both Goneril and Regan, and virtual leader of the combined English forces: the discarded kingship is but a step away. The second category consists of those characters whose lack of guile costs them their social roles, or at least the possibility of effectively fulfilling them, and who must therefore either temporarily leave the world Lear has created (as Cordelia does), or (like Kent and Edgar) engage in play-acting of their own – Kent so that he can maintain partial fulfilment of his old role in safety, Edgar as a means of protecting himself and establishing new bearings to replace the ones he has lost. The paradigm for this category is the situation Edgar articulates in his soliloquy of II. iii: he decides to assume the role of a Bedlam beggar both to 'preserve' himself (II.iii.6) and because 'Poor Turlygod! poor Tom! / That's something yet. Edgar I nothing am' (20-1). The plight of Gloucester exemplifies the third category. In III.vii, as Cornwall and Regan abuse him, he reminds them that, both as their host and as an old man, he deserves better treatment from them (III.vii. 29-30, 34-40). But he pleads in vain, since these roles have fallen with the others. With the disruption of order *per se*, there can be only temporary, moment-to-moment order, and it is established by those who control the situation. Here it is Cornwall and Regan who have the upper hand, and they have recast their host in the role of 'the traitor Gloucester' (21). Like Kent and Edgar, Gloucester lacks guile and therefore like them he stands at the mercy of those who thrive in Lear's new world. Unlike Kent and Edgar, however, he has no place to hide. He becomes one of the new world's chief victims.

Lear also belongs to the category exemplified by Gloucester, but with some significant differences. He has, of course, created the conditions that make possible his suffering, and more important, he collaborates in bringing it about. Lear's problem is that he is unwilling to play the new role his errors have cast him in and that Goneril and Regan are so eager to compel him to fulfil. Instead of playing the 'idle old man' that Goneril maintains he has become, he persists in speaking and acting as if his roles of king and father had not been nullified. And he expects that others will so respond to him. This quality of Lear's condition is quickly established by Shakespeare in I.iv through the contrasting receptions Lear accords Kent and Oswald. The disguised Kent offers to serve Lear because, as Kent says, 'you have that in your countenance which I would fain call master' – i.e., 'authority' (I.iv.27-30). Kent addresses Lear, in other words, as a king, and therefore he is welcomed, though with proper aloofness: 'Follow me; thou shalt serve me. If I like thee no worse after dinner, I will not part from thee yet' (40-2). But when Oswald very deliberately refuses to perceive any vestige of authority in the face of the man he can now call simply 'My lady's father,' he becomes in Lear's eyes 'my lord's knave,' a 'whoreson dog,' a 'slave,' and a 'cur' (79-80). He becomes a recreant deserving the blow he receives from the king he has slighted and the kick he receives from the king's new follower, who thus once again defines his master as king and thus once again is rewarded with the king's approval: 'I thank thee, fellow; thou serv'st me, and I'll love thee' (86-7).

Throughout the first two acts of the play, Lear steadily searches for others who will acknowledge his kinghood and fatherhood by treating him in the appropriate manner and feeding him the proper cues. His decision to leave Goneril for Regan is an attempt to find a setting that will correspond to the roles he is still determined to play:

> Ha! Is't come to this?
> Let it be so. I have another daughter,
> Who, I am sure, is kind and comfortable.
> When she shall hear this of thee, with her nails
> She'll flay thy wolvish visage. Thou shalt find
> That I'll resume the shape which thou dost think
> I have cast off for ever. (304-10)

But apart from Kent and, more problematically, the Fool, he can find no one who will respond to him as to a king, and no one at all whose treatment of him defines him as a father. The cues he hears when he finally reaches Regan are obviously not the ones he expects to hear:

> Deny to speak with me! They are sick! They are weary!
> They have travell'd all the night! Mere fetches;
> The images of revolt and flying off.
> Fetch me a better answer. (II.iv.86-9)

And so he directs that Regan and Cornwall be reminded who he is:

> The King would speak with Cornwall; the dear father
> Would with his daughter speak; commands their service. (99-100)

Yet even before they enter to confirm that their 'remotion ... / Is practice only' (112-13), Lear's eyes light on inescapable proof that he has not found the setting he sought, for to him Kent's imprisonment in the stocks is 'Death on my state!' (110). He soon realizes, moreover, that the setting he has entered is no more congenial to his intention of continuing to play the father. What

he discovers when he confronts Regan is not a daughter who is 'kind and comfortable' but a new enemy, one who denies the relationship he assumes she
holds towards him by directing him to perform an act for Goneril's benefit
which completely negates his conception of fatherhood:

> Ask her forgiveness?
> Do you but mark how this becomes the house:
> 'Dear daughter, I confess that I am old;
> Age is unnecessary; on my knees I beg
> That you'll vouchsafe me raiment, bed, and food.' (150-4)

This lack of co-operation from his fellow players means that the only
way Lear can continue to speak like a king is to adopt the tone of righteous
indignation he has already tried out on Kent in I.i and Oswald in I.iv. This is
why the formal and florid maledictions he pronounces against Goneril in I.iv
and II.iv are simultaneously so appropriate and so pathetic. They constitute
Lear's last valiant attempt to keep hold of the roles he still feels are rightly his
and thus to keep hold of his identity. Yet he cannot sustain even this last vestige of his sense of himself as king and father. The complete loss of self that
he will demonstrate in acts III and IV begins to set in as early as II.iv, when he
interrupts his cursing of Cornwall in order to fabricate possible excuses that
will account for Cornwall's neglect (103-10). When Regan turns out to be exactly like her sister, Lear capitulates. He responds not with a new formal curse
but with the 'reason not the need' speech, which doubly reveals his inability to
sustain any longer the fiction of his kinghood. In this speech for the first time
Lear stops trying to talk like a king; instead he is now desperately fighting
merely to hang on to the material properties that allow him to *look* like a king.
In doing so, moreover, he sounds for the first time as if he actually fits the conception of him that Goneril and Regan hold, that of the helpless old man whose
lack of status compels him to beg rather than demand.

In I.iv, after mistreatment from Oswald and Goneril, Lear had asked:

> Does any here know me? This is not Lear.
> Does Lear walk thus? speak thus? Where are his eyes?
> Either his notion weakens, or his discernings
> Are lethargied. – Ha! waking? 'Tis not so. –
> Who is it that can tell me who I am? (I.iv.225-9)

These questions were, however, merely rhetorical, Lear's way of commenting
not upon changes in himself but only on changes in his surroundings. The process carried out in the succeeding scenes converts these rhetorical questions into substantial ones; it turns Lear into the 'O without a figure' (I.iv.191), the

'nothing' (192) that the Fool had seen him to be as early as I.iv. For the loss that Lear experiences in these succeeding scenes is defined not only by his realization that he can no longer perform his roles of king and father but also by the further realization that he (like Macbeth) is losing a role more basic than either of these: his manhood.

As early as I.iv, he feared the loss of his manhood, but then he was able to resist it:

> Life and death! I am asham'd
> That thou hast power to shake my manhood thus;
> That these hot tears, which break from me perforce,
> Should make thee worth them. (296-9)

In II.iv, his plea to Goneril and Regan makes this ultimate loss imminent once again, and once again he tries to resist it:

> You see me here, you gods, a poor old man,
> As full of grief as age; wretched in both.
> If it be you that stirs these daughters' hearts
> Against their father, fool me not so much
> To bear it tamely; touch me with noble anger,
> And let not women's weapons, water-drops,
> Stain my man's cheeks! (II.iv.271-7)

The 'noble anger' would allow him to retain his manhood and at the same time regain him his lost kinghood, and so he tries once more to adopt the tone of righteous indignation. This time he cannot sustain it at all. This time, although he insists he will never give way to 'these hot tears,' the 'noble anger' quickly dissipates into the constant reiteration of the word 'weep':

> No, you unnatural hags,
> I will have such revenges on you both
> That all the world shall – I will do such things –
> What they are yet I know not; but they shall be
> The terrors of the earth. You think I'll weep.
> No, I'll not weep.
> I have full cause of weeping; but this heart
> Shall break into a hundred thousand flaws
> Or ere I'll weep. (277-85)

'O fool, I shall go mad!' forms the only possible appropriate conclusion to this speech. Unable to play the roles of king and father and unwilling to play the 'idle old man,' Lear already necessarily experiences the madness that is simultaneously a condition caused by his plight and a metaphor to represent its exact nature. Without roles to perform, either his old ones or makeshift substitutes, Lear lacks bearings to place him in relation to reality and no longer possesses an identity. His feeling of madness and the speeches about universal disorder this feeling allows him to give free vent to record the sense of dislocated reality he now experiences, while the madness itself records his identity loss. As a concrete dramatic fact Lear's madness consists primarily of the absence of an identifiable voice. His madness is not itself a role, as is Edgar's feigned version of a similar condition; it is, instead, the presence of all possible roles simultaneously, and Shakespeare establishes the absence of an identifiable voice through the ease, rapidity, and inexplicability with which Lear shifts from one new role to another. What the spectators hear in the mad scenes of acts III and IV is not a voice they can call 'Lear' but rather a series of voices that must be given separate names, including 'poor, infirm, weak and despis'd old man,' castigator of vice, pitier of 'Poor naked wretches,' 'unaccommodated man,' prosecutor, philosopher, fool, and even, occasionally, king. Separately, none of these voices provides an accurate representation of its speaker; in their confused intermingling, however, they quite accurately represent the nothing he has become.

Through the care of Cordelia and the Doctor, Lear is finally cured of his madness. The dressing of Lear in new garments, the calculated use of music, and the Doctor's manipulation of the action –

> CORDELIA He wakes; speak to him.
> DOCTOR Madam, do you; 'tis fittest. (IV.vii.42-3)

– makes the scene of Lear's recovery every bit as stagy as the playlet in I.i. Cordelia and the Doctor have, in other words, adopted the mode of action sanctioned by Lear and practised by Goneril and Edmund; but in doing so, like Edgar at 'Dover cliff' they have converted it to a benevolent instrument and thus purged it of evil.

As the change of garments and other indications of rebirth suggest, they have used it to help Lear acquire a new identity. The new identity includes many of the roles he had played during his madness and even some of those he had sought or refused to play during the period of suffering that induced his madness. At the core of the new identity stand both his role as man and his role as father – 'Do not laugh at me; / For, as I am a man, I think this lady / To be my child Cordelia' (IV.vii.68-70) – but the concern with the feelings and welfare of others is much in evidence, and so also is the strong sense of himself as sinner, fool, and 'idle old man.' What distinguishes Lear's new condition from his madness, then, is not a total lack of continuity but rather the fact that these miscellaneous roles have coalesced to form a consistent and identifiable voice. And the voice is one that has not been heard before. In finding Cordelia, Lear finds what he had sought in vain during the first two acts, for Cordelia's responses to him – 'No cause, no cause' (75); 'In your own kingdom, sir' (76); 'Will't please your Highness walk?' (83) – define him as both the king and the honoured father he had originally seen himself to be. But in this respect Cordelia's responses are ironic. The man she addresses now speaks with a voice totally devoid of the role of king as Lear had originally conceived it and thus totally devoid as well of his conception of the father as king within the family. The new voice, in contrast to the old, is characterized by its humility, simplicity, and directness, and above all by its clear evidence of a desire to communicate rather than rule:

> Pray, do not mock me:
> I am a very foolish fond old man,
> Fourscore and upward, not an hour more nor less;
> And, to deal plainly,
> I fear I am not in my perfect mind. (59-63)

There can be no question that Lear has found an identity – a blending of roles – which is wholly congenial to him, and in the following act he can be heard experimenting with his new voice, improvising in order to define it even more concretely. Gone now are all traces of the original desire for public self-glorification, of the need for justification through the responses of others. The relation to external reality that Lear has now achieved is one in which only Cordelia and his feeling for her matter:

> Have I caught thee?
> He that parts us shall bring a brand from heaven
> And fire us hence like foxes. Wipe thine eyes;
> The good years shall devour them, flesh and fell,
> Ere they shall make us weep. We'll see 'em starv'd first. (v.iii.21-5)

As long as he has Cordelia, the rest of external reality, whatever it may actually be in itself, will in Lear's mind become transformed into an appropriate setting where they can act out their love for each other. Prison is to be welcomed because it provides them a place where they can be alone to 'sing like birds i' th' cage' (9). Mutability and the threats posed by the ambitions of others no longer need to be feared, for through their love they will be able to 'wear out / In a wall'd prison packs and sects of great ones / That ebb and flow by th' moon' (17-19).

Lear's resumption of an identity – his return to a personal order – coincides with a restoration of order for the entire kingdom as the masters of deceit who had thrived on disorder are serially exposed and destroyed. The return to order is gradual but firm, and it finds fitting expression in the later career of Edgar, who during IV.vi and V.iii undergoes a number of rapid changes from one role to another - from 'Poor Tom' to the guide of Gloucester whose 'voice is alter'd' and who speaks 'in better phrase and matter' than Poor Tom (IV.vi.7-8), to the 'bold peasant' with rustic dialect who kills Oswald (233), and finally to the nameless knight in armour who challenges and destroys Edmund. These changes move Edgar smoothly back up the social ladder from his temporary status as social outcast to his final position as restored nobleman, from 'Edgar I nothing am' to:

> I am no less in blood than thou art, Edmund;
> If more, the more th' hast wrong'd me.
> My name is Edgar, and thy father's son. (V.iii.167-9)

Edgar's statement of his restored identity is accompanied by a proper reidentification of all the characters: of Goneril and Regan; of 'Kent ... the banish'd Kent, who in disguise / Follow'd his enemy king, and did him service / Improper for a slave' (219-21); of Edmund, whom Edgar identifies as 'a traitor ... a most toad-spotted traitor' (133, 138); and of Gloucester, whose death is the direct result of his rediscovery of himself as a loved and loving father. Edgar's progress parallels the similar rise of Edmund in the first half of the play, and just as Edmund's rise betokened increasing disorder, Edgar's symbolizes its elimination; as Edmund remarks, 'The wheel is come full circle' (174).

Shakespeare's stage is now set for an ending like that which Tate later substituted. But in defiance of minds like Tate's, all other known versions of the Lear story, and the expectations carefully aroused in his spectators, Shakespeare provides a much different 'promis'd end' (V.iii.263). There is no logic in Cordelia's death, dramatic or otherwise, no explanation for it, any more than Lear can explain the 'cause in nature that make these hard hearts' (III.vi.76-7). This is why Dr Johnson found the ending to be too painful to re-read and also, I suppose, why we find it so dramatically right: it is true *because* it is painful. The source of our pain, however, is not Cordelia's death but its effect on Lear. For Lear loses not only Cordelia but with her his new identity, the new relation to reality his rediscovery of her had brought him, and thus he loses himself as well.

Lear's first sound upon entering with Cordelia dead in his arms is 'Howl, howl, howl, howl!' (V.iii.257), and what follows merely reiterates in various forms this initial response. The fact of Lear's pain is always present in our consciousness, but not because he carefully articulates it. In contrast to Macbeth with his sure, controlled discursive account of the nothingness, or to Othello

with his fully elaborated but (under the circumstances) fictional self-concep-
tion, Lear at the end of *his* tragic career lacks all coherence; he can no longer
produce a recognizable voice, not even a desperately manufactured one as
Othello has done. Lear's first two speeches set the pattern for all that is to
follow. He begins by saying that Cordelia is 'gone for ever' and that he knows
'when one is dead and when one lives' (259-60). But he actually knows nothing of the kind, nor can he really believe that Cordelia is dead, otherwise he
would not see the feather stir or hear her voice or expend so much energy to
prove that she still lives. As his speeches addressed to others indicate, he does
not even know where he is, for Albany, Edgar, and Kent are not 'murderers,
traitors all!' as he calls them (269), nor is Caius (Kent's false identity) 'dead
and rotten' (285). Lear has completely lost contact with external reality, and
his tendency to leap from thought to thought while speaking of – and to –
Cordelia suggests that he has not compensated for this lost contact by dis-
covering (as Othello does) a sure inner reality. Each of the things Lear says
while focusing on the only fact in his experience that now matters to him
makes sense in itself, but the several utterances do not jell into a coherent
whole. Since, moreover, the utterances related to Cordelia's death coexist with
his unresponsive replies to Kent and the others, the impression of incoherence is greatly magnified. The common source of Lear's speeches – the pain
he feels – comes through consistently, but the speeches themselves seem no
more than noises forced from him, no more than additional 'howls.'

In Lear's final speech (305-11), the incoherence is even more pronounced:
he has moved from disjointed speeches to a speech of disjointed elements. And
here, also, his use of words gains a new characteristic, the inability to express
unequivocal meaning. The first line of this speech – 'And my poor fool is
hang'd!' – loses certainty of meaning through the ambiguity of 'fool.' The next
few lines are unequivocal enough, but it is the logic of pain rather than the
laws of exposition which determines their continuity, and by ending with the
repetition of 'Never, never, never, never, never,' they veer back toward the
howl of Lear's entrance. It is impossible to determine the function of 'Pray you
undo this button. Thank you, sir.' Is it a request and the acknowledgment of
the request's having been granted? Or is it simply an echo from the stripping
scene in the storm? And it is also impossible to determine the significance of
Lear's final line and a half. To read 'Do you see this? Look on her. Look, her
lips. / Look there, look there!' as an indication that Lear dies joyfully, content
in his belief that Cordelia still lives is an act of wishful thinking not unlike the
act this reading attributes to Lear. These words no more surely indicate that
Lear is calling attention to some sign of life than they do that he has discovered some equally convincing testimony of death. These words in themselves
do not and cannot make any kind of statement or convey with clarity any definite fact – about Cordelia, Lear himself, or anything else. And this is as it

should be, for the words are spoken by a man who, in every sense, has been reduced to a howl.

He is a speaker without language, and he is so because he has no identity, no roles to provide him with language. But he has not returned to his earlier state of madness. Once more it is impossible to hear a recognizable voice, but this time the failure is owing to the fact that his speeches are only a prolonged cry of pain. Lear's final condition makes us realize that madness, in Edgar's words, is 'something yet,' that it does provide, after all, some kind of relation to external reality. For in this last speech Lear is experiencing an even emptier state of nothingness. He dies (in our sense) when he does because he is already dead. Without roles, without an identity, without the language they provide, he cannot continue to exist.

King Lear constitutes Shakespeare's most fully wrought dramatization of his primary tragic pattern. Through the temporary restoration of Lear (his acquiring a valid identity again after having once confronted the void), the play tends to veer away from the form Shakespeare had given the pattern in *Richard II*, *Othello*, and *Macbeth*. But the ultimate effect of this temporary restoration is to make the final glimpse of the nothingness even more blinding and all-destructive, so that, for example, Lear cannot, like the earlier tragic heroes, escape into a substitute role, even a histrionic version of his original self. Only *King Lear*, therefore, succeeds in fully revealing to us the void that lies in wait just beyond the edge of our fragile shell of order and, by its imminence, makes experience tragic. *Macbeth* tells us what the experience of this void feels like, but the action of *King Lear* makes us virtually live it ourselves. *King Lear* is of all Shakespeare's tragedies the one that seems most to justify the term 'tragic illumination.' It is not, however, speeches like those Lear delivers upon awaking at the end of act IV which contain this quality, for moral illumination and tragic illumination, though often confused, are not the same. Tragic illumination involves discovery of the void and is therefore something that the hero and his audience can share, not something the hero experiences in order that his audience might learn. It is, moreover, an extremely rare phenomenon, probably because it is so incredibly painful. The first tragic hero ever to experience it, after all, recorded its impact by gouging out his own eyes.

With its almost constant focus on its hero, *Timon of Athens* has greater unity of action than most of Shakespeare's tragedies, and this action seems on the surface to reproduce the pattern previously shaped by the careers of Richard II, Othello, Macbeth, and Lear. Despite the greater concentration of *Timon of Athens*, however, something is obviously lacking, for the play falls far short of producing the tragic impact ordinarily resulting from the pattern. Like Lear and the others, Timon is deprived of his original identity (in his case, that of the magnanimous patron), but he does not, like them, genuinely experience its loss; instead of suffering a fall into the void, he accomplishes a leap into a different identity – and, for the sake of the play at any rate, a better one.

The ravings of the new voice Timon adopts upon leaving Athens are reminiscent of some of Lear's speeches on the barren heath and, like them, could be said to reflect the vision of universal disorder that tends to accompany loss of identity and exposure to nothingness. But Timon's curses and denunciations go too far. They acquire an aura of absurd exaggeration which associates the new voice with excessively histrionic mannerism. One feels that the new voice is less a genuine response to glimpsing the void than a substitute role Timon has seized in compensation for his inability to play the old role any longer. It is not surprising, therefore, that he identifies himself to Alcibiades by saying, 'I am Misanthropos, and hate mankind' (iv.iii.52), that Apemantus regards Timon as having taken over *his* role by 'putting on the cunning of a carper' (208), or that acts iv and v tend to form a series of brief incidents, almost little playlets, in which Timon has the opportunity to perform his role of misanthrope under a variety of circumstances.

At one point, Timon speaks of his recipients' betrayal of him as a 'winter's brush' that left him 'open, bare / For every storm that blows – I to bear this, / That never knew but better, is some burden' (263-6). But moments like this are rare; there is almost nothing else to help define the role of misanthrope as only a desperate substitute that evokes the void through its obvious function of offering its user protection from the void. Timon expresses a desire for death (e.g., 373-8), but this mood seems just one more dimension of his role. In the final act, he vaguely echoes Richard ii by regarding the nothingness of death as beneficial – 'My long sickness / Of health and living now begins to mend, / And nothing brings me all things' (v.i.184-6) – but Richard's words follow after a powerful evocation of the nothingness of life, and Timon's do not. Nor does Timon, in one sense, really experience the nothingness of death, because although he dies his epitaph preserves him for ever as Timon the misanthrope. For Timon, obviously, this role is not the fragile kind of thing Richard, Othello, and Macbeth sought refuge in (or that Lear momentarily found) but a solid, substantial solution to the problem of identity loss, an alternative to it that succeeds. Timon has more opportunity than his predecessors to give direct vent to his feelings, but Shakespeare does not allow him, ultimately, to use this opportunity to best advantage. *Timon of Athens* does not reveal the nothingness that makes experience tragic; it evades it.

Shakespeare's last two tragedies, *Coriolanus* and *Antony and Cleopatra*, also lack the tragic impact of *Othello*, *Macbeth*, and *King Lear*, though certainly by no means as much so as *Timon of Athens*. One reason for this dilution of the tragic effect is that in these two plays Shakespeare has developed a particular role-playing theme to such an extent as to create a variation in the tragic pattern. Macbeth's invocation of night and darkness as an appropriate setting for the imperial drama he decides to enact is echoed by Lear's rushing out into the storm as if in search of a setting to harmonize with the disorder that loss of identity has sprung loose in his mind. Having become nothing, Lear moves towards the barren heath and the hovel with the same sure sense of proper goal that Timon expresses in 'Timon will to the woods, where he shall find / Th' unkindest beast more kinder than mankind' (IV.i.35-6). In *Coriolanus* and *Antony and Cleopatra*, Shakespeare's interest in the scene-agent ratio – in the relationship between role and setting – develops into a major preoccupation. Each of these two final tragedies derives its action as a whole from its hero's search for a setting in which he can perform his identity with greatest effectiveness.

When Coriolanus enters in the opening scene of his play, he nearly shatters the very delicate calm Menenius has painstakingly built among the restless citizens of Rome, and this effect quickly and decisively dramatizes the central fact of Coriolanus' situation: that he, though a native Roman, is even more out of place in his community than Othello was in his. Coriolanus is a superb warrior whose proper costume consists of armour and his enemies' blood. He has been well trained for his role and performs it brilliantly. Already at sixteen, according to Cominius' report, he refused to 'act the woman in the scene,' even though his age entitled him to, and instead 'prov'd best man i' th' field' (II.ii. 94-5). He thrives on the battlefield, and during the first act wins there the name by which he is primarily known and which he acquires because he has almost single-handedly conquered the enemy city of Corioli. As his name indicates, the role of warrior is the dominant element of his identity – as far as he is concerned, its determining factor. Unfortunately, residence in Rome calls for something more than just the talents of a warrior; it calls for something that Coriolanus is unable to produce.

To thrive not just as warrior but as the *Roman* warrior he is, Coriolanus must be able to comprehend and accommodate the needs and demands of all elements of a highly complicated and potentially volatile political entity, or at least create the impression that he can. This capacity, lacking in Coriolanus, is symbolized by the ceremony in which the candidate for consul appears in the market place, displays his wounds as token of his service to the state, and pleads for the people's approval of his appointment. Residence in Rome requires, in other words, that Coriolanus must play an additional 'part' – as the ceremony is frequently called. He must convincingly execute a series of clear and specific histrionic gestures, a series that his mother defines during her effort to get him to return to the market place for a second try at the ceremony (III.ii.52-86). Coriolanus regards the ceremony beforehand as 'a part / That I shall blush in acting' (II.ii.142-3), and his fears are prophetic. He puts on the proper costume – 'The napless vesture of humility' (II.i.224) – but does not know himself in the role (II.iii.144) and cannot bring his tongue to the correct pace (49-50); he miserably botches his performance.

When his mother shows displeasure with his failure, Coriolanus explains that he cannot play the role of humble pleader because he has another role that he must act instead:

Why did you wish me milder? Would you have me
False to my nature? Rather say I play
The man I am. (III.ii.14-16)

He who at sixteen would not 'act the woman' will also not now violate his role of warrior ('The man I am') by adopting false gestures. But his mother and his friends realize what residence in Rome requires. They give him a short course in executing the alien part, promise to 'prompt' him (106), and virtually force him back to the market place. Coriolanus, who still feels it to be 'a part which never / I shall discharge to th' life' (105-6), fails again, however, this time more miserably than before, with the result that his exile is ordered. He in turn exiles the Romans, or, rather, the citizens and their political leaders: 'Despising / For you the city, thus I turn my back; / There is a world elsewhere' (III.iii.135-7). The banishment of Coriolanus symbolically enacts the incompatibility between his identity as warrior, the only identity he is capable of playing, and his setting, which calls for further roles and thus a more complex identity. His defiant claim about a world elsewhere, on the other hand, witnesses his belief that a compatible setting can be found, and that in leaving Rome he is not just accepting banishment but also actively seeking this compatible setting.

Nonetheless, the first glimpse of Coriolanus away from Rome finds him dressed 'in mean apparel, disguis'd and muffled' (IV.iv.,s.d.), and at the beginning of the next scene he participates in a bit of low comedy with Aufidius' servants. These details indicate the result of Coriolanus' search. When Aufidius enters, Coriolanus unmuffles and, as if certain he has found the compatible setting, formally identifies himself:

My name is Caius Marcius, who hath done
To thee particularly, and to all the Volsces,
Great hurt and mischief; thereto witness may
My surname, Coriolanus. (IV.v.65-68)

He goes on to define his new relation to Rome, but these opening words have already branded his discovered 'world elsewhere' as an enemy camp, a setting in which he cannot simply act out his role of warrior but, as enemy, must either conquer or be conquered. His arrival in disguise has therefore been a highly appropriate image, for the identity he wishes to preserve is threatened here as much as in Rome, if not more so. Aufidius' plans to dispose of Coriolanus after they have conquered Rome together suggest that in coming to the enemy city Coriolanus has merely made himself Aufidius' puppet, an actor in another's drama.

Coriolanus does not for some time consciously perceive that he has failed to find what he sought, but his subsequent performance is nonetheless an appropriate response to such failure. For one thing, he experiences a taste of the nothingness his position exposes him to – at least, according to Cominius, he speaks as if he does:

> 'Coriolanus'
> He would not answer to; forbad all names;
> He was a kind of nothing, titleless,
> Till he had forg'd himself a name i' th' fire
> Of burning Rome. (v.i.11-15)

And, as the last clause of this speech signifies, he has resolved to destroy Rome, which has prevented him from continuing to act out his desired identity and transformed him from hero into exile. He will, therefore, simultaneously punish it for its crimes and destroy it as a means of wiping out for ever the false identity it has imposed on him. And in laying it waste, he will also be making *it* his unfound 'world elsewhere': he will succeed in reshaping it into a compatible setting, partly because it will have become, like Corioli, a testimony to his conquering might, and partly because his loss of identity has already turned *him* into a kind of wasteland. His cry of 'Wife, mother, child, I know not' (v.ii.78) sums up both his responses. It expresses, to the extent he can express it, his sense of identity loss, and it makes clear the fullness of his resolve with regard to Rome.

He cannot sustain this resolve, however, because his cry is not ultimately true. When his wife, mother, and child arrive, he tries to break the 'bond and privilege of nature' (v.iii.25), to 'stand / As if a man were author of himself / And knew no other kin' (35-7), but this self-projection quickly strikes him as just one more unsuitable, inappropriate external role – 'Like a dull actor now / I have forgot my part and I am out, / Even to a full disgrace' (40-2) – and he comes to see his effort at maintaining this self-projection as an 'unnatural scene' that the gods look down on and laugh at (183-5). Mostly through ridicule his mother finishes shattering for him the identity of 'author of himself' he has grasped at as a substitute. He is forced to acknowledge the familial roles that make him a Roman, and this means he must again know himself as exiled Roman. He cannot destroy Rome, and as exiled Roman he can neither return there nor find himself a setting anywhere else.

All that remains to him, therefore, is to suffer the consequences of his having spared Rome. This act puts Coriolanus fully in Aufidius' power, so that Coriolanus' 'tale' becomes 'pronounc'd' Aufidius' way (v.vi.58). Coriolanus must hear Aufidius define him as 'traitor' (85) and – a far worse blow to his

sense of himself as man-warrior – 'thou boy of tears' (101). Just before Aufidius and his conspirators kill him, Coriolanus tries to fight off this last label
by using Othello's device of reasserting his original identity. But Othello was
able to substantiate his imaginative self-projection and preserve it from the
interference of others by shaping an appropriate action for it. Coriolanus cannot. His reassertion of himself as the conqueror of the Volscians is met by the
attack that makes him their victim. In death, through the words of others, he
regains something of his initial reputation. He shall 'be regarded / As the most
noble corse that ever herald / Did follow to his urn' (143-5), and he shall 'have
a noble memory' (154). But these words are too few and come too soon after
his fall: they cannot adequately offset the impression his fall has made.

   Coriolanus' failure to discover a congenial setting nullifies his identity as
heroic warrior and brings him close to the basic Shakespearian tragic experience. But only close. Coriolanus cannot fully participate in this experience because Shakespeare has not provided him with the necessary sensibility. He cannot, like Macbeth, describe the nothingness, nor, like Lear, mirror it in his
language. He is not, perhaps, even fully aware of it, and it is significant that the
spectators must hear at second hand, through Cominius' report, Coriolanus'
surest acknowledgment of felt identity loss. It is difficult to say why Shakespeare has limited Coriolanus so much – perhaps his conception of the heroic
warrior demanded it; perhaps the great interest he here shows in the scene-
agent ratio caused him to neglect other considerations; perhaps he could himself no longer endure the impact of the tragic vision. At any rate, the limitation
exists, and because of it the tragic pattern in *Coriolanus* can produce only a
cold, remote effect, making the play as distant in its way from the great tragedies as *Timon of Athens* is in its.

   One aspect of Coriolanus' limitation is that the identity he acknowledges
and seeks to perform has less scope and complexity than the identity called
for by his setting. *Antony and Cleopatra* avoids this impediment to the full
tragic effect because the search its hero undertakes is for a setting that will
be sufficiently spacious and diverse. Antony has ties with both Rome and
Egypt and, more important, he possesses the qualities these ties symbolize.
His potential identity is vast and various, but he cannot actually perform it
because neither of his settings will allow him to play all the specific roles he
must assume if he is to make his potential identity actual.

   Lear does not learn for some time to ask who he is, and even then he does
not at first truly believe in the relevance of his question. Antony himself never
asks a similar question, but the issue of his identity is nonetheless raised immediately. Philo's Antony, the Antony Philo exhibits as if he were upon a
stage ('Behold and see,' I.i.13), is a figure that has undergone a transformation
from his former worthy self as responsible warrior, military leader, and head
of state to the baseness of being 'a strumpet's fool' (13). As Philo will soon add

through implication, this figure can best be described by saying that he is no longer Antony:

> Sir, sometimes when he is not Antony,
> He comes too short of that great property
> Which still should go with Antony. (57-9)

These words of Philo's take on added weight because of what has preceded them. Antony has entered in company with Cleopatra and has insisted that, contrary to Philo's notion, not Rome but Egypt constitutes his proper setting ('Here is my space,' 34). In place of mere clay, Egypt offers 'new heaven, new earth' (17), and only it permits a location suitable for the kind of gesture Antony is compelled to execute, the kind he refers to in 'The nobleness of life / Is to do thus' (36-7). Philo is wrong, for 'Antony / will be himself' only when 'stirr'd by Cleopatra' (42-3).

This opening scene assigns the contrasting notions of who or what Antony is to different sources, but Shakespeare quickly indicates that Antony himself is aware of and accepts both versions of his identity. Despite his strong insistence of i.i, when he next appears he has not only been struck by a 'Roman thought,' as Cleopatra says (i.ii.80); he has wholly adopted the language and manner of Rome and so completely accepted the Roman version of his identity that he now sees his continued stay in Egypt not as a means of realizing his identity but as a threat to it:

> These strong Egyptian fetters I must break,
> Or lose myself in dotage. (113-14)

His Roman ties and qualities have been restored to dominance in him, and he is returning to Rome to find a setting where these elements of his nature can be expressed through appropriate roles, as they cannot in Egypt. However, this purely Roman mood does not last much longer than the purely Egyptian one of the first scene. Soon Antony tries to express both major dimensions of his identity. He is returning to Rome, as his affairs demand, but he goes there as Cleopatra's 'soldier, servant, making peace or war / As [she] affects' (i.iii.70-1). She mocks him and claims that this is not a role he genuinely assumes but one he merely feigns: 'Good now, play one scene / Of excellent dissembling, and let it look / Like perfect honour' (78-80). But he is not dissembling. He needs Egypt as well as Rome, and as he exits for Rome, he tries to eliminate the vast distance dividing his two settings by creating a verbal fusion of them:

> Our separation so abides and flies
> That thou, residing here, goes yet with me,
> And I, hence fleeing, here remain with thee. (102-4)

Antony's stay in Rome gives him an opportunity to exhibit the importance of honour to the Roman dimension of his identity; in Rome he can not only feel his behaviour to be worthy of respect, he can also find those who know how to accord him publicly the respect he deserves, if they so choose. And he tries, while there, to strengthen his Roman ties by adding a new one in his marriage to Octavia. But Rome is not the answer. As the soothsayer points out in II.iii (and he merely utters what Antony already knows) Rome is Caesar's setting. Caesar must thrive there, defeating Antony in the process, because Caesar is perfectly attuned to Rome in a way that Antony, who is not so limited, can never be. Antony's remaining in Rome merely provides occasion for Caesar to thwart his efforts to play the man of honour (III.iv.1-10), and this, Antony realizes, threatens his identity as a whole: 'If I lose mine honour, / I lose myself' (22-3). Rome is not the answer, and neither is the attempt to make Athens (in company with Octavia) a substitute setting. Antony cannot help being struck by an Egyptian thought: 'I will to Egypt ... / I' th' East my pleasure lies' (II.iii.39, 41). Something else lies there also, however, which hints at losses as serious as any Rome can effect. In the next scene, moments after Antony has had this Egyptian thought, Cleopatra gleefully recalls the time she unmanned Antony by reducing the part he must play for her from her soldier-servant to the dominated mistress of herself as soldier: 'I drunk him to his bed, / Then put my tires and mantles on him, whilst / I wore his sword Philippan' (II.v.21-3).

The war with Caesar that follows Antony's return to Egypt brings to a climax Antony's search for a setting. Antony's victory would mean fusion of his two settings and the creation of a new setting in which all his potential roles could be fully realized and he would rule supreme as Caesar does in Rome. But of course Rome must win any war with Egypt and in winning destroy Egypt, leaving Antony with no location in which he can function. His military defeats therefore appropriately occasion various effects suggesting identity loss. As Shakespeare has implied, Antony's return to Egypt unmans him, and his decision to fight Caesar by sea at Actium persuades Canidius that 'our leader's led, / And we are women's men' (III.vii.69-70). After his defeat – after fleeing in pursuit of Cleopatra – he has become a 'noble ruin'; he has violated 'Experience, manhood, honour' and become something other than himself, for 'Had our general / Been what he knew himself, it had gone well' (III.x.19, 23, 26-7); most of those whose service to him helped define him as the great leader he has been now begin to leave him.

Antony himself is well aware of what is happening to him. He experiences the familiar sensation of dislocated reality, of lost bearings:

Hark! the land bids me tread no more upon't;
It is asham'd to bear me ...

> I am so lated in the world that I
> Have lost my way for ever. (III.xi.1-4)

He knows his identity is slipping away like the authority that melts from him (III.xiii.90), and he knows he cannot allow the slippage to complete itself. He boldly insists 'I am / Antony yet' (92-3), but to back up his claim he can do little more than pretend that Cleopatra has been transformed and, worse, betray his own identity by his ferocious abuse of the innocent Thyreus. These devices do not satisfy him for long, and he must soon restore Cleopatra to her proper self and to his favour because of his great need for her in the performance of his identity. He accepts her vow of fidelity to him with quickness and relief, and even interprets it as a sign that *all* things are right once more. When he then pronounces a speech that simultaneously reflects both the Egyptian and the Roman dimensions of his identity (178-85), Cleopatra declares full restoration for him as well as her: 'since my lord / Is Antony again, I will be Cleopatra' (186-7). To Enobarbus, however, Antony's new mood seems rather a 'diminution in [his] brain' (198), and Enobarbus now adds himself to the company whose desertion of Antony helps signify his more general diminution.

Antony's many quickly changing moods in these scenes between the battles create an impression vaguely similar to Lear's madness, and, like Lear's madness, Antony's instability of mood suggests a decomposition of identity, though in Antony's case it would be more accurate to speak of the decomposition of a *potential* identity or, better yet, the symbolic representation of the impossibility of his ever being able to bring his potential identity to full existence. Similarly, Antony's brief success in battle, celebrated in IV.viii, is like Lear's discovery of a new role after his madness: it makes the final rupture worse. Antony's final defeat thus takes him 'to the very heart of loss' (IV.xii. 29), where the melting he once slightly felt becomes his chief sensation. The play in which he has tried to act his parts now seems to him to be as unsubstantial and devoid of basis in the real world as 'black vesper's pageants,' the clouds that 'mock our eyes with air' by seeming to resemble something familiar before suddenly dislimning so that the once familiar object becomes 'indistinct, / As water is in water' (IV.xiv.7-8, 9-11). Antony is himself, he feels, 'Even such a body,' for now to be Antony is to dissolve, to melt away to nothing: 'Here I am Antony; / Yet cannot hold this visible shape' (13-14). He is, moreover, now fully unmanned; Cleopatra has robbed him of his sword once and for all (23).

Belief that Cleopatra has killed herself prompts him to reject his momentary loathing for her and deepens in him the sense of his own loss. He now wants death since he has become nothing, wants his body to cleave and crack as his non-physical being has done. But no more bravely than his predecessors in the tragedies can he face the nothingness while awaiting death. He too must shape, however fragmentarily, various substitute roles. In his vision of himself and Cleopatra in Elysium, he tries briefly to create in words the setting he has always sought:

> Where souls do couch on flowers, we'll hand in hand,
> And with our sprightly port make the ghosts gaze.
> Dido and her Æneas shall want troops,
> And all the haunt be ours. (51-4)

He also defines himself, because of his suicide, as Caesar's conqueror and tersely reasserts his former self with 'I, that with my sword / Quarter'd the world, and o'er green Neptune's back / With ships made cities' (57-9). None of these efforts avail. He will, he claims, be 'A bridegroom in my death, and run into't / As to a lover's bed' (100-1); but the bungled suicide mars all in much the same way that Aufidius' attack mocks the claims of Coriolanus. Antony must repeat his assertion of what he was (and still is, according to the purpose for asserting it) in even more elaborate terms when his dying carcass is brought to Cleopatra, and the words with which he begins sound as if he implores her to find some way of preserving the assertion for him: 'please your thoughts / In feeding them with those my former fortunes' (IV.xv.52-3).

Cleopatra inherits from the dead Antony both the centre of focus and the tragic experience he has gone through. His death suddenly dislocates her by removing her from the reality she has known and placing her 'In this dull world, which in [Antony's] absence is / No better than a sty':

> The crown o' th' earth doth melt ...
> O, wither'd is the garland of the war,
> The soldier's pole is fall'n! Young boys and girls
> Are level now with men. The odds is gone,
> And there is nothing left remarkable
> Beneath the visiting moon. (61-8)

She then swoons, and although the swoon does not signify her death, as Iras fears, it is followed by Cleopatra's expression of her own identity loss. No longer 'Royal Egypt, Empress!' she is now

> No more but e'en a woman, and commanded
> By such poor passion as the maid that milks
> And does the meanest chares. (71-5)

Full loss of identity seems unavoidable for her, since it is not only the death of Antony that has altered her circumstances. She can never again even be the Cleopatra she was before her meeting with Antony. Rome has conquered Egypt, she is Caesar's prisoner, and since he plans to crown his victory with a triumphal show to 'Let the world see / His nobleness well acted' (v.ii. 44-5), the former queen can look forward only to being a puppet in her conqueror's play (207-12). Soon, moreover, she will have been reduced even further and become no more than a crudely acted theatrical role:

> the quick comedians
> Extemporally will stage us, and present
> Our Alexandrian revels; Antony
> Shall be brought drunken forth, and I shall see
> Some squeaking Cleopatra boy my greatness
> I' th' posture of a whore. (215-20)

On Shakespeare's stage the effect must have been a bold one indeed: for a moment the spectator is forced to perceive in his proper person the boy who speaks these words of Cleopatra, and during that moment her loss of identity is utter and absolute.

But only for a moment; Cleopatra's allusion to the play as a play does not put its stamp on the entire action as does the speech by Cassius after the assassination of Julius Caesar. The impact of her allusion cannot last because of the magnificent moment that follows. Cleopatra refuses to accept the oblivion of identity loss. She responds to the threat in the manner of Richard II and Othello by creating her own imaginative drama to replace the unbearable action of reality; and she rises to the occasion with a fullness and perfection of execution that neither they nor any of their partial emulators can quite manage. She decides to conquer Caesar by conquering fortune, which rules him. He has been a master dramatist on a world stage and now intends a final triumphant act involving her, but she will thwart him by performing instead her own counter-drama. Part of this drama consists of pretending to submit herself wholly to her conqueror, and her play-acting to this end helps establish the play-like quality of her counter-drama; but its core is made up of two magnificent moments: her dream of Emperor Antony and her suicide scene.

The episode of her suicide, like that of Lady Macbeth's sleep-walking, is a scene in the full theatrical sense. She calls it a 'noble act' (283), and her imagery is echoed by Dolabella after the scene has ended, when he tells Caesar he is 'coming / To see perform'd the dreaded act which thou / So sought'st to hinder' (328-30). This notion of performance is amply substantiated by Cleopatra's manner, both in her careful setting of the stage –

> Show me, my women, like a queen. Go fetch

> My best attires. I am again for Cydnus,
> To meet Mark Antony (226-8)

– and in the highly histrionic way in which she presents several manifestations of herself to her audience during her final speeches. Cleopatra performs in these last speeches her own complex identity, her many roles as queen, 'gypsy,' lover and wife of Antony, aspiring spirit, jealous woman, mother, and the latest addition to her repertory: conqueror of Caesar. Unlike Antony's, her suicide is flawlessly performed (mechanically as well as histrionically), and thus she succeeds in validating through her actions her imaginative projection of herself. She genuinely earns the title of 'lass unparallel'd' which Charmian applies to her in death (314).

Cleopatra's brilliant and successful performance during the final act of *Antony and Cleopatra* is as much a victory for Antony as it is for herself. Her attempt to impose her own will on reality, to become a dramatist of life, constitutes a new and striking example of an action motif that often appears in the tragedies and forms a chief element of Shakespeare's earliest tragic pattern. In sharp contrast to the earlier plays, however, in which the hero's attempt to realize his imaginative drama in concrete terms is consistently thwarted by a destructive counter-action, Cleopatra's attempt itself forms the counter-action. She succeeds in achieving for herself and Antony what, setting aside the doubtful and inconsequential case of Titus Andronicus and the only partial success of Romeo and Juliet, none of the other tragic heroes is able to achieve. She succeeds in making reality conform to her vision of what it should be. One measure of her success is her forcing Caesar to change his scheduled drama and make its final act not the triumphant pageant he had planned but a very different kind of 'show': 'our army shall / In solemn show attend this funeral, / And then to Rome. Come, Dolabella, see / High order in this great solemnity' (360-3). A further and far more important measure of her success is an audience's tendency to respond so wholly to the splendid poetry Shakespeare has written for her that elements of reality like Caesar's military triumph and Antony's death (or Cleopatra's own) lose their normal magnitude in the face of the greater reality created by Cleopatra's words.

Cleopatra's performance has an additional significance, one especially pertinent to Antony. Through her dream of Emperor Antony, which endows him with mythic dimensions (76-100), and through her validation of that dream by conferring immortality upon him during her suicide scene, Cleopatra shapes her imagination into the setting Antony had searched for in vain, the setting within which his whole identity can finally and freely unfold itself in all its fullness and amplitude. Nature, which abhors paradox as much as it abhors a vacuum, keeps it Egypts separated from its Romes. It cannot unassisted provide Antony with the setting he needs, for to do that requires the invention of 'new heaven, new earth.' In the fifth act, Cleopatra fulfils the request Antony makes to her at the beginning of the play. She 'finds out' new heaven, new earth. She expands reality so that it includes not only nature but also, as a sort of higher adjunct of nature, her own creative imagination.

The brilliance of Cleopatra's achievement removes *Antony and Cleopatra* from the domain of tragedy as it is defined by such plays as *Macbeth* and *King Lear*. Antony experiences to some extent the felt loss of identity and the accompanying glimpse of the void which stand at the core of the tragic pattern, but, unlike any tragic hero before him, he passes through the void to the other side, so that the audience's final awareness of him is as of someone who has triumphed – and without having to delude himself. Cleopatra's brilliance also makes this play an answer of sorts to the drift of the two early tragedies whose special handling of role-playing materials prompted me to label them history plays genuinely deserving of the name: *Julius Caesar* and *Troilus and Cressida*. These two plays are tragic because they dramatize the way in which the reality of history thwarts and destroys the dreams of the individuals whose destinies it shapes. The eulogies over the fallen in *Julius Caesar* constitute an element of concession to the power of imagination, but this element does not acquire so much strength that it can obscure or blunt the central import of the play. In *Antony and Cleopatra*, Shakespeare greatly expands this concession to the power of imagination. Here it is the dream that triumphs and, in its triumph, reduces history to insignificance. *Antony and Cleopatra* thus rejects tragedy and history both. *Coriolanus* may have been written after it, as the usual dating goes, but the predominant mood of the romances has already set in.

9 The internal dramatist

The King's will be perform'd! (*The Winter's Tale,* II.i.115)

Of the countless playwrights of experience, the dramatists of life, who fill and enliven Shakespeare's stage, a large number, perhaps the majority, belong to a special sub-type that I have chosen to call the internal dramatist. This figure has its origins in a number of sources (especially the stereotype stage Machiavel, the clever slave-servant of comedy, and the vice of the morality play), and he functions with equal ease in comedy and tragedy. He differs from playwrights of experience like Richard II, or Othello, or most of the characters of *Twelfth Night* through the emphasis on plotting and manipulation which characterizes his activity.

An Orsino or an Othello devises and acts out imagined dramas (devises them *by* acting them out), either because of self-delusion or in order to establish some kind of bearings in a vast and seemingly formless universe. If his dramas require him to assign parts to his fellow characters, he will behave towards them accordingly, and he may even go so far in making them fit into his drama as Othello does in killing Desdemona. But the inclusion of others need not occur, and when it does, this kind of playwright of experience almost never forces his fellow characters *actively* to play a part – that is, by adopting certain gestures and moves and acting out prescribed episodes: he acts upon them, but he does not manipulate them. The internal dramatist, on the other hand, of which Iago provides a perfect example, rarely acts from self-delusion or loss of bearings. He always has a firm goal in mind, usually a materialistic one, and he tends to plot with care before he acts, although, like Iago or Richard III, he often plots only one scene at a time. Like the more self-preoccupied playwright of experience, the internal dramatist is a skilled actor in his own right, but he seems even more impressive as a director. He manipulates his fellow characters as if they were characters of his own invention rather than Shakespeare's. The usual climax of his drama is the conversion of his victim by compelling him to accept a new role, and much of the intrigue leading up to this climax is acted out not by the internal dramatist but by those he has in one way or another enlisted to help him, with the victim himself often unwittingly included.

The figure of the internal dramatist is obviously a familiar one in Shakespeare and of considerable importance to the action of his plays. He is usually a by-figure, a more or less subordinate character who initiates things, or keeps them astir, thereby providing occasion for the comic or tragic sufferings of the protagonists. But not always. In *Richard III* and *Measure for Measure* the internal dramatist is himself the protagonist. This is true also of the last two major plays of Shakespeare, *The Winter's Tale* and *The Tempest*, in both of which the thoughtful examination of this figure and his activity assumes a position of central dramatic importance.

Some of the differences that distinguish comedy from tragedy in Shakespeare pertain directly to the role-playing materials of the plays. One of these differences (to repeat a distinction made in the preceding chapter) has to do with the issue of identity loss, which in comedy tends to form a crucial and necessary stage in the process of full self-discovery but in tragedy constitutes the end result of a destructive process that carries its victim into the void. Another of these differences involves Shakespeare's attitude towards the internal dramatist. Titus Andronicus and Friar Lawrence of *Romeo and Juliet* somewhat complicate the picture in so far as tragedy is concerned, because Shakespeare fails to establish a clear-cut attitude towards their activity, but they stem from quite early plays; in most of the tragedies the manipulation of others and of events is something to be highly deplored. Many of the internal dramatists of tragedy, such as Aaron the Moor, Iago, Edmund, and Goneril are unequivocally evil and so seen. (By the end of his career Richard III has also joined this category.) Others, for one reason or another, themselves tend to elude the brand of unequivocal evil (this group includes Cassius, Claudius, Lear, the Tribunes of *Coriolanus*, and Octavius Caesar), but their activity does not. It always issues in destruction, usually the destruction of someone of great worth. And although the activity may succeed in fulfilling its primary purpose, as the dramatic design requires, almost invariably it also ultimately recoils upon those who perform it.

In the comedies, however, especially the early ones, Shakespeare reveals a quite different attitude towards the internal dramatist. The first of these comic manipulators is the Lord of *The Taming of the Shrew*, who acts purely to further his own pleasure and who, if his activity could be taken seriously, would have to be seen in a highly dubious light. Shakespeare does not take him seriously, however, and does not emphasize his potentially sinister quality. His activity merely provides a useful dramatic device and remains as morally neutral as Lucentio's automatic fulfilment of the conventions of the *amoroso* in *his* use of dramatic manipulation. It is not these internal dramatists that a spectator of *The Taming of the Shrew* is likely to take a moral stance to but Petruchio, and Petruchio is an attractive figure whose manipulation of events and his fellow characters proves entirely beneficial. This is not to say that Shakespeare expresses no uneasiness about the internal dramatist in the early comedies. *A Midsummer Night's Dream* contains the ambiguous Theseus, who helps to create the difficulty even as, still acting arbitrarily, he eventually corrects it. Don John of *Much Ado About Nothing* and Oliver and the usurping Duke of *As You Like It* should probably not be stressed, since they are conventional villains whose efforts merely help get things going, but *Much Ado* also contains the fussy – and morally fuzzy – Don Pedro. Nevertheless, even Theseus and Don Pedro manage to work towards the fulfilment of the comic theme (what they eventually accomplish is pleasing even if they themselves are not entirely so), and to this extent they resemble the prominent comic manipulators who also appeal through their personal attractiveness: Petruchio, Portia, the Friar of *Much Ado,* the Merry Wives, and Rosalind.

What necessitates this isolation of the early comedies is a conspicuous change in Shakespeare's comic attitude. From first to last, the comedies all tend to imply that for every character there exists an ideal role (or perhaps an ideal combination of roles), which suits him perfectly, which he is capable of fulfilling successfully (in *The Taming of the Shrew,* the relevant terms are 'aptly fitted' and 'naturally perform'd'), and which, if successfully and steadily fulfilled, ensures personal well-being for the character and stability for his society. This conception of the ideal role does not, I believe, undergo any change in the course of the comedies. What does change is Shakespeare's optimism about the possibility of realizing the ideal. Early on, he seems to view the possibility with great optimism and to assume that such realization is readily available through human effort alone: some individuals may not be able to realize the ideal for themselves, but this does not ultimately matter, because they will benefit from the assistance of those who manipulate them. As the comedies follow one upon another, however, and especially in those comedies written after tragedy begins to become Shakespeare's primary dramatic mode, his optimistic assumptions about man tend to disappear.

Twelfth Night achieves only a partial resolution, and even it depends upon the fortuitous arrival of Sebastian. Viola and Feste may be able to remain psychologically true to themselves, but they cannot avoid all personal difficulties, and they have no effect whatever on ridding the others of their delusions. Sebastian manages to fulfil the function of the beneficial manipulator, but not through any conscious effort of his own; his contribution is purely the product of good fortune. The pattern from the early comedies of the beneficent manipulator acting upon his lucky victim recurs in *All's Well That Ends Well* (in the relationship between Helena and Bertram), but an intensely bitter irony deprives it of its force, while at the same time Helena is made to realize that her 'success' is less the product of her own work than that of heaven. *Measure for Measure* then culminates the concern with the discrepancy between the actor and his role which preoccupied Shakespeare during the middle of his career. No character of importance in this play manages, aided or unaided, to achieve an ideal performance of his office, nor, despite (or perhaps because of) the considerable manipulation practised by Duke Vincentio, does any character ever attain to any real degree the satisfying equivalence between role and actor that had once so consistently defined the conclusion of the comic action. After *Measure for Measure*, therefore, the shift to the romance pattern seems inevitable. Each of the romances contains a single character or a small handful who persistently adhere to their roles with fidelity, but in every case the satisfying resolution is unequivocally the gift of providence, whose work is now viewed without any trace of the bitter irony of *All's Well That Ends Well.*

Accompanying this loss of optimism about man's capacity to bring the comic theme to a successful resolution is Shakespeare's increasing suspicion of the comic manipulator and his activity. The tricks practised against Malvolio in *Twelfth Night* betray a quality of cruelty and mercilessness which is quite new in Shakespearean comedy. This quality becomes even more prominent in the French Lords' treatment of Parolles in *All's Well That Ends Well*, while the work of the major internal dramatist in that play, as I have noted, is mocked by the ironic nature of its achievement. With the morally inept, self-indulgent, and empty duke of dark corners from *Measure for Measure*, the figure of the comic manipulator has begun to resemble its counterpart in the tragedies. *The Winter's Tale*, the next comedy with a prominent internal dramatist, carries this process one step further, for the internal dramatist of this play is a madman whose work must be carefully undone.

The first scene of *The Winter's Tale* is a kind of prologue designed to stress the ancient love between Leontes and Polixenes and the importance of Prince Mamillius to Leontes and his kingdom. The action proper then begins in scene ii, which opens with a playlet already in progress. One quality of 'The Leave-taking of Polixenes' which helps endow it with the aura of a playlet is the ceremony employed by Polixenes and Hermione, who say the sort of thing appropriately said on such an occasion. Ceremony by itself, however, especially ceremony that, as here, is simply the formal embodiment of feeling, should connote not drama but ritual. What transforms the leave-taking from a ritual act to a playlet is the contribution of Leontes. His curt replies, which show no trace of ceremony, set him apart from the action in which Polixenes and Hermione are engaged. Instead of participating, he directs the participation of Hermione: 'Tongue-tied, our Queen? Speak you' (i.ii.27). In his aside, he becomes an onstage spectator, describing and interpreting the drama going on before him:

Too hot, too hot!

> To mingle friendship far is mingling bloods.
> I have tremor cordis on me; my heart dances,
> But not for joy, not joy. This entertainment
> May a free face put on; derive a liberty
> From heartiness, from bounty, fertile bosom,
> And well become the agent. 'T may, I grant;
> But to be paddling palms and pinching fingers,
> As now they are, and making practis'd smiles
> As in a looking-glass; and then to sigh, as 'twere
> The mort o' th' deer. O, that is entertainment
> My bosom likes not, nor my brows! (108-19)

What Leontes sees is not an innocent ceremony but an 'entertainment' which, as the putting on of 'a free face' and the 'practis'd smiles' indicate, involves deliberate play-acting, and his characterization of what he sees is reinforced by his own relation to it.

In the speech that Leontes addresses only incidentally to his son, Mamillius, he develops the idea of the playlet far more explicitly even as he also makes clear that, contrary to the initial impression, he is not just the director/spectator of the playlet but rather one of its principal actors. 'Go, play, boy, play,' he tells his son:

> thy mother plays, and I
> Play too; but so disgrac'd a part, whose issue
> Will hiss me to my grave. (187-9)

The 'disgrac'd' part he has been assigned is that of the cuckold, and he is so intensely aware of being upon a stage playing it that he forgets Mamillius and lapses into an eerie version of the standard comic cuckold-soliloquy, complete with the usual gibes at the husbands in the audience:

> There have been,
> Or I am much deceiv'd, cuckolds ere now;
> And many a man there is, even at this present,
> Now while I speak this, holds his wife by th' arm
> That little thinks she has been sluic'd in's absence,
> And his pond fish'd by his next neighbour, by
> Sir Smile, his neighbour ...
> ...
> Be it concluded,
> No barricado for a belly. Know't,
> It will let in and out the enemy

> With bag and baggage. Many thousand on's
> Have the disease, and feel't not. (190-6, 203-7)

But this speech does more than merely emphasize the sense of an on-going playlet; by focusing so clearly on Leontes' imagination and the extent to which (as
in the rapid shift from one meaning of the word 'play' to another) his mind is
capable of reshaping the raw material of experience to its own uses, this speech
indicates how the playlet has come into being. For some reason that Shakespeare makes no attempt to suggest, either here or elsewhere, Leontes seems
able to cope with experience only by translating it into theatrical conventions.

   Before scene ii concludes, Leontes has extended his playlet beyond himself and the ceremony taking place in front of him to encompass his entire
world. In a further aside after the exit of Polixenes and Hermione, he devotes
his attention to the subordinate characters of the playlet, the attendants who
have stood by, silently witnessing the earlier episode:

> They're here with me already; whisp'ring, rounding,
> 'Sicilia is a so-forth.' 'Tis far gone
> When I shall gust it last. (217-19)

When Camillo observes that Polixenes agreed to stay 'At the good Queen's entreaty,' Leontes responds to his remark as if it were a line of dialogue requiring
revision:

> 'At the Queen's' be't. 'Good' should be pertinent;
> But so it is, it is not. (220-2)

And when Camillo denies the truth of Leontes' suspicions, Leontes retaliates
by assigning him a role as one of the villains of the playlet:

> you lie, you lie.
> I say thou liest, Camillo, and I hate thee;
> Pronounce thee a gross lout, a mindless slave,
> Or else a hovering temporizer that
> Canst with thine eyes at once see good and evil,
> Inclining to them both. (299-304)

   In shaping his playlet, Leontes thus assigns new, alien roles both to himself and to those who help determine his identity: his wife, his lifelong friend,
his attendants, and even his son, whom he asks at one point, 'Mamillius, /
Art thou my boy?' (119-20). In his imagination, Leontes has already relinquished
his identity; all he need do to make the loss an actuality is to deal with external

reality as if his version of it were true, and, shortly after Polixenes and Hermione have left the stage, he proceeds to do so by deciding to seize control of the play-let he thinks they have initiated and turn it from a comedy of cuckoldry into a tragedy of revenge. In thus imposing his imagination on reality, in proceeding to manipulate its people and events, he also undergoes a significant change. Up to this point he has been a playwright of experience of the Orsino-Othello variety; he now becomes more truly an internal dramatist. He has already, as it were, been an Iago for himself, and he now assumes that function in relation to the others.

His first move is to try to assign the 'hovering temporizer' Camillo a new part, that of Polixenes' poisoner. Camillo's refusal to perform this role (he instead helps Polixenes escape) assures Leontes that his distorted version of reality is true. He now knows 'There is a plot against my life, my crown' (II.i.47) and that he must act quickly to counteract his enemies' purpose. Two of them have fled his kingdom, but the third, Hermione, still lies within his power. He separates her from her son, so that she can no longer contaminate him, and publicly exposes her by asserting, ' 'tis Polixenes / Has made thee swell thus' (61-2). He then assigns his attendants their parts:

> You, my lords,
> Look on her, mark her well; be but about
> To say 'She is a goodly lady' and
> The justice of your hearts will thereto add
> ' 'Tis pity she's not honest – honourable.' (64-8)

As he elaborates upon the contrast between Hermione's 'without-door form' (69) and the corruption it conceals, he momentarily becomes confused and catches himself with 'O, I am out!' (72). The unreality and fragility of the play-world he is constructing here betrays itself, but Leontes resists the implications of his failure to speak his part correctly and through force of will restores the illusion he has momentarily shattered. He brands Hermione as an adultress and orders her to be taken to prison. Antigonus, who foresees the losses towards which Leontes is heading, warns, 'Be certain what you do, sir, lest your justice / Prove violence, in the which three great ones suffer, / Yourself, your queen, your son' (127-9). But his interference and that of Leontes' other attendants merely lead to additional losses, for them and Leontes, as the king now rejects his courtiers as well as his queen.

In most cases, what resistance there is to Leontes takes the form of an attempt to do what he believes he has done: convert one kind of play into another. In replying to the charge of adultery, Hermione tries to stop Leontes by opening his eyes – by defining the action in which she finds herself as a melodrama with Leontes as villain:

> Should a villain say so,
> The most replenish'd villain in the world,
> He were as much more villain: you, my lord,
> Do but mistake. (78-81)

But she soon realizes that resistance is useless, and so she pronounces the pun that informs the action of the first half of *The Winter's Tale:* 'The King's will be perform'd!' (115). Antigonus' choice is a farce – his reply to Leontes' 'this business / Will raise [i.e., rouse] us all' is 'To laughter, as I take it, / If the good truth were known' (197-9) – but since he has learned not to interfere, he confines himself to merely hoping and will express himself only in an aside. Paulina, who has not learned Antigonus' lesson, thinks she can convert the tragedy into a comedy by showing Leontes his new daughter (ii.ii.35-42), but her effort also fails. Since it leads to the loss of both Perdita and Antigonus, it becomes just one more episode in the revenge tragedy Leontes continues to press relentlessly toward its climax.

This climax is Hermione's trial scene. Here once again formal ceremony helps to establish the impression of a playlet, but the idea is also made explicit in Hermione's speech of defence. Because she is unjustly treated, she argues, her unhappiness 'is more / Than history can pattern, though devis'd / And play'd to take spectators' (iii.ii.33-5). Her use of personifications –

> if pow'rs divine
> Behold our human actions, as they do,
> I doubt not then but innocence shall make
> False accusation blush, and tyranny
> Tremble at patience; (26-30)

– suggests that the kind of play she has in mind is a morality; at any rate, she has been miscast:

> for behold me –
> A fellow of the royal bed, which owe
> A moiety of the throne, a great king's daughter,
> The mother to a hopeful prince – here standing
> To prate and talk for life and honour fore
> Who please to come and hear. (35-40)

But she cannot persuade her judge; Leontes is also familiar with the morality play, and therefore he knows that Hermione is merely fulfilling one of its standard conventions:

> I ne'er heard yet

That any of these bolder vices wanted
Less impudence to gainsay what they did
Than to perform it first. (52-5)

And so he intones the scene's (and his playlet's) climactic words: 'thou / Shalt feel our justice; in whose easiest passage / Look for no less than death' (87-9).

But the trial scene is the climax of Leontes' playlet in more than one sense, for it is also the occasion of the permanent shattering of the illusion he has so carefully fashioned. When the 'seal'd-up oracle, by the hand deliver'd / Of great Apollo's priest' (125-6) proclaims Hermione's innocence and his own tyrannic jealousy, Leontes tries to extend his playlet even to the heavens:

There is no truth at all i' th' oracle.
The sessions shall proceed. This is mere falsehood. (137-8)

And with these words his play-world crumbles about him. At once a servant announces the sudden death of Prince Mamillius, and Hermione swoons: according to Paulina, 'This news is mortal to the Queen' (145). Leontes now realizes his injustice, and he prays to Apollo for pardon. He also realizes full well what his theatrical manipulation of the real world has cost him, for he vows, 'I'll reconcile me to Polixenes, / New woo my queen, recall the good Camillo – ' (152-3). But his realizations come too late; his courtiers, his friend, his daughter, his son, and his wife are all lost to him. As a result, he no longer has an identity, not even the fictional one he has been playing throughout. As if also realizing this, he now chooses for himself a new role and thus a new identity, the only one through which he can still maintain some kind of relationship with the two people who have had the most to do with determining his original identity:

Prithee, bring me
To the dead bodies of my queen and son.
...
Once a day I'll visit
The chapel where they lie; and tears shed there
Shall be my recreation. So long as nature
Will bear up with this exercise, so long
I daily vow to use it. Come, and lead me
To these sorrows. (231-2, 235-40)

Leontes' loss of identity is a dramatic fact of some importance, but it is by no means a source of tragic illumination; his discovery of a substitute role allows him and Shakespeare to evade tragedy. Tragedy is also evaded in *The*

Winter's Tale by the shifts in focus that immediately follow upon the double climax to Leontes' playlet, the shifts from Sicilia to Bohemia, from hatred to love, from destructive imagination to 'great creating nature' (IV.iv.88), from 'things dying' to 'things new-born' (III.iii.110-11). Perhaps the most significant shift is that the play-world now falls to the control of a new and entirely different kind of figure. The action of the second half of *The Winter's Tale* is also governed by an internal dramatist, but this one is not a fallible human being; it is, instead, Time, who enters in IV.i to mend the plot so that, despite Leontes, it can have a happy outcome:

> Impute it not a crime
> To me or my swift passage that I slide
> O'er sixteen years, and leave the growth untried
> Of that wide gap, since it is in my pow'r
> To o'erthrow law, and in one self-born hour
> To plant and o'erwhelm custom. (IV.i.4-9)

Time makes it clear that the story unfolding on the stage has become *his* 'tale' (14) and that what is about to be shown is *his* 'scene' (16). And now that the action has become his, it will focus not on Leontes but on 'Perdita, now grown in grace / Equal with wond'ring':

> A shepherd's daughter,
> And what to her adheres, which follows after,
> Is th' argument of Time. (24-5, 27-9)

Time's assumption of control by no means ends the emphasis upon role-playing, for there is even more of it, and more varied examples of it, in Bohemia than in Leontes' Sicilia. Camillo and Polixenes believe that Florizel is violating his role of prince by wooing the daughter 'of a most homely shepherd' (IV.ii. 36), and they decide to disguise themselves and investigate. Autolycus, in order to disarm the Clown and thus have a chance to pick his pocket, pretends to be a victim of that famous thievish rogue – Autolycus (IV.iii). Florizel, using the name Doricles, has 'obscur'd' his 'high self ... With a swain's wearing' (IV.iv. 7-9), though in his own eyes he has rather come to resemble Apollo (29-31). Perdita's 'unusual weeds to each part of [her] / Do give a life – no shepherdess, but Flora' (1-2); she is 'Most goddess-like prank'd up' (10), and all her 'acts are queens' (146). 'Methinks I play as I have seen them do / In Whitsun pastorals,' she says (133-4), and thereby not only helps call attention to her own role-playing but also provides a metaphor to encompass and place as spectacle the jokes, songs, dances, and other 'turns' of the sheep-shearing festival.

As this last example especially suggests, the role-playing of Bohemia tends to express joy rather than madness. It also differs from that of Leontes in another important respect; while his is both sign and cause of identity loss, that of Perdita and Florizel, at least, symbolizes the fidelity with which they cling to their true identities. When the disguised Polixenes and Camillo arrive at the feast, the Shepherd, the supposed father of Perdita, objects to her behaviour, which he sees as violating her proper role:

> You are retired,
> As if you were a feasted one, and not
> The hostess of the meeting. Pray you bid
> These unknown friends to's welcome, for it is
> A way to make us better friends, more known.
> Come, quench your blushes, and present yourself
> That which you are, Mistress o' th' Feast. (62-8)

He is wrong to object, of course, for in playing the queen, she is, like Guiderius and Arviragus in *Cymbeline,* instinctively acting out what she is in reality. Yet, as far as she knows, he is right, and thus in a new demonstration of fidelity, this time to what she assumes to be her identity, she immediately accepts the role her 'father' assigns her:

> Sir, welcome.
> It is my father's will I should take on me
> The hostess-ship o' th' day. (70-2)

Florizel, according to his father, violates his roles as prince and son by wooing Perdita, but as Florizel himself understands his behaviour, he pursues Perdita in order to *realize* his identity, including those elements of it deriving from his position as Polixenes' son:

> Or I'll be thine, my fair,
> Or not my father's; for I cannot be
> Mine own, nor anything to any, if
> I be not thine. To this I am most constant,
> Though destiny say no. (42-6)

The primary difference between the role-playing of Bohemia and that of Sicilia emerges from the one moment in this long scene in which the spirit of Leontes intrudes upon the action. When Polixenes has heard enough, he breaks up the mirth by throwing off his disguise and disowning his son. Immediately thereafter, like a new Leontes, he characterizes his adversaries – the Shepherd he sees as an 'old traitor,' Perdita as a 'fresh piece / Of excellent witchcraft,'

Florizel as a 'fond boy' (412, 414-15, 418) – and then plots the course of any further action:

> I'll have thy beauty scratch'd with briers and made
> More homely than thy state. For thee, fond boy,
> If I may ever know thou dost but sigh
> That thou no more shalt see this knack – as never
> I mean thou shalt – we'll bar thee from succession;
> ...
>   And you, enchantment,
> Worthy enough a herdsman – ...
> ...
>   – if ever henceforth thou
> These rural latches to his entrance open,
> Or hoop his body more with thy embraces,
> I will devise a death as cruel for thee
> As thou art tender to't. (417-21, 426-7, 429-33)

The most interesting aspect of this episode is that in approximating Leontes, Polixenes does not assume an alien role but instead throws off the one he has been playing. In Bohemia, play-acting is the source of harmony, and its abandonment is the destructive force.

The Winter's Tale thus dramatizes a contrast similar to those which help structure *A Midsummer Night's Dream* and *As You Like It,* a contrast between two realms, the second of which offers role-playing possibilities that counteract the difficulties enforced by the laws governing role-playing in the first. In Sicilia role-playing originates from a diseased imagination and leads to destruction; in Bohemia, it is natural and spontaneous and productive of joy. In terms of dramatic structure, the role-playing of Bohemia offsets and purges the gloom created by Leontes' role-playing; in terms of action, it becomes the means through which Leontes regains almost everything he had lost and the world he has nearly destroyed is finally redeemed.

The counter-movement in the romance pattern of loss and reacquisition begins in iv.iv with the exit of Polixenes, at which point all of Bohemia's role-playing becomes directed to the achievement of a single end, the union of Perdita and Florizel, and through this at least partial restoration of the original situation Leontes had disrupted. Taking over the function of plotter already held by Leontes and Time, Camillo devises a new playlet, the flight of Florizel and Perdita to Leontes in Sicilia. Camillo urges the lovers to 'embrace but my direction' (515), promises to work out a detailed script (550-6), and even volunteers to oversee the costuming: 'It shall be so my care / To have you royally appointed as if / The scene you play were mine' (583-5). For the new playlet's first episode, however, the escape from Bohemia, emergency costumes are needed; therefore Florizel exchanges garments with Autolycus, and Perdita, who realizes 'the play so lies / That I must bear a part' (645-6), fashions herself a costume out of her own clothing and Florizel's hat. Camillo tells the lovers that his part in their playlet will consist of an attempt to 'qualify' Florizel's 'discontenting father ... And bring him up to liking' (524-5), but in an aside he reveals his true intention of telling Polixenes about the flight, in order

> To force him after; in whose company
> I shall re-view Sicilia, for whose sight
> I have a woman's longing. (655-7)

Camillo thus acts primarily for selfish reasons, but he nonetheless makes possible not only the permanent union of the lovers but also the reconciliation between Leontes and Polixenes and the reunion of Leontes and his daughter.

Once Camillo has set his plot in motion, all that is needed to ensure the result it points toward is the one thing Camillo does not know exists: proof that Perdita is Leontes' lost daughter. And this item is supplied when, in keeping with a standard practice of Shakespeare's time, another plotter furnishes Camillo's playlet with a comic underplot. For even Autolycus puts his penchant for play-acting to the lovers' use when he overhears the Shepherd and the Clown discussing the proof they have that Perdita is a changeling, proof they intend to give Polixenes in order to escape his wrath. To prevent them from interfering with Florizel's flight, Autolycus, whose exchange of garments with Florizel has already equipped him with an appropriate costume, 'pocket[s] up [his] pedlar's excrement' (703) so that he can play the courtier and thus trick them into giving him their bundle. Autolycus acts even more selfishly than Camillo, for he expects his efforts to win him some reward from Florizel, but he too contributes, however unwittingly, to the joyful conclusion; it is more than the Shepherd and the Clown that Autolycus can include among 'those I have done good to against my will' (v.ii.120).

The care with which Shakespeare develops and emphasizes the Camillo-Autolycus playlet indicates its importance to the basic pattern of action. It is counteractant to the playlet of Leontes, a successful attempt to accomplish what his adversaries had vainly sought to do in the first half of the play – convert his plot into a drama of another genre. Eventually, as the ultimate step in fulfilling its function, the Camillo-Autolycus playlet even enlists Leontes in a subordinate role. That Leontes is ready to succeed in such a part is shown at once when the focus shifts back to Sicilia, for by conscientiously playing the new role he had set for himself sixteen years before, he has atoned; as Cleomenes remarks, 'Sir, you have done enough, and have perform'd / A saint-like sorrow' (v.i.1-2). But Leontes denies this; he cannot forget the evil he has created, and

as he dwells upon it, he re-establishes himself and his losses as the central focus
of the action:

> Whilst I remember
> Her and her virtues, I cannot forget
> My blemishes in them, and so still think of
> The wrong I did myself; which was so much
> That heirless it hath made my kingdom, and
> Destroy'd the sweet'st companion that e'er man
> Bred his hopes out of. (6-12)

The speech also serves to substantiate the validity of Cleomenes' statement:
by dramatizing Leontes' adherence to the role of penitent mourner, it demonstrates that he has indeed acquired the capacity to play the kind of part his
circumstances render appropriate. Similarly, by agreeing not to remarry until
Paulina approves a wife for him, he shows that he has also learned how to take
direction from others. The wilful playwright-director of the first half of *The
Winter's Tale* has disappeared, his place now filled by a conscientious actor
whose sole desire consists of learning his proper role and performing it with all
the skill and fidelity he can muster. Thus he has no hesitancy in accepting the
role Florizel begs him to assume:

> Step forth mine advocate; at your request
> My father will grant precious things as trifles. (221-2)

The 'stage' Leontes mentions (58) is now set for the climactic scene of
the Camillo-Autolycus playlet – the identifying of Perdita and the reconciliation between Leontes and Polixenes – and this scene is narrated in v.ii. One
reason, evidently, why the scene is narrated rather than performed is to ensure
its being experienced as a scene in the playlet. The three Gentlemen who describe it and stress the 'wonder' it evoked also emphasize its stagy quality:

> There might you have beheld one joy crown another, so and in such
> manner that it seem'd sorrow wept to take leave of them; for their joy
> waded in tears. There was casting up of eyes, holding up of hands, with
> countenance of such distraction that they were to be known by gar-
> ment, not by favour. (42-7)

So stagy is it, in fact, that it can finally be spoken of only as a play: 'The dignity of this act was worth the audience of kings and princes; for by such was
it acted' (77-8). And by twice likening what they have witnessed to 'an old
tale' (28, 59), the Gentlemen also identify the kind of play it is. Time, working

through Camillo and Autolycus, has finally managed to convert Leontes' revenge tragedy into a different kind of play. What Time has produced is not the farce hoped for by Antigonus, the melodrama urged by Hermione, or the comedy imagined by Paulina, but instead an example of the dramatic genre that most resembles 'an old tale,' the romance.

With the climax of the Camillo-Autolycus playlet, *The Winter's Tale* would seem to have reached its ending. There follows, however, the climax of Autolycus' comic underplot – in which the Shepherd and the Clown try out their new roles as 'gentlemen born' (123) – and then, far more unexpectedly, Paulina's unveiling of Hermione's statue. There was, it now becomes clear, a second and even better reason for narrating the climax of the Camillo-Autolycus playlet, the fact that it is not the true climax of *The Winter's Tale*. It restores to Leontes his lost daughter and his lost friend, but it leaves his primary loss, that of his wife, unaffected. As the audience knows, what is needed to restore that loss is an impossible miracle; but through Paulina's magic the impossible miracle occurs. Paulina's manipulation of her miracle – her request for 'music' (v.iii.98) and her directions to Hermione and the assembled spectators (99-107) – make it a new playlet, the last in the rich series dramatized within *The Winter's Tale*. And although it is perhaps inspired by the Camillo-Autolycus playlet, it has its own independent source, its own dramatist, who thus completes the purgation of Leontes' errors by associating with Sicilia the kind of play-making that before had sprung only from Bohemia. Yet, despite its independent source, Paulina's playlet forms part of the same master plot to which Camillo and Autolycus have contributed, for Paulina's playlet, too, is 'Like an old tale' (117). As Leontes says, the whole preceding sixteen years have encompassed but a single action:

> Good Paulina,
> Lead us from hence where we may leisurely
> Each one demand and answer to his part
> Perform'd in this wide gap of time since first
> We were dissever'd. (151-5)

Camillo, Autolycus, and Paulina help restore what Leontes had destroyed, but their activity by no means redeems the internal dramatist from the thorough condemnation Leontes has won for this figure in the first half of the play. The true internal dramatist of the second half of *The Winter's Tale* is not a human character, but Time. Camillo, Autolycus, and Paulina, who do not quite realize what they are accomplishing, work independently of one another and to a considerable extent for more or less selfish reasons. Their final joint masterpiece is produced not through their own unaided efforts but only because they unknowingly assist Time in the staging of his 'old tale.'

The final speech of the play defines the union of Perdita and Florizel as the work of heaven (149-51), and as other passages make clear, all the miracles wrought by Time can be attributed to the same source. In *The Winter's Tale*, as in the other romances, heaven is seen to be the guiding force in the action, and in *The Winter's Tale* the verbal assertions about the intervention of heaven are emotionally validated by the miracle that the audience participates in along with the characters: the restoration of Hermione. Hermione's age, her evident inability to speak to Leontes even as she embraces him, and the absence of Mamillius indicate that some of the things which have been lost cannot be re-acquired, and this gives the ending of the play an unusual, anti-romance touch of realism. The touch of realism does not, however, undermine the celebration of providential assistance. If anything, it provides another striking source of emotional validation.

The gap between play-world and real world seems most of the time to be a fairly narrow one. As spectators we do not make the mistake of Partridge in *Tom Jones* and assume that the activity before us on the stage is actually happening, now, in the real world. But we do assume that in so far as the play we are watching dramatizes some sort of coherent vision the content of this vision can and should be applied to the real world. We assume, in other words, that the play constitutes at least in part a commentary on the real world by the dramatist. Some dramatists narrow this gap even further through one means or another: a satiric tone, explicit moralizing, the obviousness with which they define their characters and events as representative cases, or perhaps (to suggest a means of a quite different kind) the use of topical allusions. Shakespeare is fond of topical allusions, but he tends to avoid the other means of narrowing the gap, and this is as true of his treatment of role-playing as it is of his treatment of the other themes and materials exploited in his plays. There are, however, with respect to role-playing, a number of interesting real or apparent exceptions to this practice, especially in the earlier plays of his career.

If Shakespeare's plays *can* pass for an image of life, the continual histrionic activity and allusions to such activity in these plays cause them to characterize life as a theatrical enterprise, to assert, in keeping with the primary metaphor from which Shakespeare works, that the (real) world's a stage. In *The Taming of the Shrew*, one of the first of the plays thoroughly to adopt role-playing as an explicit dramatic subject, Shakespeare seems to dramatize this assertion deliberately by making his main action a play-within-the-play performed by the company of actors that appear in the Induction. This effect places the adventures of Christopher Sly which comprise the Induction on a par with the real world, but since no spectator forgets that the Induction is itself a theatrical fiction, and since role-playing also constitutes its chief activity, the real world as it is here defined inevitably acquires the attributes of a play.

A similar but subtler effect occurs in *Love's Labour's Lost* after the Princess and Rosaline have penalized their wooers to a year's wait. The King and Berowne agree to fulfil their ladies' demands, but Berowne is clearly disappointed:

Our wooing doth not end like an old play:
Jack hath not Jill. These ladies' courtesy
Might well have made our sport a comedy.

The King consoles him with 'it wants a twelvemonth an' a day, / And then 'twill end,' but Berowne remains dissatisfied: 'That's too long for a play' (v.ii. 862-6). By emphasizing the difference between the outcome of their adventure and the conventional ending of comedy, Berowne acknowledges that until this point he and his comrades have conducted their adventure as if it were a comedy. There is also the further implication that only if it had been a comedy and had thus been immune to such grim facts of existence as the death of the Princess' father would their theatrical kind of role-playing have served. These dimensions of Berowne's speeches comment only on the affairs of the play-world, but his role-playing images also have a further effect that pertains more to the real world, for by equating what has previously occurred with a play, Berowne's images assert that this play has ended and that the present moment, like the Induction to *The Taming of the Shrew*, is equivalent to life in the real world. Nevertheless, as with the Induction, no spectator can forget that Berowne is in fact a character and that his speeches advance what is unquestionably a play. Once again, therefore, Shakespeare equates a portion of one of his plays with the real world in such a way as to suggest the essential theatrical quality of the real world. This time, moreover, he does not merely make the suggestion but complicates it by letting it absorb everything *Love's Labour's Lost* has dramatized about the defective role-playing that the King and his Lords have practised.

This way of narrowing the gap between play-world and real world does not look particularly promising, and, so far as I can see, Shakespeare did not employ it again until the very end of his career; in the meantime, if he was at all concerned with asserting the theatrical nature of life, he let his preoccupation with role-playing speak for itself. A far more promising means of narrowing the gap he also used sparingly: the extension of the play-world to include the performance itself. I do not have in mind here such things as the use of the aside (in Shakespeare's theatre the aside seldom becomes anything more than one further means of defining the play-world verbally) nor the usual direct addressing of the audience in prologue or epilogue. A good example of what I mean – the first of its sort – occurs near the end of *A Midsummer Night's Dream* when Theseus compares Peter Quince's actors to 'The best in this kind' (v.i.209)

and thus directs the spectators' attention to a contrast between the bad performance of the 'base mechanicals' and the highly successful theatrical venture simultaneously carried off by Shakespeare's company. Later examples
of this means of narrowing the gap, most of which have been discussed incidentally in the two preceding chapters, consist of Cassius' prophecy about
future dramatizations of the assassination of Caesar, several speeches from
Troilus and Cressida, especially the one with which Pandarus closes the play,
the allusions in *Hamlet* to the Globe Theatre and other phenomena of the
London theatrical world, occasional speeches by Iago in *Othello* and the Fool
in *King Lear,* and Cleopatra's despairing vision of 'Some squeaking Cleopatra'
boy-ing her greatness (*Antony and Cleopatra,* v.ii.219). The example from *A
Midsummer Night's Dream* points outward to the real world because it offers
a definition of good theatrical art as a kind of waking dream, a means of temporarily escaping the rigid restrictions of the real world. But at the same time
the contrast Theseus establishes also points inward to the play-world because
of its special relevance to the theme of the relationship between fairyland and
Athens, and pointing inward to comment upon and enrich the play-world is
unquestionably the chief, if not the sole, function of the subsequent examples
of this device.

These sure or fairly sure cases of Shakespeare's narrowing the gap between play-world and real world with respect to the role-playing material of
his dramas prompts one to perceive other cases that are perhaps less sure. *The
Merchant of Venice,* as I indicate in chapter 3, seems to me to constitute in
large measure a comment on dramatic form, a comparison of two contrasting
types of dramatic character. And several of the history plays, which are often
thought of as narrowing the gap through their didacticism, seem to me to do
so rather (or at least also) through their reflection of Shakespeare's experience
with the actors for whom he was writing. The tragedy dramatized by the three
parts of *Henry VI* is in one sense a tragedy about a role no one can fill, and this
treatment of the material perhaps springs from the circumstances of its writing. Shakespeare is already drawn to Henry V, as the attempt to celebrate him
at the beginning of Part I shows, but he must start with his death and directly
dramatize only the lesser figures of the period that succeeded it. Speculation
about the reasons for these choices is necessarily idle, and they may not be
choices at all but merely accidents of one kind or another, yet it is tempting to
see Shakespeare's refusing the opportunity to write about Henry V either because he does not yet feel equal to the task or because (as the theme of the trilogy suggests) he doubts whether the company for which he is writing possesses
an actor fit to play the part.

Richard III is unmistakably a study of an actor who can deliver a superb
performance when creating his own little playlets on the stage, but who lacks
the discipline that would make him capable of doing justice to a part someone

else has written. *Richard II*, in Richard and Henry, contains two further studies of inadequate actors, and together with *Richard III* and early comedies like *The Two Gentlemen of Verona* and *Love's Labour's Lost,* the play helps establish the important theme of the discrepancy between the actor and his role which becomes especially prominent during the middle of Shakespeare's career. A different kind of study of actors and their ways forms one dimension of *1 Henry IV*, which begins with King Henry's vigorous efforts to put himself in the best possible light. One can see why Shakespeare has him behave this way (for play-acting is a key element in Henry's nature and in his resemblance to his son), but one wonders why Henry himself chooses such an occasion for play-acting, why he picks for his audience a group of courtiers who must be able to see through a good share, if not all, of the deception in his managing of the news. When Falstaff and Hal appear, and both produce their versions of the kind of thing Henry has done, one ceases to wonder. Henry has not been playing to the audience onstage but to the audience in the theatre. Like Falstaff and Hal, he tries to impress this audience and win its approval. He, like them, is advancing his claim to the title role in the sub-drama of *1 Henry IV*, 'Who Shall Play the King' – or, perhaps, simply behaving as the vain, career-wise actor he is.

Whether or not these problematic examples from the history plays can be included, most of these cases of Shakespeare's narrowing the gap between play-world and real world fall fairly early in his career. Following *Troilus and Cressida,* examples of this effect become rather scattered, until suddenly, at the end of his career, it finds in *The Tempest* its most impressive exemplification. Here Shakespeare works carefully in an attempt to bridge the gap completely and create a powerful effect that is designed to point in both directions, to comment on both worlds simultaneously. Once again, as in *The Taming of the Shrew* and *Love's Labour's Lost,* a Shakespearian play asserts the theatrical nature of the real world, though not, this time, simply to do so, but as an important element of Shakespeare's final comment about the internal dramatist in particular and role-playing in general.

Prospero is Shakespeare's most accomplished internal dramatist, for the action of *The Tempest* consists almost exclusively of his manipulation of others and of the events in which they participate. As early as I.ii, the play becomes Prospero's play, and in more than one sense. Act I scene i is a scene of pure, objective drama; it is (to the extent this term can apply to Elizabethan drama) a 'slice of life' presenting a number of characters involved in a lifelike situation (the storm) and responding to it in recognizably human ways. Once scene ii begins, however, this opening is redefined as a 'spectacle' (I.ii.26) devised by Prospero's art and so controlled by him that its outcome bears no resemblance to the ending such a situation would lead to in ordinary experience: 'there is no soul – / No, not so much perdition as an hair / Betid to any creature in the vessel / Which thou heard'st cry, which thou saw'st sink' (29-32). Equally important, the movement from scene i to scene ii is a shift from drama to narrative. At line 25 of the second scene, Prospero removes the 'magic garment' in which he practises his art because, as he says to Miranda, ' 'Tis time / I should inform thee farther'; the time has come, that is, for Prospero to supply the exposition needed to give his 'spectacle' its full meaning. He thus further demonstrates his control of the action by becoming, like Time in *The Winter's Tale,* its presenter.

Prospero's two roles make the action wholly his. As narrator, he determines the way in which the action is seen by deciding what portions of the past shall be introduced and how they shall be defined, by establishing the characterizations of the central figures, and by continuing throughout the play to offer comments on both people and events. As mage, the wearer of the 'magic garment,' he controls the action more directly, not simply by speaking of it in a particular way but by shaping it to meet his wishes. Prospero's success with the storm and its outcome as well as the power he holds over the spirit Ariel demonstrate his capacity for this direct control, but that which assures the spectators they are to witness a drama of his creation is the speech in which he first alludes to what he will later call his 'project':

> By accident most strange, bountiful Fortune,
> Now my dear lady, hath mine enemies
> Brought to this shore; and by my prescience
> I find my zenith doth depend upon
> A most auspicious star, whose influence
> If now I court not, but omit, my fortunes
> Will ever after droop. (178-84)

Exactly what Prospero intends, the spectators cannot know: 'Here,' he commands Miranda, 'cease more questions' (184). They must, therefore, wait to see the dimensions of his drama take shape as it unfolds. For Prospero himself does not know exactly what he plans to do; it soon becomes evident that in fashioning his drama he is partly working from a prepared scenario and partly improvising.

The division of the visitors to the island into three groups furnishes Prospero's drama with three separate plot strands, the first of which begins in I.ii and centres upon Ferdinand and Miranda. Prospero has fully prepared this portion of his drama, and it rapidly unfolds as he has planned it, for Ferdinand and Miranda have scarcely met before Prospero can say, 'They are both in either's pow'rs' (I.ii.450). Nevertheless, Prospero feels that their love story cannot properly develop without complications: 'but this swift business / I must uneasy make, lest too light winning / Make the prize light' (450-2); and so, by

Is identity a given or something we discover, something that opens before us?

abusing Ferdinand and forcing him to 'remove / Some thousands of these logs, and pile them up, / Upon a sore injunction' (III.i.9-11), he imposes on Ferdinand what he will later call 'trials of thy love' (IV.i.6). As Prospero is eventually to note, Ferdinand has 'strangely stood the test' (7) – that is, he has proven himself worthy to play husband to Miranda by first demonstrating his capacity to play the temporary role of slave.

In keeping with the romance pattern Prospero is compelling Ferdinand to enact, Ferdinand's success is also a demonstration of his fidelity to his true identity. His distinction between the 'baseness' of his task and the 'executor' so incongruously enjoined to perform it (III.i.12-13) indicates that he, like Miranda, is highly conscious of the discrepancy between himself and the role Prospero has imposed; yet he performs this role with pleasure, and in so doing he demonstrates both his princeliness (because, although the task is base, it is 'nobly undergone') and the sincerity of his love for Miranda:

> There be some sports are painful, and their labour
> Delight in them sets off; some kinds of baseness
> Are nobly undergone, and most poor matters
> Point to rich ends. This my mean task
> Would be as heavy to me as odious, but
> The mistress which I serve quickens what's dead,
> And makes my labours pleasures. (1-7)

But in the final analysis, it is the product of Prospero's drama, Ferdinand's love for Miranda, which takes precedence, for, as Ferdinand tells Miranda, were it not for his love, his rank as prince would force him to rebel; it is for her sake that he becomes 'this patient log-man' (67).

While Ferdinand pauses in his labours so that he and Miranda can explore the theme of their love for each other, Prospero watches 'at a distance, unseen.' His presence as onstage spectator and the asides he speaks reinforce the association between the Ferdinand-Miranda love plot and the theatre already implied by Prospero's earlier manipulation of the action, and although Prospero's comments on what he sees are remarks that a mere spectator might make, his implied connection with what he sees causes his presence to stress not just the play-like quality of the Ferdinand-Miranda love plot but also the dramatist who has devised it. The chief link between this plot strand and the theatre, however, is the formal masque Prospero stages to entertain and reward the newly formed couple (IV.i.60-138). Like all else in this plot strand, it too is evidently part of his original plan; at any rate, it forms an appropriate climax, and its theme of the blessings pronounced on Ferdinand and Miranda by Juno and Ceres (106-17) commemorates an outcome exactly like that which Prospero had hoped and expected to produce.

The second plot strand, which focuses on the fortunes of Alonso and his group, involves more improvisation. At first glance, in fact, it would seem to concern itself not with Prospero's drama but with one fashioned by Antonio and Sebastian. As this plot strand begins to evolve in II.i, these two, through their asides and their mockery of Gonzalo, Adrian, and even Alonso, remain aloof from the others, placing themselves between the action and Shakespeare's spectators, so that the spectators are encouraged to view the action in the perspective Antonio and Sebastian supply. Once the others drowse off under the influence of Ariel's 'solemn music,' moreover, it becomes clear that Antonio, at least, has more in mind than merely interpreting someone else's play. He has conceived a fully formed plot of his own. 'Th' occasion speaks thee,' he tells Sebastian, 'and / My strong imagination sees a crown / Dropping upon thy head' (II.i.198-200). He can direct Sebastian how to play his part – 'I'll teach you how to flow' (213) – and between them, seizing the occasion destiny has given them, they will 'perform an act / Whereof what's past is prologue, what to come / In yours and my discharge' (243-5). But Antonio and Sebastian never manage to perform their 'act.' If Prospero has not entirely foreseen what his brother will do, he has had every reason to anticipate a show of evil, and he has apparently had Ariel put Alonso and the others to sleep in order to give Antonio an opportunity to betray his true intentions. At any rate, no sooner has Antonio's idea for a play of his own become explicit than Prospero reseizes control of the action. Just as Antonio and Sebastian are about to act, Ariel quickly returns and sings in Gonzalo's ear to warn him of the danger, stressing as he does so Prospero's management of his activity:

My master through his art foresees the danger
That you, his friend, are in; and sends me forth –
For else his project dies – to keep them living. (288-90)

After this, Antonio and Sebastian no longer have any effect upon what is now clearly a phase of Prospero's evolving 'project'; they continue to talk about their plot, but it never again even comes close to being transformed into action.

Prospero's subverting of the plans of Antonio and Sebastian has the air of improvisation, but this plot strand also includes material that has been carefully planned: the formal playlet Ariel executes in III.iii as a parallel to the masque with which Prospero entertains Ferdinand and Miranda. The playlet begins as a dumb show, with '*Solemn and strange music*' and Prospero, '*invisible,*' watching from the top of the theatre: '*Enter several strange Shapes, bringing in a banquet; and dance about it with gentle actions of salutations; and inviting the King, &c, to eat, they depart.*' As Alonso and the others respond with awe and wonder, dumb show gives way to dialogue, and once again Prospero uses asides to comment on the action and stress his control of it (III.iii.

34-6, 39). Because of their hunger, the amazement felt by Alonso's group is short-lived, but as they are about to accept the invitation and eat, the second scene of the playlet prevents them: '*Thunder and lightning. Enter Ariel, like a harpy; claps his wings upon the table; and, with a quaint device, the banquet vanishes.*' This time, before anyone can react, Ariel, identifying Alonso, Antonio, and Sebastian as 'three men of sin' (53), proceeds to interpret the dumb show they have seen. All efforts of theirs to control their own actions are fruitless, for they are, he assures them while Prospero watches from above, under the control of Destiny. Then, having reminded them what they did to Prospero, Ariel concludes by spelling out the implicit message of the playlet:

> Thee of thy son, Alonso,
> They [i.e., the 'pow'rs' of Destiny] have bereft; and do pronounce by
>   me
> Ling'ring perdition, worse than any death
> Can be at once, shall step by step attend
> You and your ways; whose wraths to guard you from –
> Which here, in this most desolate isle, else falls
> Upon your heads – is nothing but heart's sorrow,
> And a clear life ensuing. (75-82)

With this Ariel '*vanishes in thunder; then, to soft music, enter the Shapes again, and dance, with mocks and mows, and carrying out the table.*' The playlet has reached its conclusion.

Prospero's ensuing comment on the playlet explicitly locates its source in his imagination and indicates that it has effectively fulfilled its purpose:

> Bravely the figure of this harpy hast thou
> Perform'd, my Ariel; a grace it had, devouring.
> Of my instruction hast thou nothing bated
> In what thou hadst to say; so, with good life
> And observation strange, my meaner ministers
> Their several kinds have done. My high charms work,
> And these mine enemies are all knit up
> In their distractions. They now are in my pow'r. (83-90)

What happens after his exit suggests that the playlet has had an even more important effect. Sebastian and Antonio rush out to fight the 'fiends' that have beset them, but Alonso, who is deeply moved, has clearly understood the point:

> O, it is monstrous, monstrous!

> Methought the billows spoke, and told me of it;
> The winds did sing it to me; and the thunder,
> That deep and dreadful organ-pipe, pronounc'd
> The name of Prosper; it did bass my trespass.
> Therefore my son i' th' ooze is bedded; and
> I'll seek him deeper than e'er plummet sounded,
> And with him there lie mudded. (95-102)

The third plot strand of Prospero's drama traces the fortunes of Caliban, the 'savage and deformed slave,' Trinculo, the 'jester,' and Stephano, the 'drunken butler.' The main emphasis of this plot strand falls on the familiar Shakespearian theme of discrepant role-playing, as Caliban, through his responses, continually defines the drunken butler as god or noble lord and soon decides this god should kill Prospero and become lord of the island in Prospero's place. Here, too, therefore a 'plot' (III.ii.105) of their own is conceived by characters in Prospero's drama, and this one, if successful, would result in the climax Stephano describes, the absurdity of which far outweighs any sense of potential disaster: 'Monster, I will kill this man; his daughter and I will be King and Queen – save our Graces! – and Trinculo and thyself shall be viceroys' (102-4). Prospero has clearly not anticipated this development in his drama; his handling of it is entirely improvised. But, acting through Ariel, he appropriates it as a farcical subplot with an ease that provides special testimony of his capacity to control all actions.

Prospero's adroitness enables him to ignore Caliban and his confederates until 'the minute of their plot / Is almost come' (IV.i.141-2), at which time Prospero quickly whips up a farcical counterpart to the formal playlets of the other plot strands. He has Ariel set the stage by hanging 'glistering apparel' and other 'trumpery' on a lime tree 'For stale to catch these thieves' (187), and to Caliban's despair, his confederates forget their purpose in their greedy haste to make this 'trash' their own. The second scene of the playlet then follows: *'A noise of hunters heard. Enter divers Spirits, in shape of dogs and hounds, hunting them about; Prospero and Ariel setting them on.'* And Prospero even orders a third scene, though, mercifully, it is to take place offstage:

> Go charge my goblins that they grind their joints
> With dry convulsions, shorten up their sinews
> With aged cramps, and more pinch-spotted make them
> Than pard or cat o' mountain. (257-60)

Like the other playlets, this one also has a theme or moral, which Caliban, once his senses are restored, pronounces:

> I'll be wise hereafter,
> And seek for grace. What a thrice-double ass
> Was I to take this drunkard for a god,
> And worship this dull fool! (v.i.294-7)

The immediate effect of this playlet is that, as Prospero observes, 'At this hour / Lies at my mercy all mine enemies' (iv.i.261-2). In v.i, therefore, Prospero assembles them for the climax of his drama, the play-like quality of which is established by two highly stagy effects, his own change of costume so that he can present himself as he 'was sometime Milan' (v.i.86) and his 'discovery' of *'Ferdinand and Miranda playing at chess.'* As his 'project gather[s] to a head' (v.i.1), Prospero, realizing that 'The rarer action is / In virtue than in vengeance' (27-8), decides not to exploit the power he holds over his enemies: 'they being penitent, / The sole drift of my purpose doth extend / Not a frown further' (28-30). As a result, the most important aspect of the climax of his drama is the responses of the others, who, freed from Prospero's magic spells, can now act on their own. His presentation of himself as he 'was sometime Milan' provokes from Alonso the resignation of Prospero's dukedom and an entreaty for pardon. The discovery of Ferdinand and Miranda occasions Miranda's awe at the 'brave new world' (183), Ferdinand's attribution of his good fortune to 'immortal Providence' (189), Gonzalo's celebration of the gods that 'have chalk'd forth the way / Which brought us hither' (203-4), and his and Alonso's evocation of the joy they should all feel in finding what seemed irretrievably lost (205-15). Since even Sebastian views the discovery of Ferdinand and Miranda as 'A most high miracle!' (177), Alonso's final comment on their experience evidently expresses the general sentiment:

> This is as strange a maze as e'er men trod;
> And there is in this business more than nature
> Was ever conduct of. (242-4)

Nevertheless, one of the characters in Prospero's drama does not participate in the general wonder and rejoicing – the character that has most harmed Prospero, his brother Antonio, who has nothing to say during the entire scene except for a wisecrack about Caliban of the sort he was making in ii.i (v.i.265-6). Although Prospero forgives him (131-2), Antonio's silence makes it clear that he has not merited this forgiveness by becoming penitent like the others.

Except for Antonio's response, or non-response, the climax of Prospero's drama defines it (and therefore *The Tempest,* with which Prospero's drama is largely co-extensive) as a full-scale version of a device Shakespeare has frequently utilized, especially in *Much Ado About Nothing, The Merry Wives of*

Windsor, and *All's Well That Ends Well:* the staged action that transforms its victims' identities. Prospero is by and large the most admirable practitioner of this device in all Shakespeare. Because of his intentions, as they finally take shape, and because of the distinctions he makes in dealing with his various victims, Prospero emerges as a character whose actions the spectators would be likely to approve and whose manipulations seem fully justified by the consequences they produce. But his failure to achieve full success (his failure to convert his brother) is not to be ignored. It indicates, rather, the way in which his activity is finally to be seen. For just as the work of Camillo, Autolycus, and Paulina cannot overcome the impression created by Leontes, the portrait of Prospero does not ultimately redeem the figure of the internal dramatist from the opprobrium it has always had in tragedy and that it comes also to acquire in the later comedies. On the contrary, this portrait suggests why the internal dramatist must be condemned even when, like Prospero, he acts with sure moral soundness and for the best of motives.

The reason for Prospero's inability to achieve full success, I would say, is that in the final analysis he occupies much the same position as the other characters of *The Tempest.* The movement from scene i to scene ii consists, as I have argued, of a sort of symbolic raising of the scenery to reveal the hidden dramatist who has plotted and executed what originally looked like a free and autonomous event, happening in the same way, we believe, as similar events happen in real life. Throughout *The Tempest,* this opening effect is reproduced and its implications reinforced by the numerous episodes (such as the plotting of Antonio and Sebastian, the parody of this by Caliban and his crew, and even the love-making of Ferdinand and Miranda) in which characters who imagine themselves to be free and in control of their own actions are shown to be restricted by the will of Prospero and, in some cases, simply acting out the parts he has assigned them. The conclusion of Prospero's masque makes a similar point, for just as it is nearing its devised end, it is broken off by the intrusion of a reality more real than its own:

> *Enter certain Reapers, properly habited; they join with the Nymphs in a graceful dance; towards the end whereof Prospero starts suddenly, and speaks; after which, to a strange, hollow, and confused noise, they heavily vanish.*
> PROSPERO I had forgot that foul conspiracy
> Of the beast Caliban and his confederates
> Against my life; the minute of their plot
> Is almost come. [*To the Spirits*] Well done; avoid; no more!
> (IV.i.139-42)

The relevance of all this to Prospero is suggested by his masque in its capacity as metaphor. As Prospero's creation, the masque epitomizes his play-making; it provides an analogy for the larger drama Prospero evolves, of which the masque is also simultaneously just one episode; and therefore its conclusion calls attention to the fact that Prospero's larger drama is also encompassed within a more real reality. This is, of course, Prospero's own experience outside and apart from his drama. His narrative in 1.ii, in addition to providing necessary exposition for his own drama, also establishes for him a life prior to that drama, one in which, significantly, he has been the victim of a drama devised by another, for while he was 'neglecting worldly ends' (1.ii.89), his 'false brother,' Antonio (92), like a dramatist, 'new created / The creatures that were' Prospero's, 'or chang'd 'em, / Or else new form'd 'em' (81-3), and took whatever other steps were necessary 'To have no screen between this part he play'd / And him he play'd it for' (107-8). Towards the end of *The Tempest*, Prospero rejects the possibility of revenge because he accepts the fact that he, like those he has manipulated, is a human being (v.i.21-7), and this means that he must also reject his role as mage; thus, in becoming once more as he was when he 'was sometime Milan,' he is not only contributing to the climax of his drama, he is also readying himself for a life subsequent to his drama, the life in which he will return as Duke to Milan, 'where / Every third thought shall be [his] grave' (310-11). Furthermore, Prospero's experience outside and apart from his drama is far from merely a matter of before and after; throughout *The Tempest*, Shakespeare keeps it in focus by means of the various responses – of satisfaction, rage, etc. – with which Prospero acknowledges the evolving contours produced by his art. Prospero not only creates a drama in *The Tempest*, then, he also lives an experience. But for everyone else in *The Tempest*, to live an experience is to be subject to the manipulations of a (normally) hidden dramatist, and although for everyone else that hidden dramatist is Prospero, the insistence with which *The Tempest* continually redefines experience as drama suggests that Prospero's experience should be seen in the same light.

And for Prospero, as for the others, the scenery masking the hidden dramatist is finally lifted. For Prospero this occurs at the very end of *The Tempest*, when he remains alone onstage to speak the epilogue, in which he admits his ultimate inability fully to control his experience and – more significantly – asks the spectators to help him. The importance of this explicit acknowledgment of the audience is that it adds the final touch to a set of implications arising from the almost continuous role-playing going on in *The Tempest* and from the rigour with which *The Tempest* conforms to the unity of time in the purest sense – in other words, the three-hours' duration of the action which is twice brought to the attention of the audience in the final scene (v.i.186, 223). Prospero's acknowledgment of the spectators explicitly defines *The Tempest* in its entirety (and not just his own contribution to it) as a play, and this in turn focuses attention upon the dramatist who has created the play. But who is this dramatist? One answer (and obviously a correct one) is Shakespeare, who in writing *The Tempest* has manipulated Prospero just as, within *The Tempest,* Prospero manipulates the others.

Significantly, however, this is not the answer that *The Tempest* itself specifically suggests. The key passages here are Prospero's comment upon his masque (IV.i.148-58) and, once again, the epilogue. In the first of these passages, Prospero sees the masque that has just ended as an emblem of human life, and its dissolution as reflective of the transience of life:

> Our revels now are ended. These our actors,
> As I foretold you, were all spirits, and
> Are melted into air, into thin air;
> And, like the baseless fabric of this vision,
> The cloud-capp'd towers, the gorgeous palaces,
> The solemn temples, the great globe itself,
> Yea, all which it inherit, shall dissolve,
> And, like this insubstantial pageant faded,
> Leave not a rack behind. We are such stuff
> As dreams are made on; and our little life
> Is rounded with a sleep.

This speech explains why Prospero will decide to abandon his art, accept his humanity, and begin to contemplate his own ending, his 'grave.' For he realizes that just as the masque is an unsubstantial fiction in contrast to the higher reality of the actual life encompassing it, so also is this actual life itself a kind of unsubstantial fiction in contrast to the even higher reality that encompasses *it.* What we take to be solid and permanent objects, towers, palaces, temples, and even the earth itself, will also melt and dissolve – not simply, however, because of the law of mutability but because of that which enables the law of mutability to do its destructive work: the fact that, in contrast to the highest reality as defined by God, heaven, and eternity, our life is no more substantial than a dream. Our reality can legitimately be compared to the masque because it too is ultimately no more than a kind of 'pageant' or play, whose dramatist, since he must exist on a level of reality higher than that of the play, can be identified as God.

In identifying God as the dramatist, moreover, this speech effectively bypasses the human dramatist Shakespeare, who himself finally occupies much the same position as Prospero. The 'great globe' that will dissolve (153) necessarily refers not only to the earth but also to Shakespeare's theatre, and thus the 'all which it inherit' (154) (i.e., the 'all' who occupy the 'globe') includes not only the characters of *The Tempest* but also the audience watching the play and, by implication at least, the author who has written it. The passage, in other words, equates life outside *The Tempest* with life within, so that what Prospero has said about life in his world applies as well to life in ours. This point is reinforced by the epilogue, in which, contrary to the usual practice, the actor playing Prospero does not acknowledge his true identity. Even though the play has presumably ended, Prospero remains Prospero. He is not just a fictional character from a play, this effect suggests, but one of us. His reality is equivalent to that of the spectators whom he addresses in the epilogue, especially since, as he insists, they by their applause can affect his experience for good, can help him return to Naples and thus prevent his 'ending' from being 'despair.' Yet, of course, *The Tempest* is only a play, and Prospero is only a character in it, which means that, if Prospero is one of us, we are no different, no better. Like everyone in *The Tempest,* including Prospero, we too perform within an 'insubstantial pageant' which from the standpoint of eternity has no more reality than a play like *The Tempest* has from the standpoint of 'real life.'

Given such an attitude towards life, what matters in living more than anything else is the preparation for the ending of life. And this, I think, is the explanation for the abrupt shift in tone in the epilogue, where a sort of clever playfulness anticipatory of *Peter Pan* quickly gives way to deeply felt seriousness. At the beginning of the epilogue it is applause that is important, so important that it can be likened to that which frees one from bonds, to the gentle gale that carries a ship safely and surely towards its destination, and to prayer. By the end of the epilogue – in fact, as soon as the comparison to prayer has been hit on – applause no longer holds any importance at all. Its place is taken by the metaphor, which loses its status as metaphor (even before it fully gains it) to become the literal subject of the speech. And the speaker himself abruptly changes from someone coyly appealing for applause to (in the final lines) someone for whom prayer has become the only human activity that matters:

> Now I want
> Spirits to enforce, art to enchant;
> And my ending is despair
> Unless I be reliev'd by prayer,
> Which pierces so that it assaults
> Mercy itself, and frees all faults.
> As you from crimes would pardon'd be,
> Let your indulgence set me free.

The Tempest is Shakespeare's last work of true importance, and this fact as well as the manner of the play tempt one almost irresistibly to take it as a kind of 'summing up' or final statement – not only in the usual ways but also with respect to the themes I have been exploring. In *The Tempest*, role-playing has ceased to be a neutral but enormously fruitful source for the creation of character, action, and theme and has taken on much of the tone of *contemptus mundi* which normally characterizes the world-as-stage metaphor before Shakespeare and, to a considerable extent, outside his work during his own time. In keeping with this new (for Shakespeare) emphasis, and no doubt in part as an offshoot of it, *The Tempest* also brings to its culmination the trend of the later comedies (including the romances) with regard to the comic theme of losing oneself to find oneself. The humanistic reading of this theme that characterized its use from *The Comedy of Errors* to *Twelfth Night* has fully disappeared. The pattern of losing oneself to find oneself continues to shape the action, but in *The Tempest,* as in the other late comedies, this pattern has in large measure reassumed its usual Christian reading.

It is unnecessary, however, to let the position of *The Tempest* in the canon unduly affect one's response to these aspects of the play. I am myself inclined to believe that Shakespeare came to loathe manipulation of the sort the internal dramatist practises, and to doubt as a result the full acceptability of his own work as dramatist; but the attitudes developed in *The Tempest* (and to a lesser extent in the comedies leading up to it) do not necessarily represent genuine attitudes of Shakespeare the man. They may very well have been deliberately cultivated not as items of belief but as appropriate themes of the new romance genre. If, moreover, they do happen to be genuine attitudes, they tell us where Shakespeare ended up, not where he had been. They may very well suddenly put the raw material of the prior plays in a new and different light, but they cannot and do not alter the various and brilliant individual designs into which Shakespeare, in writing these prior plays, had shaped the raw material with which he worked.

Bibliography of related studies

Abel, Lionel *Metatheatre: A New View of Dramatic Form* New York 1963
  A study of what Abel regards as a particular type of drama – plays that are
  'theatre pieces about life seen as already theatricalized' (p. 60), consisting
  of 'characters who, having full self-consciousness, cannot but participate in
  their own dramatization' (p. 78), and exploiting the related concepts, 'the
  world is a stage, life is a dream' (p. 83). Includes provocative but over-
  ingenious discussion of the theatricalized world of *Hamlet*, dividing characters between playwrights and actors; notices Falstaff's activity as dramatist
  and actor, and Prospero's control of the action of *The Tempest* in the
  manner of a dramatist.

Bennett, Josephine Waters *Measure for Measure as Royal Entertainment*
Columbia University Press 1966
  Often focuses upon Duke Vincentio's 'play-acting' and his manipulation of
  the 'play-within-the-play' of the final act (see especially pp. 44-7 and
  chapter 8, 'The Duke as Actor and Playwright,' pp. 125-37, which provides
  a substantially different view of his activity than I do above); also notes
  (pp. 32, 67) Lucio's performing as director for Isabella.

Berg, Kent Talbot van den 'Theatrical Fiction and the Reality of Love in
As You Like It' PMLA 90 (1975): 885-93
  Sees 'theatrical artifice of the forest scenes' as affirming 'the characters'
  liberty to assert and transform themselves by deliberately playing roles and
  thereby translating the stubbornness of fortune into a variety of personal
  styles' (p. 888) and as integral to the 'mirror of love held up to the men
  and women in the audience' by the play (p. 887).

Bradbrook, Muriel C. *'King Henry IV'* in *Stratford Papers 1965-67* ed B.A.W.
Jackson, McMaster University Press, Irish University Press 1969, pp. 168-85
  Uses the concept of 'adaptability, the imaginative ability to create a part
  and to play it,' to distinguish between the characters of Falstaff and Hal
  and between the natures of the two parts of *Henry IV*.

– 'Shakespeare and the Use of Disguise in Elizabethan Drama' *Essays in
Criticism* 2 (1952): 159-68
  Defines disguise 'as the substitution, overlaying or metamorphosis of

dramatic identity, whereby one character sustains two roles' (p. 160), cites numerous examples, and provides general observations about its use in Shakespeare and his predecessors.

Burckhardt, Sigurd *Shakespearean Meanings* Princeton University Press 1968
Especially relevant for first chapter, 'How Not to Murder Caesar,' which discusses 'the metaphor of drama' in *Julius Caesar* and notes Iago's representation of Shakespeare as pure dramatic craftsman.

Calderwood, James L. *Shakespearean Metadrama* University of Minnesota Press 1971
On the related but dissimilar idea 'that Shakespeare's plays are not only about the various moral, social, political, and other thematic issues with which critics have so long and quite properly been busy but also about Shakespeare's plays' (p. 5); hence examines 'metaphor of life-as-drama' in order to get at 'Shakespeare's evolving conceptions of art' (p. 6).

Cannon, Charles K. ' "As in a Theater": *Hamlet* in the Light of Calvin's Doctrine of Predestination' *Studies in English Literature, 1500-1900* 11 (1971): 203-22
Argues that the theatrical imagery in *Hamlet* calls attention to the play as play so that 'The play as such ... becomes an image of the situation of every human being who is predestined to act in a certain way while remaining responsible for his actions' (p. 205).

Cope, Jackson I. *The Theater and the Dream: From Metaphor to Form in Renaissance Drama* The Johns Hopkins University Press 1973
A study and history of the 'structural power of the metaphors which make life into spectacle or dream, drama or vision' (p. 16); includes numerous fairly extensive play analyses, several from English Renaissance drama, in which the author notes much role-playing in my senses; with Shakespeare this mainly involves *The Tempest*, which he is primarily concerned with as an exemplification of life as a dream.

Coursen, Herbert R. Jr 'Henry V and the Nature of Kingship' *Discourse* 13 (1970): 279-305
Some attention to Henry's conscious playing of King and hence much recognition of role as role.

- '*Love's Labour's Lost* and the Comic Truth' *Papers on Language and Literature* 6 (1970): 316-22
Also sees Pageant of the Nine Worthies as analogous to the behaviour of the King and his Lords.

- 'Prospero and the Drama of the Soul' *Shakespeare Studies* 4 (1968): 316-33
Emphasizes metaphor of Prospero as dramatist but utilizes it more as if it were an imposed metaphor than an organic one.

Daiches, David 'Imagery and Meaning in *Antony and Cleopatra' English Studies* 43 (1962): 343-58
Focuses on acting imagery to discuss relation between roles and identity in the characterization of Antony and Cleopatra.

Dawson, Lawrence N. 'The Device of Wonder: *Titus Andronicus* and Revenge Tragedies' *Texas Studies in Literature and Language* 16 (1974): 27-43
Notices Titus' creation of a play-within-the-play as a 'device' for representing and alleviating his tragic suffering.

Dean, Leonard F. *'Richard II:* The State and the Image of the Theater' *PMLA* 67 (1952): 211-18
Fairly thorough examination of the 'play-acting' of both Richard and Bolingbroke; relates it to some 'examples of the state-theater comparison from More and Machiavelli.'

Egan, Robert *Drama Within Drama: Shakespeare's Sense of His Art in King Lear, The Winter's Tale, and The Tempest* Columbia University Press 1975
Studies the 'characters' attempts to control or alter reality directly through the exercise of dramatic illusion' as a means of discerning the artistic purpose of the play.

Ellis-Fermor, Una *Shakespeare the Dramatist and Other Papers* ed Kenneth Muir, London 1961
The chapter on Coriolanus (pp. 60-77) studies 'the contradiction between his outward seeming and his hidden self.'

Evans, Gareth Lloyd 'Shakespeare, Seneca, and the Kingdom of Violence' in *Roman Drama* ed T.A. Dorey and Donald R. Dudley, New York 1965, pp. 123-59
Perceptive remarks about Richard III and Hamlet as actors, with briefer appropriate references to intervening plays.

Fisch, Harold 'Shakespeare and "The Theatre of the World" ' in *The Morality of Art* ed D.W. Jefferson, London 1969, pp. 76-86
General survey of examples of the trope, in word and action, with excellent readings of the imagery in *Macbeth* and *Hamlet* which differ from mine.

– *Hamlet and the Word* New York 1971
Chapter 9, 'All the World's a Stage,' pp. 153-66, develops the points made in Fisch 'Shakespeare and "The Theatre of the World." '

Flower, Annette C. 'Disguise and Identity in *Pericles, Prince of Tyre' Shakespeare Quarterly* 26 (1975): 30-41
Detailed study of the roles assumed by Pericles, Thaisa, and Marina.

Forker, Charles R. 'Shakespeare's Theatrical Symbolism and Its Function in *Hamlet' Shakespeare Quarterly* 14 (1963): 215-29
Full discussion of theatrical images and of the characters as 'actors' engaged in 'play-acting.'

Frost, William 'Shakespeare's Rituals and the Opening of *King Lear' Hudson Review* 10 (1958): 577-85
> On the disadvantages of 'ceremonial situations' (p. 577) in drama and the transcending of these disadvantages in *King Lear.*

Garber, Marjorie B. *Dream in Shakespeare: From Metaphor to Metamorphosis* Yale University Press 1974
> Much concern with disguising, the play-within-the-play, the 'stage metaphor,' and the 'stage-manager figure' but from a point of view different from mine – as 'metaphorical gestures analogous to the activities of dream condensation and dream displacement.'

Gottschalk, Paul A. 'Hal and the "Play Extempore" in *1 Henry IV' Texas Studies in Literature and Language* 15 (1974): 605-14
> Excellent analysis of the 'play extempore' (with important similarities to mine) and of its place in the play as a whole.

Grivelet, Michel 'Shakespeare et "The Play within the Play" ' *Revue des sciences humaines* 145 (1972): 35-52

Hawkins, Harriett *Likenesses of Truth in Elizabethan and Restoration Drama* Oxford at the Clarendon Press 1972
> Chapter 2 (pp. 27-50) examines 'intersecting levels of theatricality' and characters who serve as 'the dramatic embodiments of the playwright's art' in *A Midsummer Night's Dream, The Tempest,* and Kyd's *The Spanish Tragedy,* while later chapters include a consideration of theatrical imagery and role-playing in *Macbeth* (pp. 152-60) and important discussions of role-playing in the comedies of Etherege and Congreve.

Henze, Richard 'Role Playing in *The Taming of the Shrew' Southern Humanities Review* 4 (1970): 231-40
> Detailed study of the play as a 'comedy of life' with many specific similarities to my treatment.

Holly, Marcia *'King Lear:* The Disguised and Deceived' *Shakespeare Quarterly* 24 (1973): 171-80
> Glances at some of the 'physical and non-physical' disguises in *Lear* in pursuing the idea 'that there is an inverse proportion between masks and self-deception in [Shakespeare's] plays.'

Homan, Sidney R. 'Iago's Aesthetics: *Othello* and Shakespeare's Portrait of an Artist' *Shakespeare Studies* 5 (1969): 141-8
> Discusses Iago as director and actor to argue that he represents a portrait of the artist as bad artist.

Hyman, Stanley Edgar 'Portraits of the Artist: Iago and Prospero' *Shenandoah* 21, no. 2 (1970): 18-42
> Studies Iago and Prospero as internal dramatists; contrasts Iago 'as a type of the artist or playwright, in his criminal aspect' with his antithesis,

Prospero, 'the caricature of the benign artist' (p. 18). This material also forms a chapter of Hyman's book *Iago: Some Approaches to the Illusion of His Motivation* (New York 1970).

Jacquot, Jean 'Le théâtre du monde de Shakespeare à Calderon' *Revue de littérature comparée* 31 (1957): 341-72
  Surveys and discusses numerous explicit citations of the metaphor, from the ancients through Calderon, including several by Shakespeare.

Kantak, V.Y. 'An Approach to Shakespearian Tragedy: The "Actor" Image in "Macbeth" ' *Shakespeare Survey* 16 (Cambridge at the University Press 1963): 42-52
  Despite its title, the discussion touches only minimally on the idea of role-playing.

Kernan, A.B. 'This Goodly Frame, The Stage: The Interior Theater of Imagination in English Renaissance Drama' *Shakespeare Quarterly* 25 (1974): 1-5
  General observations about the examination of their medium by Shakespeare and others through utilization of the play-within-the-play and the character's sense of himself as an actor on the stage of the world.

Kott, Jan *Shakespeare Our Contemporary* trans Boleslaw Taborski, Garden City, N.Y. 1964
  Sees Richard III as an 'actor' but book is most relevant for its discussion of *The Tempest:* 'All that happens on the island will be a play within a play, a performance produced by Prospero' (p. 170).

Latham, Jacqueline E.M. 'The Imagery in *Hamlet* – Acting' *Educational Theatre Journal* 14 (1962): 197-202
  Using imagery of 'masking, playing and acting,' focuses on Hamlet's 'tendency to dramatize' (p. 197).

Lyons, Bridget Gellert *Voices of Melancholy* London 1971
  Includes discussions of the melancholy man as a theatrical and literary role and of Hamlet's role-playing as a reflection of his melancholy.

McAlindon, T. *Shakespeare and Decorum* New York 1973
  Often aware of Shakespearian characters' play-acting, their efforts to create shows, and their failures of 'constancy' in fulfilling the demands of their roles.

McGuire, Richard L. 'The Play-within-the-Play in *1 Henry IV*' *Shakespeare Quarterly* 18 (1967): 47-52

Mack, Maynard 'Engagement and Detachment in Shakespeare's Plays' in *Essays on Shakespeare and the Elizabethan Drama in Honor of Hardin Craig* ed Richard Hosley, University of Missouri Press 1962, pp. 275-96
  Discusses numerous examples of role-playing imagery as well as the actual role-playing of Falstaff.

Mack, Maynard Jr *Killing the King: Three Studies in Shakespeare's Tragic Structure* Yale University Press 1973
See pp. 186-203: 'Merely Players?'

McNeir, Waldo F. 'The Masks of Richard the Third' *Studies in English Literature, 1500-1900* 11 (1971): 167-86
Sees Richard as actor playing to the other characters and to us, and as plotter – i.e., as manipulator, director of others.

Mehl, Dieter 'Forms and Functions of the Play within a Play' *Renaissance Drama* 8 (Northwestern University Press 1965): 41-61
Includes comments suggesting how these plays within plays can reflect the role-playing of the characters participating in them. More concerned with Shakespeare's contemporaries than with Shakespeare's own plays.

Mendelsohn, Leonard R. 'The Player as Director: An Approach to Character' *Comparative Drama* 6 (1972): 115-24
Argues that 'the character, and most certainly the character in Renaissance drama, is very much an actor [and director] in his own right' (p. 116), and consists largely of an extensive analysis of this idea as exemplified in Greene's *Friar Bacon and Friar Bungay*. Incidental references to Shakespeare.

Neill, Michael 'Shakespeare's Halle of Mirrors: Play, Politics, and Psychology in *Richard III'* *Shakespeare Studies* 8 (1975): 99-129
Constantly directs attention to Richard's theatricality, his 'delight in his prowess as an actor [and] the bustling energy of his performances' (p. 103).

Nelson, Robert J. 'Shakespeare: The Play as Mirror' in *Play Within a Play: The Dramatist's Conception of His Art: Shakespeare to Anouilh* Yale University Press 1958, pp. 11-35

Penlington, Norman 'The Terrible Sickness in Shakespeare's *Othello'* *Motive* 18, no. 4 (January 1958): 14-15, 30-2
Interesting but overly general analysis of how the four leading male characters 'fearing and concealing their essential meaninglessness are unwilling to face their empty selves. Instead each one plays a role: Roderigo pictures himself as a worthy but rejected lover; Cassio, as a loyal but disgraced companion; Othello, as a noble warrior; and Iago, as a superman' (p. 14). Also much on Iago's manipulative role-playing.

Rabkin, Norman 'The Great Globe Itself' chapter 5 of *Shakespeare and the Common Understanding* New York 1967, pp. 192-237
Argues that in his last plays (from *Pericles* on) 'Shakespeare focuses his complementary vision ... on the very art to which he has devoted his career' (p. 192).

Righter, Anne *Shakespeare and the Idea of the Play* London 1962
Pioneering, book-length study of the explicit theatrical imagery in

Shakespeare's plays. Often discusses the plays in terms similar to mine, especially in her consideration of Richard II and other 'Player-Kings,' but her primary concern is to trace Shakespeare's 'changing attitudes towards the relation of illusion and reality' (p. 86) as well as his changing attitudes towards the theatre itself.

Rosenberg, Marvin 'Shakespeare's Fantastick Trick: *Measure for Measure*' *The Sewanee Review* 80 (1972): 51-72
A good reading of the play heightened by its awareness of Duke Vincentio as theatrical 'fantastical trickster.'

Ross, John F. 'Hamlet: Dramatist' in *Five Studies in Literature* University of California Publications in English, vol. 8, no. 1, University of California Press 1940, pp. 55-72
Sees Hamlet as 'consistently a creative dramatist and actor' (p. 56), the most thorough figure of that sort in Shakespeare's tragedies; discusses not just his role-playing and manipulation of others but also his more general tendency for self-conscious display.

Rousset, Jean *La Littérature de l'age baroque en France: Circé et le paon* Paris 1954
Discusses metaphor portraying 'the world [as] a theater and life [as] a comedy wherein one must assume a role' and its ramifications of man as a 'quick-change artist, a role-adapter, an actor' in the baroque (described by Cope *The Theater and the Dream* pp. 3-4)

Sanford, Wendy Coppedge *Theater as Metaphor in Hamlet* Harvard University Press 1967
Emphasizes the various characters' contriving and directing of the episodes of the play and Hamlet's play-acting as a metaphor for his 'inner search for ... his own real image' (p. 27).

Schäfer, Dorothea 'Die Bedeutung des Rollenspiels in Shakespeares "Wie es euch gefällt" ' *Shakespeare Jahrbuch* 94 (1958): 150-74

Siemon, James Edward 'Disguise in Marston and Shakespeare' *Huntington Library Quarterly* 38 (1975): 105-23
Particularly concerned with *Coriolanus, Measure for Measure*, and Marston's *The Malcontent*, this essay focuses on 'role playing as a means by which characters achieve self-definition, or fail of it, and ... its close association with distinctive dress.'

Simmons, J.L. '*Antony and Cleopatra* and *Coriolanus*, Shakespeare's Heroic Tragedies: A Jacobean Adjustment' *Shakespeare Survey* 26 (Cambridge at the University Press 1973): 95-101
Explores one of the implications of the 'image of a demeaning theatrical performance' (p. 96) which these two plays share.

– 'Shakespeare's *Julius Caesar:* The Roman Actor and the Man' *Tulane Studies in English* 16 (1968): 1-28
Discusses the theatre imagery of the play in general terms.

Soellner, Rolf *Shakespeare's Patterns of Self-Knowledge* Ohio State University Press 1972
Studies 'movement from self-loss to self-recovery in the plays,' a movement he sees as linked with the theme of identity throughout Shakespeare's work; often attentive to implications of the world-as-stage metaphor; discusses Hamlet's role-playing.

Sternlicht, Sanford *'Hamlet:* Six Characters in Search of a Play' *College English* 27 (1966): 528-31
Study of Hamlet as an example of the 'actor-personality' who plays 'six parts: the student prince, the mourner, the melancholy philosopher, the mad hero of a revenge play, the disappointed lover, and in death – the soldier.' Some attention to the theatre imagery of the play.

Stroup, Thomas B. *Microcosmos: The Shape of the Elizabethan Play* University of Kentucky Press 1965
Provides thorough survey of explicit manifestations of the world-as-stage metaphor in the work of Shakespeare and other English Renaissance writers.

Summers, Joseph H. 'The Masks of *Twelfth Night' The University Review* 22 (Autumn 1955): 25-32
Good, rather thorough discussion of the various 'masks,' 'disguises,' or 'roles' assumed by the characters.

Thayer, C.G. *'Hamlet:* Drama as Discovery and as Metaphor' *Studia Neophilologica* 28 (1956): 118-29
Traces much of the implicit role-playing in *Hamlet* as well as the explicit theatre images; focuses on the several 'interior play-scenes' and the discoveries they provoke in the characters.

Ure, Peter 'Character and Role from *Richard III* to *Hamlet' in Hamlet* Stratford-upon-Avon Studies 5, ed John Russell Brown and Bernard Harris, London 1963 , pp. 9-28
Ignores explicit theatre imagery but contains many suggestive remarks on subject of the relation between a character and the roles he is called on or chooses to play in *Richard III, Richard II, Julius Caesar,* and especially *Hamlet.*

Velz, John W. ' "If I Were Brutus Now ... " Role-Playing in *Julius Caesar' Shakespeare Studies* 4 (1968): 149-59
Mostly concerned with the characters' playing of roles that others have played before them; sees the 'assumption of roles' as providing 'a major force for unity in the play' and relates it to 'the process by which a new Caesar emerges from the wreckage of the conspiracy' (pp. 150, 152).

Warnke, Frank J. 'The World as Theatre' chapter 4 of *Versions of Baroque: European Literature in the Seventeenth Century* Yale University Press 1972, pp. 66-89
> Surveys some appearances of the 'world-as-stage topos' in baroque literature, including Shakespeare's plays.

Weidhorn, Manfred 'The Relation of Title and Name to Identity in Shakespearean Tragedy' *Studies in English Literature, 1500-1900* 9 (1969): 303-19
> Focusing primarily on *Lear* and *Coriolanus* and more briefly on other plays, studies how loss and restoration of the identity of the Shakespearian tragic hero is signaled by the treatment of his name and titles.

Weisinger, Herbert '*Theatrum Mundi:* Illusion as Reality' in *The Agony and the Triumph: Papers on the Use and Abuse of Myth* Michigan State University Press 1964, pp. 58-71
> Speculations on the history and implications of the metaphor.

Wierum, Anne ' "Actors" and "Play-Acting" in the Morality Tradition' *Renaissance Drama* 3 (Northwestern University Press 1970): 189-214
> Not on Shakespeare but pursues a related concern (the Vice as play-actor) in closely related, probably influential period of drama.

Wilds, Lillian *Shakespeare's Character-Dramatists: A Study of a Character Type in Shakespearean Tragedy Through Hamlet* Salzburg Series in English Literature, Salzburg, Austria 1975

Wilson, Robert F. Jr 'The Plays Within *A Midsummer Night's Dream* and *The Tempest*' *Shakespeare Jahrbuch – Weimar* 110 (1974): 101-11
> Also glances at several other 'plays within' in considering their relationships to their contexts, including to some extent other forms of role-playing.

Winny, James *The Player King: A Theme of Shakespeare's Histories* London 1968
> Explores concept of the Player-King in extensive readings of the second tetralogy, with little focus on actual theatre imagery. The reading of *Richard II* is somewhat similar to mine, and the reading of *Henry IV* is usefully supplementary.

Zacha, Richard B. 'Iago and the Commedia Dell'Arte' *Arlington Quarterly* 2, no. 2 (1969): 98-116
> Iago as 'scenarist and director' for 'the most extensive use of the play within the play' in Shakespeare: i.e., most of *Othello*.

Index